Li**v**

for
Kicks

Jim McCarthy
& Kevin Cross

a mods graphic novel

Copyright © 2016 Omnibus Press
(A Division of Music Sales Limited)

Cover illustrated by Kevin Cross
Text by Jim McCarthy
Book illustrated by Kevin Cross

ISBN: 978.1.78305.578.4
Order No: OP55902

Exclusive Distributors
Music Sales Limited,
14-15 Berners Street,
London, W1T 3LJ.

Music Sales Pty Ltd,
Australia and New Zealand,
Level 4, 30-32 Carrington Street,
Sydney NSW 2000,
Australia.

Every effort has been made to trace the copyright holders of the photographs in this
book but one or two were unreachable. We would be grateful if the photographers
concerned would contact us.

Printed in the EU.

A catalogue record for this book is available from the British Library.

Visit Omnibus Press on the web at **www.omnibuspress.com**

Living for Kicks

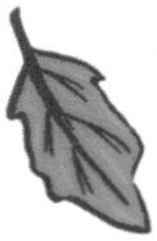

Jim McCarthy
& Kevin Cross

a mods graphic novel

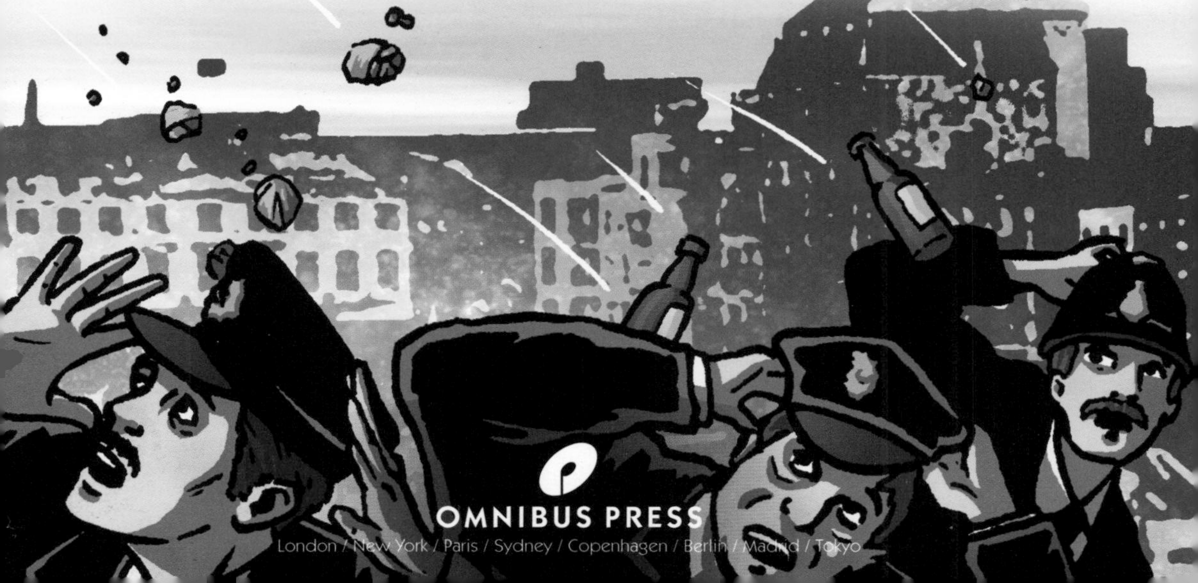

OMNIBUS PRESS
London / New York / Paris / Sydney / Copenhagen / Berlin / Madrid / Tokyo

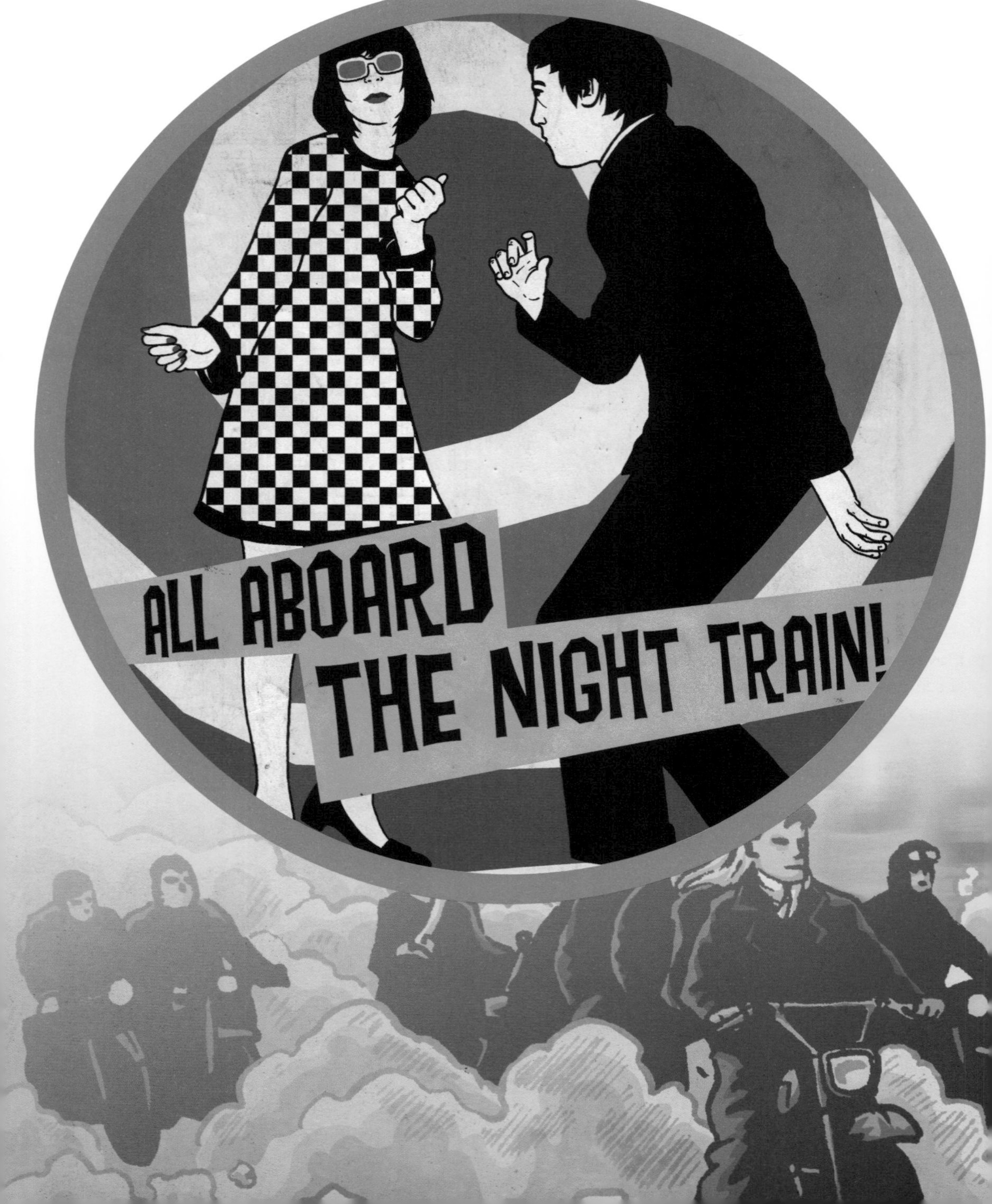
ALL ABOARD
THE NIGHT TRAIN!

mods, skins, Sta-Prest, tonics and stuff...

reflections on mods

Living for Kicks came from a great initial idea which arose during a conversation with my managing editor, David Barraclough. We agreed the early sixties world of the mods was a perfect background for a graphic novel. The first thing I did was watch *Quadrophenia*, which I remembered as a pretty good film but hadn't seen for well over 20 years. I was determined not to copy the plot, either consciously or otherwise, but quickly realised that the mods and rockers skirmishes had to be included. However, I could not hang an entire book around that brief period, despite the hype it received during its fleeting heyday.

I liked *Quadrophenia* (sort of) when I rewatched it, mostly for the colloquial lingo and the huge amount of swearing. The plot and the film's third act, much less so. The story seemed to go off the boil and Phil Daniels' character (although well acted) just petered out.

I loved writing this story, especially with it being set in pre-PC times. It made me realise just how stultifying our present day culture can be. I can still remember the amount of slang and swearing around in the second half of the sixties when I was growing up. This was just after the mod period, when it had morphed into a skinhead culture (if I can use such a 'poncey' word as 'culture').

The clothes were still sharp, with Levi jeans and Levi Sta-Prest both very prevalent. Tonic suits, Prince of Wales checks, Harrington jackets and Ben Sherman shirts, loafers or plains. I recall that people loved the heavy oxblood colour brogues, which were enlivened and deepened by applications of the right shoe polish. Mods also liked desert boots, which I don't remember skins wearing at all. Not so good for the kicking of heads, for which it needed to be thick leather. I can also clearly recall the sound they made, as many skins wore small iron Blakeys on the heels and the front of their shoes to stop the leather soles from wearing out so fast.

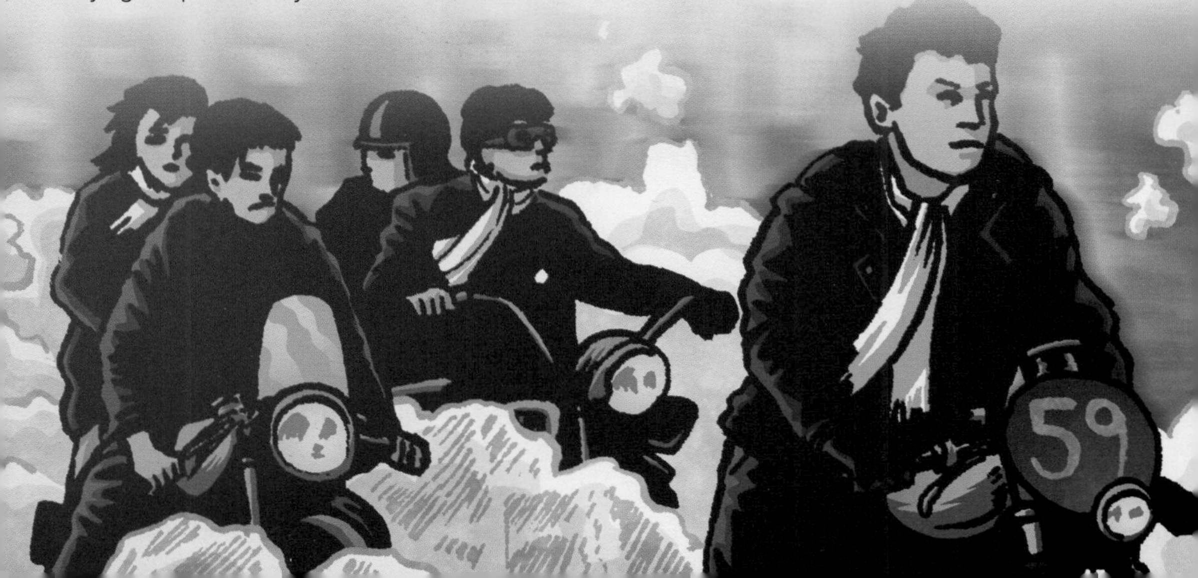
59

As a young kid, mod certainly influenced me. Especially the mod bands. I adored The Small Faces and thought Steve Marriott was practically the best thing I'd ever heard, so I had to showcase him in this book. It was important to me to mix fiction with factual events and people from that time. This book is set between late winter 1962 and late summer 1964, with a present day coda. Just over a year and a half, but so many tumultuous things happened. Apart from the John Profumo scandal and the fall of the British government, there was the mod scene, the assassination of JFK and the emergence and subsequent explosion of The Beatles. All of these events plus the arrival of ska, bluebeat, American soul and R&B music. Whew!

Many of the characters - like Christine Keeler, Lucky Gordon, Johnny Edgecombe, Georgie Fame, Ace Kefford, Trevor Burton - are real people. And there are some characters based on people I knew, such as Landy Gray. Landy was a West Indian boy who was my best friend for many years growing up in West London.

Paulette Harrison was a girl I fancied loads at school. Danny Healy was the name of another school friend. Neill Donnelly was a kid I disliked a lot at secondary modern and he became the rocker figure. Many of the others, like Karl Yelland, Eddie Emmons, Massini, Wirral, Hendry, Sales and so on, are concoctions of my imagination, but formed by paying careful attention to people I have met. Various episodes from my life have fuelled these characters in some manner or another.

The importance of amphetamines cannot be overemphasised in the mod scene. As a young kid, I discovered Philon and other speed pills very early on and this was the chemical beat all the mods were marching to. Speed was initially a revelation. When Landy and I first took it, at the age of 14 I believe, we trooped from Hanwell to

Harlesden and back in one night. We furiously put the world to rights and discovered that we had walked around ten miles, all the while chomping and talking and just speeding out of our heads. It was important for me to show how Spike comes a cropper through constant speed usage, as it can push people into semi-psychotic behaviour through constant use and abuse. Much of the mod violence will have been amphetamine

charged. It was the same with the later punk scene, where cheap 'blues' and amphetamine sulphate were (mainly) the drugs of choice.

The mod scene was the first time working class youth had a voice. As someone who believes that most of the great bands, styles and trends have arisen from the street, it is fascinating to see that as soon as youth had the opportunity to shine, it did so, utterly and brilliantly.

Youth was not only displaying great taste in clothes, but also showing open hearts and ears for great American and Jamaican imported music, which was by then landing on our shores and becoming an integral part of the mod experience. This love of black music gave many bands their initial impetus: The Beatles, The Stones, The Small Faces, The Move, The Who and many more.

Living for Kicks was a great graphic novel to write and I hope you get caught up in the excitement and surreal freshness of a fleeting, long-vanished world that was the springboard for a seminal cultural explosion that continues to reverberate to this day.

Jim McCarthy
February 2016

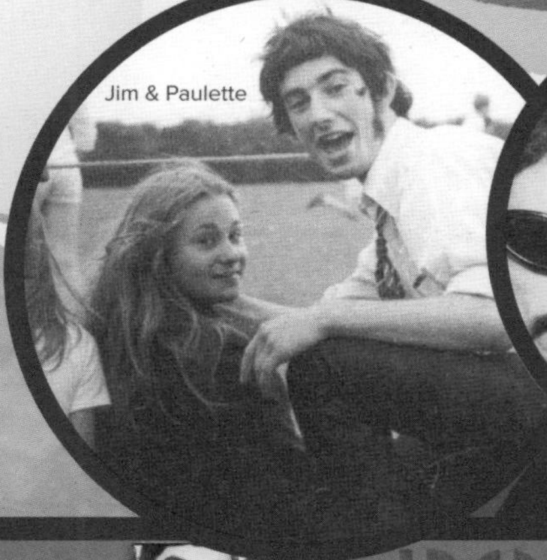

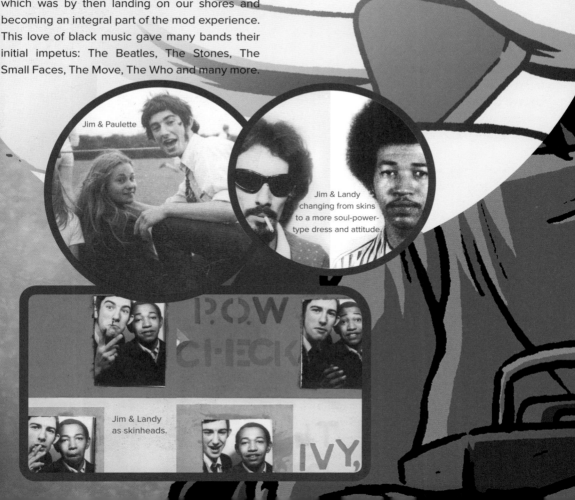

Jim & Paulette

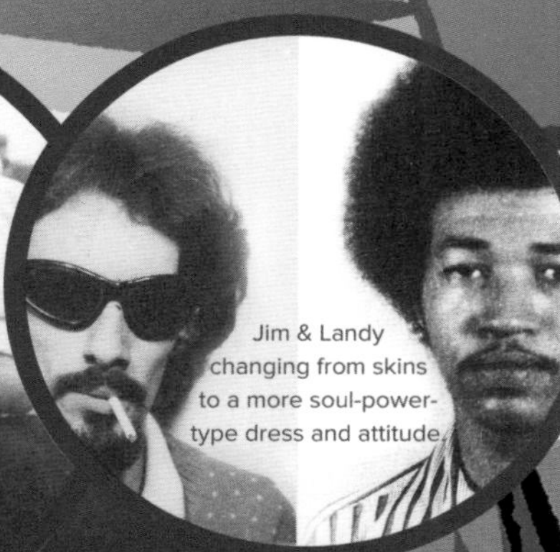

Jim & Landy changing from skins to a more soul-power-type dress and attitude.

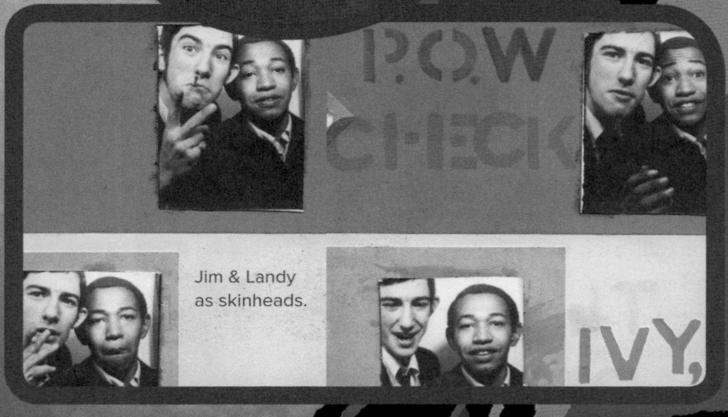
P.O.W
CHECK
IVY,

Jim & Landy as skinheads.

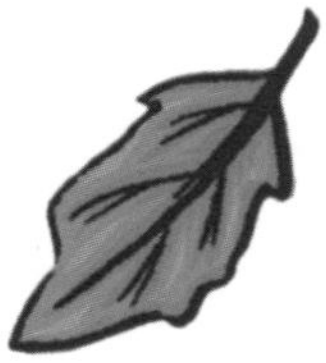

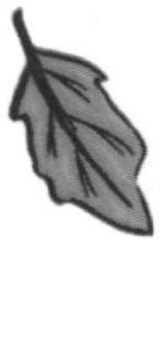

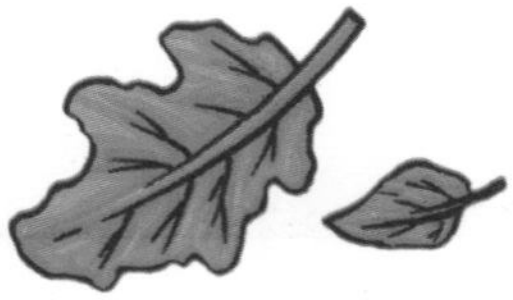

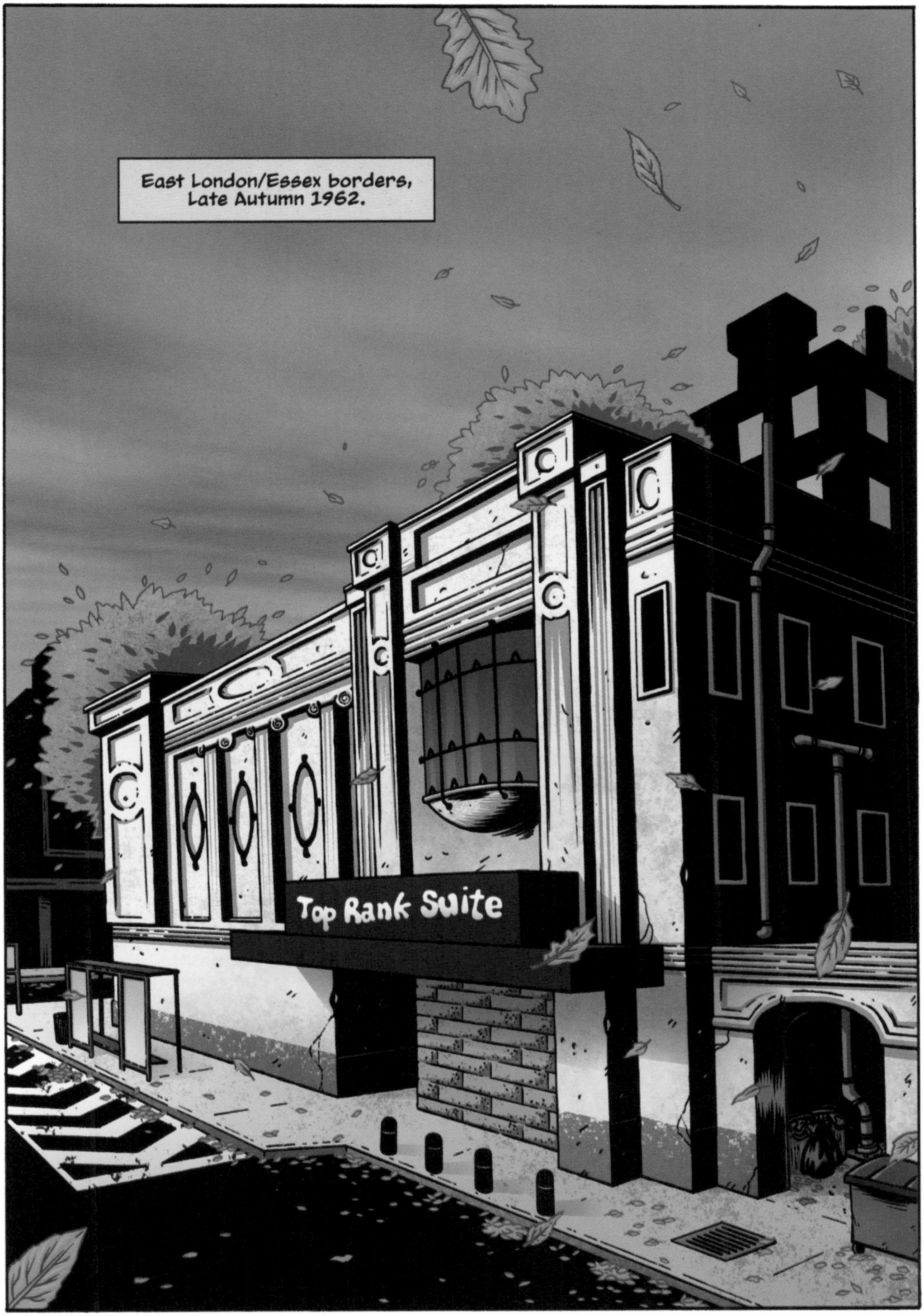
East London/Essex borders,
Late Autumn 1962.
Top Rank Suite

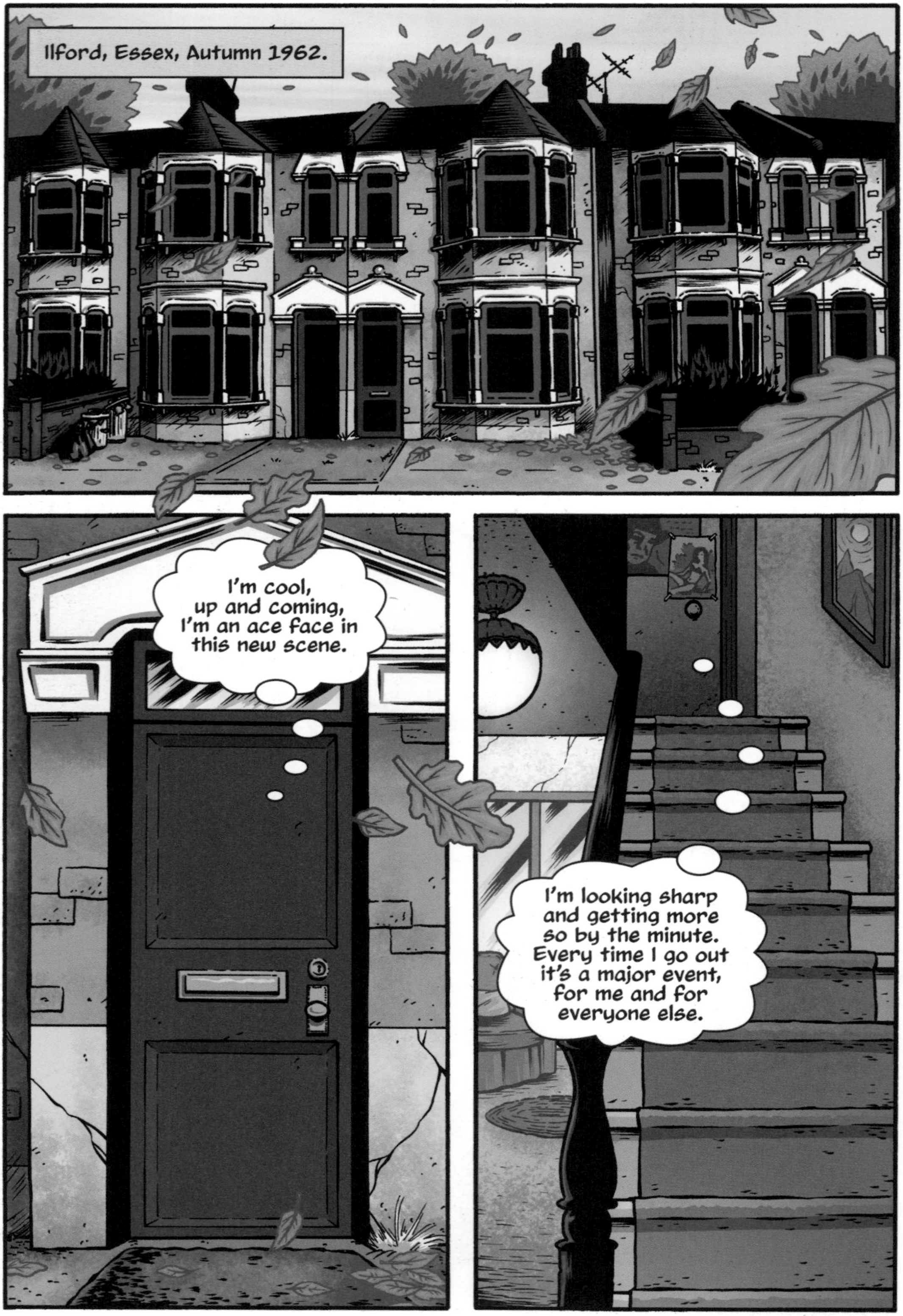
Ilford, Essex, Autumn 1962.
I'm cool, up and coming, I'm an ace face in this new scene.
I'm looking sharp and getting more so by the minute. Every time I go out it's a major event, for me and for everyone else.

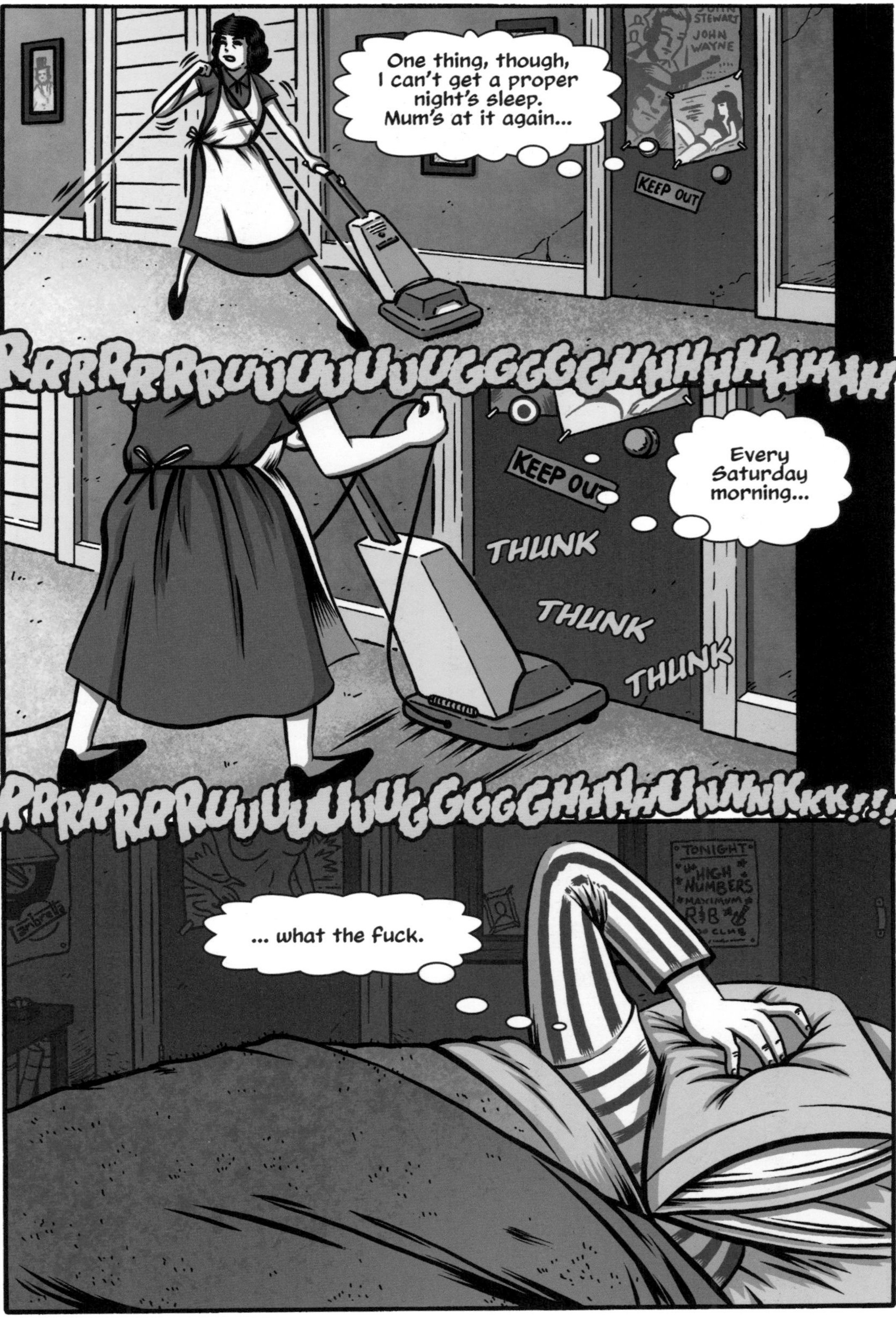

JOHN STEWART
JOHN WAYNE
One thing, though, I can't get a proper night's sleep. Mum's at it again...
KEEP OUT
RRRRRRRUUUUUUUUGGGGGHHHHHHHH
KEEP OUT
Every Saturday morning...
THUNK
THUNK
THUNK
RRRRRRRUUUUUUUUGGGGGHHHHUNNNKKK!!!
TONIGHT
HIGH NUMBERS
MAXIMUM R&B
... what the fuck.

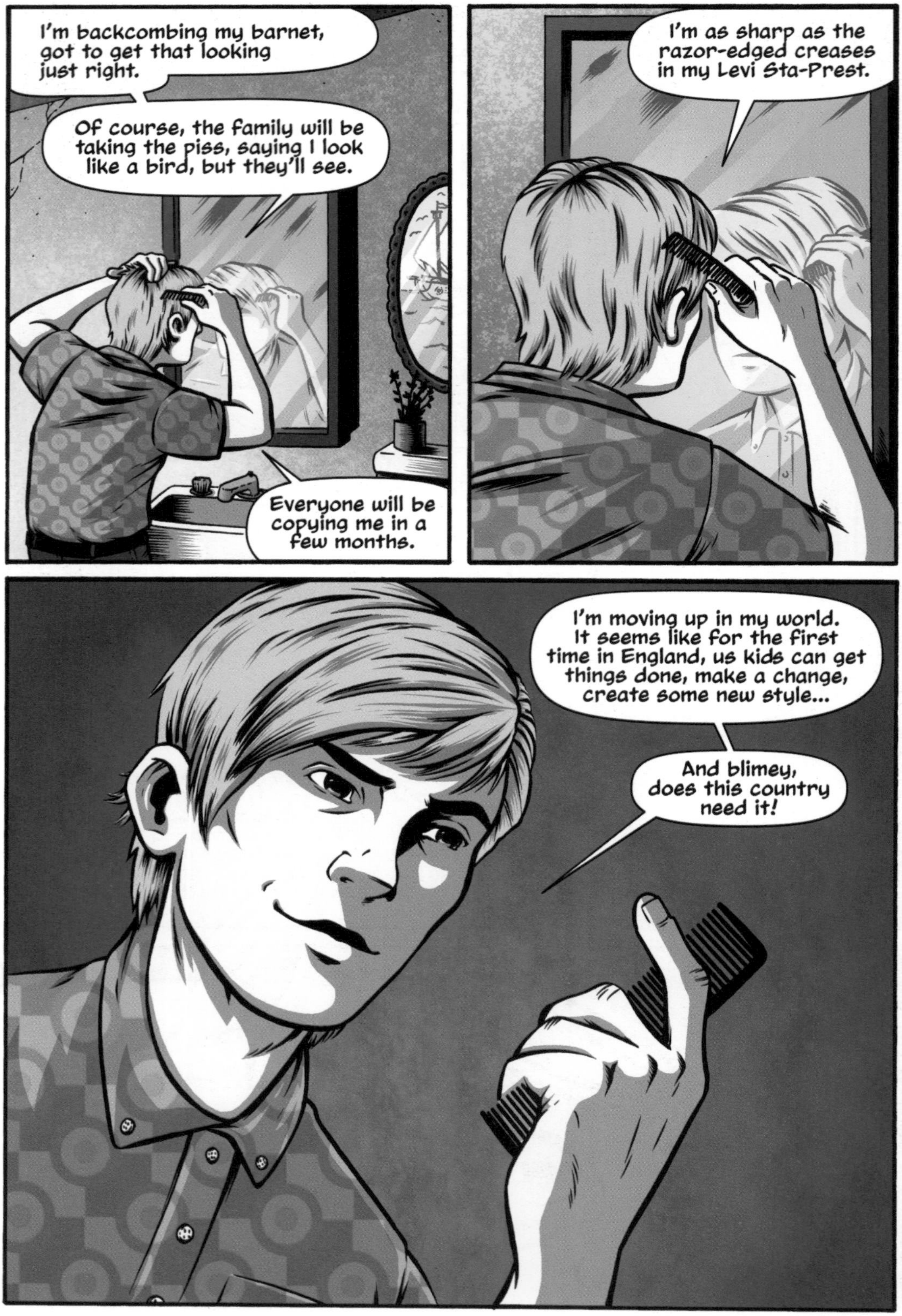
I'm backcombing my barnet, got to get that looking just right.
Of course, the family will be taking the piss, saying I look like a bird, but they'll see.
Everyone will be copying me in a few months.
I'm as sharp as the razor-edged creases in my Levi Sta-Prest.
I'm moving up in my world. It seems like for the first time in England, us kids can get things done, make a change, create some new style...
And blimey, does this country need it!

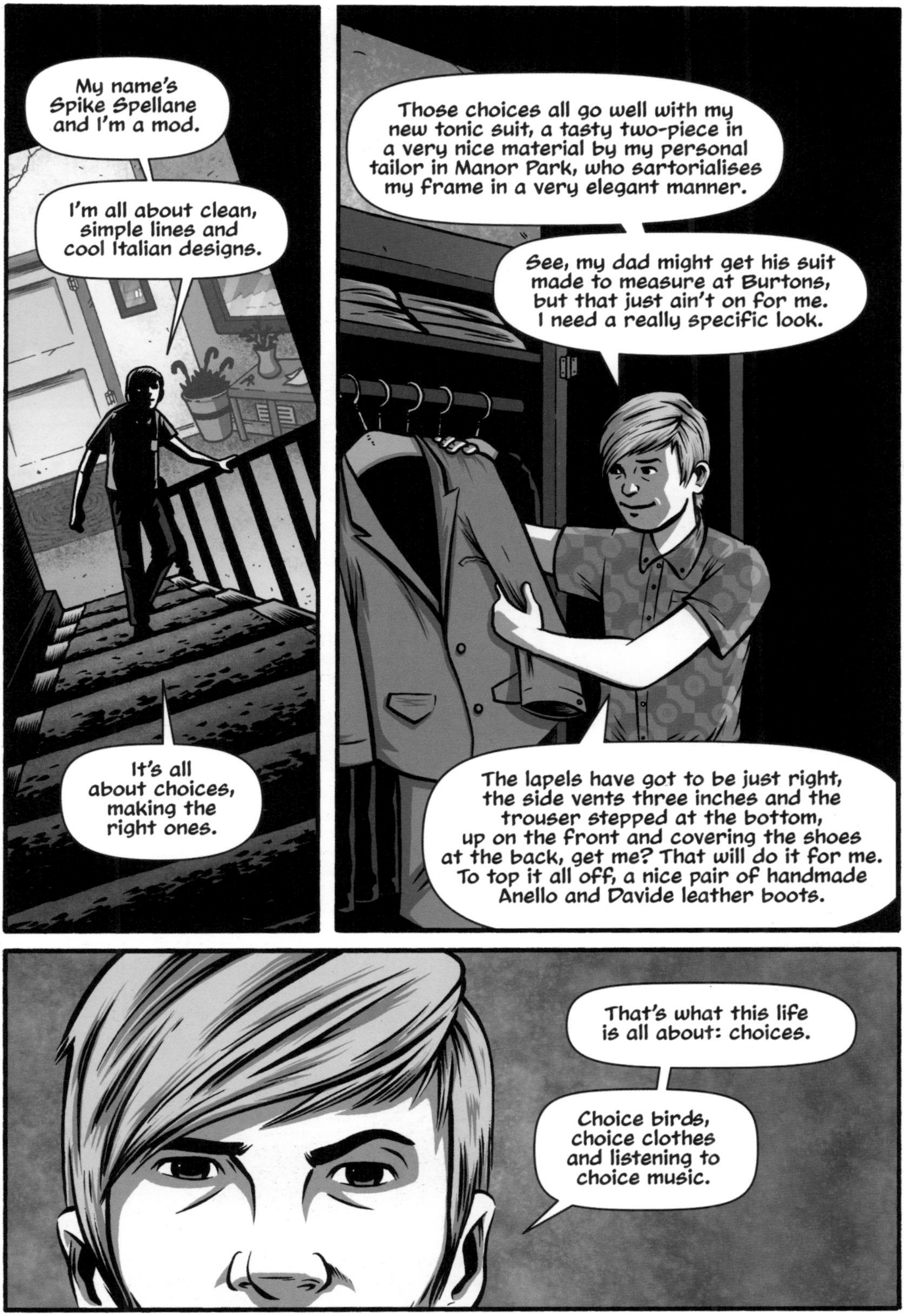
My name's Spike Spellane and I'm a mod.
I'm all about clean, simple lines and cool Italian designs.
It's all about choices, making the right ones.
Those choices all go well with my new tonic suit, a tasty two-piece in a very nice material by my personal tailor in Manor Park, who sartorialises my frame in a very elegant manner.
See, my dad might get his suit made to measure at Burtons, but that just ain't on for me. I need a really specific look.
The lapels have got to be just right, the side vents three inches and the trouser stepped at the bottom, up on the front and covering the shoes at the back, get me? That will do it for me. To top it all off, a nice pair of handmade Anello and Davide leather boots.
That's what this life is all about: choices.
Choice birds, choice clothes and listening to choice music.

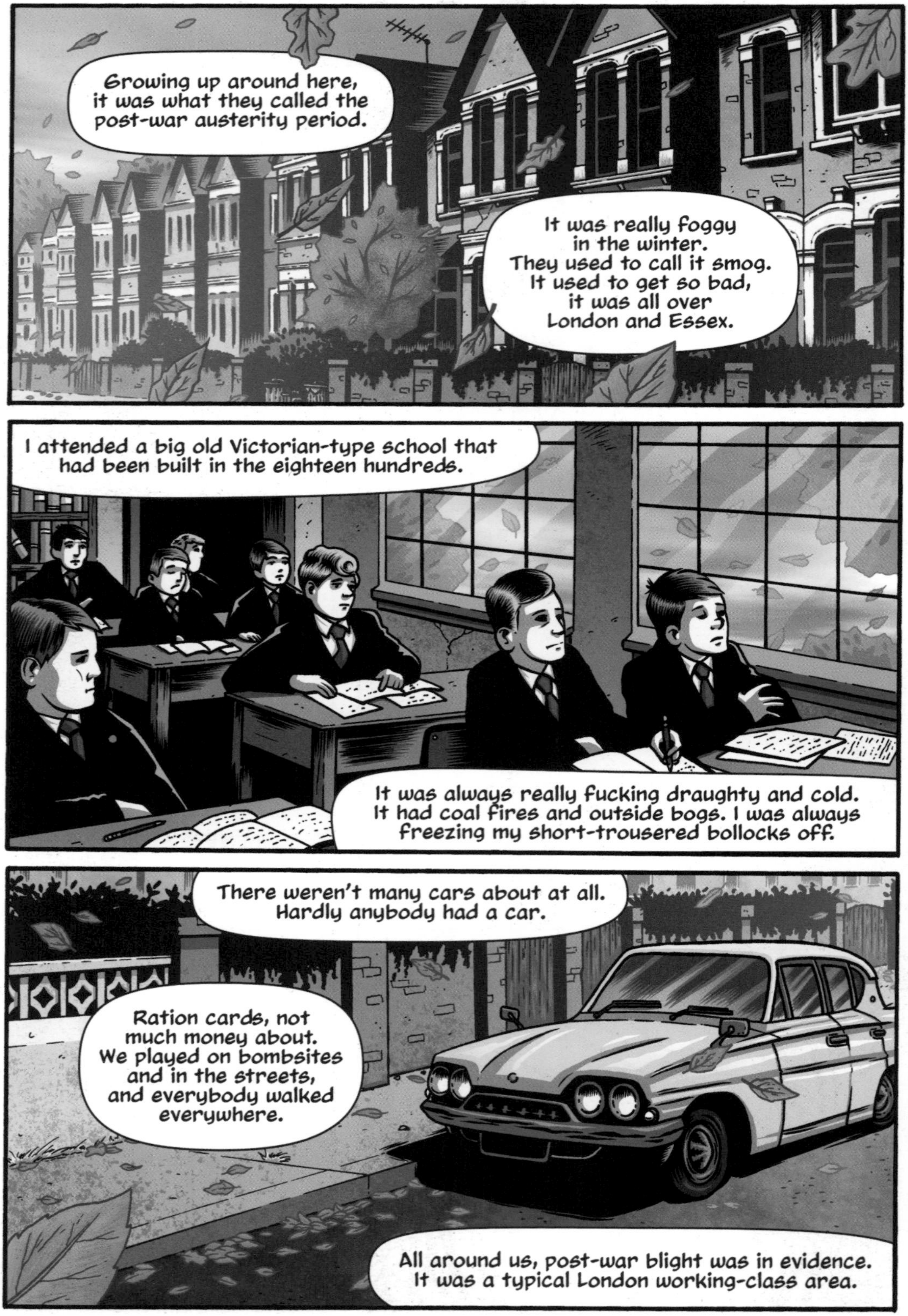
Growing up around here, it was what they called the post-war austerity period.
It was really foggy in the winter. They used to call it smog. It used to get so bad, it was all over London and Essex.
I attended a big old Victorian-type school that had been built in the eighteen hundreds.
It was always really fucking draughty and cold. It had coal fires and outside bogs. I was always freezing my short-trousered bollocks off.
There weren't many cars about at all. Hardly anybody had a car.
Ration cards, not much money about. We played on bombsites and in the streets, and everybody walked everywhere.
All around us, post-war blight was in evidence. It was a typical London working-class area.

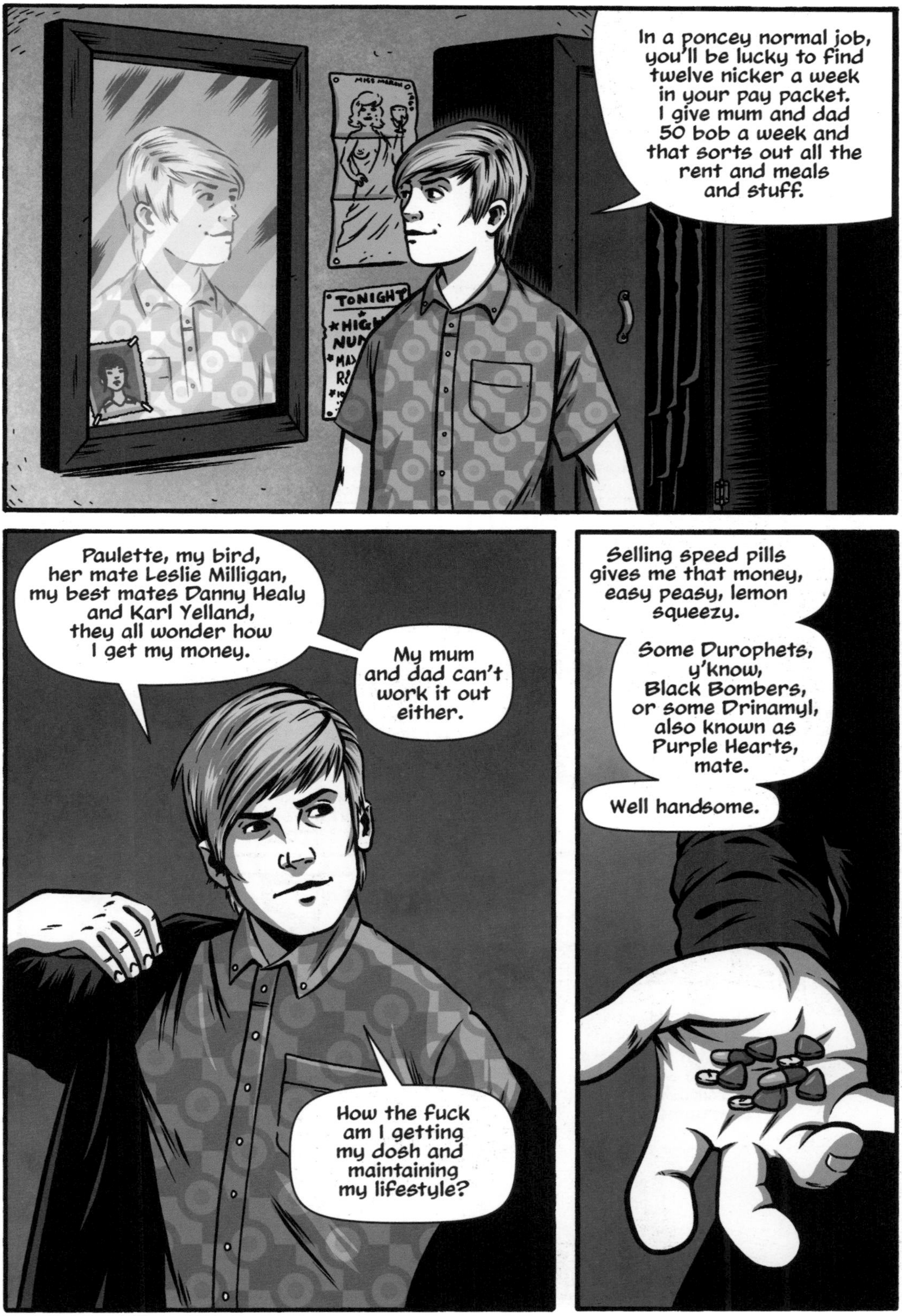
In a poncey normal job, you'll be lucky to find twelve nicker a week in your pay packet. I give mum and dad 50 bob a week and that sorts out all the rent and meals and stuff.
TONIGHT
Paulette, my bird, her mate Leslie Milligan, my best mates Danny Healy and Karl Yelland, they all wonder how I get my money.
My mum and dad can't work it out either.
How the fuck am I getting my dosh and maintaining my lifestyle?
Selling speed pills gives me that money, easy peasy, lemon squeezy.
Some Durophets, y'know, Black Bombers, or some Drinamyl, also known as Purple Hearts, mate.
Well handsome.

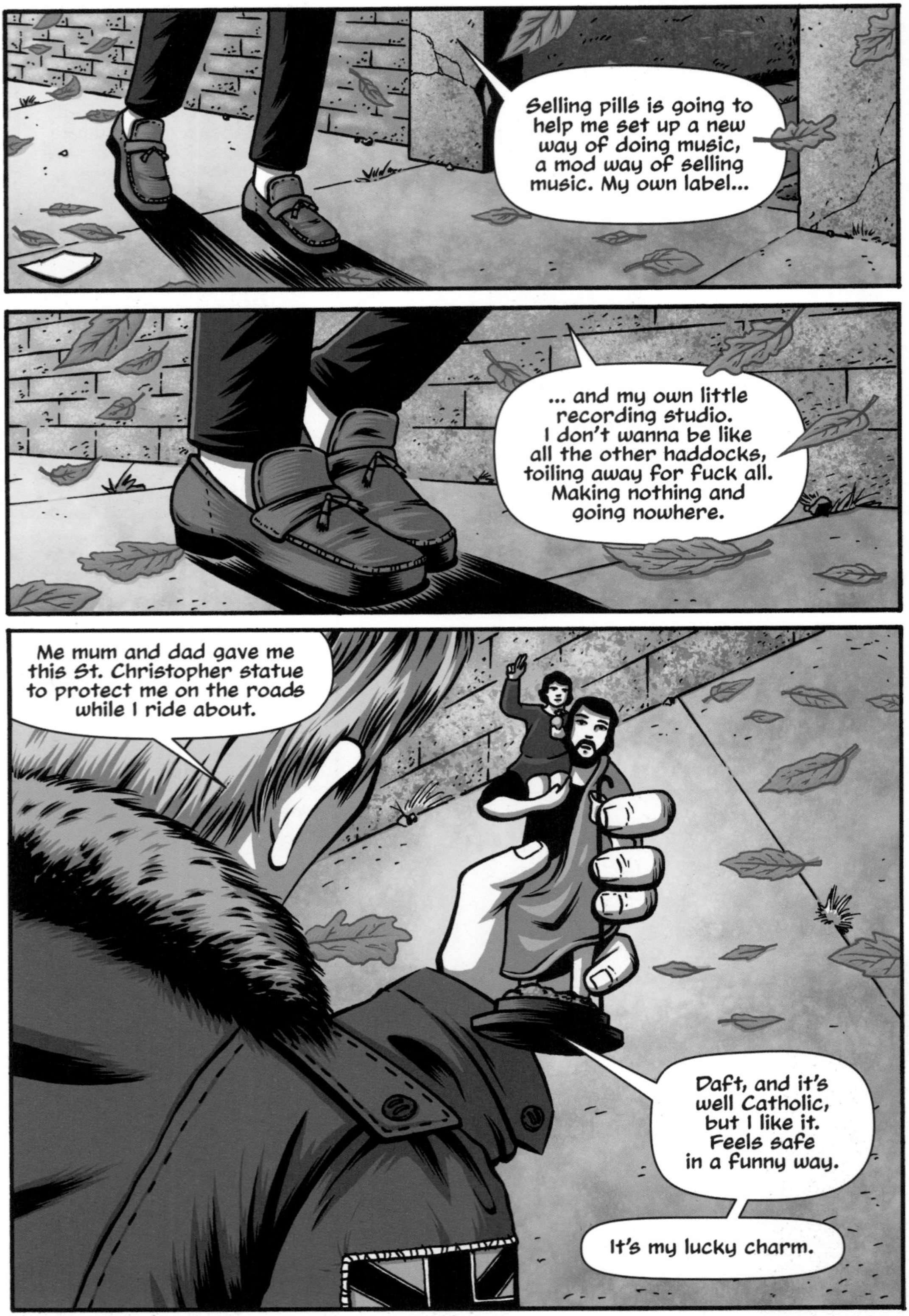
Selling pills is going to help me set up a new way of doing music, a mod way of selling music. My own label...
... and my own little recording studio. I don't wanna be like all the other haddocks, toiling away for fuck all. Making nothing and going nowhere.
Me mum and dad gave me this St. Christopher statue to protect me on the roads while I ride about.
Daft, and it's well Catholic, but I like it. Feels safe in a funny way.
It's my lucky charm.

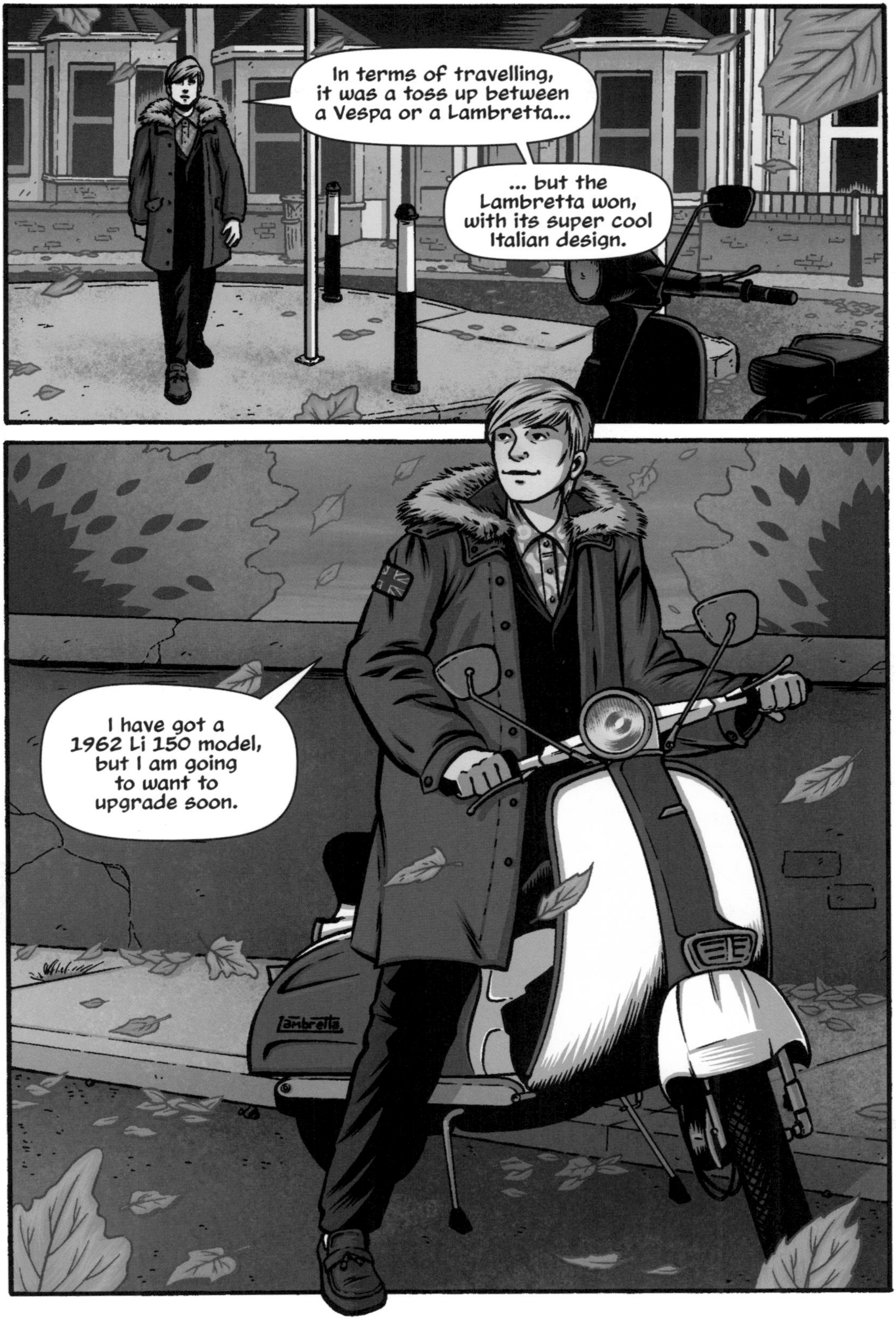
In terms of travelling, it was a toss up between a Vespa or a Lambretta...
... but the Lambretta won, with its super cool Italian design.
I have got a 1962 Li 150 model, but I am going to want to upgrade soon.

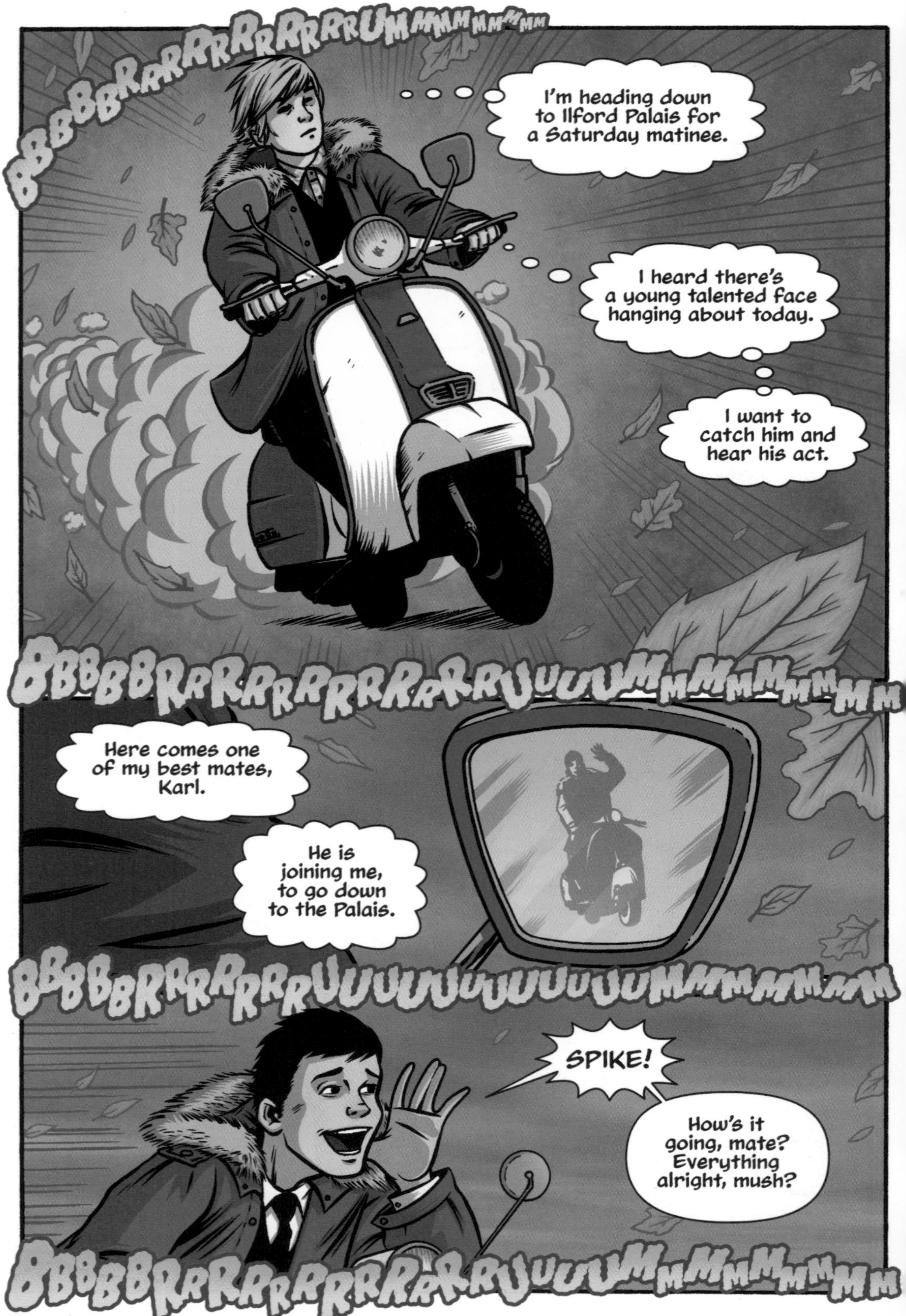
BBBBBRRRRRRRRRRRRUMMMMMMMMM
I'm heading down to Ilford Palais for a Saturday matinee.
I heard there's a young talented face hanging about today.
I want to catch him and hear his act.
BBBBBRRRRRRRRRRRRRUUUUMMMMMMMMMM
Here comes one of my best mates, Karl.
He is joining me, to go down to the Palais.
BBBBBRRRRRRRUUUUUUUUUUUUUMMMMMMMMMM
SPIKE!
How's it going, mate? Everything alright, mush?
BBBBBRRRRRRRRRRRRRUUUUMMMMMMMMMM

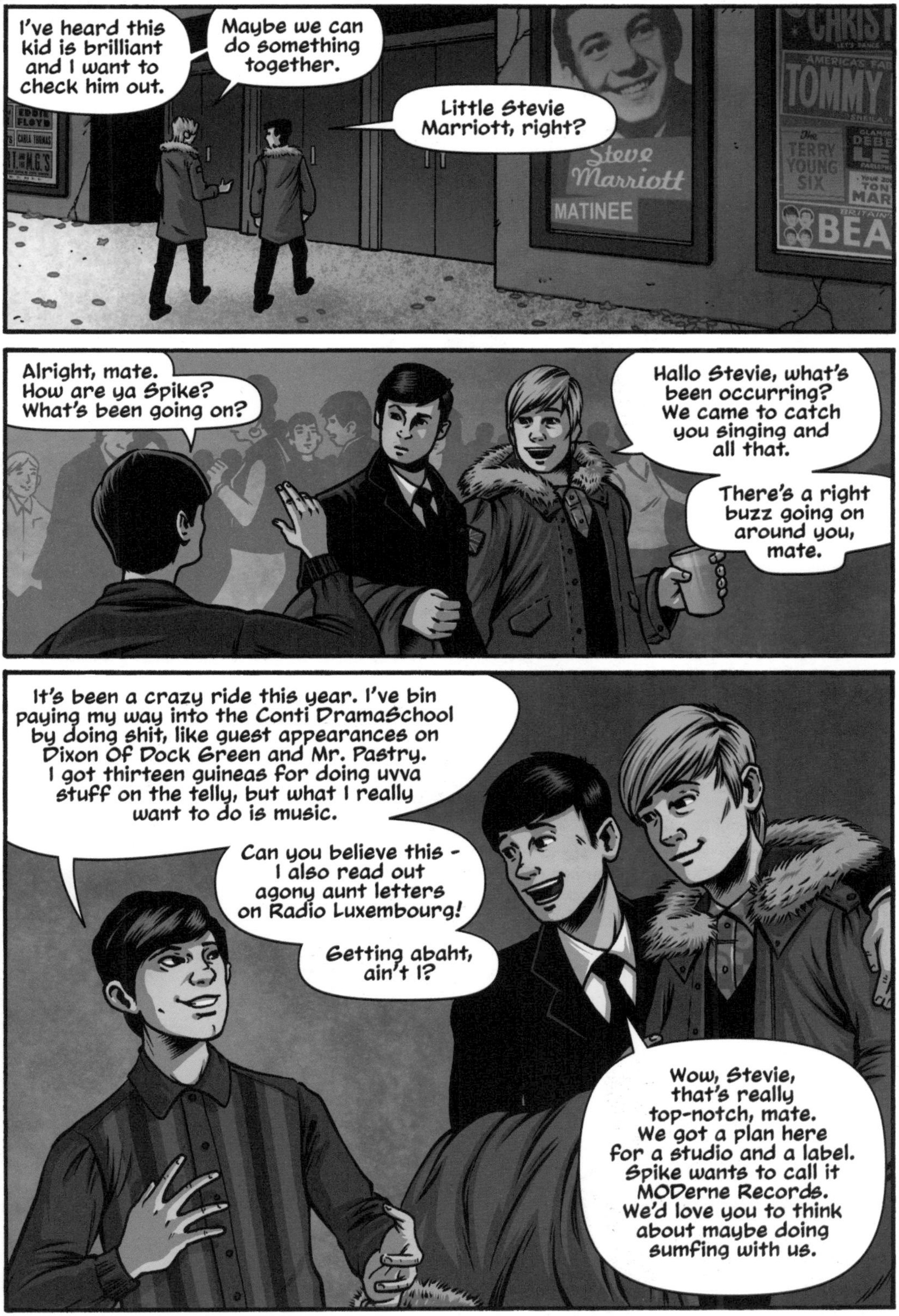
I've heard this kid is brilliant and I want to check him out.
Maybe we can do something together.
Little Stevie Marriott, right?
Steve Marriott
MATINEE
Alright, mate. How are ya Spike? What's been going on?
Hallo Stevie, what's been occurring? We came to catch you singing and all that.
There's a right buzz going on around you, mate.
It's been a crazy ride this year. I've bin paying my way into the Conti DramaSchool by doing shit, like guest appearances on Dixon Of Dock Green and Mr. Pastry. I got thirteen guineas for doing uvva stuff on the telly, but what I really want to do is music.
Can you believe this - I also read out agony aunt letters on Radio Luxembourg!
Getting abaht, ain't I?
Wow, Stevie, that's really top-notch, mate. We got a plan here for a studio and a label. Spike wants to call it MODerne Records. We'd love you to think about maybe doing sumfing with us.

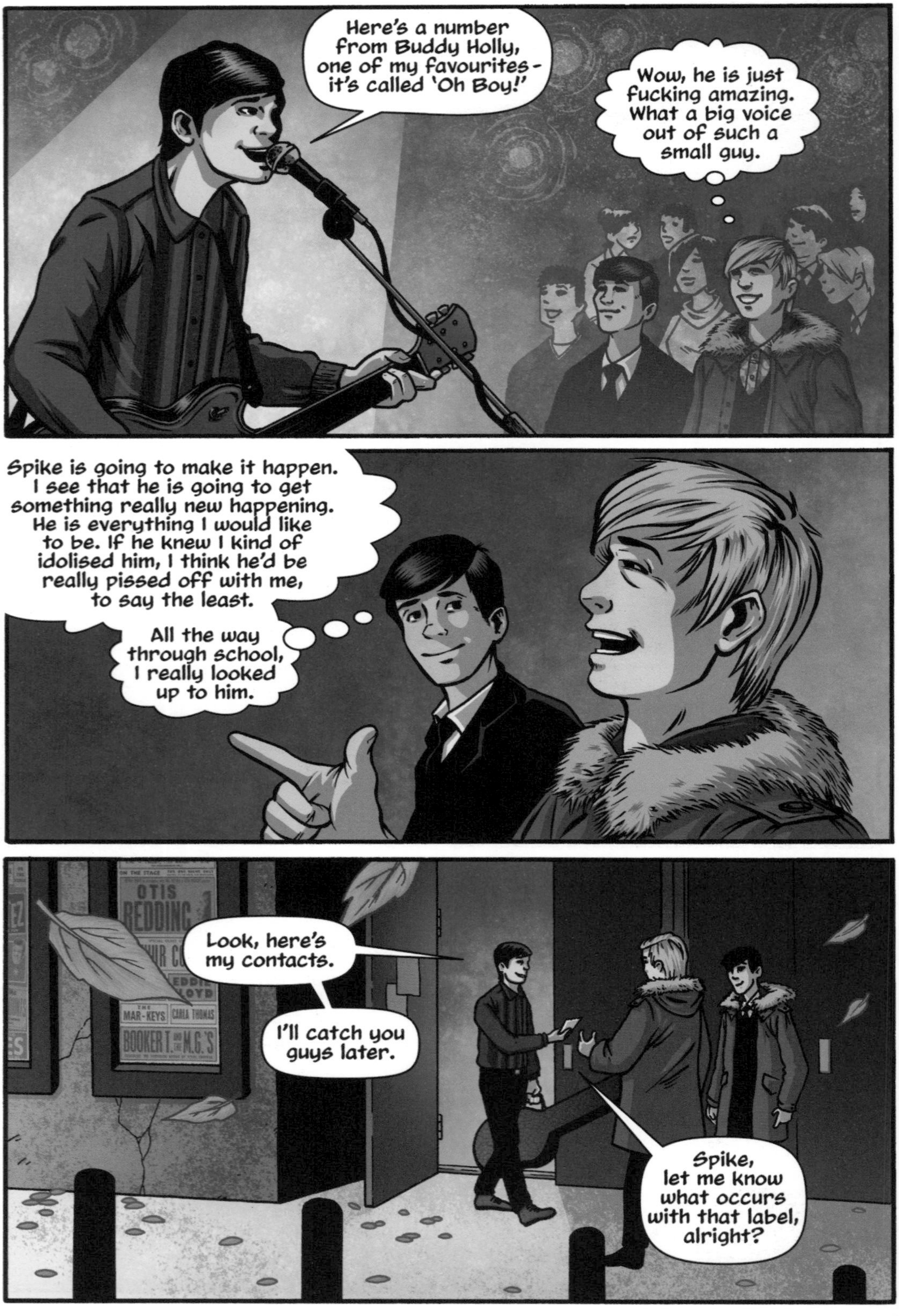
Here's a number from Buddy Holly, one of my favourites - it's called 'Oh Boy!'
Wow, he is just fucking amazing. What a big voice out of such a small guy.
Spike is going to make it happen. I see that he is going to get something really new happening. He is everything I would like to be. If he knew I kind of idolised him, I think he'd be really pissed off with me, to say the least.
All the way through school, I really looked up to him.
OTIS REDDING
THE MAR-KEYS
CARLA THOMAS
BOOKER T.
M.G.'S
Look, here's my contacts.
I'll catch you guys later.
Spike, let me know what occurs with that label, alright?

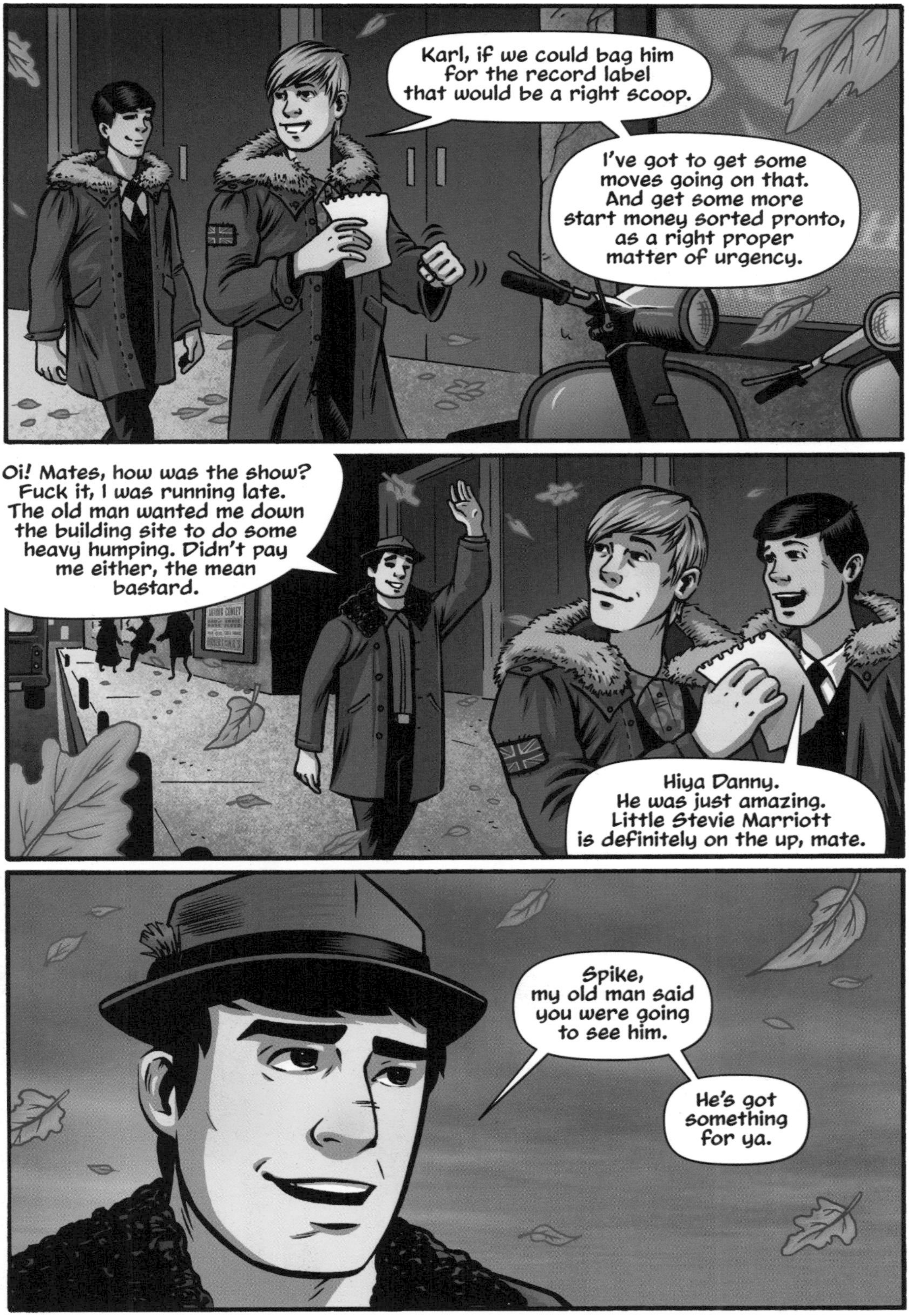
Karl, if we could bag him for the record label that would be a right scoop.
I've got to get some moves going on that. And get some more start money sorted pronto, as a right proper matter of urgency.
Oi! Mates, how was the show? Fuck it, I was running late. The old man wanted me down the building site to do some heavy humping. Didn't pay me either, the mean bastard.
Hiya Danny. He was just amazing. Little Stevie Marriott is definitely on the up, mate.
Spike, my old man said you were going to see him.
He's got something for ya.

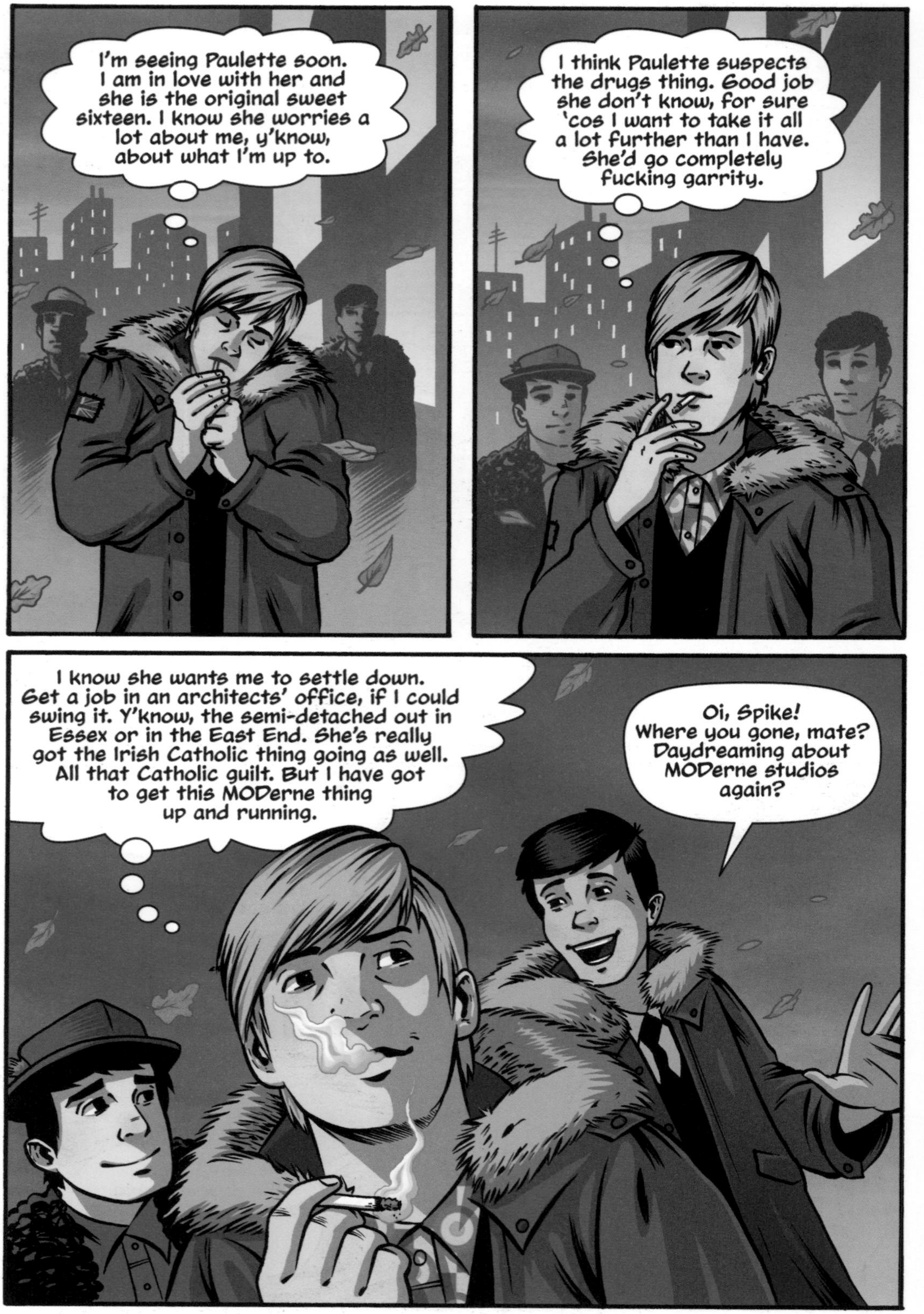
I'm seeing Paulette soon. I am in love with her and she is the original sweet sixteen. I know she worries a lot about me, y'know, about what I'm up to.
I think Paulette suspects the drugs thing. Good job she don't know, for sure 'cos I want to take it all a lot further than I have. She'd go completely fucking garrity.
I know she wants me to settle down. Get a job in an architects' office, if I could swing it. Y'know, the semi-detached out in Essex or in the East End. She's really got the Irish Catholic thing going as well. All that Catholic guilt. But I have got to get this MODerne thing up and running.
Oi, Spike! Where you gone, mate? Daydreaming about MODerne studios again?

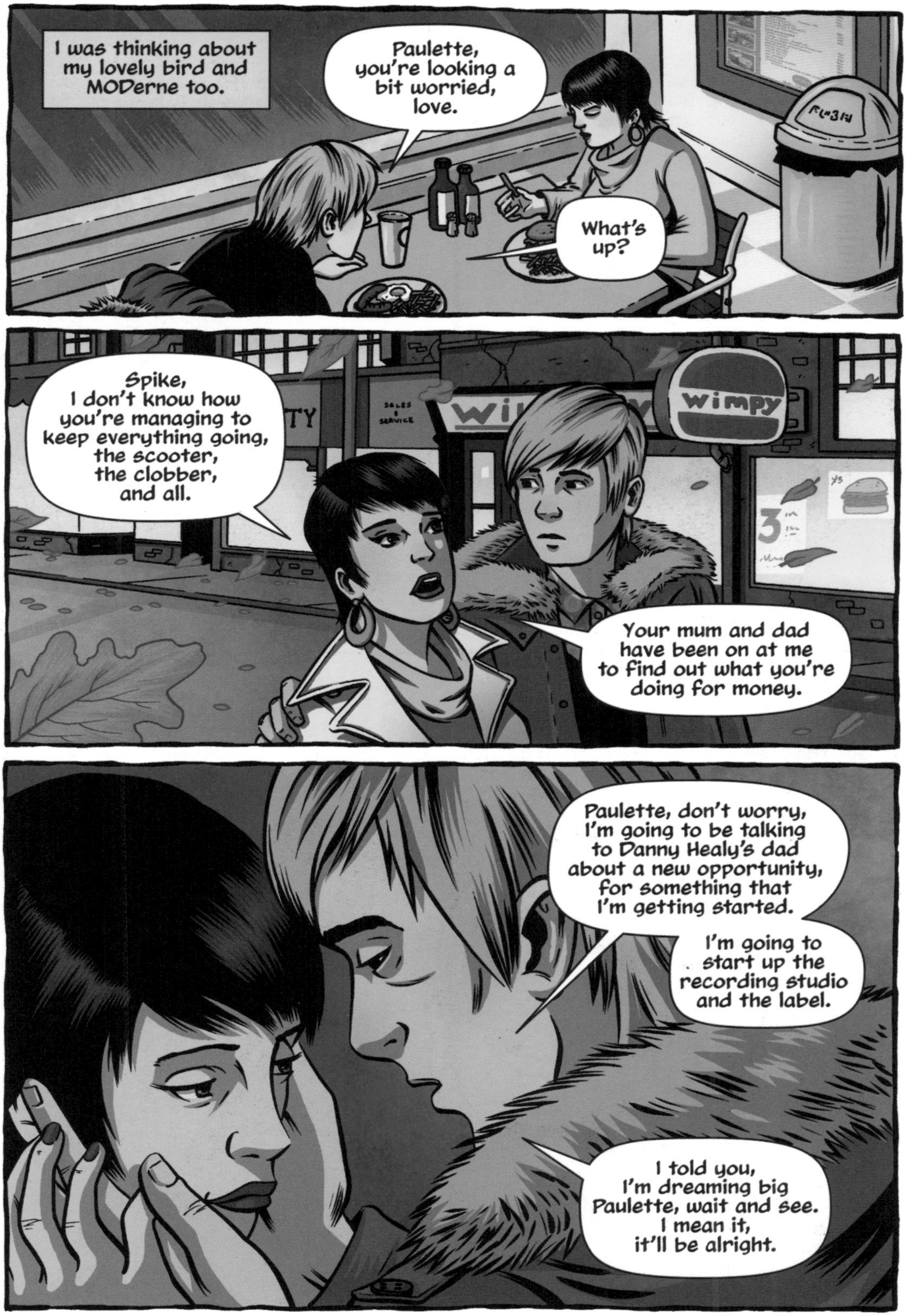
I was thinking about my lovely bird and MODerne too.
Paulette, you're looking a bit worried, love.
What's up?
wimpy
Spike, I don't know how you're managing to keep everything going, the scooter, the clobber, and all.
Your mum and dad have been on at me to find out what you're doing for money.
Paulette, don't worry, I'm going to be talking to Danny Healy's dad about a new opportunity, for something that I'm getting started.
I'm going to start up the recording studio and the label.
I told you, I'm dreaming big Paulette, wait and see. I mean it, it'll be alright.

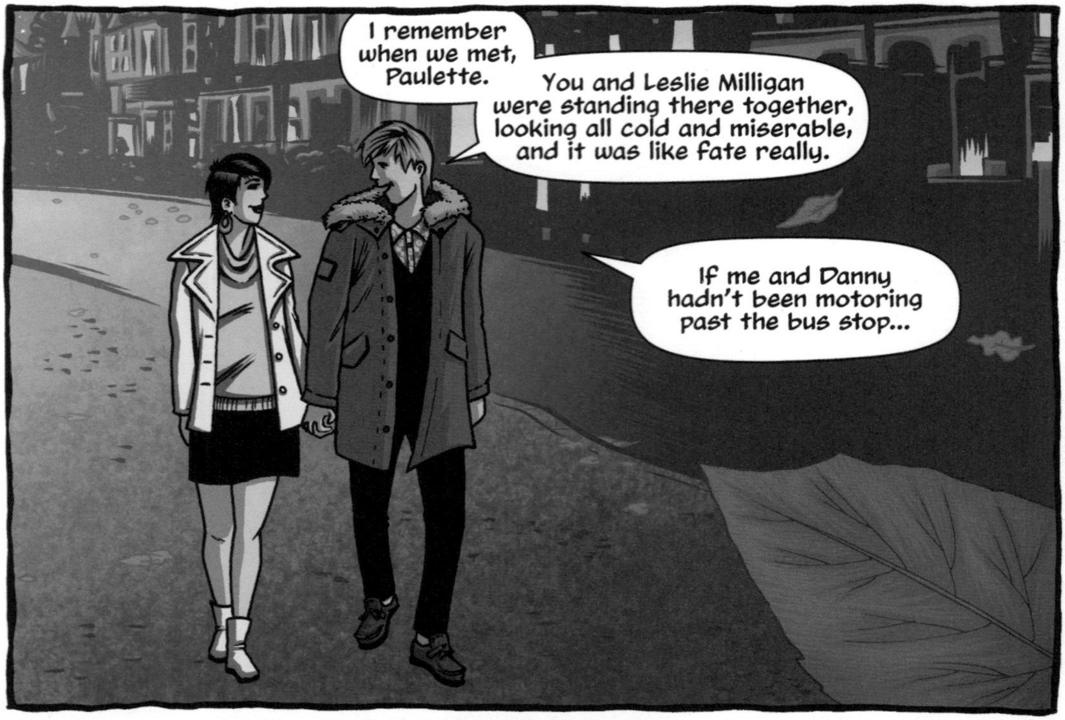
I remember when we met, Paulette.
You and Leslie Milligan were standing there together, looking all cold and miserable, and it was like fate really.
If me and Danny hadn't been motoring past the bus stop...

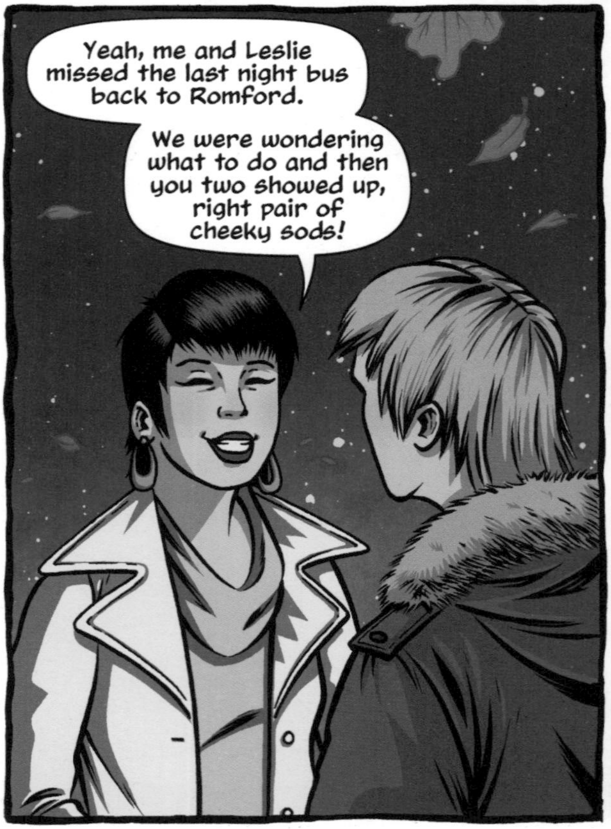
Yeah, me and Leslie missed the last night bus back to Romford.
We were wondering what to do and then you two showed up, right pair of cheeky sods!

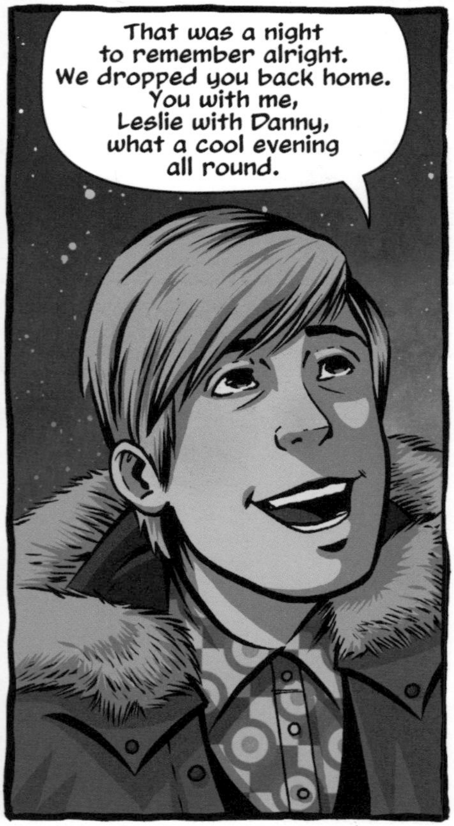
That was a night to remember alright. We dropped you back home. You with me, Leslie with Danny, what a cool evening all round.

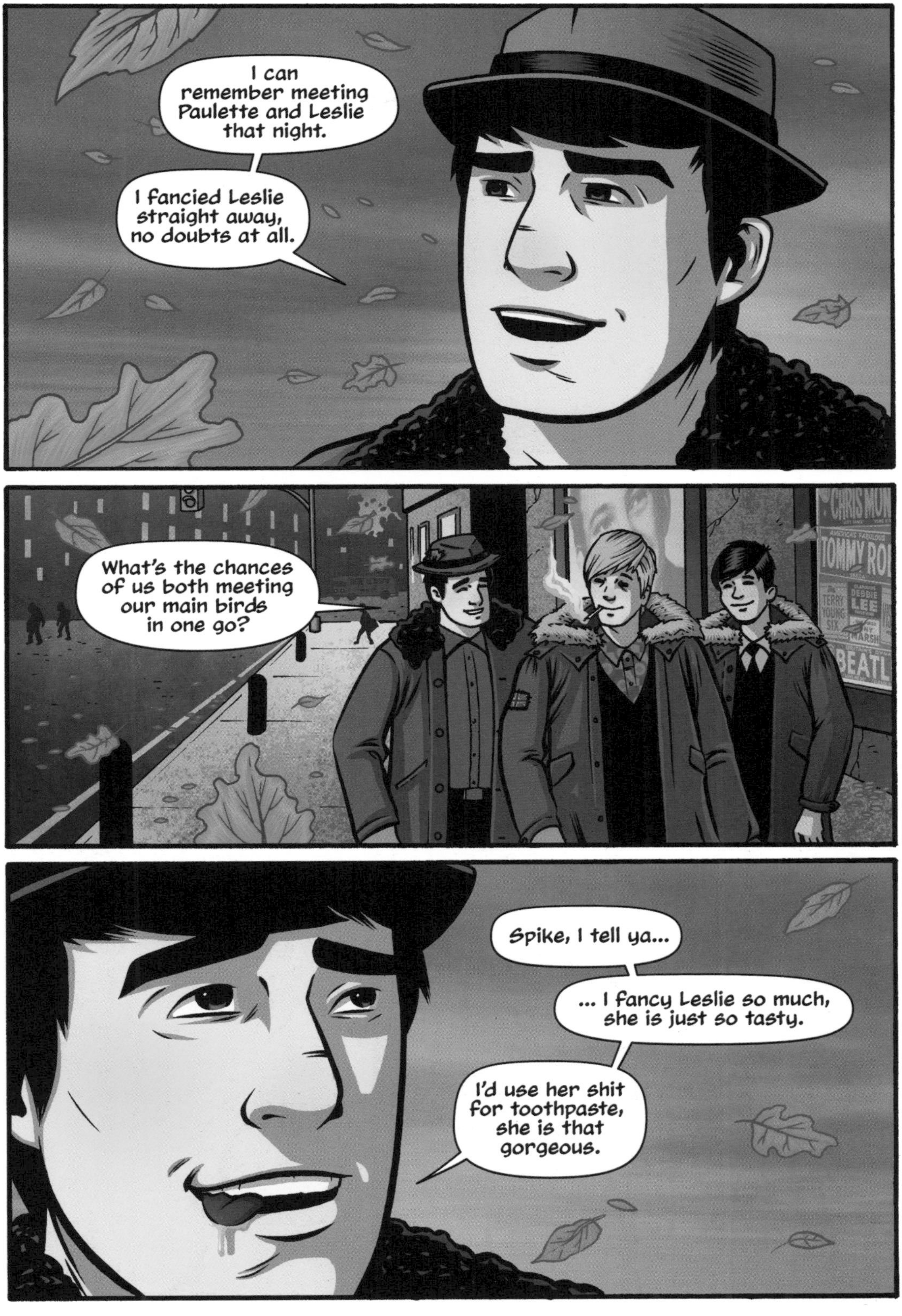
I can remember meeting Paulette and Leslie that night.
I fancied Leslie straight away, no doubts at all.
AMERICA'S FABULOUS
TERRY YOUNG SIX
DEBBIE LEE
What's the chances of us both meeting our main birds in one go?
Spike, I tell ya...
... I fancy Leslie so much, she is just so tasty.
I'd use her shit for toothpaste, she is that gorgeous.

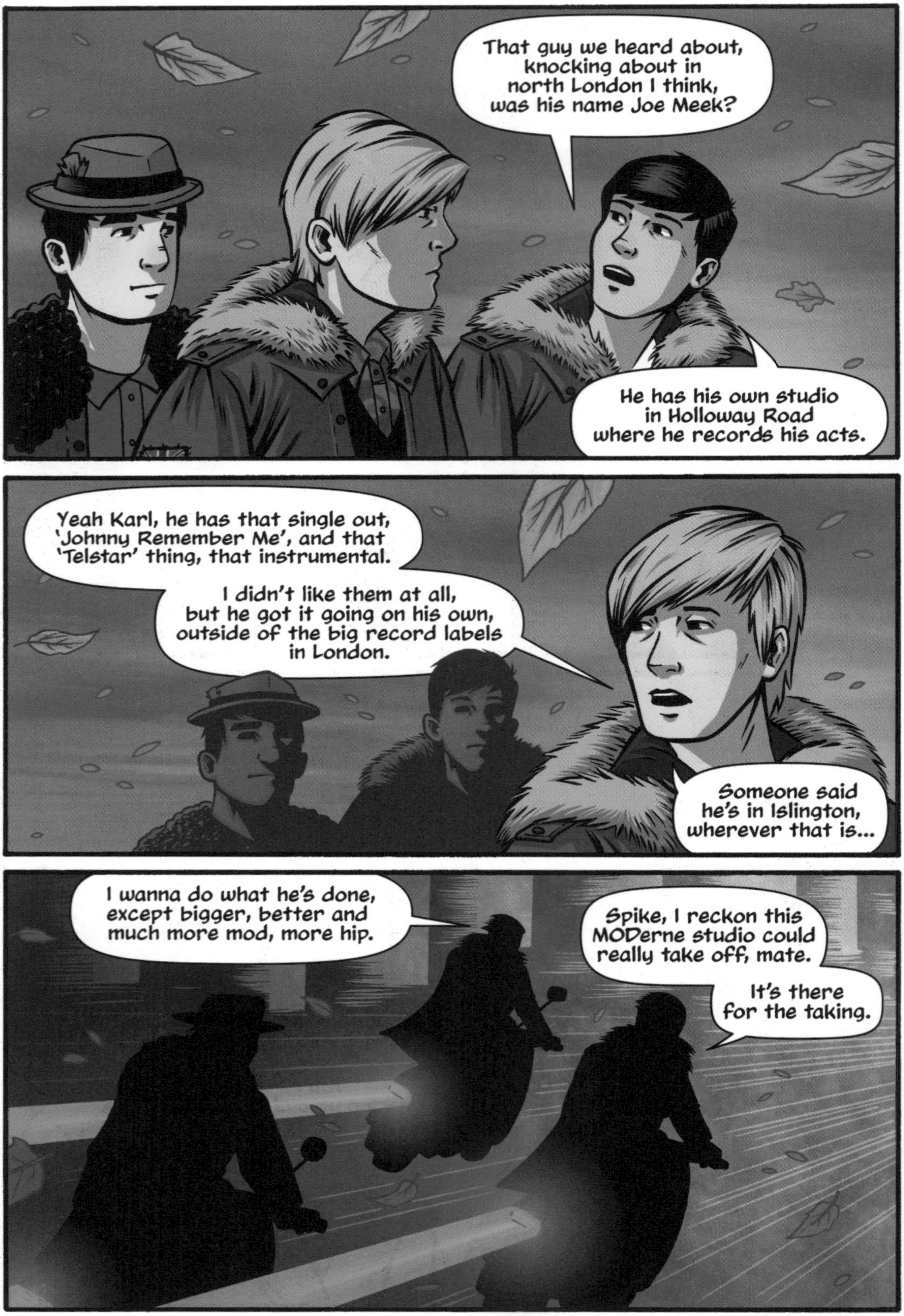
That guy we heard about, knocking about in north London I think, was his name Joe Meek?
He has his own studio in Holloway Road where he records his acts.
Yeah Karl, he has that single out, 'Johnny Remember Me', and that 'Telstar' thing, that instrumental.
I didn't like them at all, but he got it going on his own, outside of the big record labels in London.
Someone said he's in Islington, wherever that is...
I wanna do what he's done, except bigger, better and much more mod, more hip.
Spike, I reckon this MODerne studio could really take off, mate.
It's there for the taking.

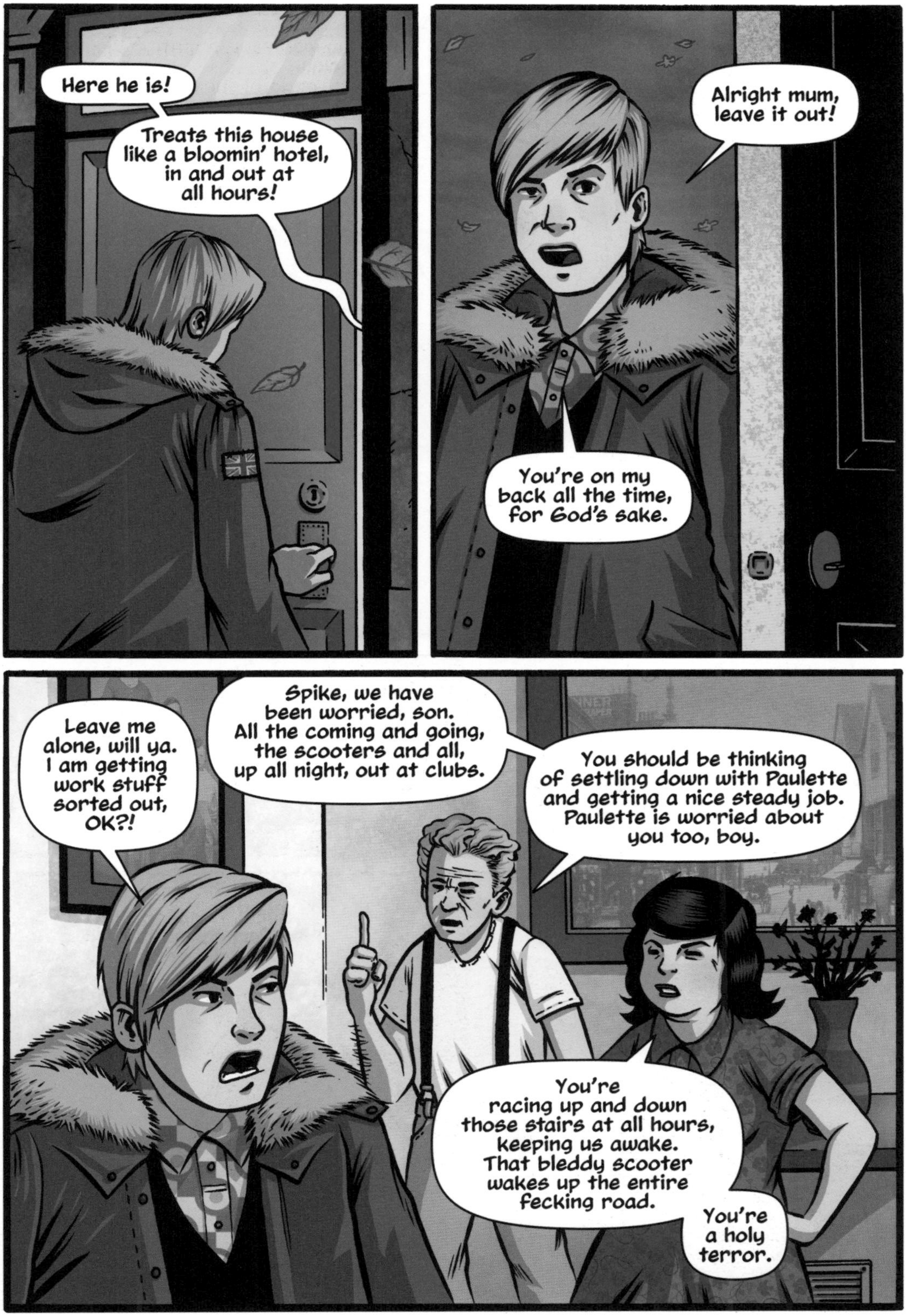
Here he is!
Treats this house like a bloomin' hotel, in and out at all hours!
Alright mum, leave it out!
You're on my back all the time, for God's sake.
Leave me alone, will ya. I am getting work stuff sorted out, OK?!
Spike, we have been worried, son. All the coming and going, the scooters and all, up all night, out at clubs.
You should be thinking of settling down with Paulette and getting a nice steady job. Paulette is worried about you too, boy.
You're racing up and down those stairs at all hours, keeping us awake. That bleddy scooter wakes up the entire fecking road.
You're a holy terror.

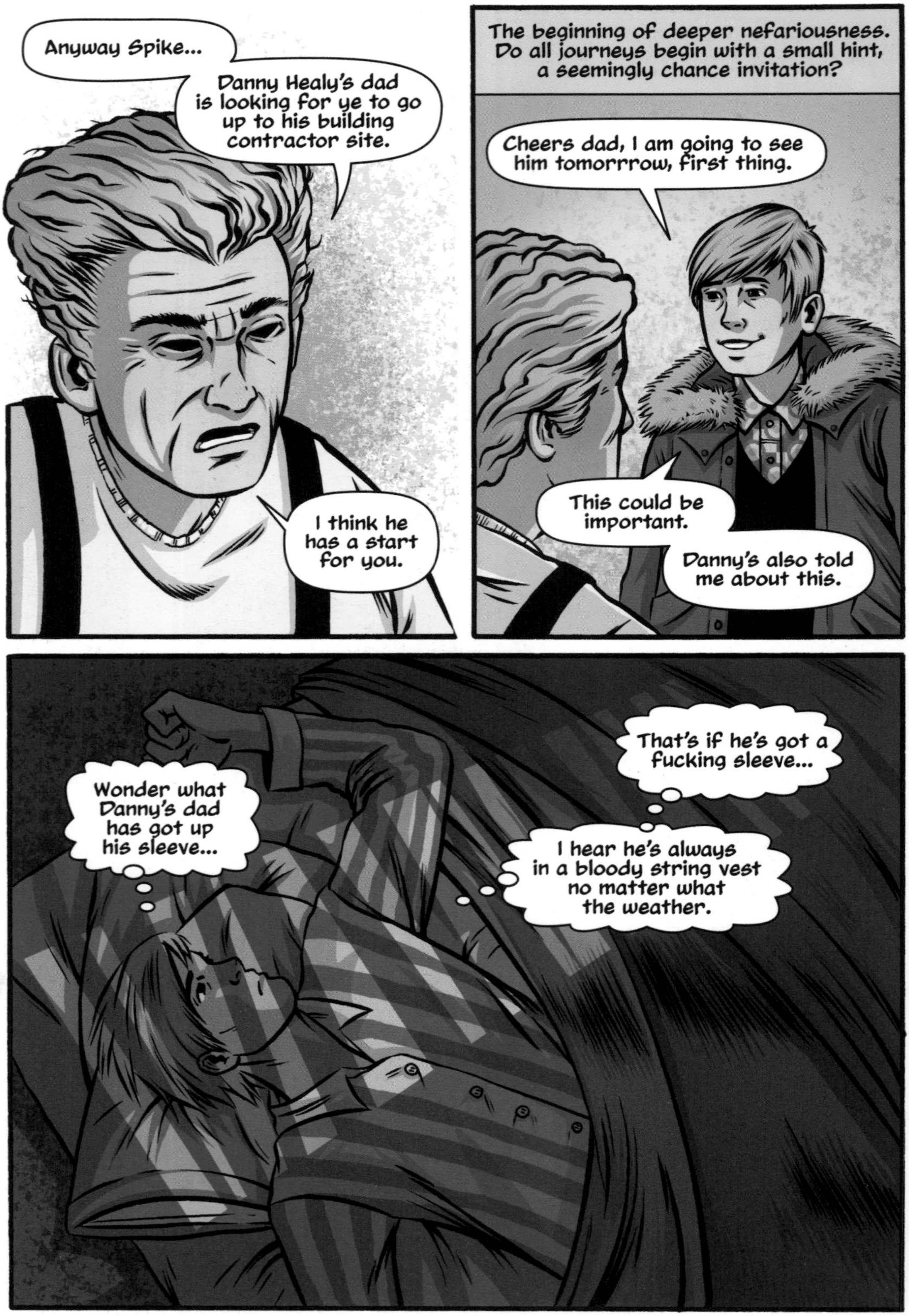
Anyway Spike...
Danny Healy's dad is looking for ye to go up to his building contractor site.
I think he has a start for you.
The beginning of deeper nefariousness. Do all journeys begin with a small hint, a seemingly chance invitation?
Cheers dad, I am going to see him tomorrow, first thing.
This could be important.
Danny's also told me about this.
Wonder what Danny's dad has got up his sleeve...
That's if he's got a fucking sleeve...
I hear he's always in a bloody string vest no matter what the weather.

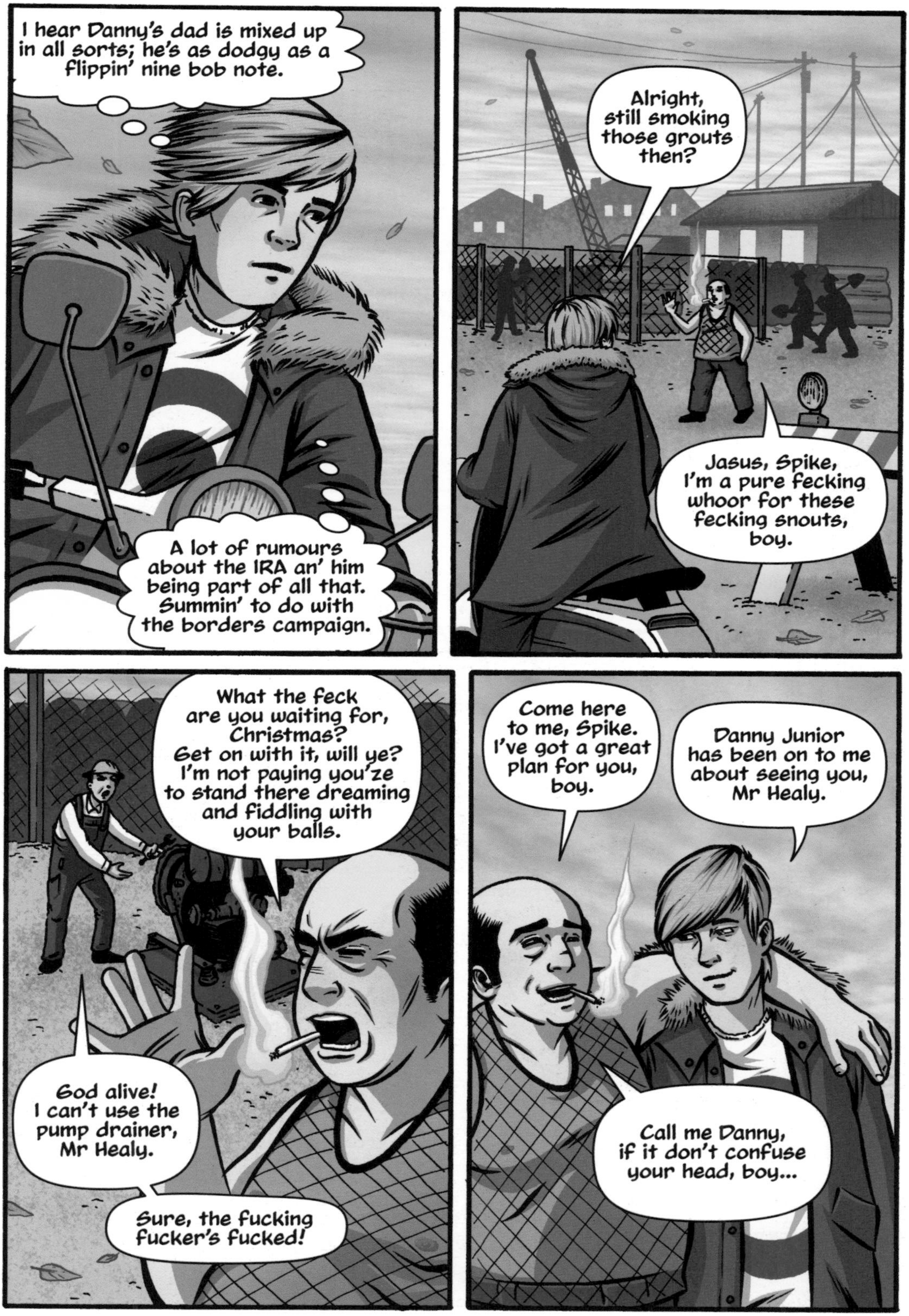
I hear Danny's dad is mixed up in all sorts; he's as dodgy as a flippin' nine bob note.
A lot of rumours about the IRA an' him being part of all that. Summin' to do with the borders campaign.
Alright, still smoking those grouts then?
Jasus, Spike, I'm a pure fecking whoor for these fecking snouts, boy.
What the feck are you waiting for, Christmas? Get on with it, will ye? I'm not paying you'ze to stand there dreaming and fiddling with your balls.
God alive! I can't use the pump drainer, Mr Healy.
Sure, the fucking fucker's fucked!
Come here to me, Spike. I've got a great plan for you, boy.
Danny Junior has been on to me about seeing you, Mr Healy.
Call me Danny, if it don't confuse your head, boy...

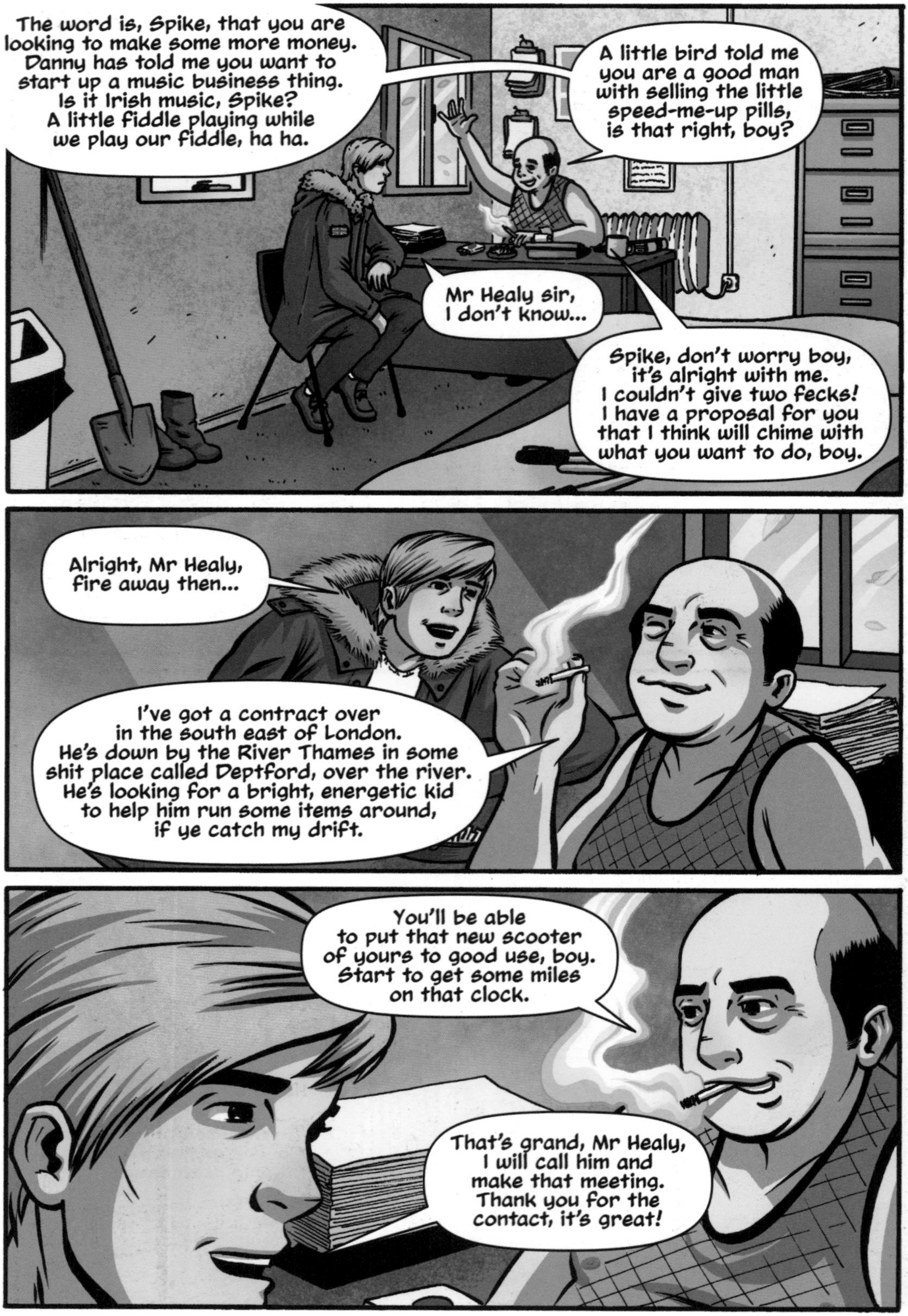
The word is, Spike, that you are looking to make some more money. Danny has told me you want to start up a music business thing. Is it Irish music, Spike? A little fiddle playing while we play our fiddle, ha ha.
A little bird told me you are a good man with selling the little speed-me-up pills, is that right, boy?
Mr Healy sir, I don't know...
Spike, don't worry boy, it's alright with me. I couldn't give two fecks! I have a proposal for you that I think will chime with what you want to do, boy.
Alright, Mr Healy, fire away then...
I've got a contract over in the south east of London. He's down by the River Thames in some shit place called Deptford, over the river. He's looking for a bright, energetic kid to help him run some items around, if ye catch my drift.
You'll be able to put that new scooter of yours to good use, boy. Start to get some miles on that clock.
That's grand, Mr Healy, I will call him and make that meeting. Thank you for the contact, it's great!

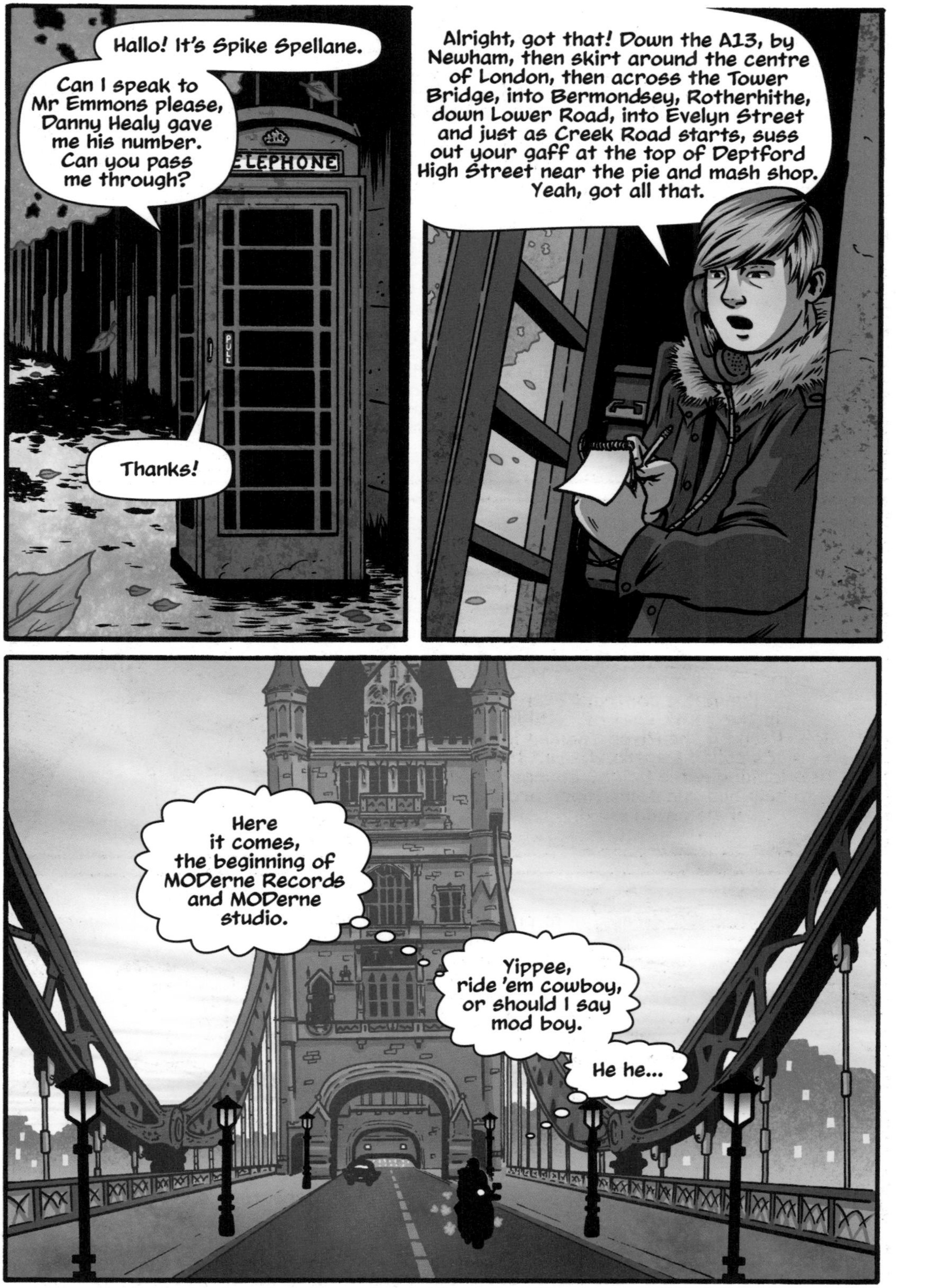
Hallo! It's Spike Spellane.
Can I speak to Mr Emmons please, Danny Healy gave me his number. Can you pass me through?
ELEPHONE
PULL
Thanks!
Alright, got that! Down the A13, by Newham, then skirt around the centre of London, then across the Tower Bridge, into Bermondsey, Rotherhithe, down Lower Road, into Evelyn Street and just as Creek Road starts, suss out your gaff at the top of Deptford High Street near the pie and mash shop. Yeah, got all that.
Here it comes, the beginning of MODerne Records and MODerne studio.
Yippee, ride 'em cowboy, or should I say mod boy.
He he...

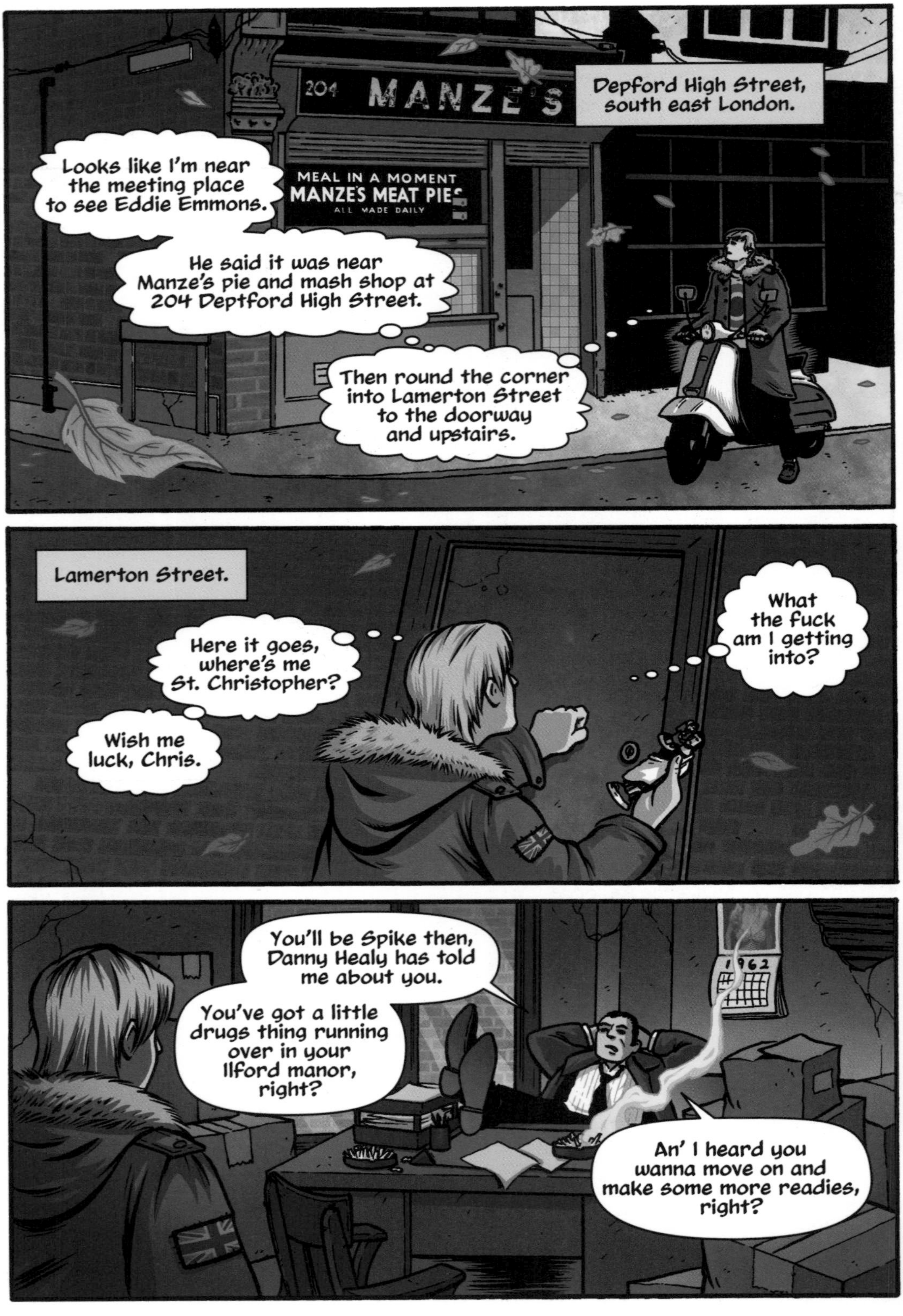
204 MANZE'S
Depford High Street,
south east London.
Looks like I'm near the meeting place to see Eddie Emmons.
MEAL IN A MOMENT
MANZE'S MEAT PIES
ALL MADE DAILY
He said it was near Manze's pie and mash shop at 204 Deptford High Street.
Then round the corner into Lamerton Street to the doorway and upstairs.
Lamerton Street.
Here it goes, where's me St. Christopher?
Wish me luck, Chris.
What the fuck am I getting into?
You'll be Spike then, Danny Healy has told me about you.
You've got a little drugs thing running over in your Ilford manor, right?
1962
An' I heard you wanna move on and make some more readies, right?

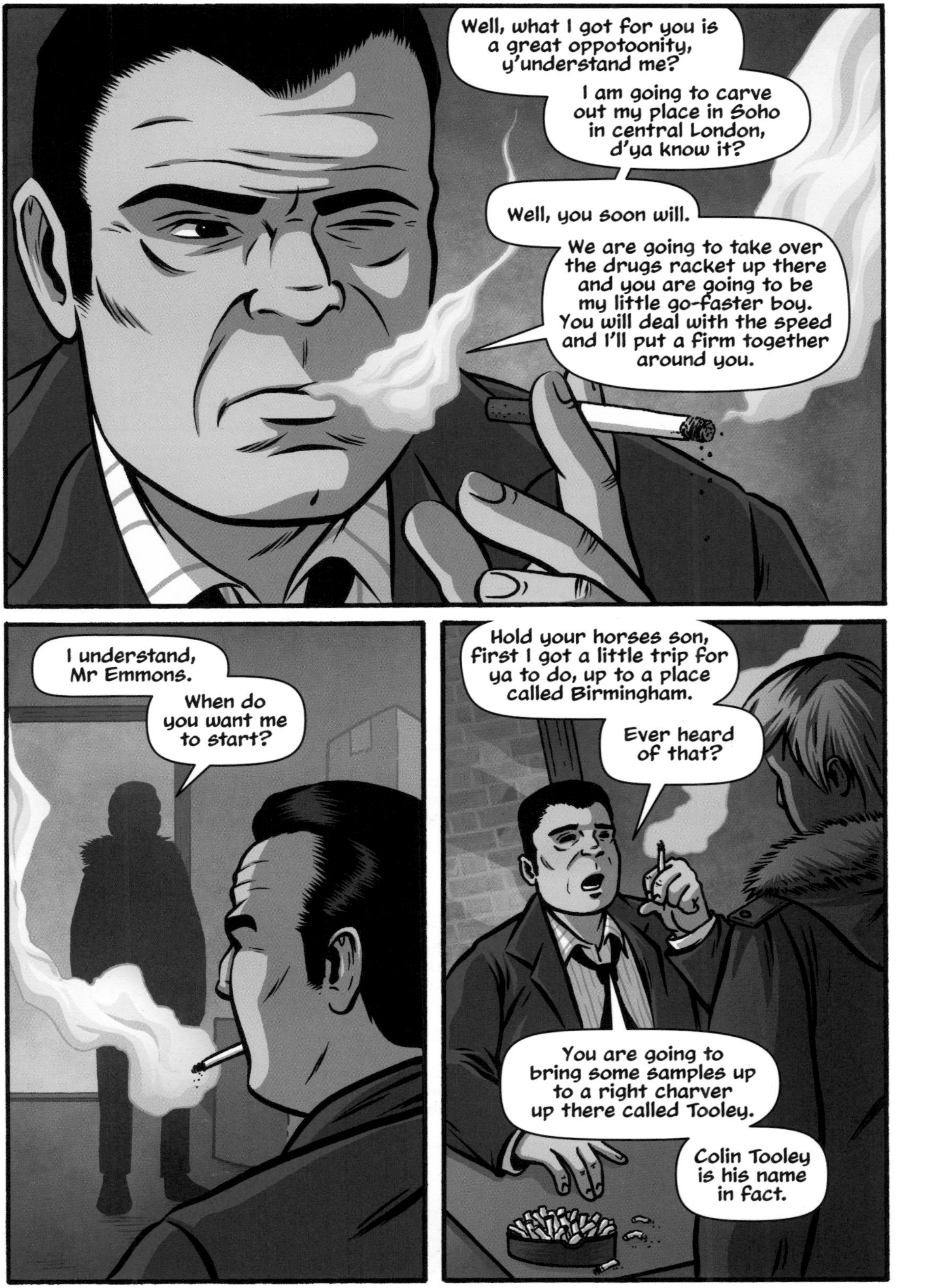
Well, what I got for you is a great oppotoonity, y'understand me?
I am going to carve out my place in Soho in central London, d'ya know it?
Well, you soon will.
We are going to take over the drugs racket up there and you are going to be my little go-faster boy. You will deal with the speed and I'll put a firm together around you.
I understand, Mr Emmons.
When do you want me to start?
Hold your horses son, first I got a little trip for ya to do, up to a place called Birmingham.
Ever heard of that?
You are going to bring some samples up to a right charver up there called Tooley.
Colin Tooley is his name in fact.

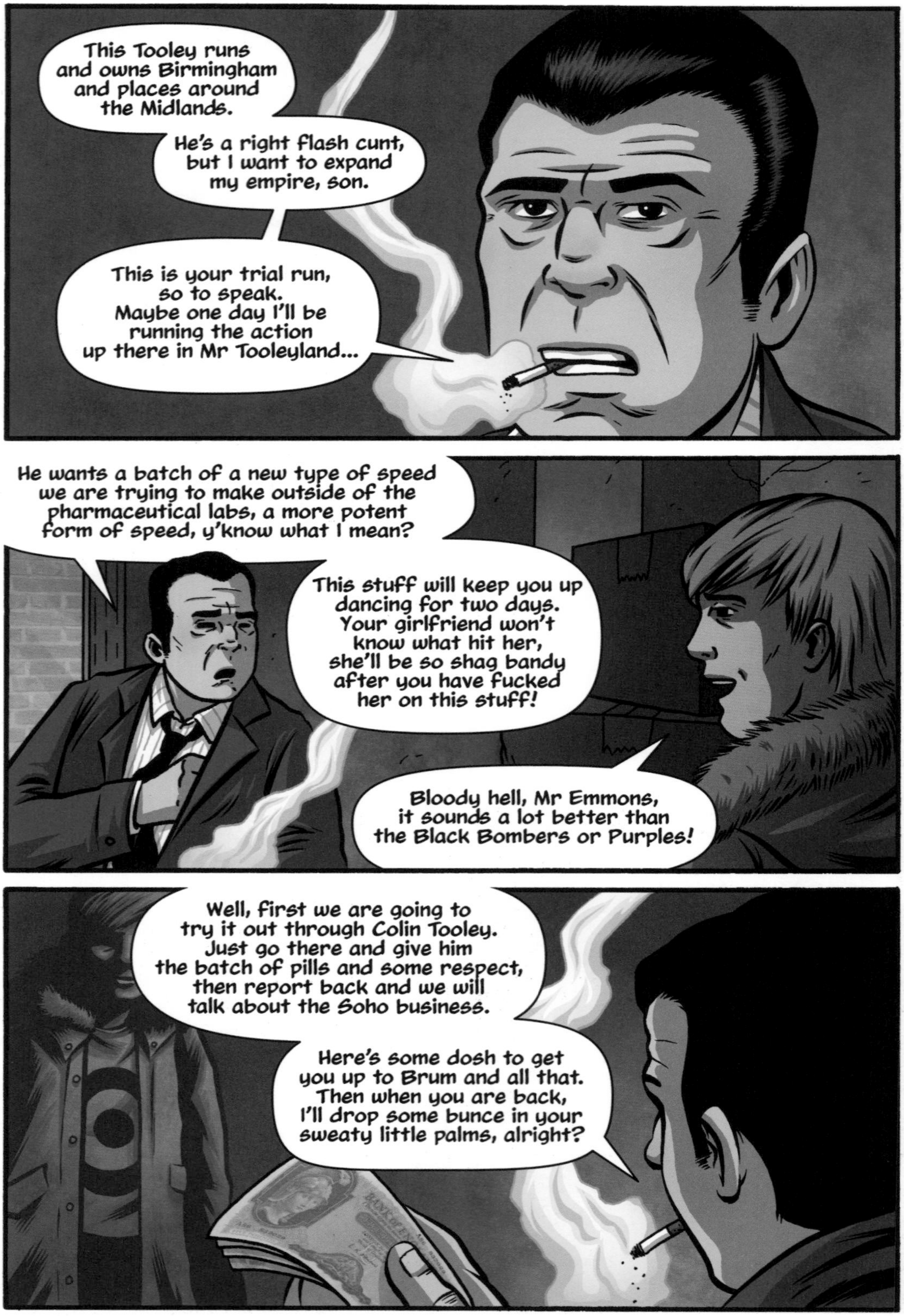
This Tooley runs and owns Birmingham and places around the Midlands.
He's a right flash cunt, but I want to expand my empire, son.
This is your trial run, so to speak. Maybe one day I'll be running the action up there in Mr Tooleyland...
He wants a batch of a new type of speed we are trying to make outside of the pharmaceutical labs, a more potent form of speed, y'know what I mean?
This stuff will keep you up dancing for two days. Your girlfriend won't know what hit her, she'll be so shag bandy after you have fucked her on this stuff!
Bloody hell, Mr Emmons, it sounds a lot better than the Black Bombers or Purples!
Well, first we are going to try it out through Colin Tooley. Just go there and give him the batch of pills and some respect, then report back and we will talk about the Soho business.
Here's some dosh to get you up to Brum and all that. Then when you are back, I'll drop some bunce in your sweaty little palms, alright?

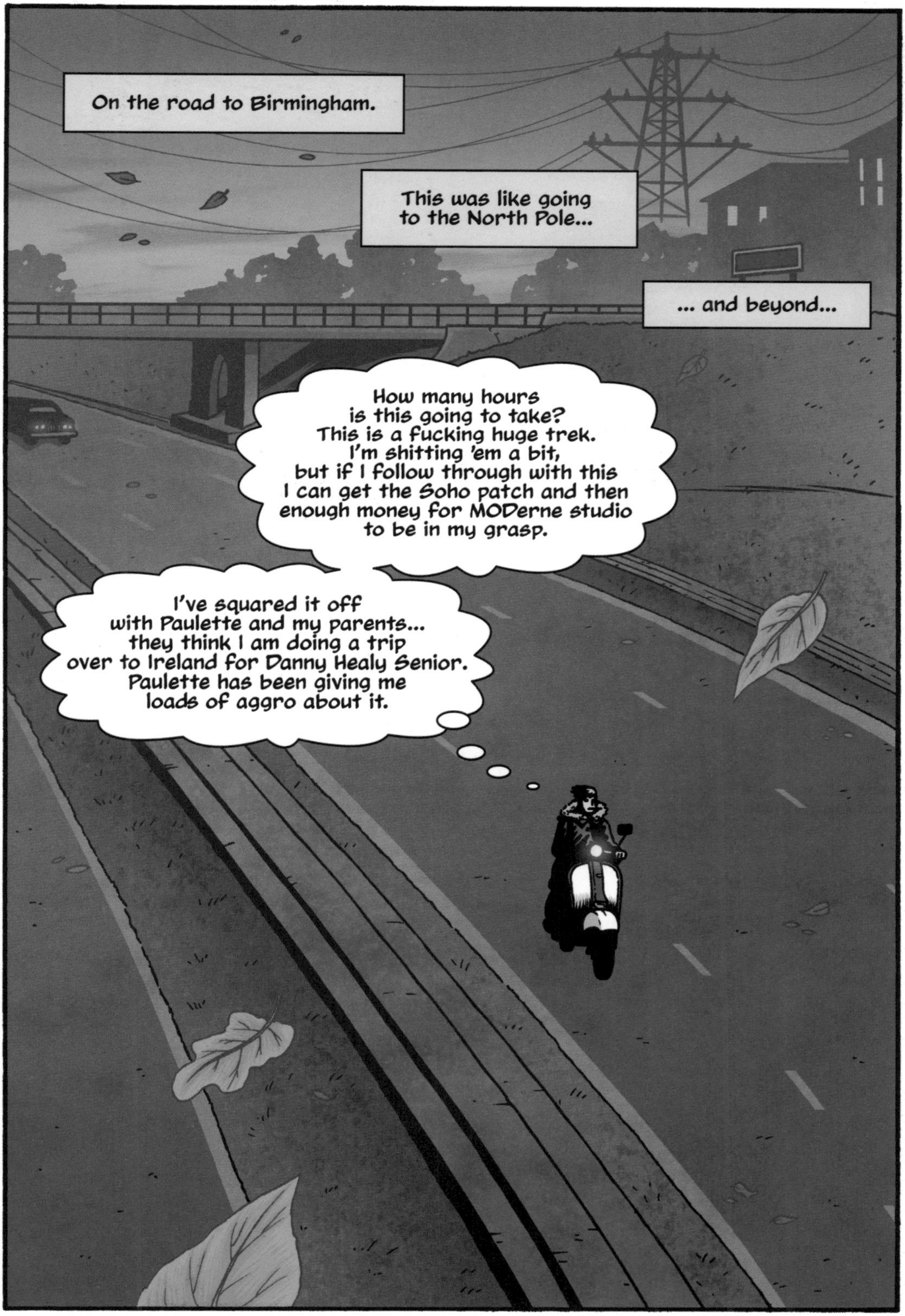
On the road to Birmingham.
This was like going to the North Pole...
... and beyond...
How many hours is this going to take? This is a fucking huge trek. I'm shitting 'em a bit, but if I follow through with this I can get the Soho patch and then enough money for MODerne studio to be in my grasp.
I've squared it off with Paulette and my parents... they think I am doing a trip over to Ireland for Danny Healy Senior. Paulette has been giving me loads of aggro about it.

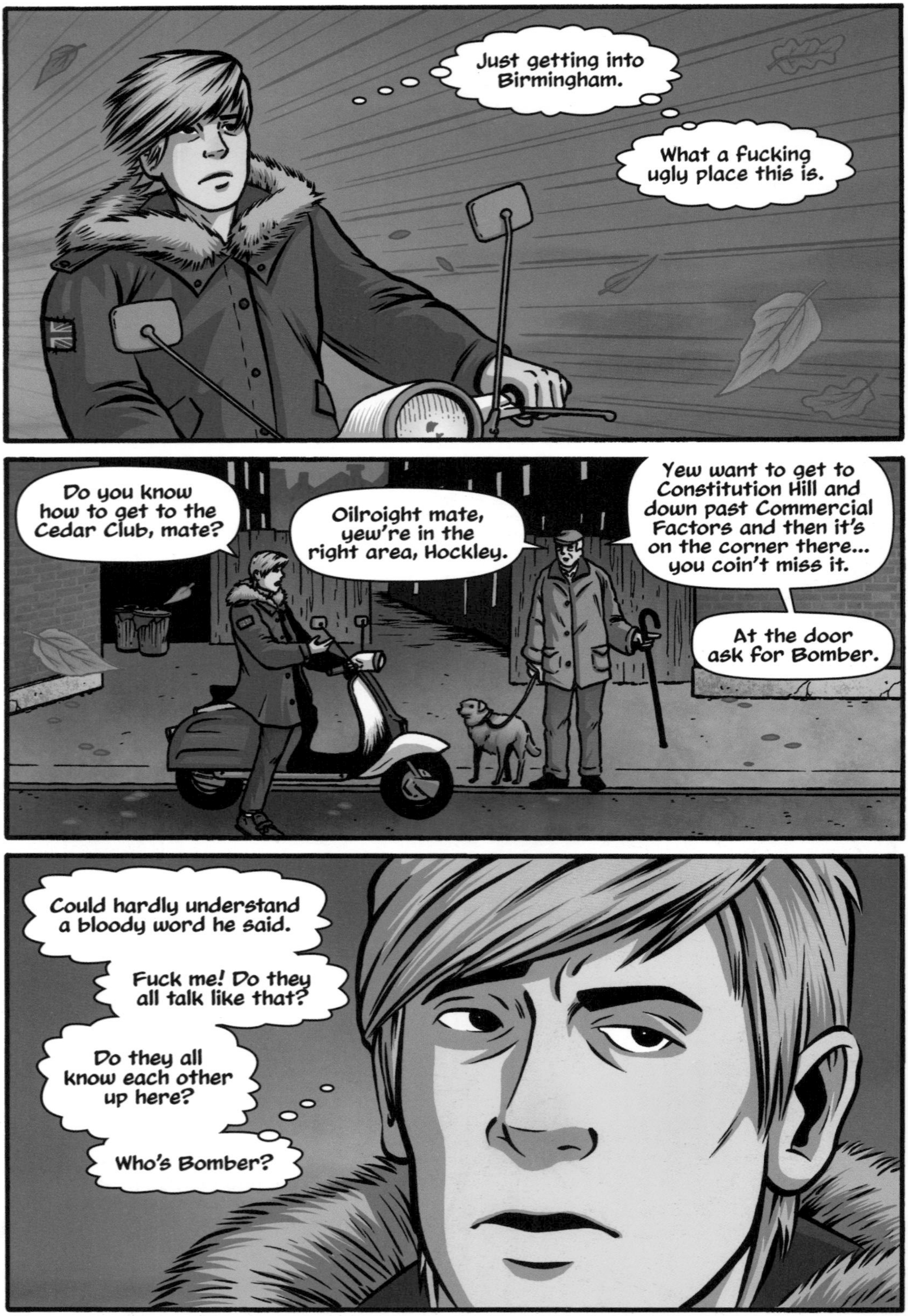
Just getting into Birmingham.
What a fucking ugly place this is.
Do you know how to get to the Cedar Club, mate?
Oilroight mate, yew're in the right area, Hockley.
Yew want to get to Constitution Hill and down past Commercial Factors and then it's on the corner there... you coin't miss it.
At the door ask for Bomber.
Could hardly understand a bloody word he said.
Fuck me! Do they all talk like that?
Do they all know each other up here?
Who's Bomber?

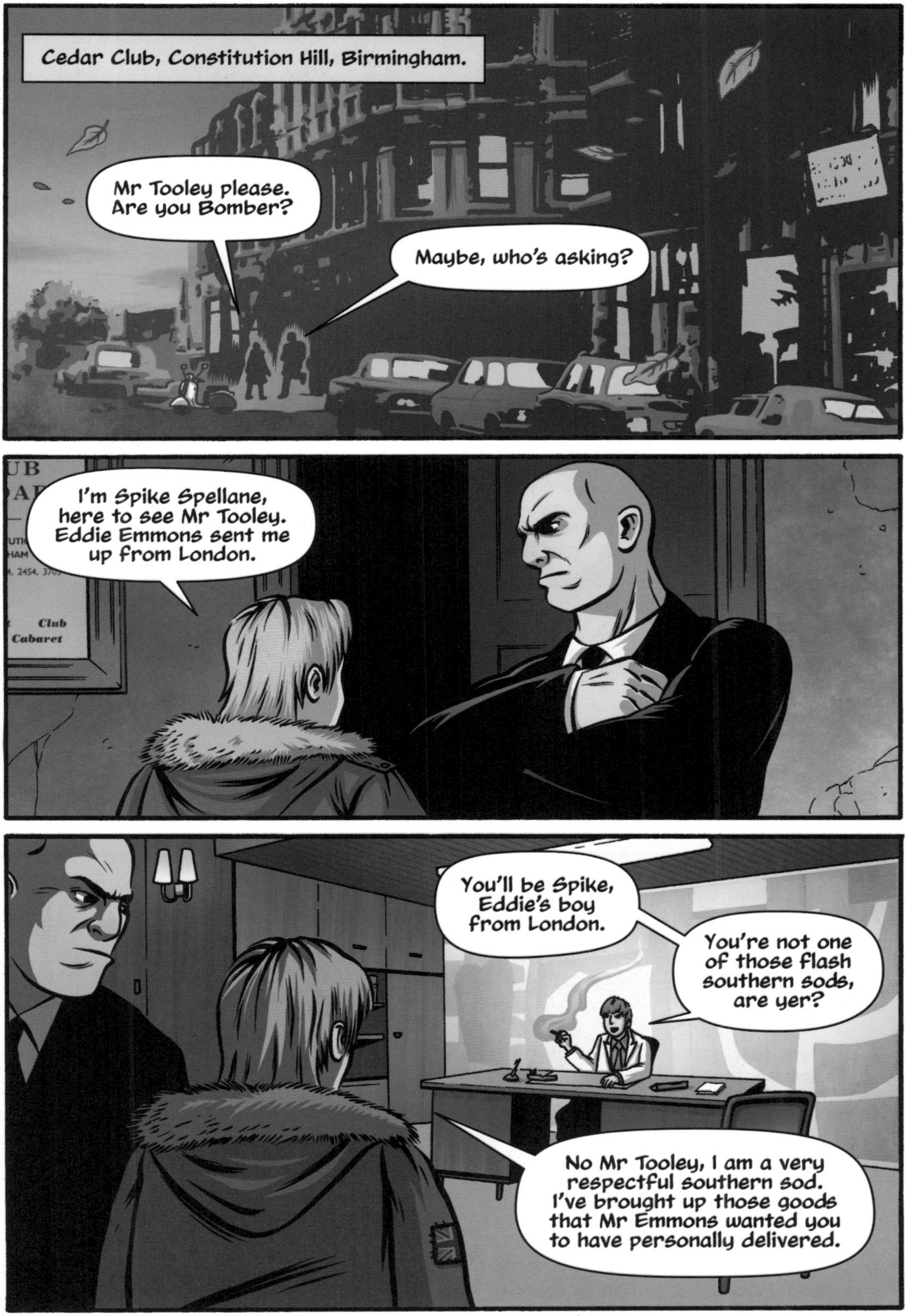
Cedar Club, Constitution Hill, Birmingham.
Mr Tooley please. Are you Bomber?
Maybe, who's asking?
I'm Spike Spellane, here to see Mr Tooley. Eddie Emmons sent me up from London.
Club
Cabaret
You'll be Spike, Eddie's boy from London.
You're not one of those flash southern sods, are yer?
No Mr Tooley, I am a very respectful southern sod. I've brought up those goods that Mr Emmons wanted you to have personally delivered.

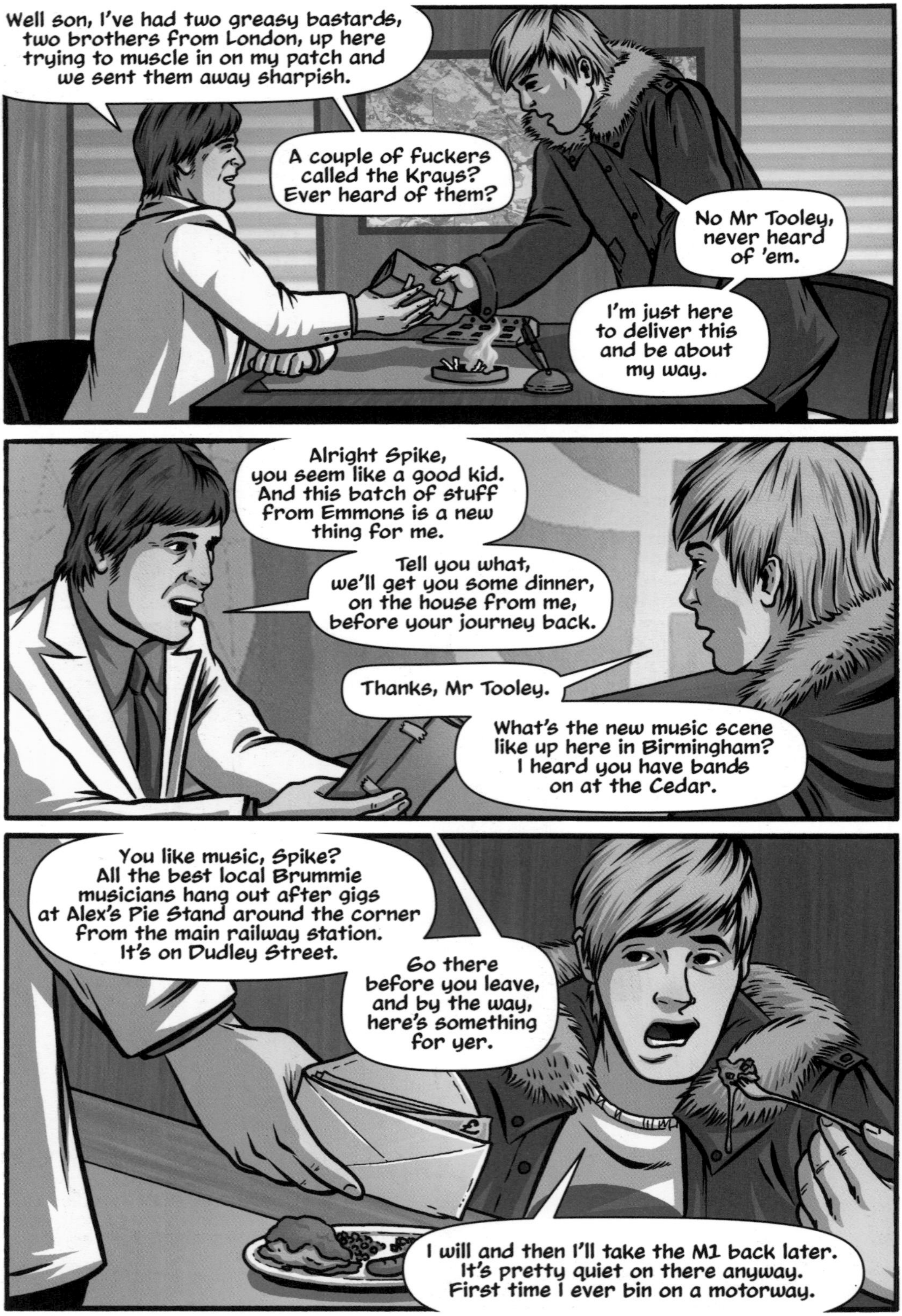
Well son, I've had two greasy bastards, two brothers from London, up here trying to muscle in on my patch and we sent them away sharpish.
A couple of fuckers called the Krays? Ever heard of them?
No Mr Tooley, never heard of 'em.
I'm just here to deliver this and be about my way.
Alright Spike, you seem like a good kid. And this batch of stuff from Emmons is a new thing for me.
Tell you what, we'll get you some dinner, on the house from me, before your journey back.
Thanks, Mr Tooley.
What's the new music scene like up here in Birmingham? I heard you have bands on at the Cedar.
You like music, Spike? All the best local Brummie musicians hang out after gigs at Alex's Pie Stand around the corner from the main railway station. It's on Dudley Street.
Go there before you leave, and by the way, here's something for yer.
I will and then I'll take the M1 back later. It's pretty quiet on there anyway. First time I ever bin on a motorway.

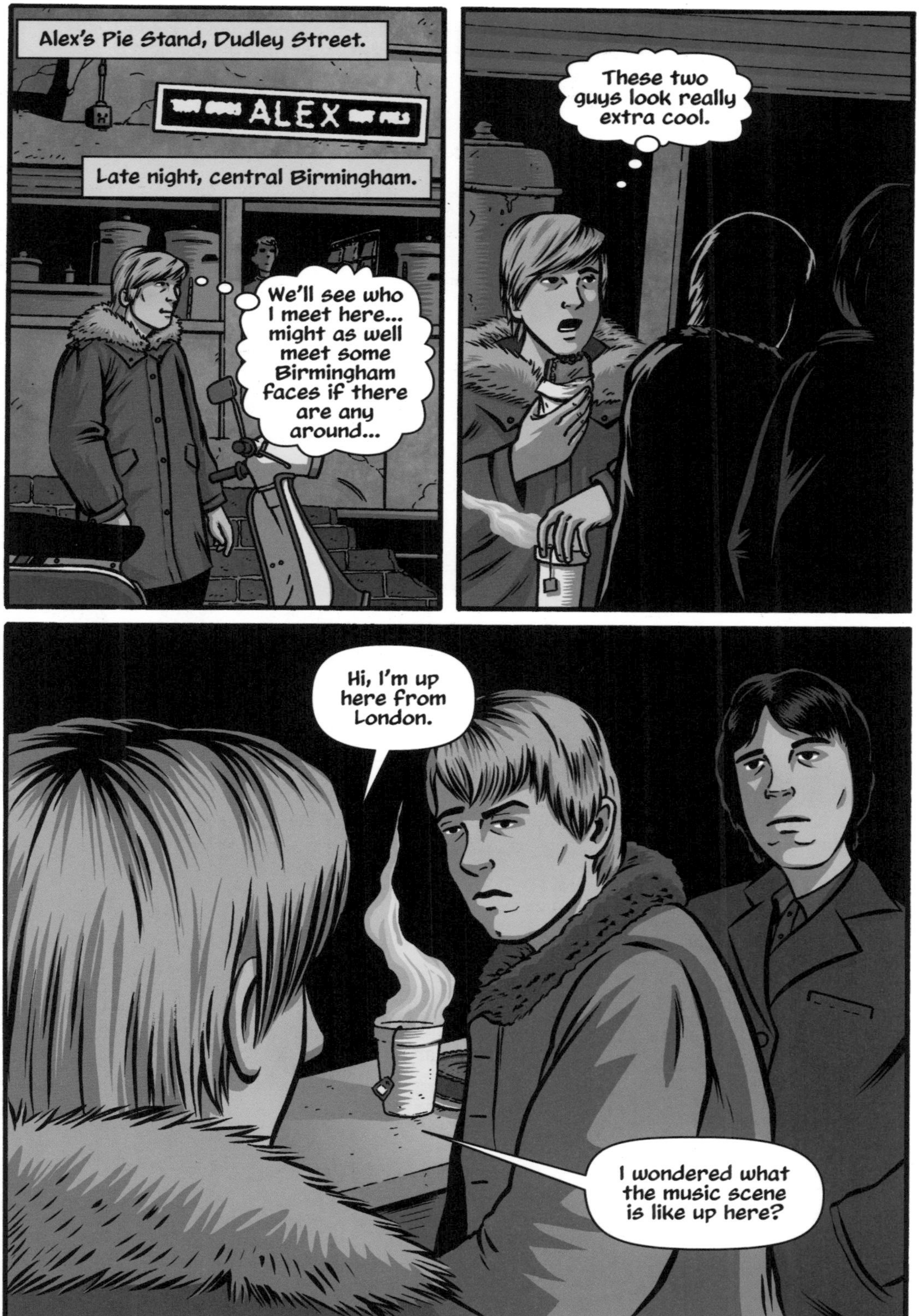
Alex's Pie Stand, Dudley Street.
ALEX
Late night, central Birmingham.
We'll see who I meet here... might as well meet some Birmingham faces if there are any around...
These two guys look really extra cool.
Hi, I'm up here from London.
I wondered what the music scene is like up here?

Wow! This guy almost looks like me! How bloody weird, he's almost a dead ringer.

Bloody hell! This guy almost looks like me! Is it my twin or summat?

I'm Spike Spellane from London, I'm about to set up a label and recording studio down there. What are you guys into?

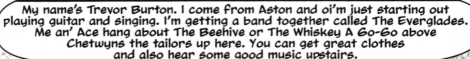

My name's Trevor Burton. I come from Aston and oi'm just starting out playing guitar and singing. I'm getting a band together called The Everglades. Me an' Ace hang about The Beehive or The Whiskey A Go-Go above Chetwyns the tailors up here. You can get great clothes and also hear some good music upstairs.

And I'm Chris Kefford, but I'm also called Ace, Ace the face, mate! Me and Trev are looking to get a band started at some stage. I play bass and sing in The Shantelles with my uncles.

You guys look so young but you're getting things going up here, right?

There's a big scene happening up here but a lot of it is just local bands doing cover versions. One day me and Trev will break out with some new happening stuff.

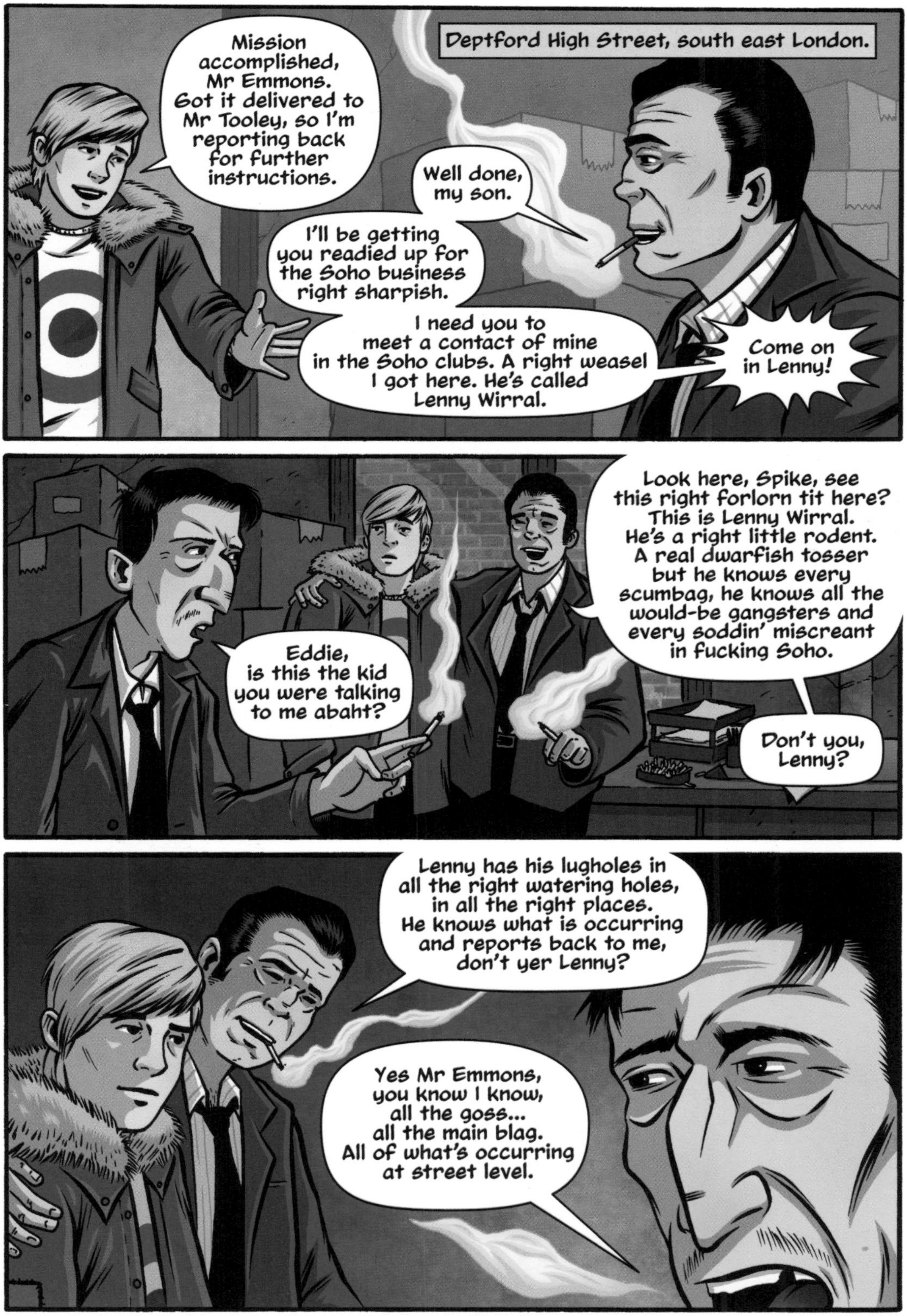
Deptford High Street, south east London.
Mission accomplished, Mr Emmons. Got it delivered to Mr Tooley, so I'm reporting back for further instructions.
Well done, my son.
I'll be getting you readied up for the Soho business right sharpish.
I need you to meet a contact of mine in the Soho clubs. A right weasel I got here. He's called Lenny Wirral.
Come on in Lenny!
Eddie, is this the kid you were talking to me abaht?
Look here, Spike, see this right forlorn tit here? This is Lenny Wirral. He's a right little rodent. A real dwarfish tosser but he knows every scumbag, he knows all the would-be gangsters and every soddin' miscreant in fucking Soho.
Don't you, Lenny?
Lenny has his lugholes in all the right watering holes, in all the right places. He knows what is occurring and reports back to me, don't yer Lenny?
Yes Mr Emmons, you know I know, all the goss... all the main blag. All of what's occurring at street level.

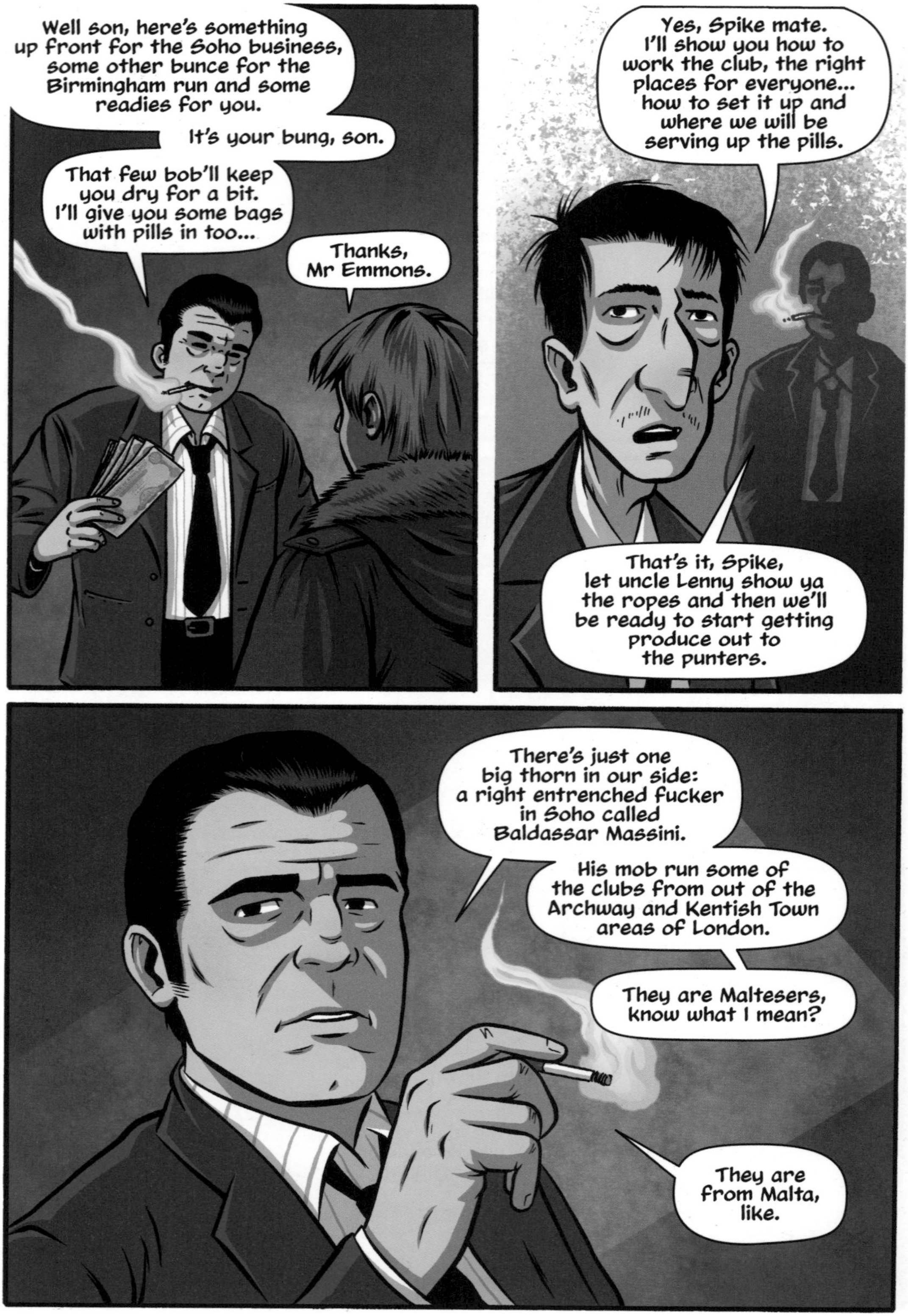

Well son, here's something up front for the Soho business, some other bunce for the Birmingham run and some readies for you.
It's your bung, son.
That few bob'll keep you dry for a bit. I'll give you some bags with pills in too...
Thanks, Mr Emmons.
Yes, Spike mate. I'll show you how to work the club, the right places for everyone... how to set it up and where we will be serving up the pills.
That's it, Spike, let uncle Lenny show ya the ropes and then we'll be ready to start getting produce out to the punters.
There's just one big thorn in our side: a right entrenched fucker in Soho called Baldassar Massini.
His mob run some of the clubs from out of the Archway and Kentish Town areas of London.
They are Maltesers, know what I mean?
They are from Malta, like.

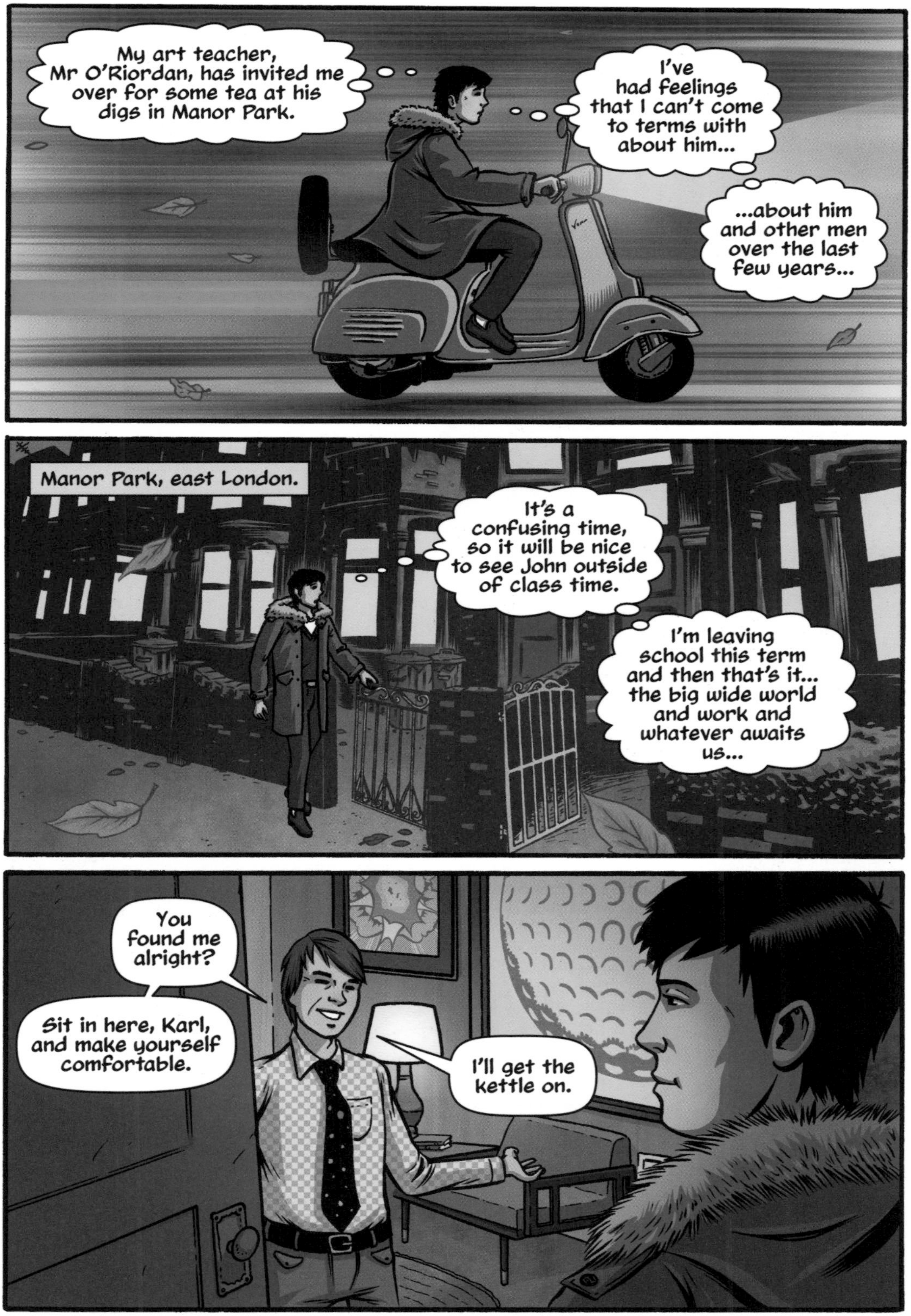
My art teacher, Mr O'Riordan, has invited me over for some tea at his digs in Manor Park.
I've had feelings that I can't come to terms with about him...
...about him and other men over the last few years...
Manor Park, east London.
It's a confusing time, so it will be nice to see John outside of class time.
I'm leaving school this term and then that's it... the big wide world and work and whatever awaits us...
You found me alright?
Sit in here, Karl, and make yourself comfortable.
I'll get the kettle on.

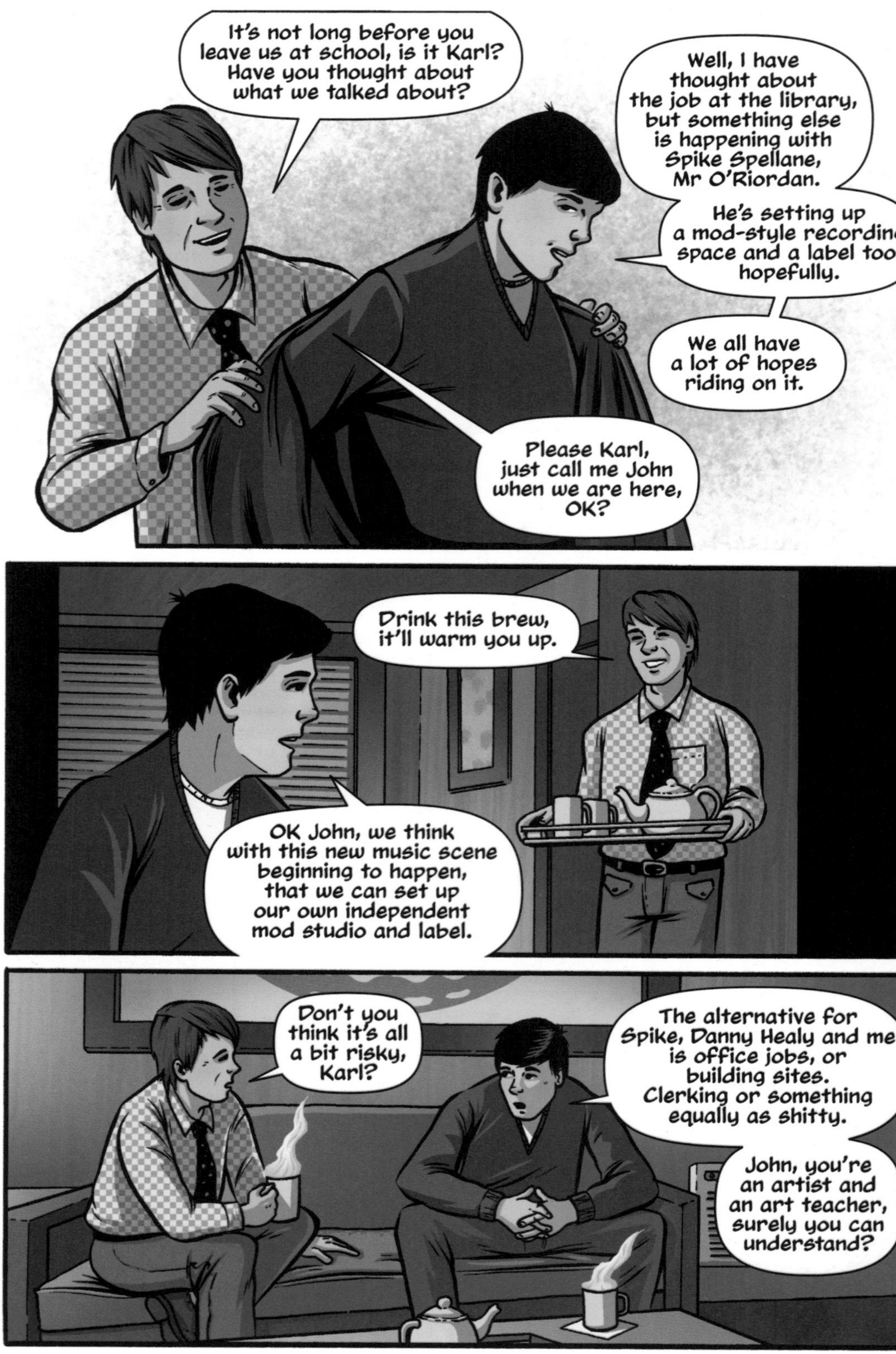
It's not long before you leave us at school, is it Karl? Have you thought about what we talked about?
Well, I have thought about the job at the library, but something else is happening with Spike Spellane, Mr O'Riordan.
He's setting up a mod-style recording space and a label too, hopefully.
We all have a lot of hopes riding on it.
Please Karl, just call me John when we are here, OK?
Drink this brew, it'll warm you up.
OK John, we think with this new music scene beginning to happen, that we can set up our own independent mod studio and label.
Don't you think it's all a bit risky, Karl?
The alternative for Spike, Danny Healy and me is office jobs, or building sites. Clerking or something equally as shitty.
John, you're an artist and an art teacher, surely you can understand?

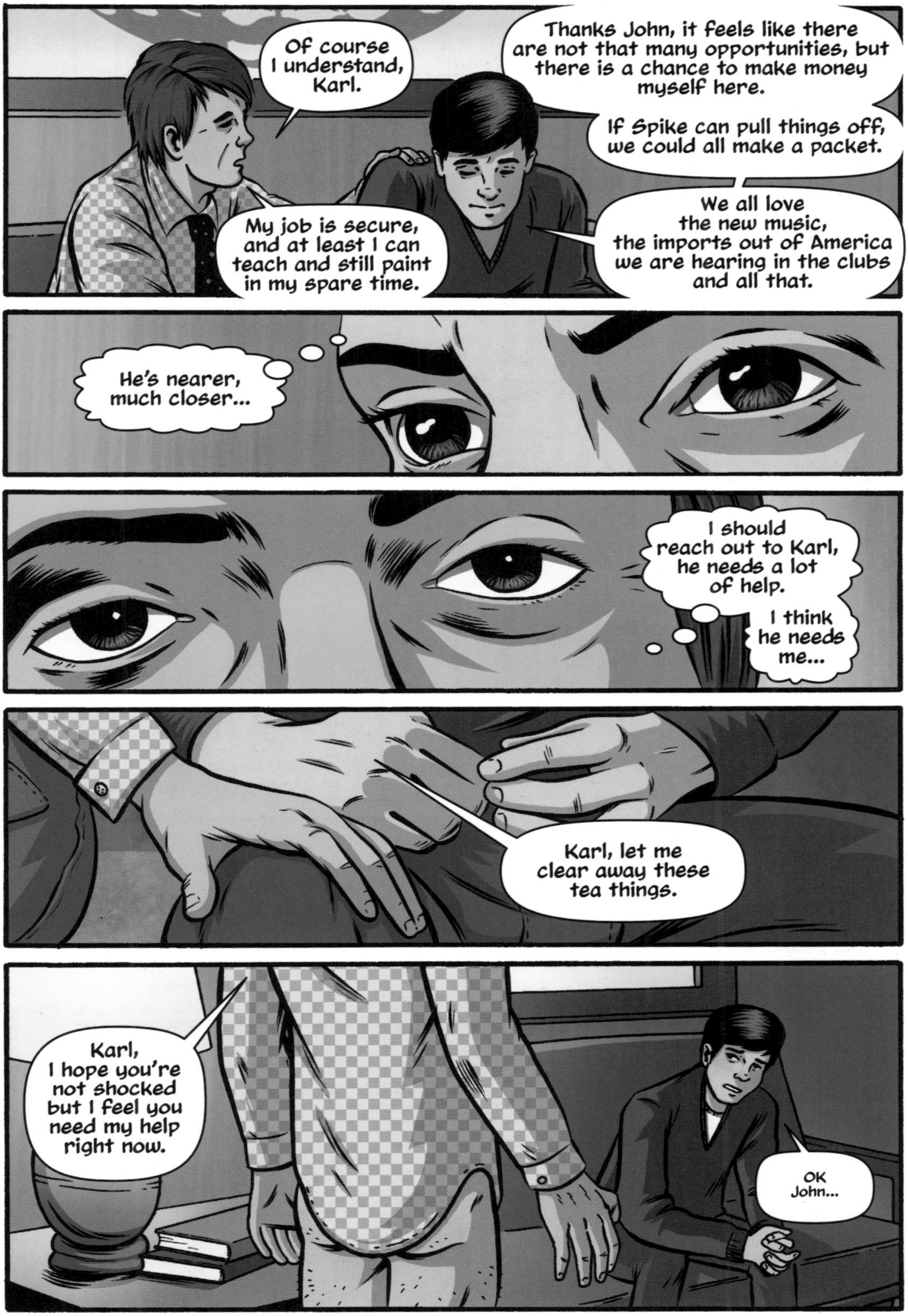
Of course I understand, Karl.
Thanks John, it feels like there are not that many opportunities, but there is a chance to make money myself here.
If Spike can pull things off, we could all make a packet.
My job is secure, and at least I can teach and still paint in my spare time.
We all love the new music, the imports out of America we are hearing in the clubs and all that.
He's nearer, much closer...
I should reach out to Karl, he needs a lot of help.
I think he needs me...
Karl, let me clear away these tea things.
Karl, I hope you're not shocked but I feel you need my help right now.
OK John...

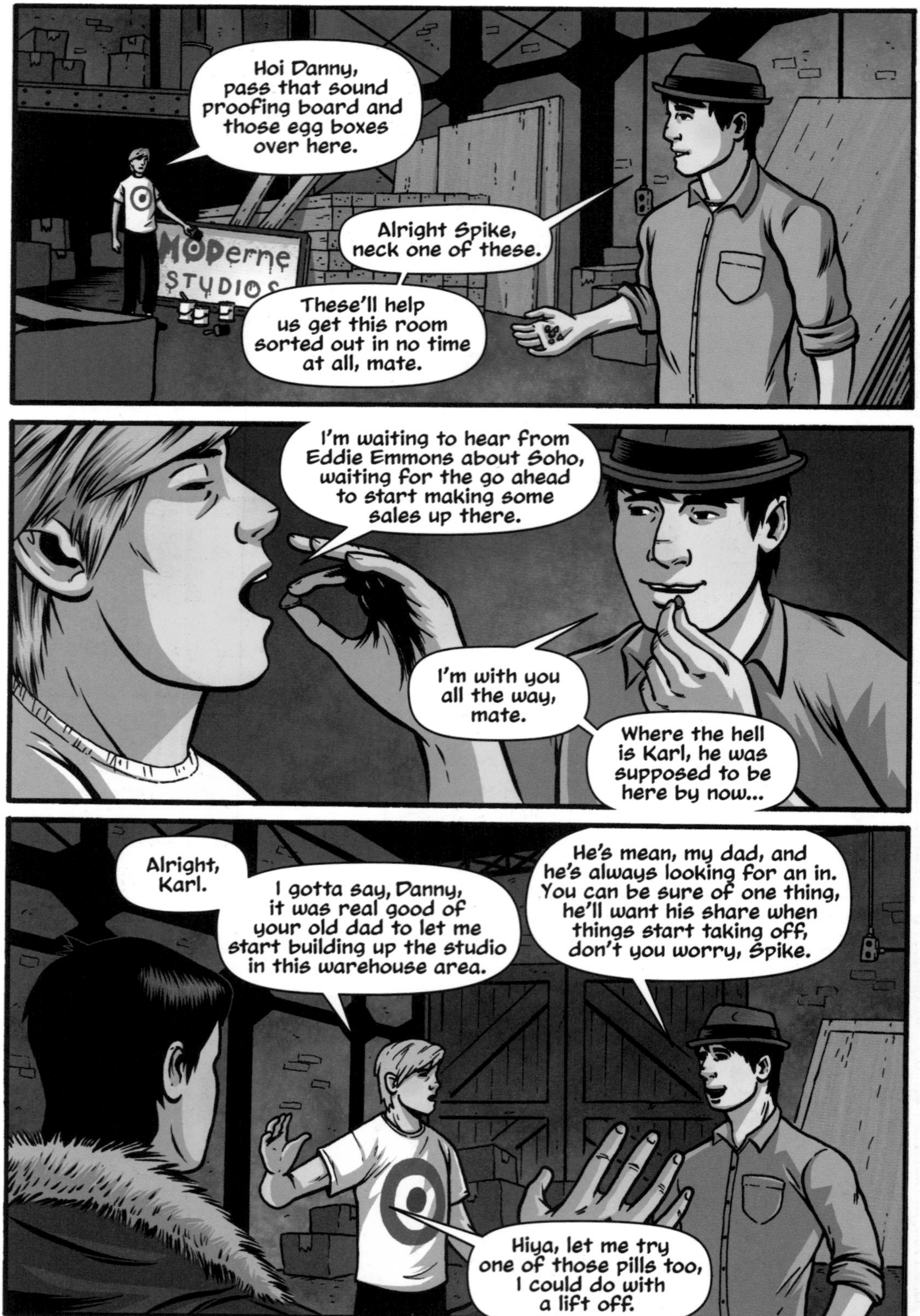
Hoi Danny, pass that sound proofing board and those egg boxes over here.
MODerne STUDIOS
Alright Spike, neck one of these.
These'll help us get this room sorted out in no time at all, mate.
I'm waiting to hear from Eddie Emmons about Soho, waiting for the go ahead to start making some sales up there.
I'm with you all the way, mate.
Where the hell is Karl, he was supposed to be here by now...
Alright, Karl.
I gotta say, Danny, it was real good of your old dad to let me start building up the studio in this warehouse area.
He's mean, my dad, and he's always looking for an in. You can be sure of one thing, he'll want his share when things start taking off, don't you worry, Spike.
Hiya, let me try one of those pills too, I could do with a lift off.

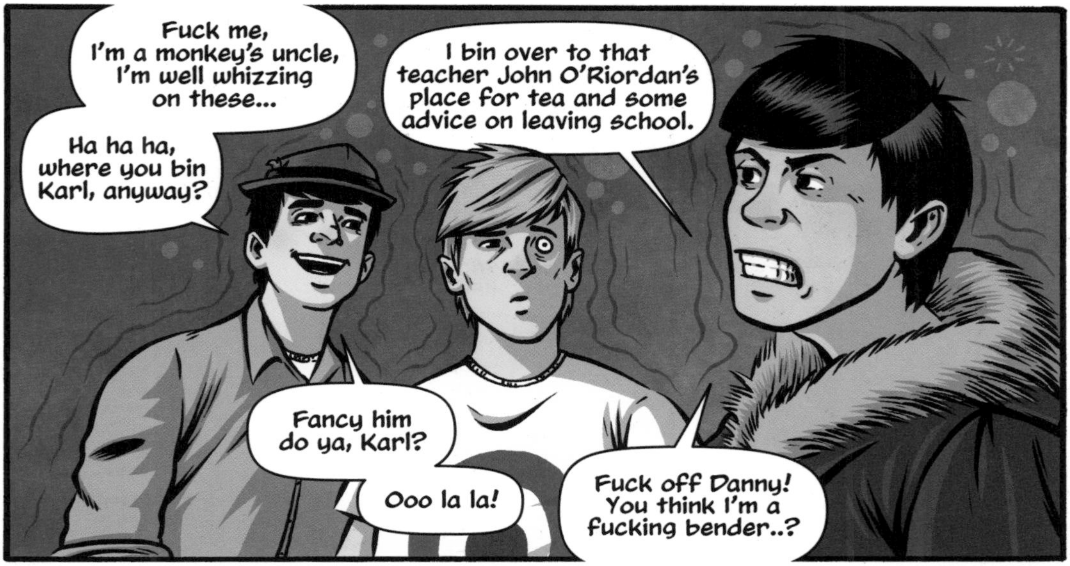
Fuck me, I'm a monkey's uncle, I'm well whizzing on these...
Ha ha ha, where you bin Karl, anyway?
I bin over to that teacher John O'Riordan's place for tea and some advice on leaving school.
Fancy him do ya, Karl?
Ooo la la!
Fuck off Danny! You think I'm a fucking bender..?
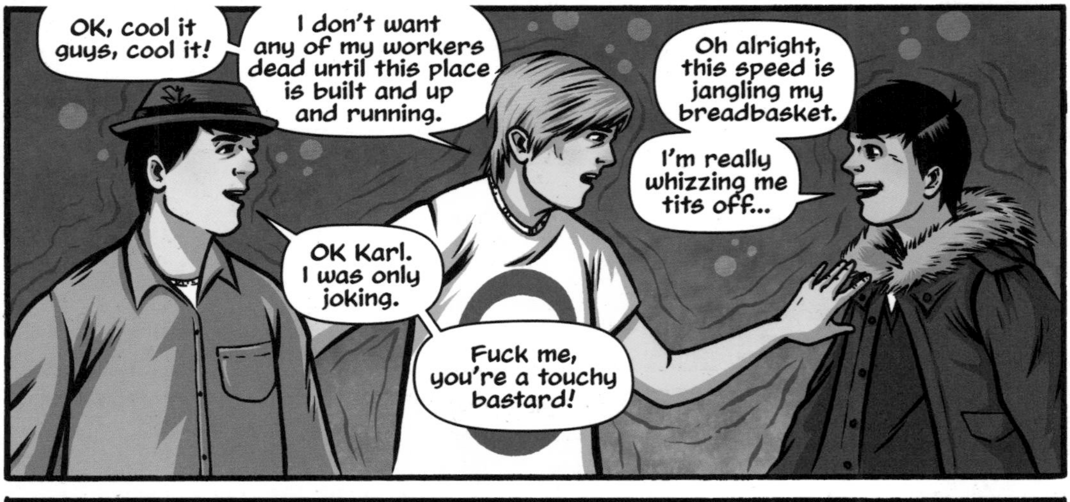
OK, cool it guys, cool it!
I don't want any of my workers dead until this place is built and up and running.
Oh alright, this speed is jangling my breadbasket.
I'm really whizzing me tits off...
OK Karl. I was only joking.
Fuck me, you're a touchy bastard!
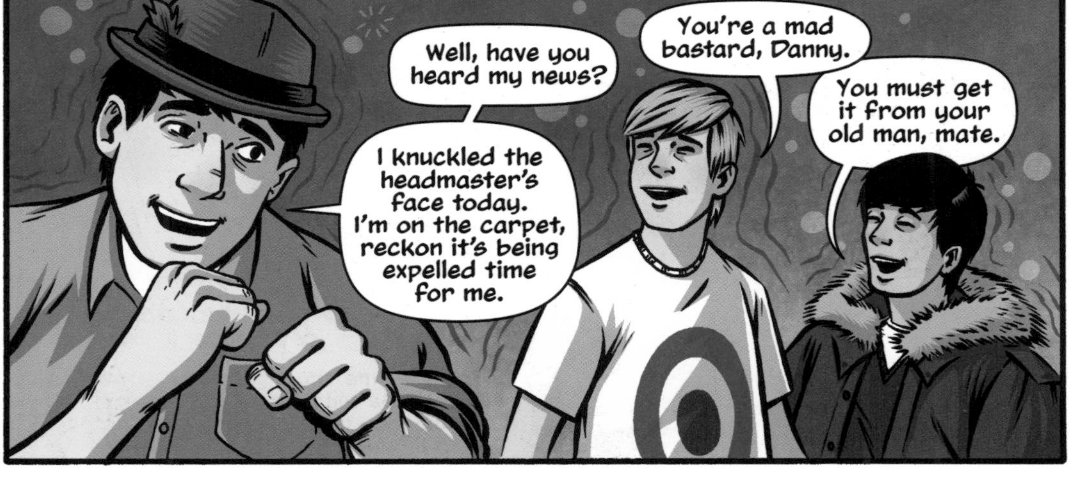
Well, have you heard my news?
I knuckled the headmaster's face today. I'm on the carpet, reckon it's being expelled time for me.
You're a mad bastard, Danny.
You must get it from your old man, mate.

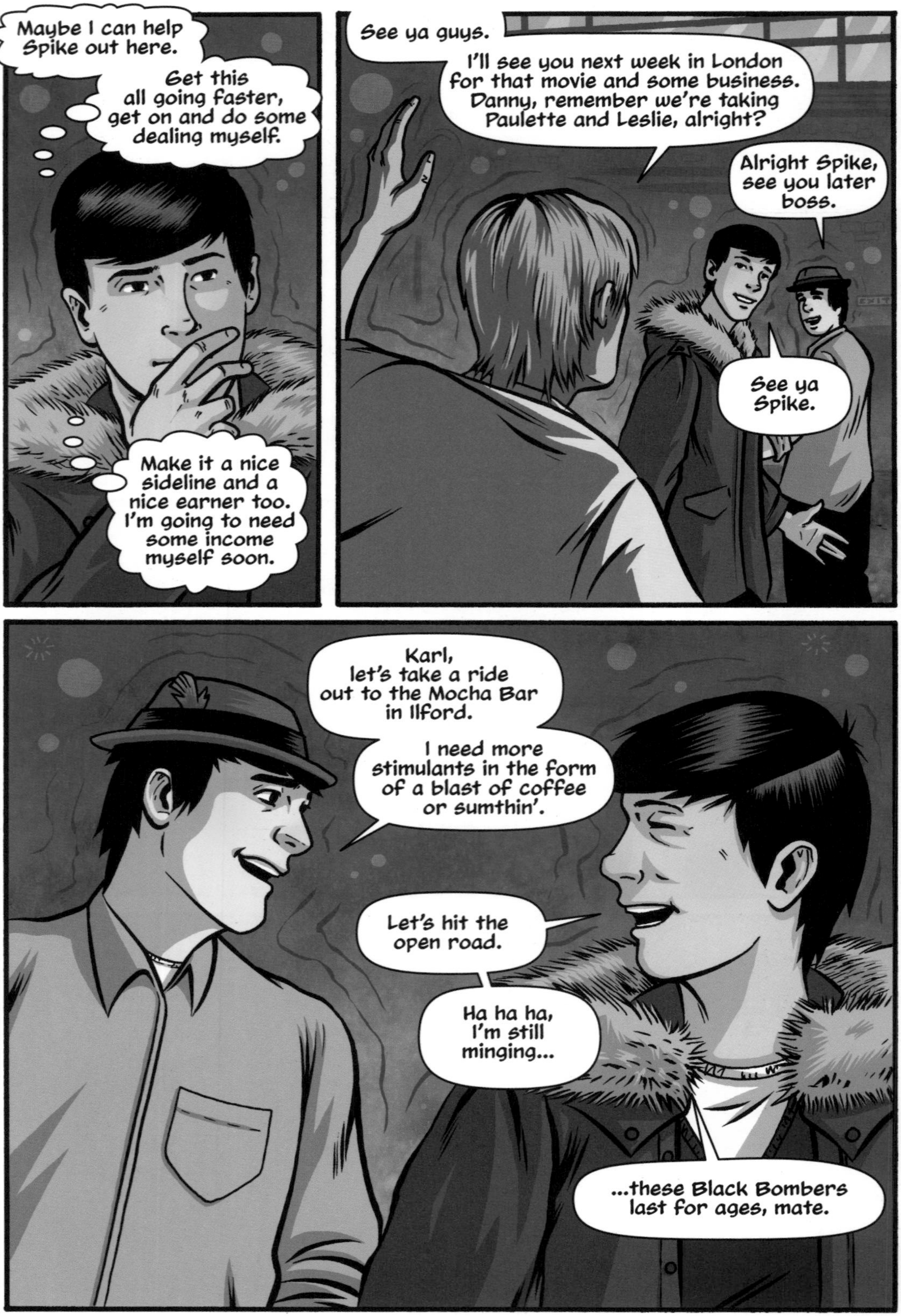
Maybe I can help Spike out here.
Get this all going faster, get on and do some dealing myself.
Make it a nice sideline and a nice earner too. I'm going to need some income myself soon.
See ya guys.
I'll see you next week in London for that movie and some business. Danny, remember we're taking Paulette and Leslie, alright?
Alright Spike, see you later boss.
See ya Spike.
Karl, let's take a ride out to the Mocha Bar in Ilford.
I need more stimulants in the form of a blast of coffee or sumthin'.
Let's hit the open road.
Ha ha ha, I'm still minging...
...these Black Bombers last for ages, mate.

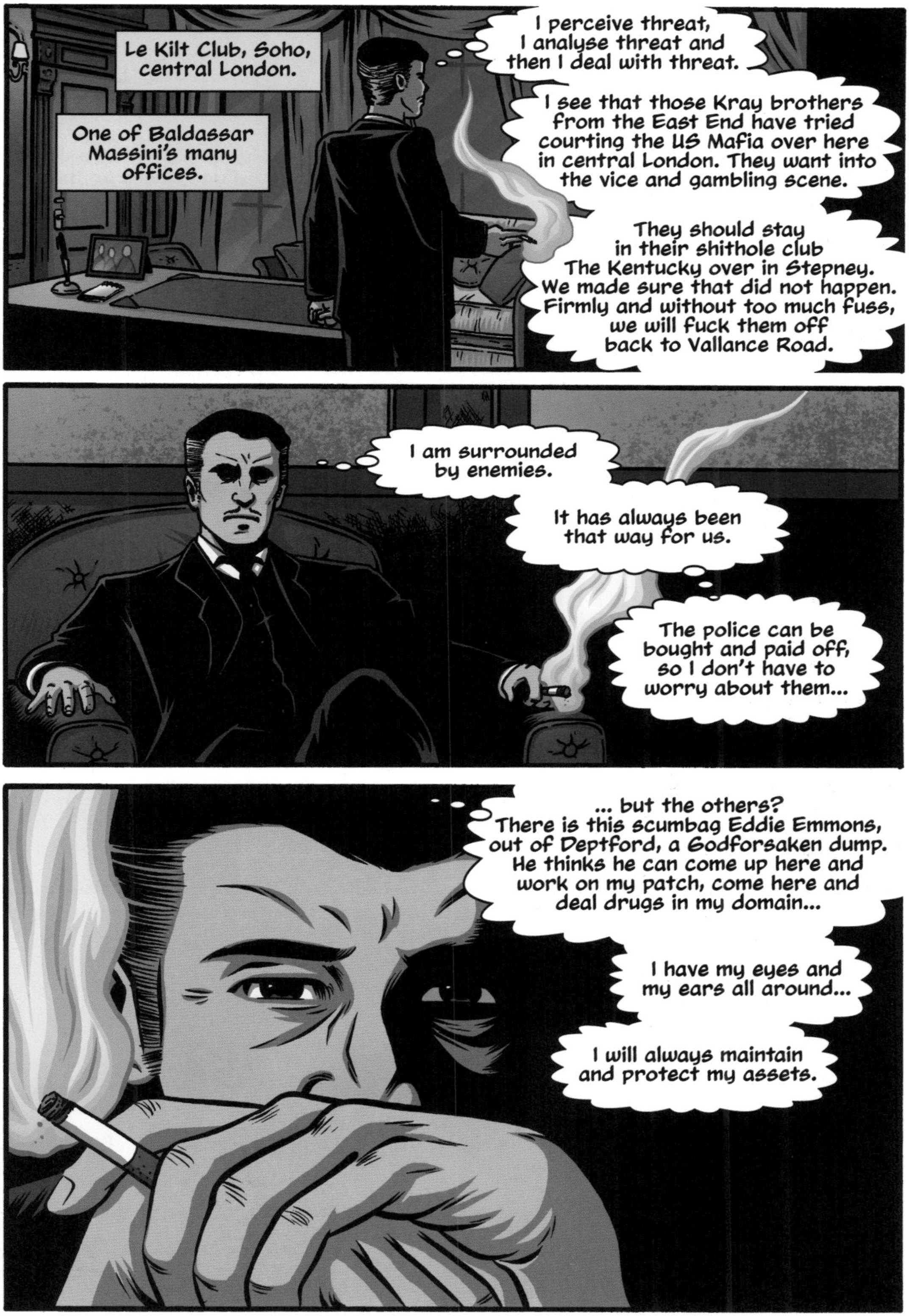

Le Kilt Club, Soho, central London.
One of Baldassar Massini's many offices.
I perceive threat, I analyse threat and then I deal with threat.
I see that those Kray brothers from the East End have tried courting the US Mafia over here in central London. They want into the vice and gambling scene.
They should stay in their shithole club The Kentucky over in Stepney. We made sure that did not happen. Firmly and without too much fuss, we will fuck them off back to Vallance Road.
I am surrounded by enemies.
It has always been that way for us.
The police can be bought and paid off, so I don't have to worry about them...
... but the others? There is this scumbag Eddie Emmons, out of Deptford, a Godforsaken dump. He thinks he can come up here and work on my patch, come here and deal drugs in my domain...
I have my eyes and my ears all around...
I will always maintain and protect my assets.

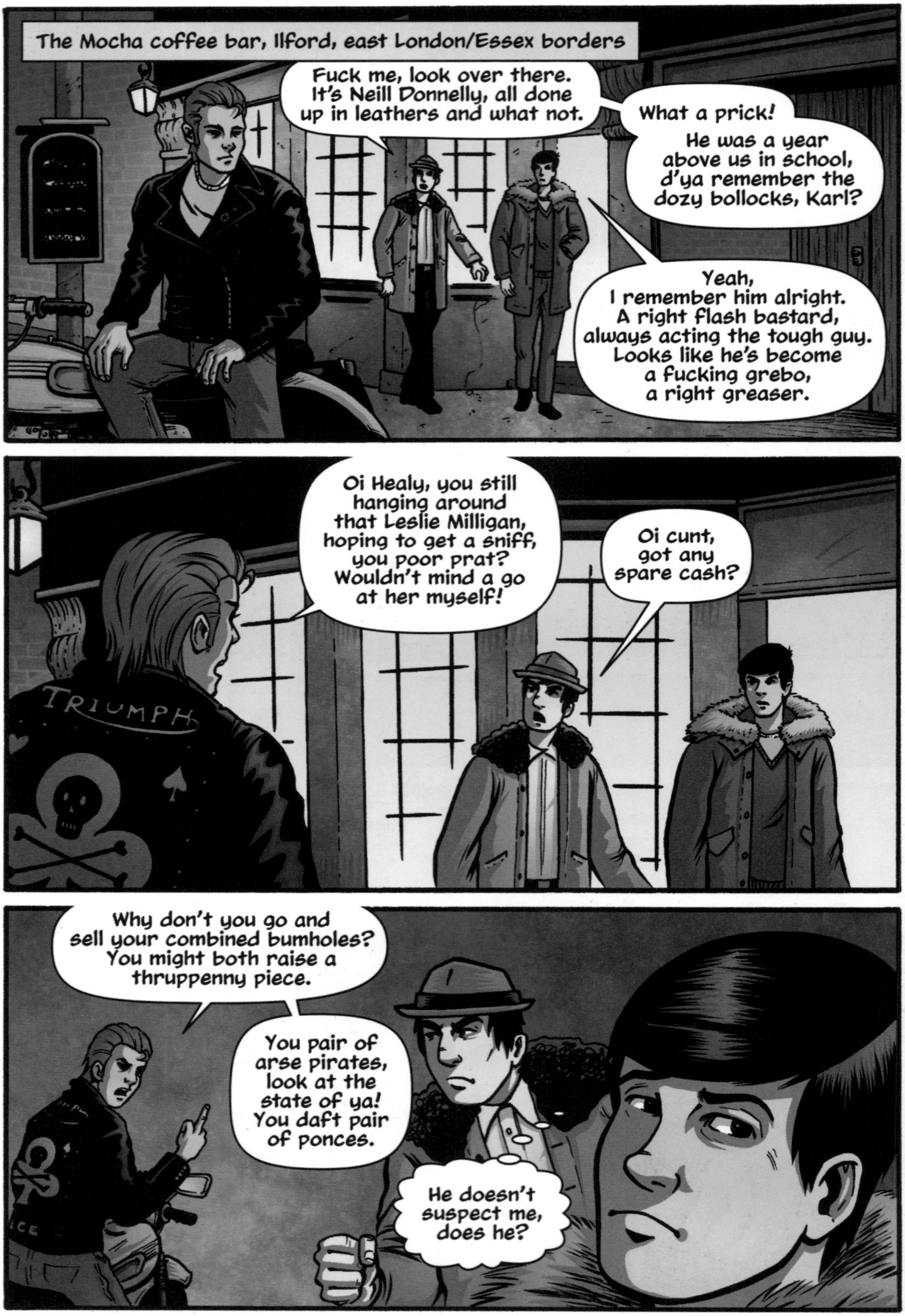
The Mocha coffee bar, Ilford, east London/Essex borders
Fuck me, look over there. It's Neill Donnelly, all done up in leathers and what not.
What a prick!
He was a year above us in school, d'ya remember the dozy bollocks, Karl?
Yeah, I remember him alright. A right flash bastard, always acting the tough guy. Looks like he's become a fucking grebo, a right greaser.
Oi Healy, you still hanging around that Leslie Milligan, hoping to get a sniff, you poor prat? Wouldn't mind a go at her myself!
Oi cunt, got any spare cash?
TRIUMPH
Why don't you go and sell your combined bumholes? You might both raise a thruppenny piece.
You pair of arse pirates, look at the state of ya! You daft pair of ponces.
He doesn't suspect me, does he?

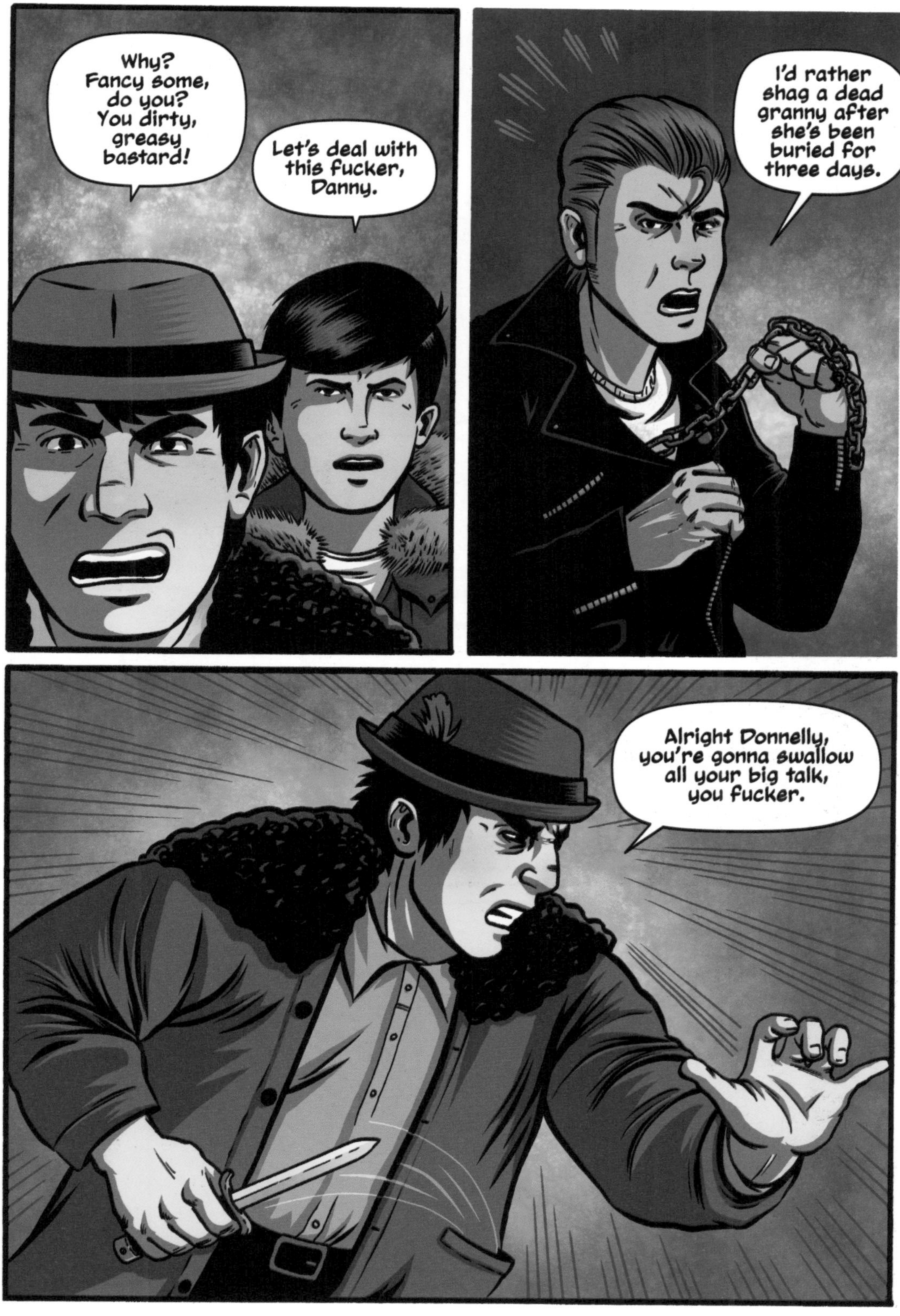

Why? Fancy some, do you? You dirty, greasy bastard!
Let's deal with this fucker, Danny.
I'd rather shag a dead granny after she's been buried for three days.
Alright Donnelly, you're gonna swallow all your big talk, you fucker.

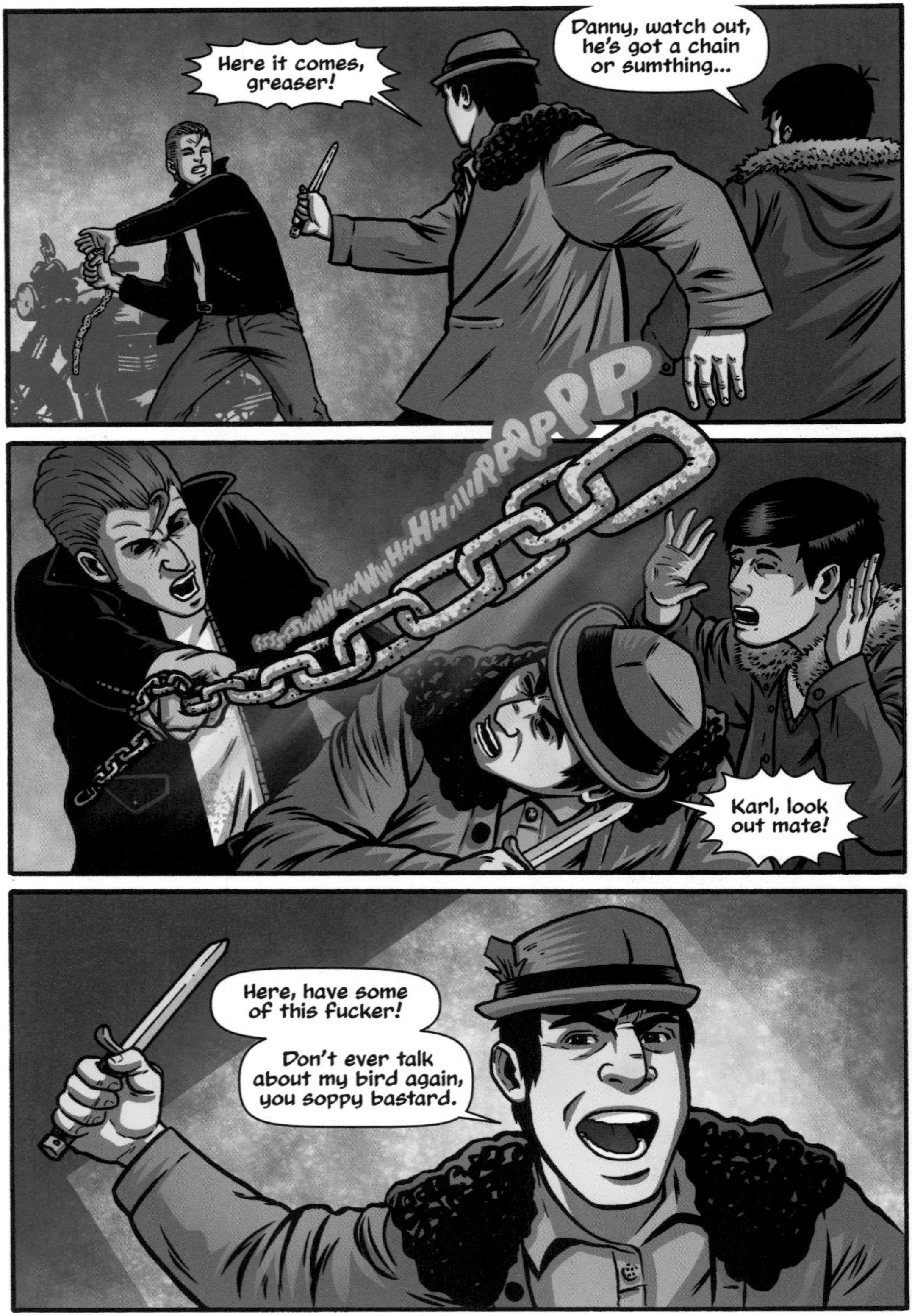
Here it comes, greaser!
Danny, watch out, he's got a chain or sumthing...
Karl, look out mate!
Here, have some of this fucker!
Don't ever talk about my bird again, you soppy bastard.

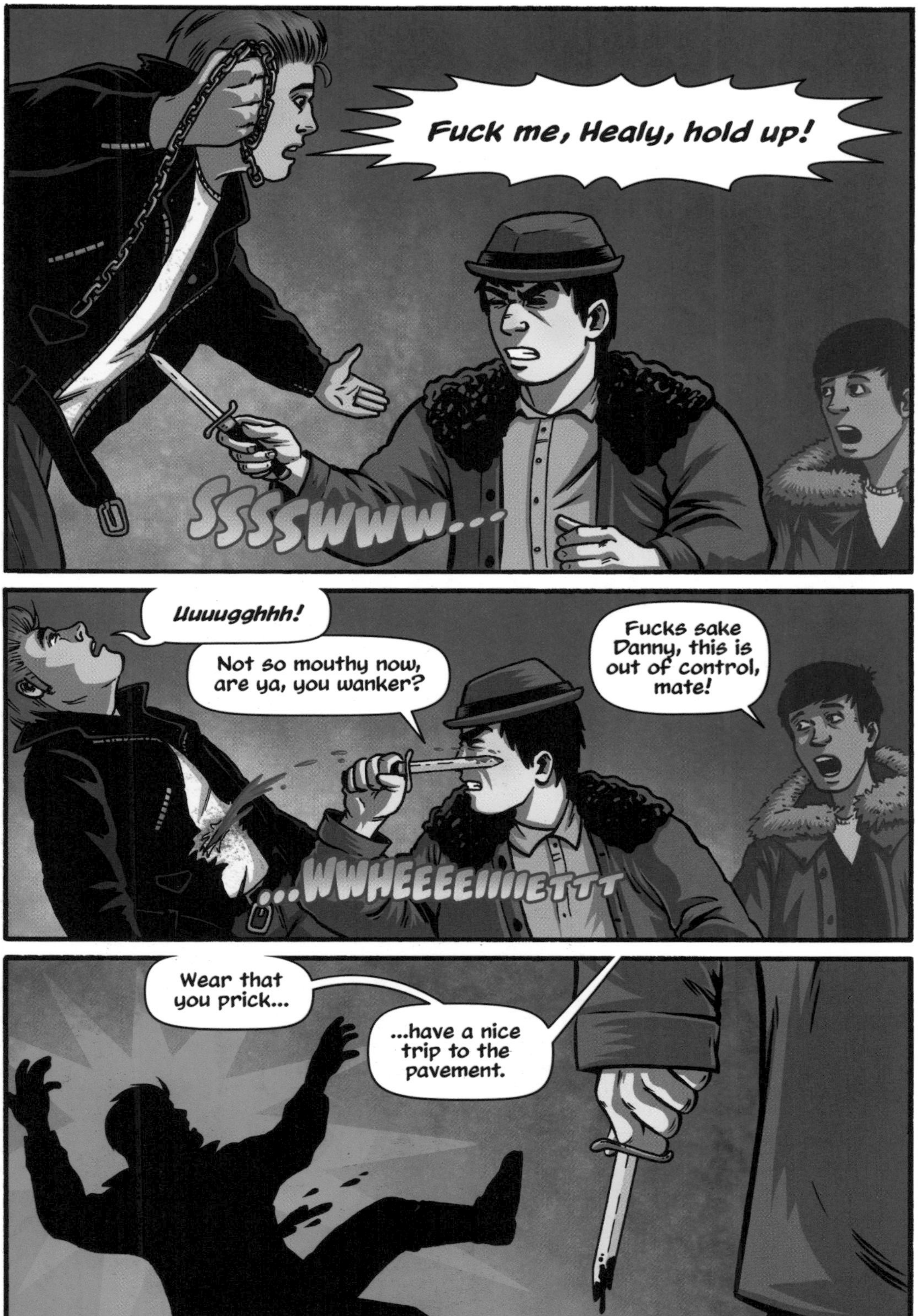
Fuck me, Healy, hold up!
SSSSWWW...
Uuuugghhh!
Not so mouthy now, are ya, you wanker?
Fucks sake Danny, this is out of control, mate!
...WWHEEEEIIIIIETTT
Wear that you prick...
...have a nice trip to the pavement.

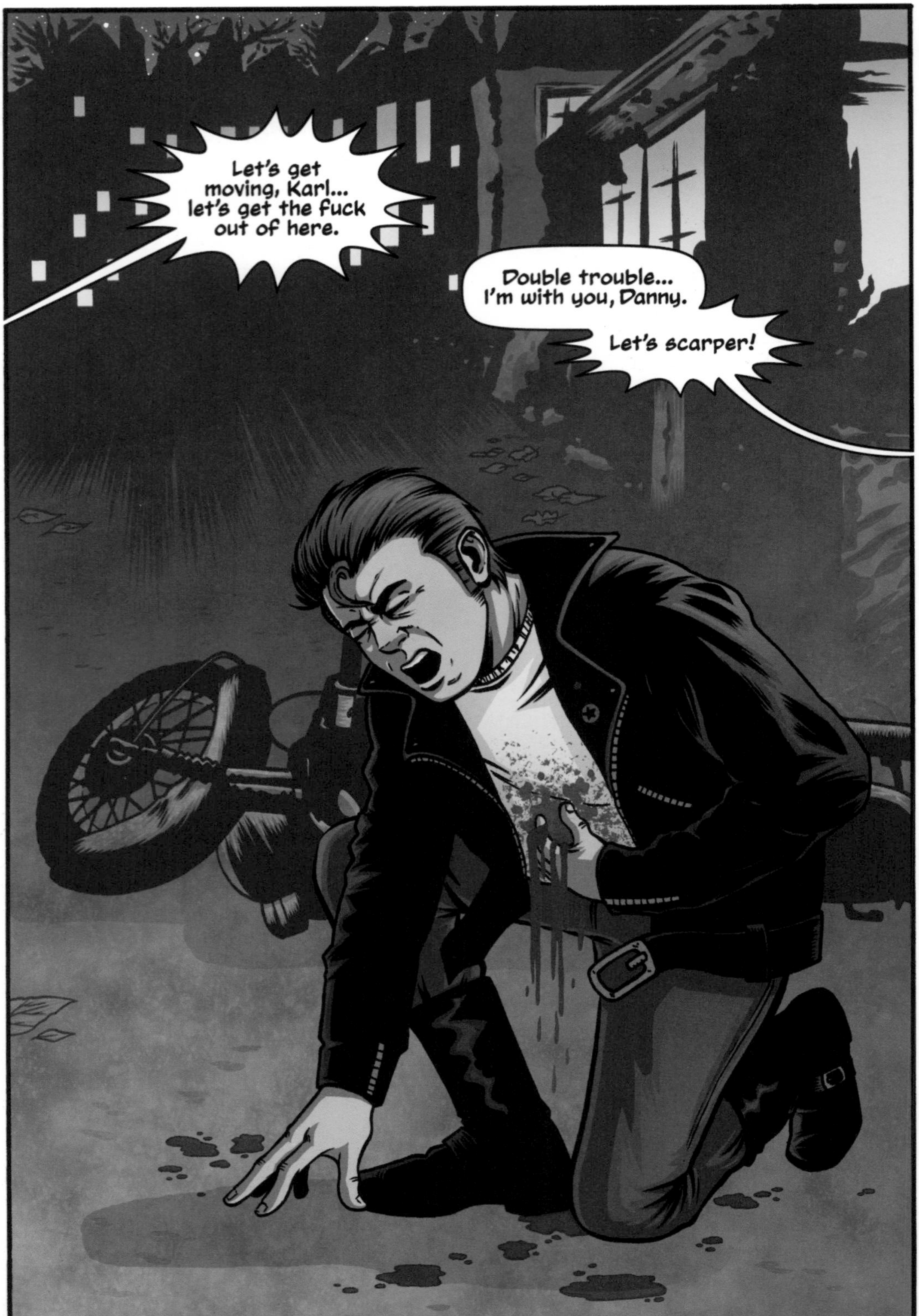
Let's get moving, Karl... let's get the fuck out of here.
Double trouble... I'm with you, Danny.
Let's scarper!

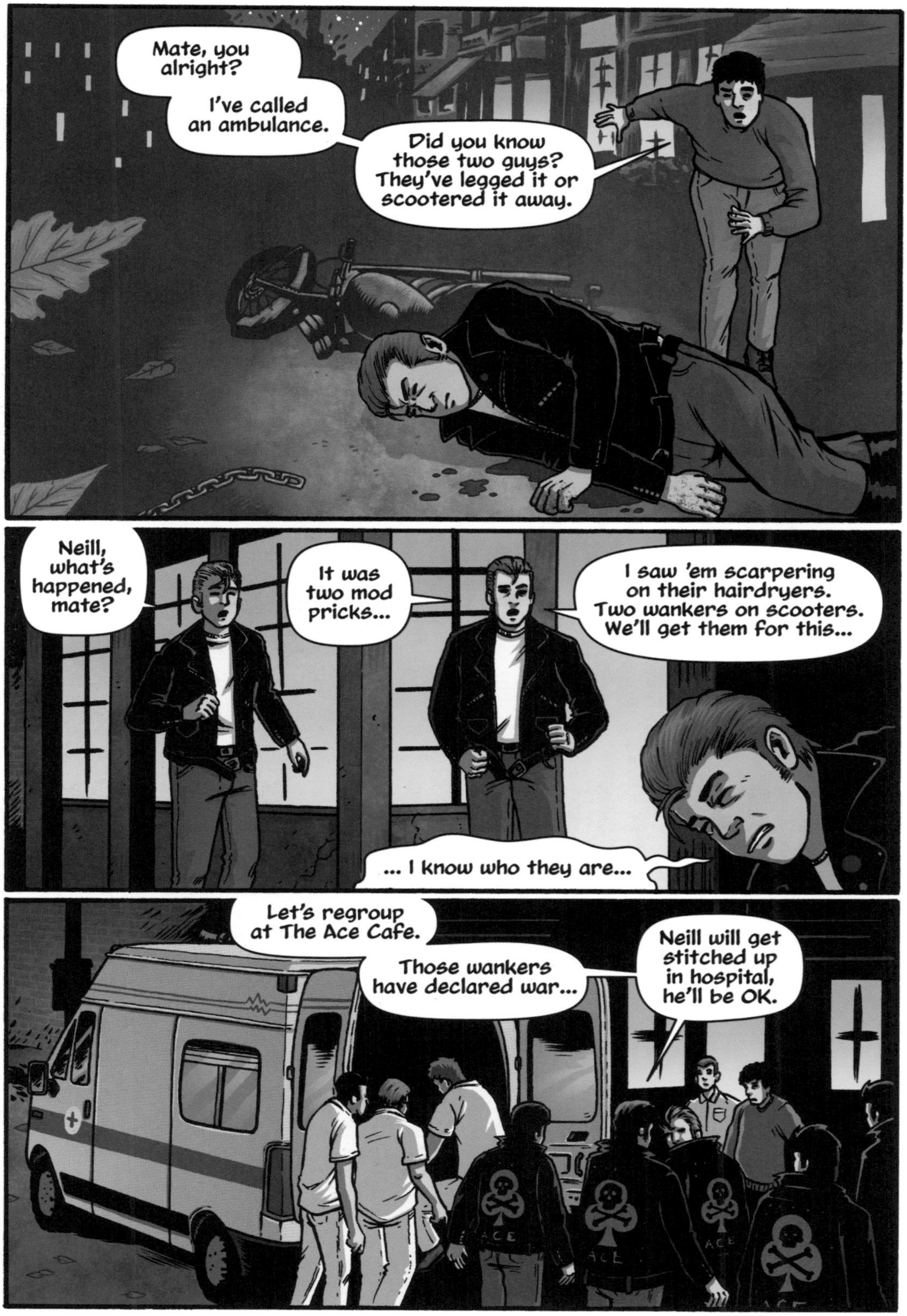
Mate, you alright?
I've called an ambulance.
Did you know those two guys? They've legged it or scootered it away.
Neill, what's happened, mate?
It was two mod pricks...
I saw 'em scarpering on their hairdryers. Two wankers on scooters. We'll get them for this...
... I know who they are...
Let's regroup at The Ace Cafe.
Those wankers have declared war...
Neill will get stitched up in hospital, he'll be OK.
ACE
ACE
ACE

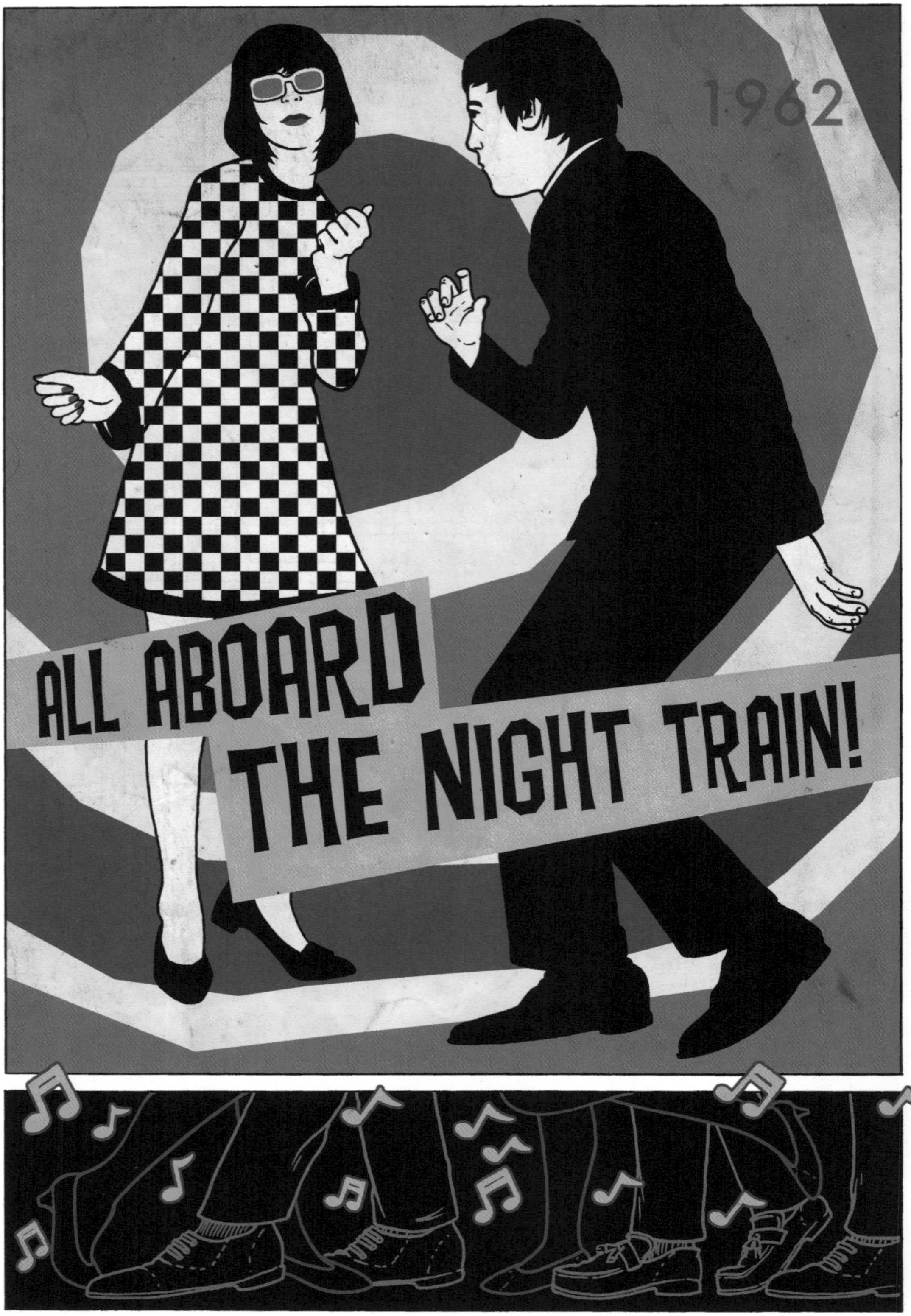
1962
ALL ABOARD
THE NIGHT TRAIN!

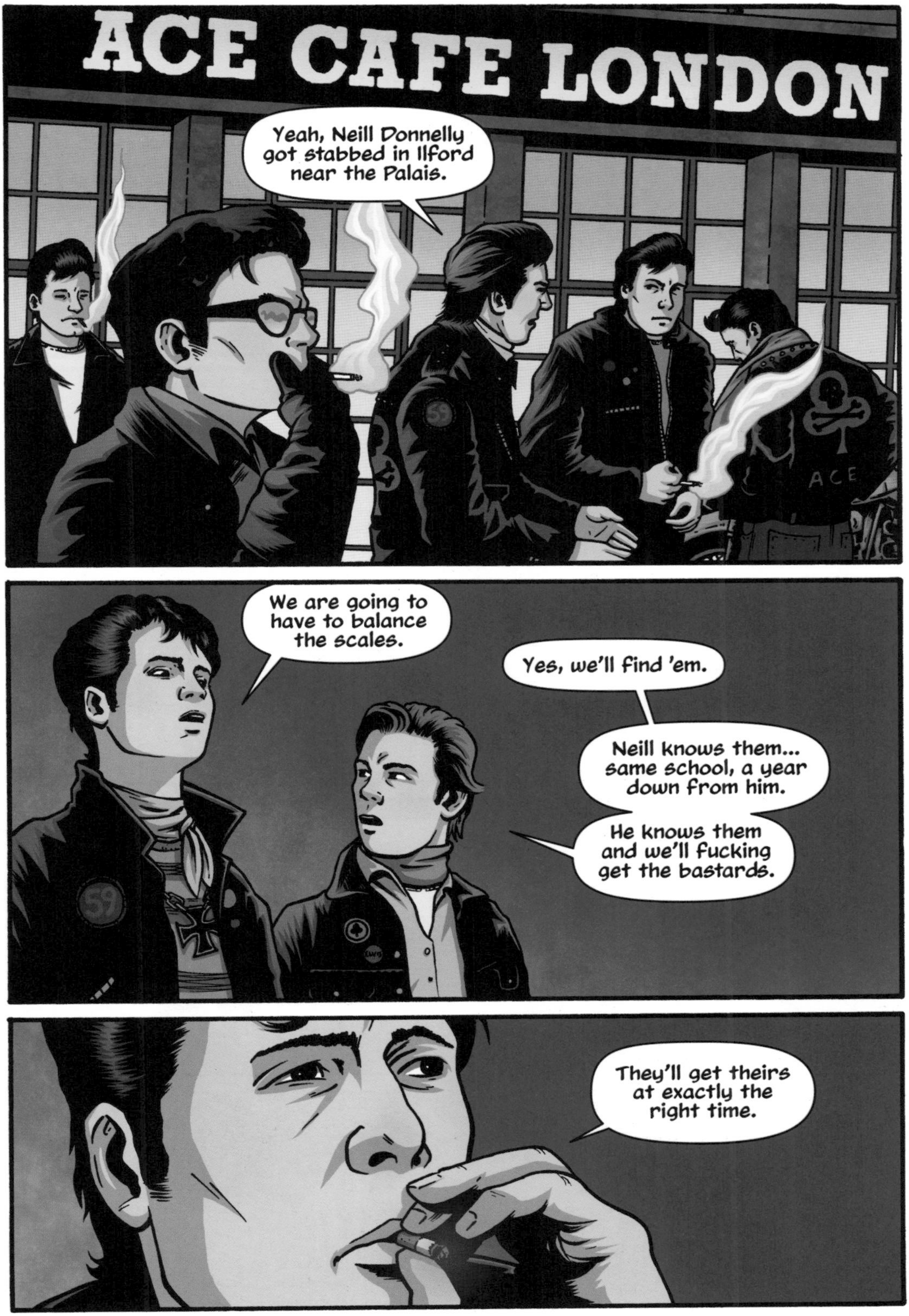
ACE CAFE LONDON
Yeah, Neill Donnelly got stabbed in Ilford near the Palais.
ACE
We are going to have to balance the scales.
Yes, we'll find 'em.
Neill knows them... same school, a year down from him.
He knows them and we'll fucking get the bastards.
They'll get theirs at exactly the right time.

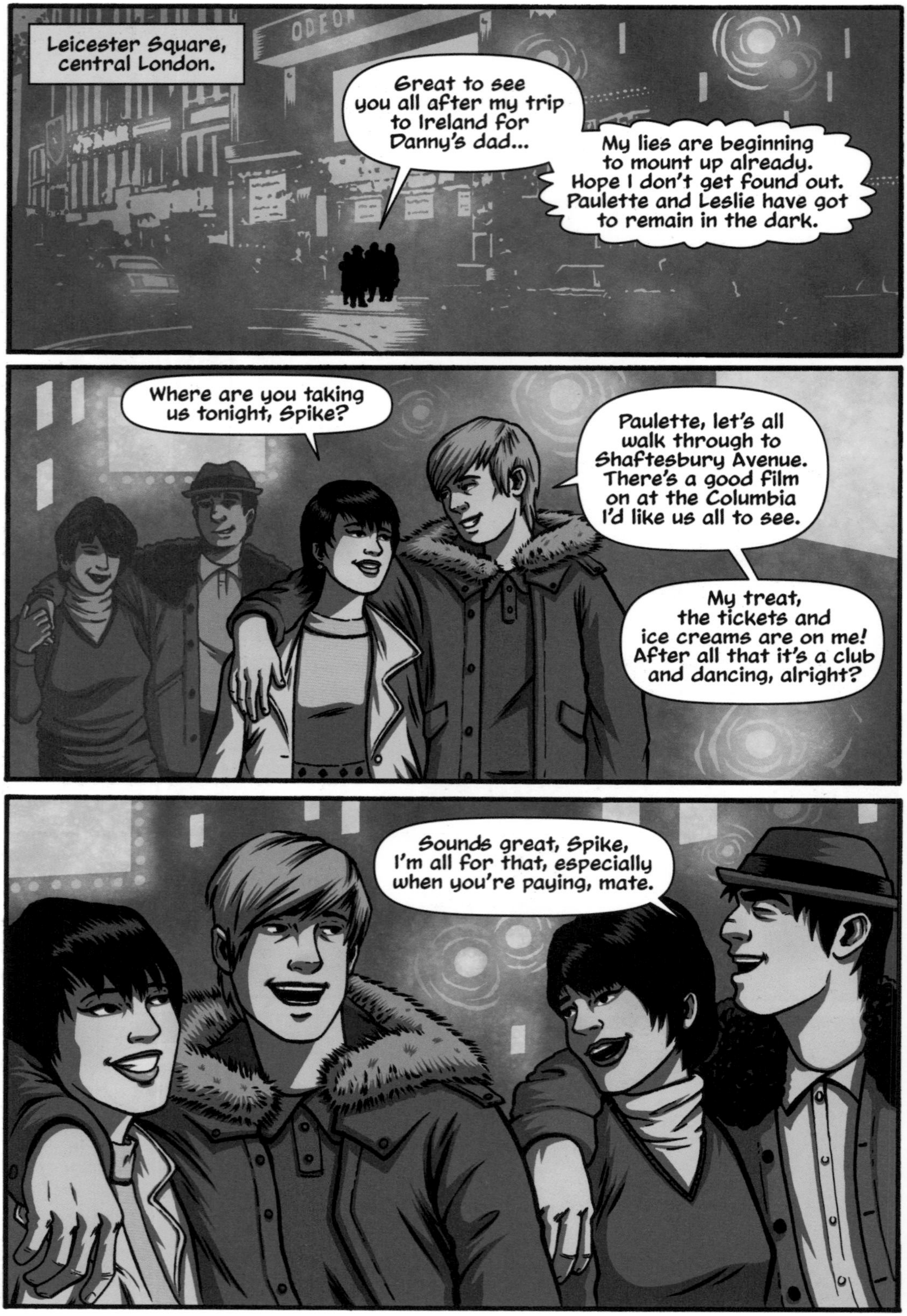
Leicester Square, central London.
Great to see you all after my trip to Ireland for Danny's dad...
My lies are beginning to mount up already. Hope I don't get found out. Paulette and Leslie have got to remain in the dark.
Where are you taking us tonight, Spike?
Paulette, let's all walk through to Shaftesbury Avenue. There's a good film on at the Columbia I'd like us all to see.
My treat, the tickets and ice creams are on me! After all that it's a club and dancing, alright?
Sounds great, Spike, I'm all for that, especially when you're paying, mate.

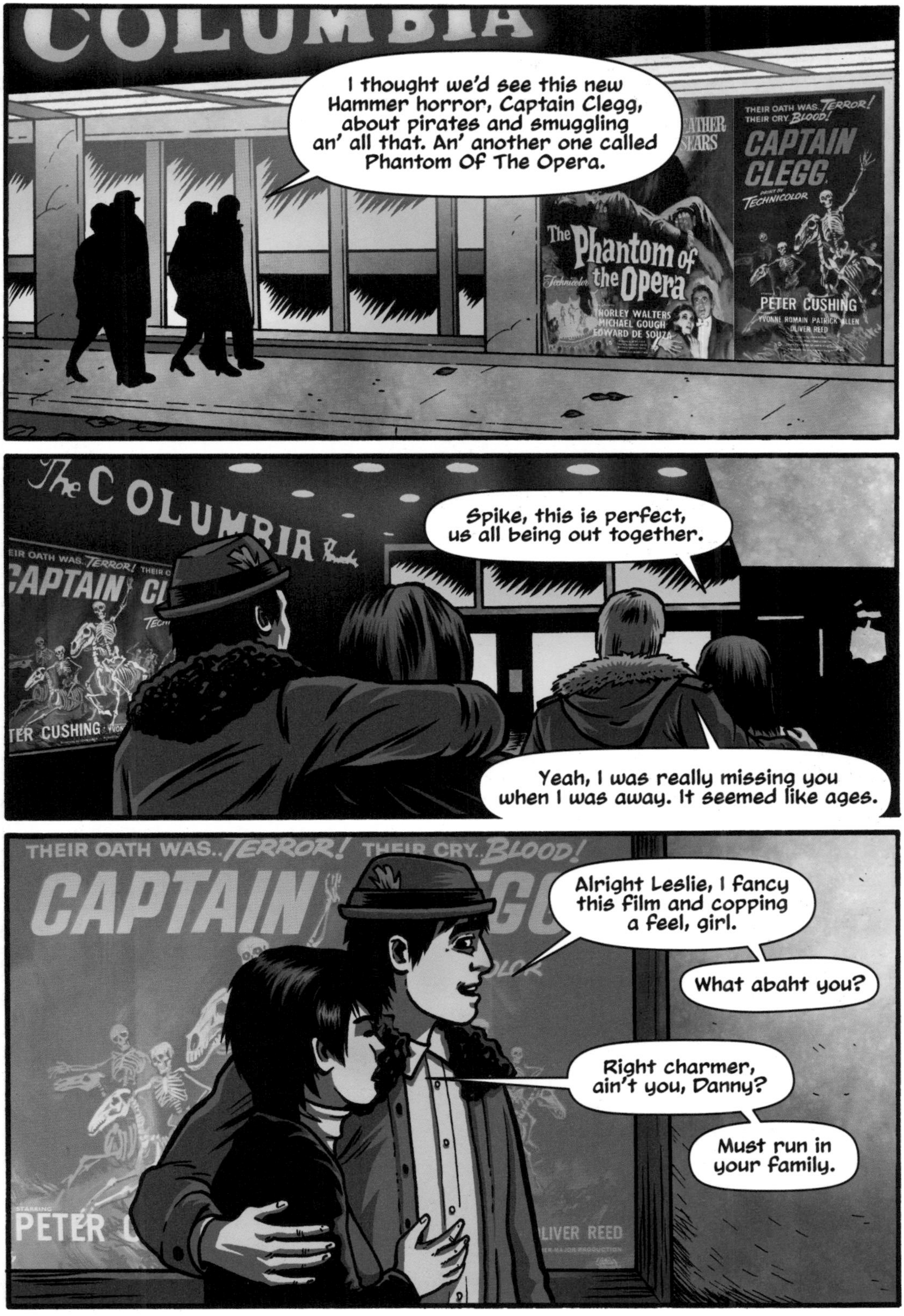
COLUMBIA
I thought we'd see this new Hammer horror, Captain Clegg, about pirates and smuggling an' all that. An' another one called Phantom Of The Opera.
The Phantom of the Opera
Technicolor
THORLEY WALTERS
MICHAEL GOUGH
EDWARD DE SOUZA
THEIR OATH WAS..TERROR! THEIR CRY..BLOOD!
CAPTAIN CLEGG
TECHNICOLOR
PETER CUSHING
YVONNE ROMAIN PATRICK ALLEN
OLIVER REED
The COLUMBIA
Spike, this is perfect, us all being out together.
Yeah, I was really missing you when I was away. It seemed like ages.
THEIR OATH WAS..TERROR! THEIR CRY..BLOOD!
CAPTAIN
Alright Leslie, I fancy this film and copping a feel, girl.
What abaht you?
Right charmer, ain't you, Danny?
Must run in your family.
PETER
OLIVER REED

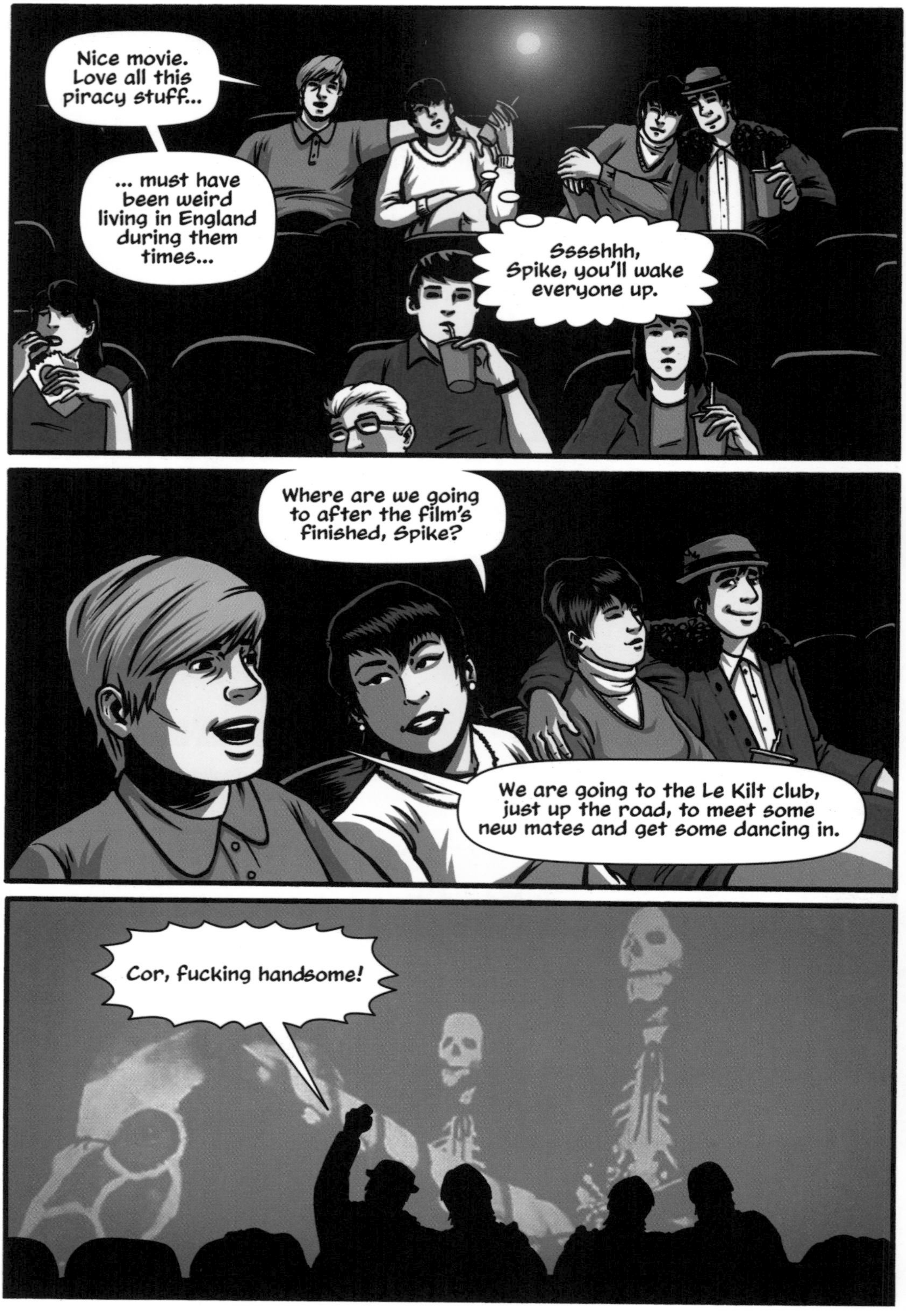
Nice movie. Love all this piracy stuff...
... must have been weird living in England during them times...
Sssshhh, Spike, you'll wake everyone up.
Where are we going to after the film's finished, Spike?
We are going to the Le Kilt club, just up the road, to meet some new mates and get some dancing in.
Cor, fucking handsome!

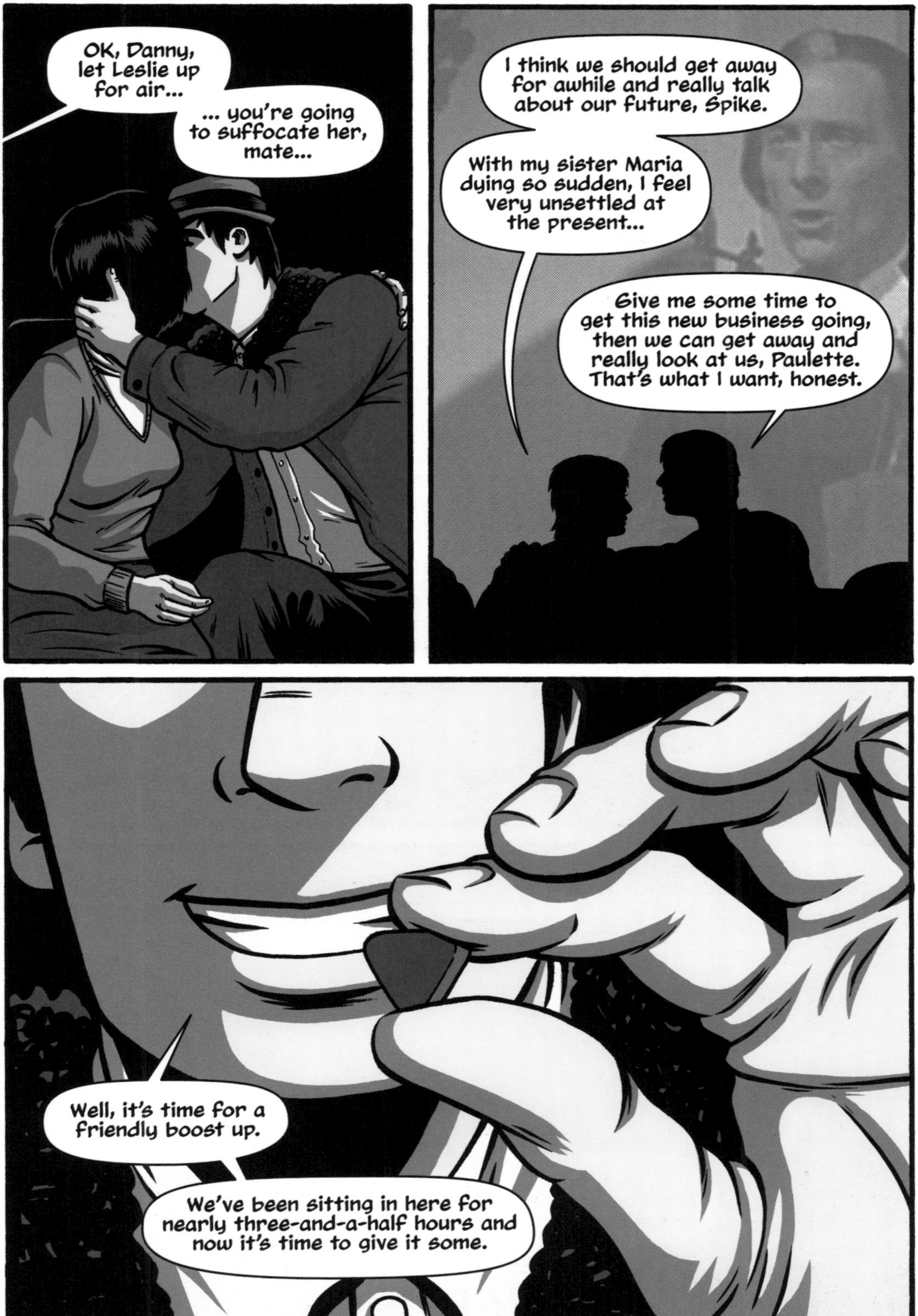
OK, Danny, let Leslie up for air...
... you're going to suffocate her, mate...
I think we should get away for awhile and really talk about our future, Spike.
With my sister Maria dying so sudden, I feel very unsettled at the present...
Give me some time to get this new business going, then we can get away and really look at us, Paulette. That's what I want, honest.
Well, it's time for a friendly boost up.
We've been sitting in here for nearly three-and-a-half hours and now it's time to give it some.

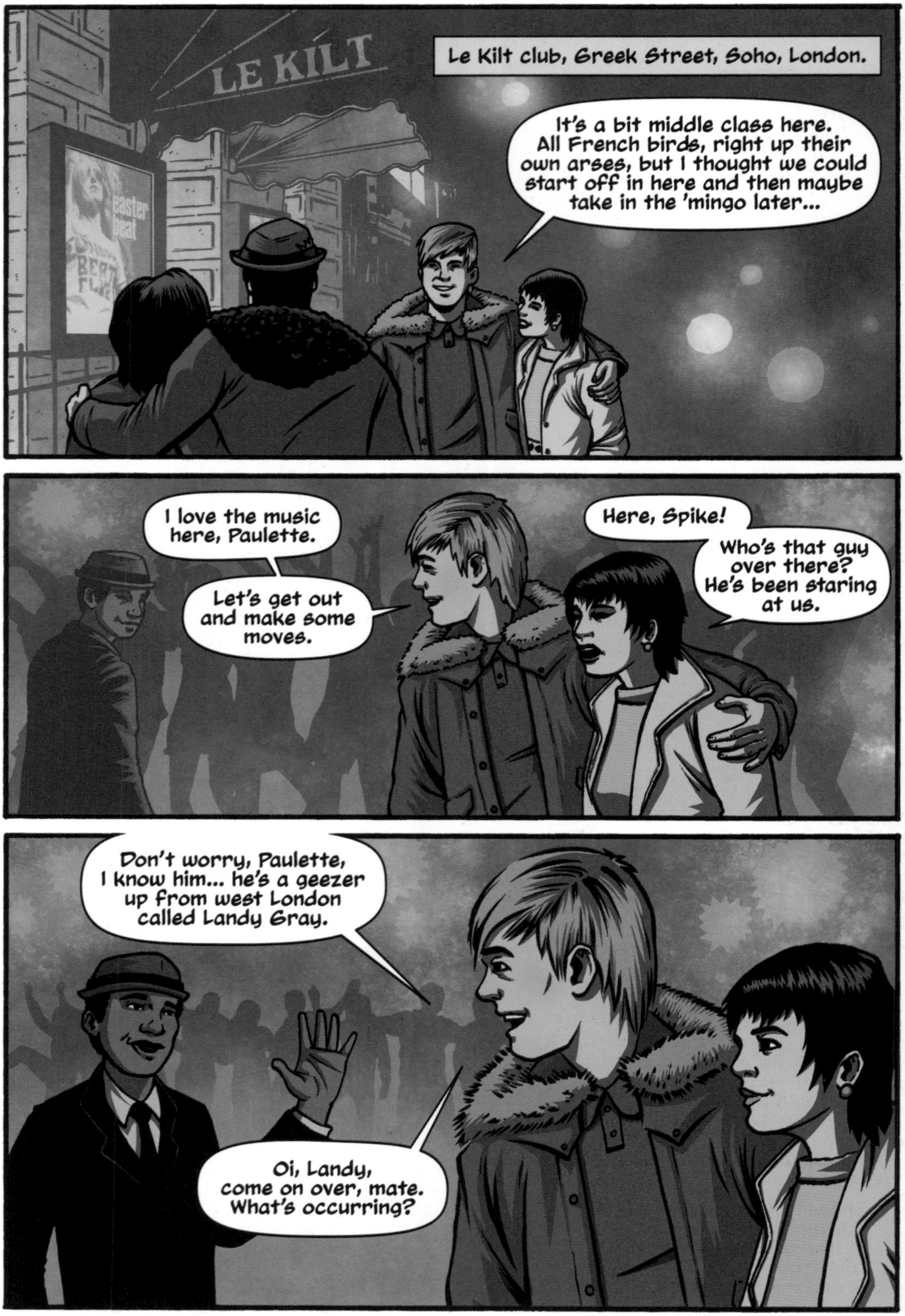
LE KILT
Le Kilt club, Greek Street, Soho, London.
easter beat
It's a bit middle class here. All French birds, right up their own arses, but I thought we could start off in here and then maybe take in the 'mingo later...
I love the music here, Paulette.
Let's get out and make some moves.
Here, Spike!
Who's that guy over there? He's been staring at us.
Don't worry, Paulette, I know him... he's a geezer up from west London called Landy Gray.
Oi, Landy, come on over, mate. What's occurring?

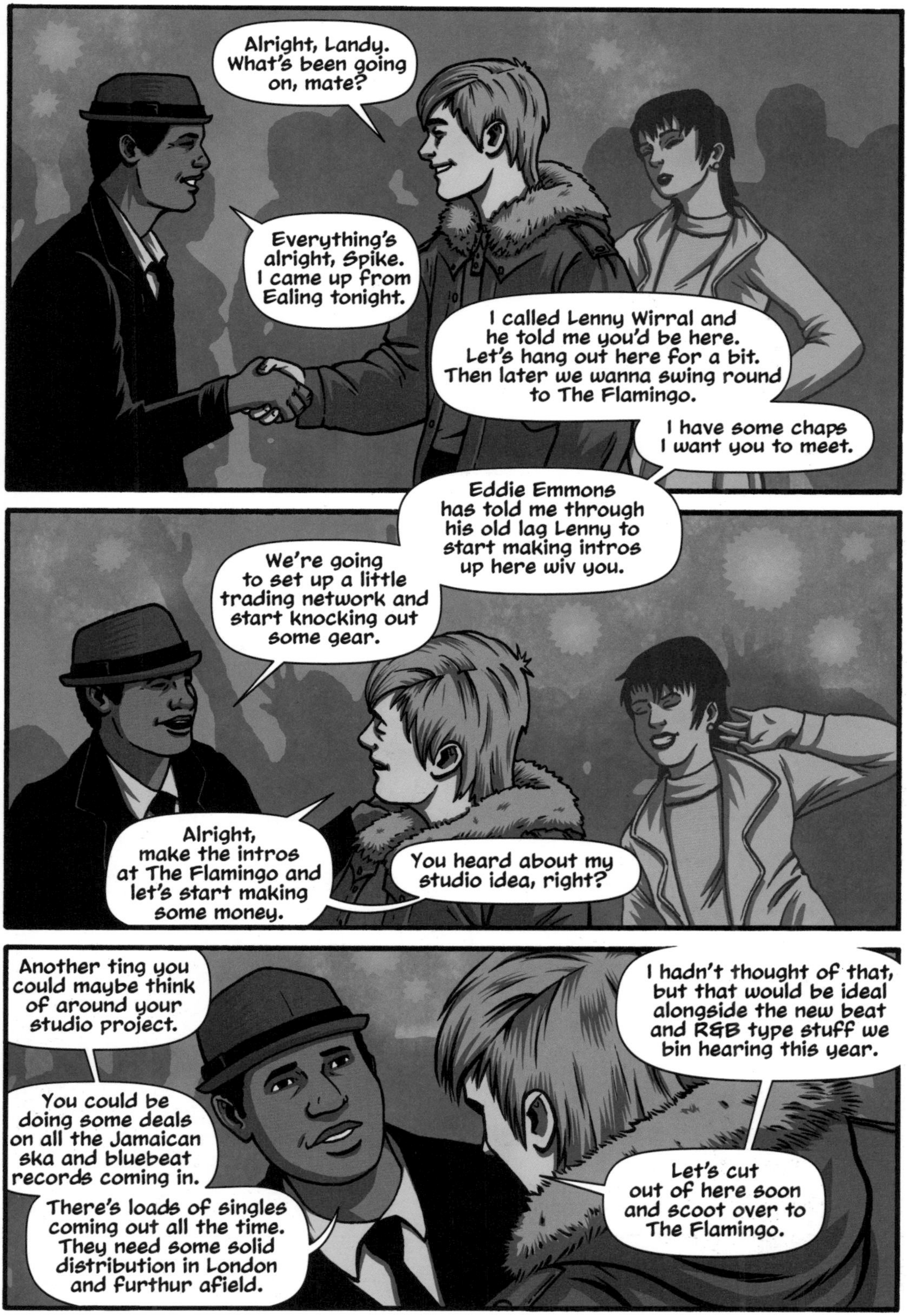
Alright, Landy. What's been going on, mate?
Everything's alright, Spike. I came up from Ealing tonight.
I called Lenny Wirral and he told me you'd be here. Let's hang out here for a bit. Then later we wanna swing round to The Flamingo.
I have some chaps I want you to meet.
Eddie Emmons has told me through his old lag Lenny to start making intros up here wiv you.
We're going to set up a little trading network and start knocking out some gear.
Alright, make the intros at The Flamingo and let's start making some money.
You heard about my studio idea, right?
Another ting you could maybe think of around your studio project.
You could be doing some deals on all the Jamaican ska and bluebeat records coming in.
There's loads of singles coming out all the time. They need some solid distribution in London and furthur afield.
I hadn't thought of that, but that would be ideal alongside the new beat and R&B type stuff we bin hearing this year.
Let's cut out of here soon and scoot over to The Flamingo.

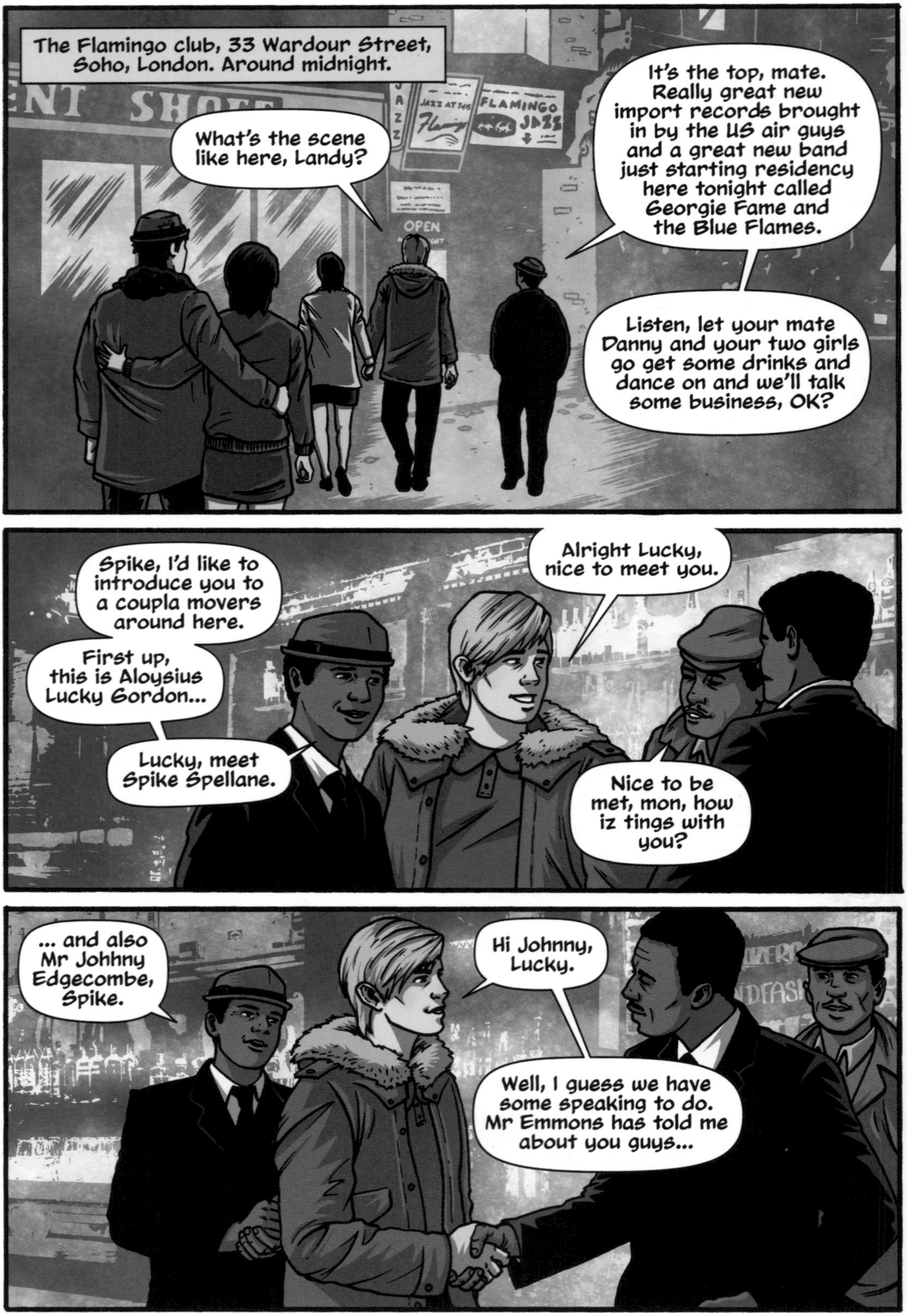

The Flamingo club, 33 Wardour Street, Soho, London. Around midnight.
FLAMINGO
JAZZ
OPEN
What's the scene like here, Landy?
It's the top, mate. Really great new import records brought in by the US air guys and a great new band just starting residency here tonight called Georgie Fame and the Blue Flames.
Listen, let your mate Danny and your two girls go get some drinks and dance on and we'll talk some business, OK?
Spike, I'd like to introduce you to a coupla movers around here.
First up, this is Aloysius Lucky Gordon...
Lucky, meet Spike Spellane.
Alright Lucky, nice to meet you.
Nice to be met, mon, how iz tings with you?
... and also Mr Johhny Edgecombe, Spike.
Hi Johnny, Lucky.
Well, I guess we have some speaking to do. Mr Emmons has told me about you guys...

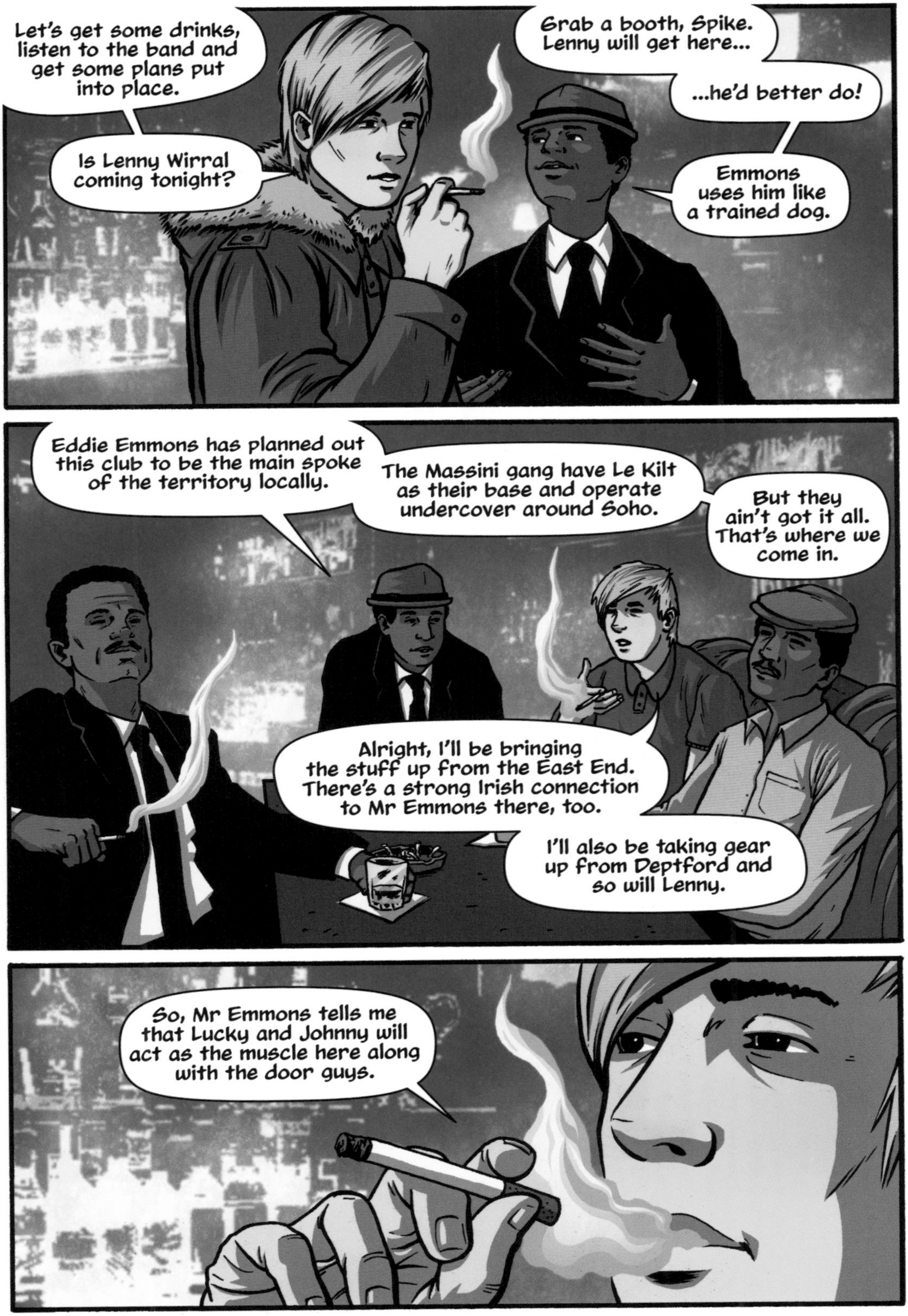
Let's get some drinks, listen to the band and get some plans put into place.
Is Lenny Wirral coming tonight?
Grab a booth, Spike. Lenny will get here...
...he'd better do!
Emmons uses him like a trained dog.
Eddie Emmons has planned out this club to be the main spoke of the territory locally.
The Massini gang have Le Kilt as their base and operate undercover around Soho.
But they ain't got it all. That's where we come in.
Alright, I'll be bringing the stuff up from the East End. There's a strong Irish connection to Mr Emmons there, too.
I'll also be taking gear up from Deptford and so will Lenny.
So, Mr Emmons tells me that Lucky and Johnny will act as the muscle here along with the door guys.

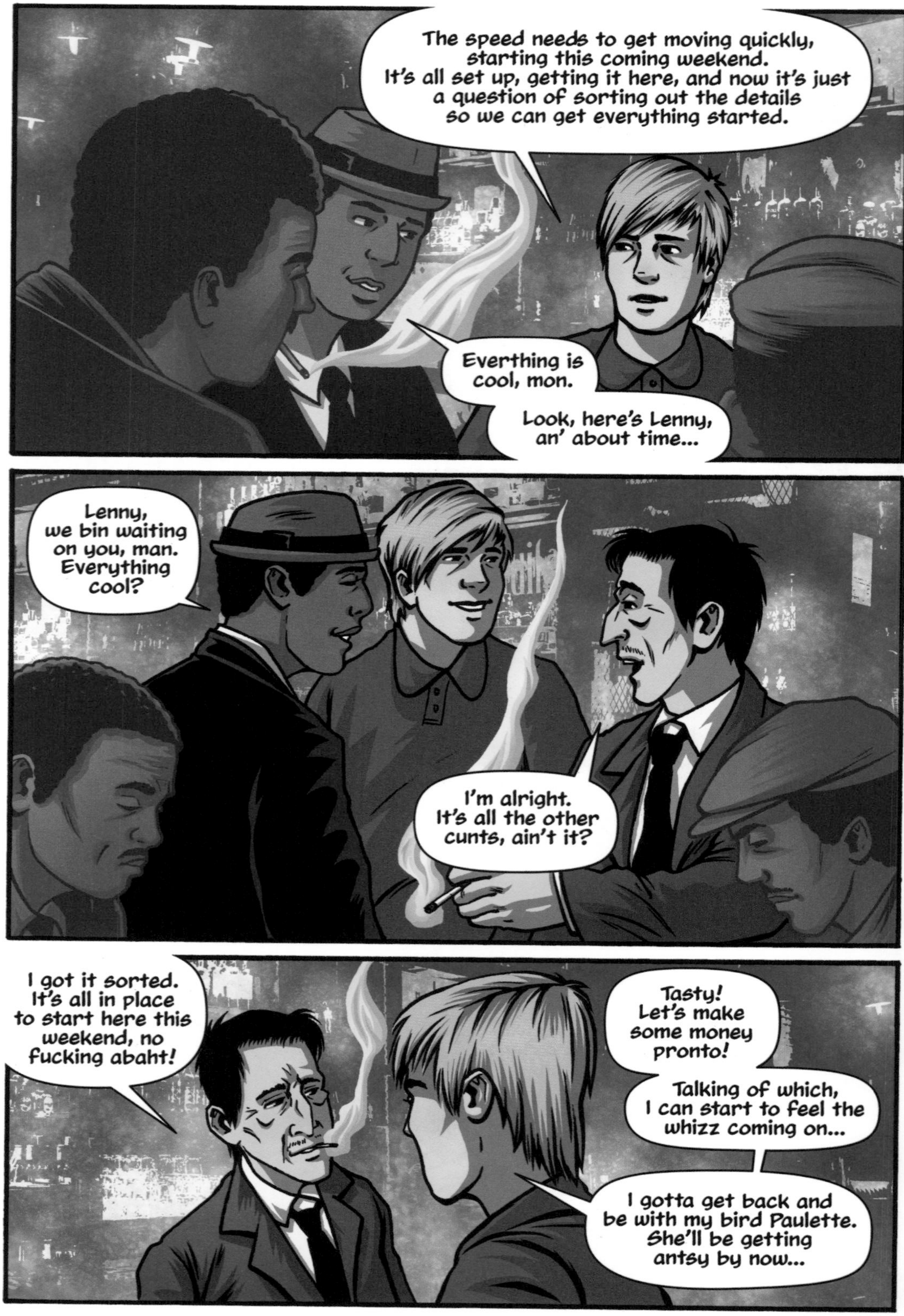
The speed needs to get moving quickly, starting this coming weekend. It's all set up, getting it here, and now it's just a question of sorting out the details so we can get everything started.
Everthing is cool, mon.
Look, here's Lenny, an' about time...
Lenny, we bin waiting on you, man. Everything cool?
I'm alright. It's all the other cunts, ain't it?
I got it sorted. It's all in place to start here this weekend, no fucking abaht!
Tasty! Let's make some money pronto!
Talking of which, I can start to feel the whizz coming on...
I gotta get back and be with my bird Paulette. She'll be getting antsy by now...

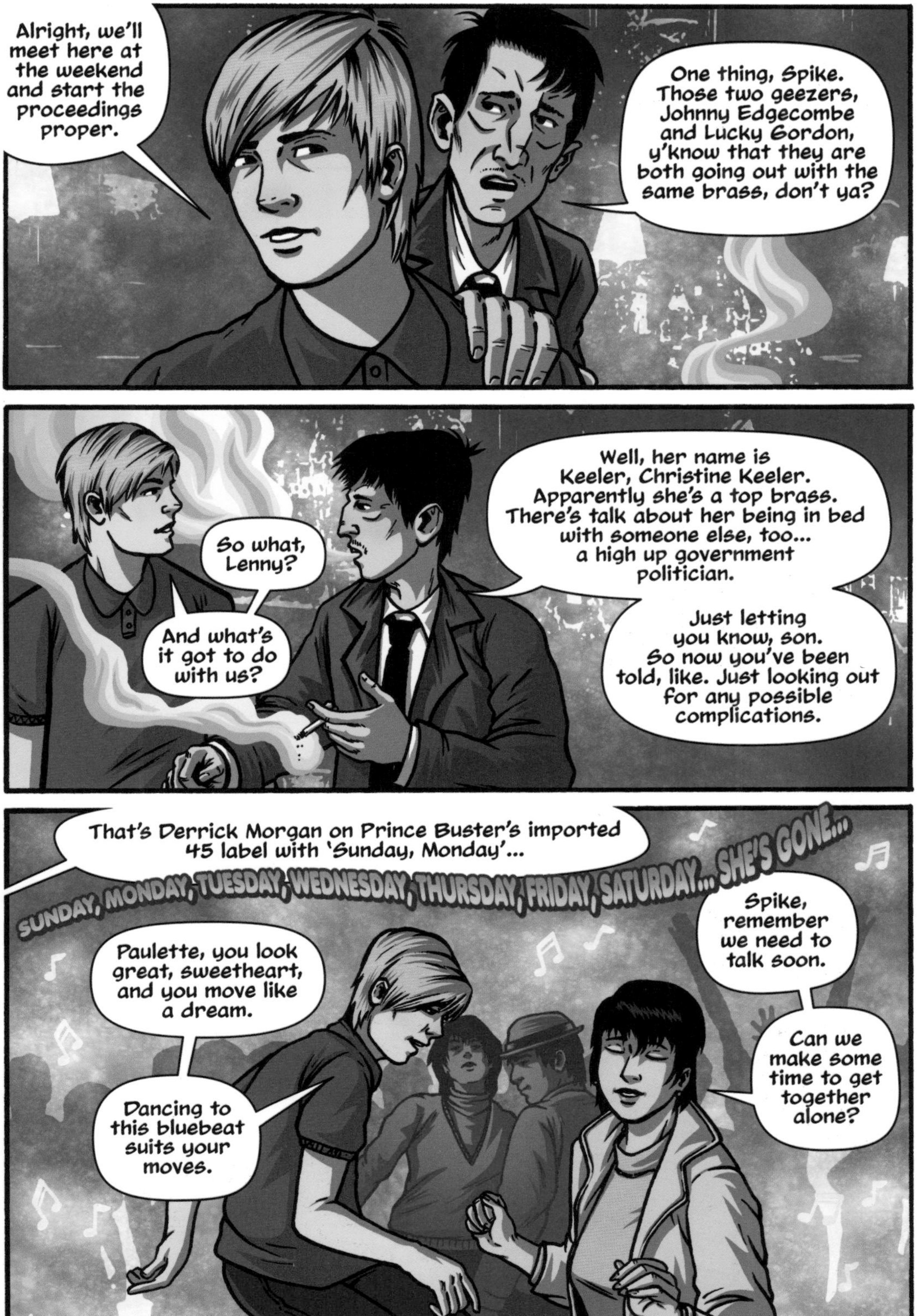
Alright, we'll meet here at the weekend and start the proceedings proper.
One thing, Spike. Those two geezers, Johnny Edgecombe and Lucky Gordon, y'know that they are both going out with the same brass, don't ya?
So what, Lenny?
And what's it got to do with us?
Well, her name is Keeler, Christine Keeler. Apparently she's a top brass. There's talk about her being in bed with someone else, too... a high up government politician.
Just letting you know, son. So now you've been told, like. Just looking out for any possible complications.
That's Derrick Morgan on Prince Buster's imported 45 label with 'Sunday, Monday'...
SUNDAY, MONDAY, TUESDAY, WEDNESDAY, THURSDAY, FRIDAY, SATURDAY... SHE'S GONE...
Paulette, you look great, sweetheart, and you move like a dream.
Dancing to this bluebeat suits your moves.
Spike, remember we need to talk soon.
Can we make some time to get together alone?

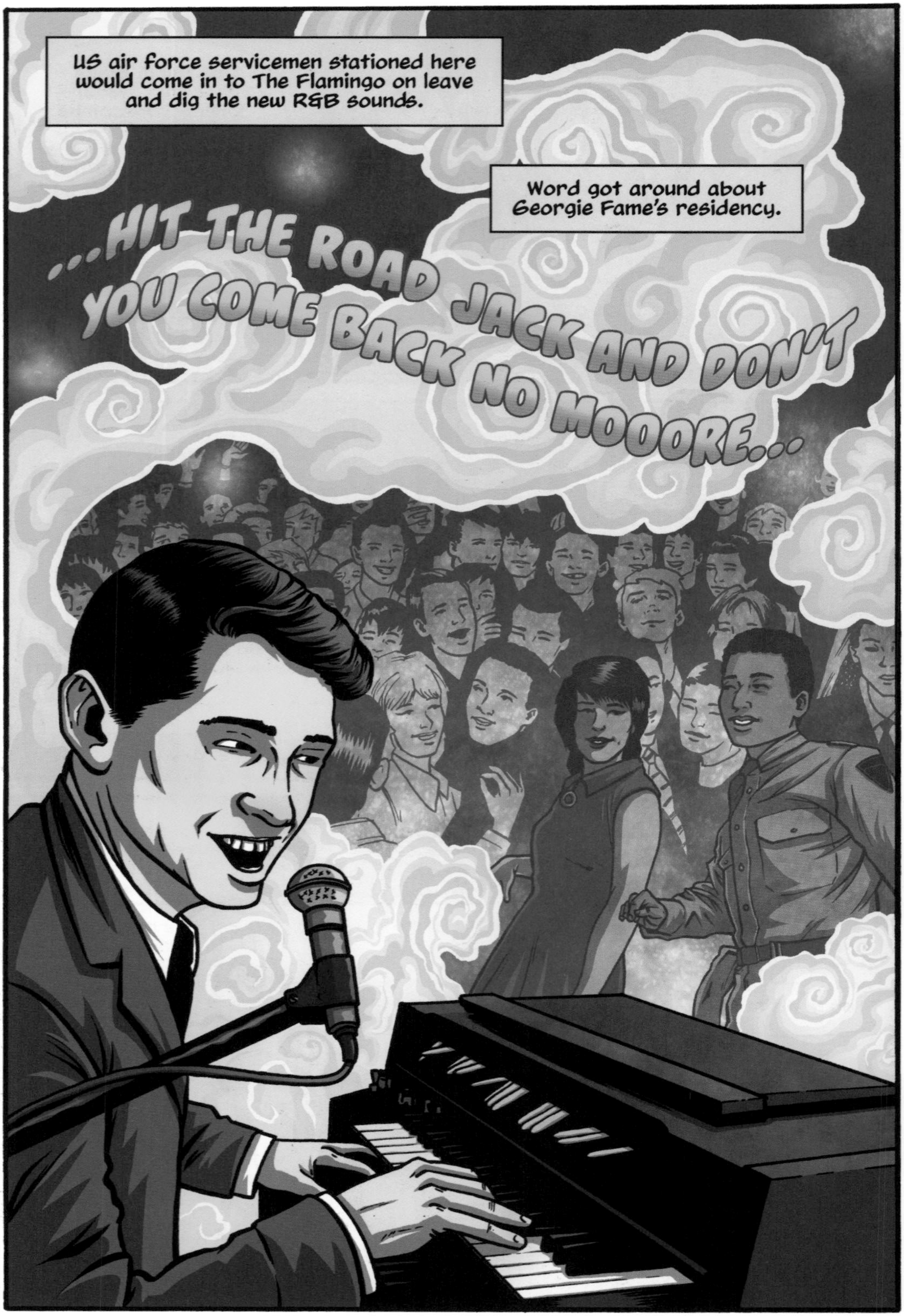
US air force servicemen stationed here would come in to The Flamingo on leave and dig the new R&B sounds.
Word got around about Georgie Fame's residency.
...HIT THE ROAD JACK AND DON'T YOU COME BACK NO MOOORE...

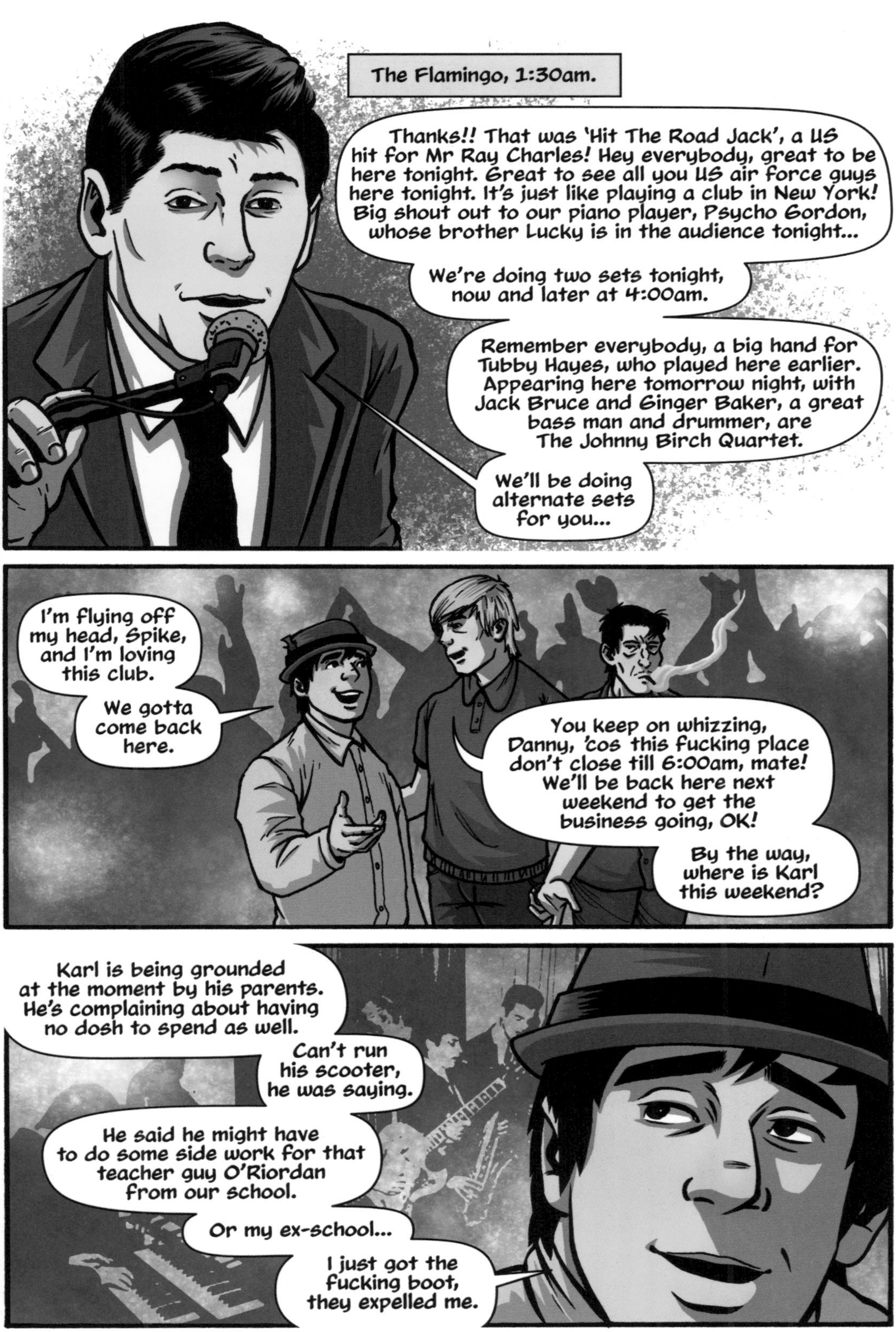
The Flamingo, 1:30am.
Thanks!! That was 'Hit The Road Jack', a US hit for Mr Ray Charles! Hey everybody, great to be here tonight. Great to see all you US air force guys here tonight. It's just like playing a club in New York! Big shout out to our piano player, Psycho Gordon, whose brother Lucky is in the audience tonight...
We're doing two sets tonight, now and later at 4:00am.
Remember everybody, a big hand for Tubby Hayes, who played here earlier. Appearing here tomorrow night, with Jack Bruce and Ginger Baker, a great bass man and drummer, are The Johnny Birch Quartet.
We'll be doing alternate sets for you...
I'm flying off my head, Spike, and I'm loving this club.
We gotta come back here.
You keep on whizzing, Danny, 'cos this fucking place don't close till 6:00am, mate! We'll be back here next weekend to get the business going, OK!
By the way, where is Karl this weekend?
Karl is being grounded at the moment by his parents. He's complaining about having no dosh to spend as well.
Can't run his scooter, he was saying.
He said he might have to do some side work for that teacher guy O'Riordan from our school.
Or my ex-school...
I just got the fucking boot, they expelled me.

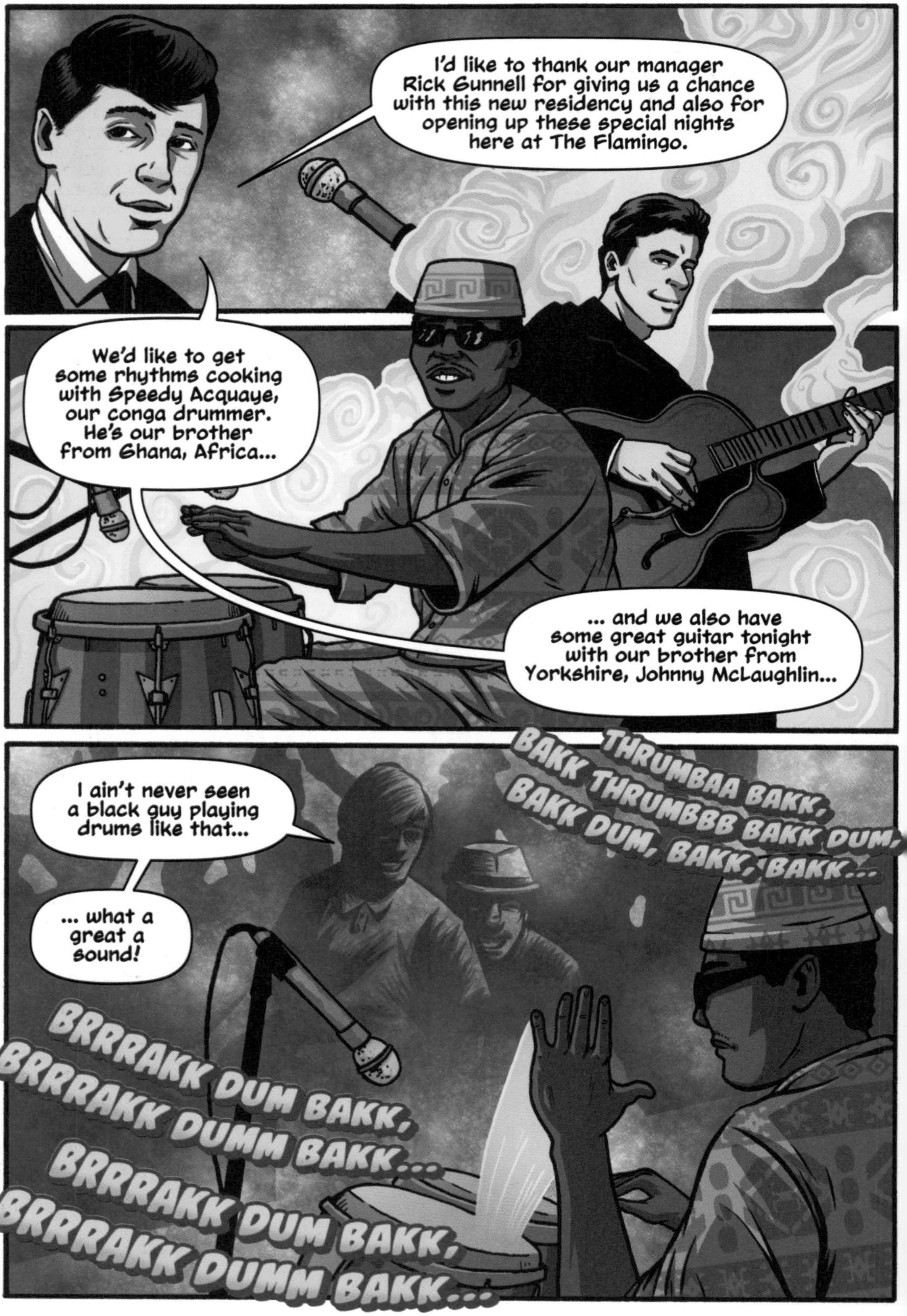
I'd like to thank our manager Rick Gunnell for giving us a chance with this new residency and also for opening up these special nights here at The Flamingo.
We'd like to get some rhythms cooking with Speedy Acquaye, our conga drummer. He's our brother from Ghana, Africa...
... and we also have some great guitar tonight with our brother from Yorkshire, Johnny McLaughlin...
THRUMBAA BAKK, BAKK THRUMBBB BAKK DUM, BAKK DUM, BAKK, BAKK...
I ain't never seen a black guy playing drums like that...
... what a great a sound!
BRRRAKK DUM BAKK, BRRRAKK DUMM BAKK... BRRRAKK DUM BAKK, BRRRAKK DUMM BAKK...

The Flamingo Club.

That next weekend, the beginning of the business rolled around...

... the end of the beginning...

Alright, so Johnny and Lucky are dealing from the front of the house and the door, keeping an eye on proceedings.

We're staying back in the club and will sell from near and around the bogs.

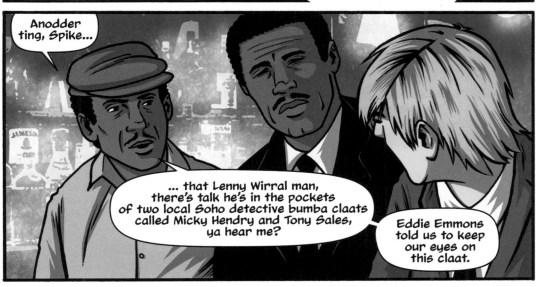

Anodder ting, Spike...

... that Lenny Wirral man, there's talk he's in the pockets of two local Soho detective bumba claats called Micky Hendry and Tony Sales, ya hear me?

Eddie Emmons told us to keep our eyes on this claat.

I'll be watching the fucker... he's watching every move I'm making.

He thinks he's the dog's nuts, but I ain't stupid.

OK chaps, let's make some money here.

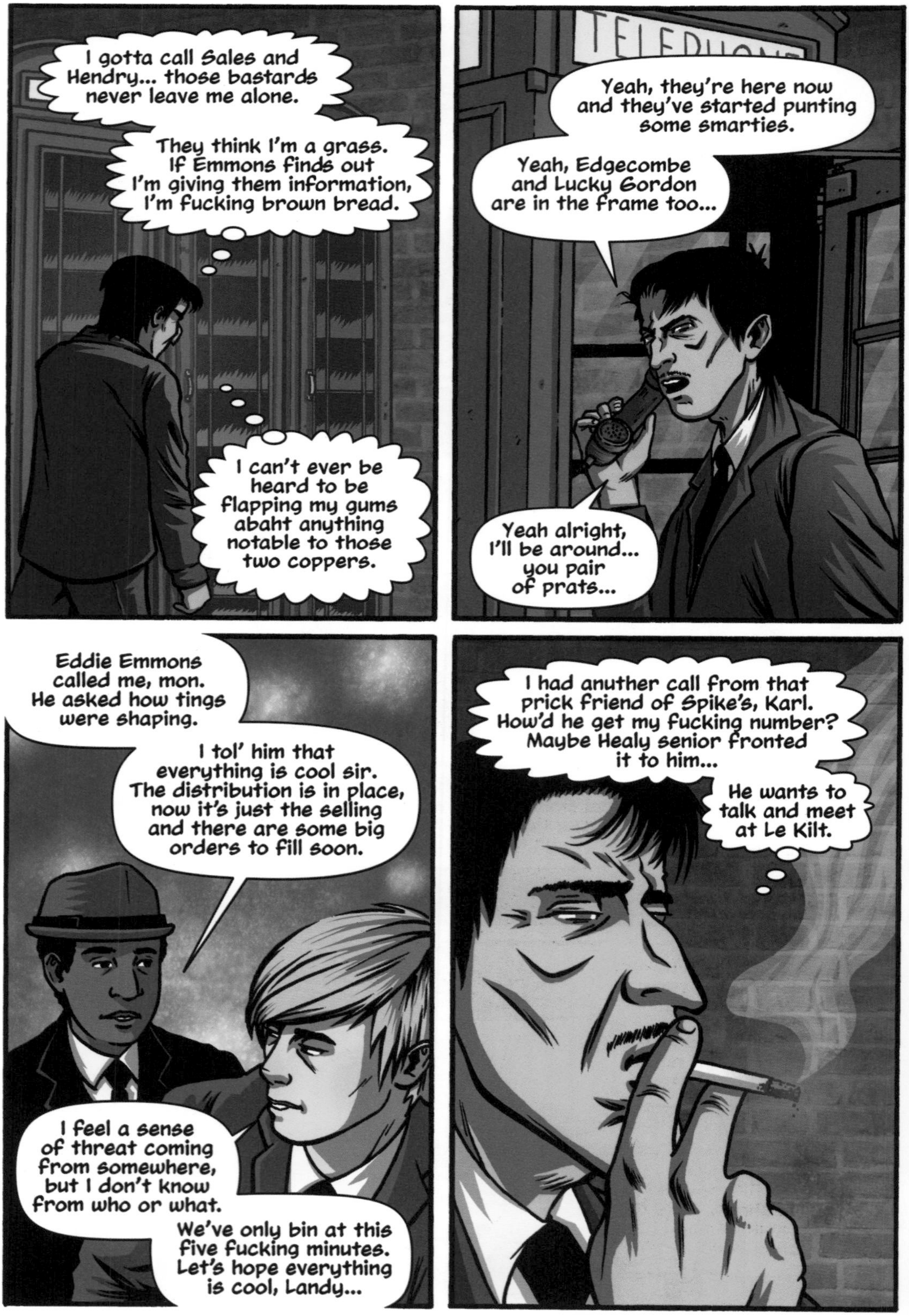
I gotta call Sales and Hendry... those bastards never leave me alone.
They think I'm a grass. If Emmons finds out I'm giving them information, I'm fucking brown bread.
I can't ever be heard to be flapping my gums abaht anything notable to those two coppers.
Yeah, they're here now and they've started punting some smarties.
Yeah, Edgecombe and Lucky Gordon are in the frame too...
Yeah alright, I'll be around... you pair of prats...
Eddie Emmons called me, mon. He asked how tings were shaping.
I tol' him that everything is cool sir. The distribution is in place, now it's just the selling and there are some big orders to fill soon.
I feel a sense of threat coming from somewhere, but I don't know from who or what.
We've only bin at this five fucking minutes. Let's hope everything is cool, Landy...
I had anuther call from that prick friend of Spike's, Karl. How'd he get my fucking number? Maybe Healy senior fronted it to him...
He wants to talk and meet at Le Kilt.

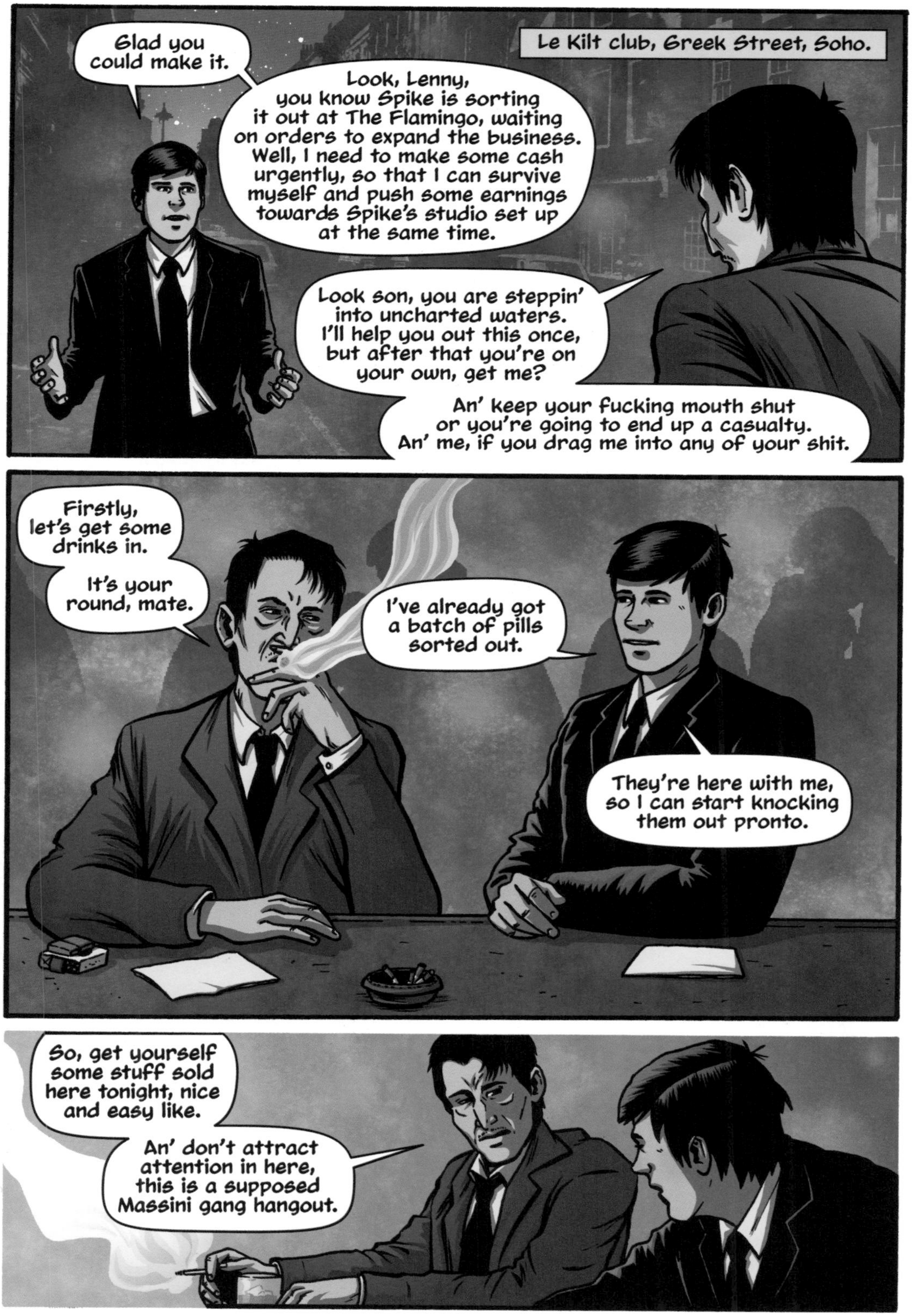
Le Kilt club, Greek Street, Soho.
Glad you could make it.
Look, Lenny, you know Spike is sorting it out at The Flamingo, waiting on orders to expand the business. Well, I need to make some cash urgently, so that I can survive myself and push some earnings towards Spike's studio set up at the same time.
Look son, you are steppin' into uncharted waters. I'll help you out this once, but after that you're on your own, get me?
An' keep your fucking mouth shut or you're going to end up a casualty. An' me, if you drag me into any of your shit.
Firstly, let's get some drinks in.
It's your round, mate.
I've already got a batch of pills sorted out.
They're here with me, so I can start knocking them out pronto.
So, get yourself some stuff sold here tonight, nice and easy like.
An' don't attract attention in here, this is a supposed Massini gang hangout.

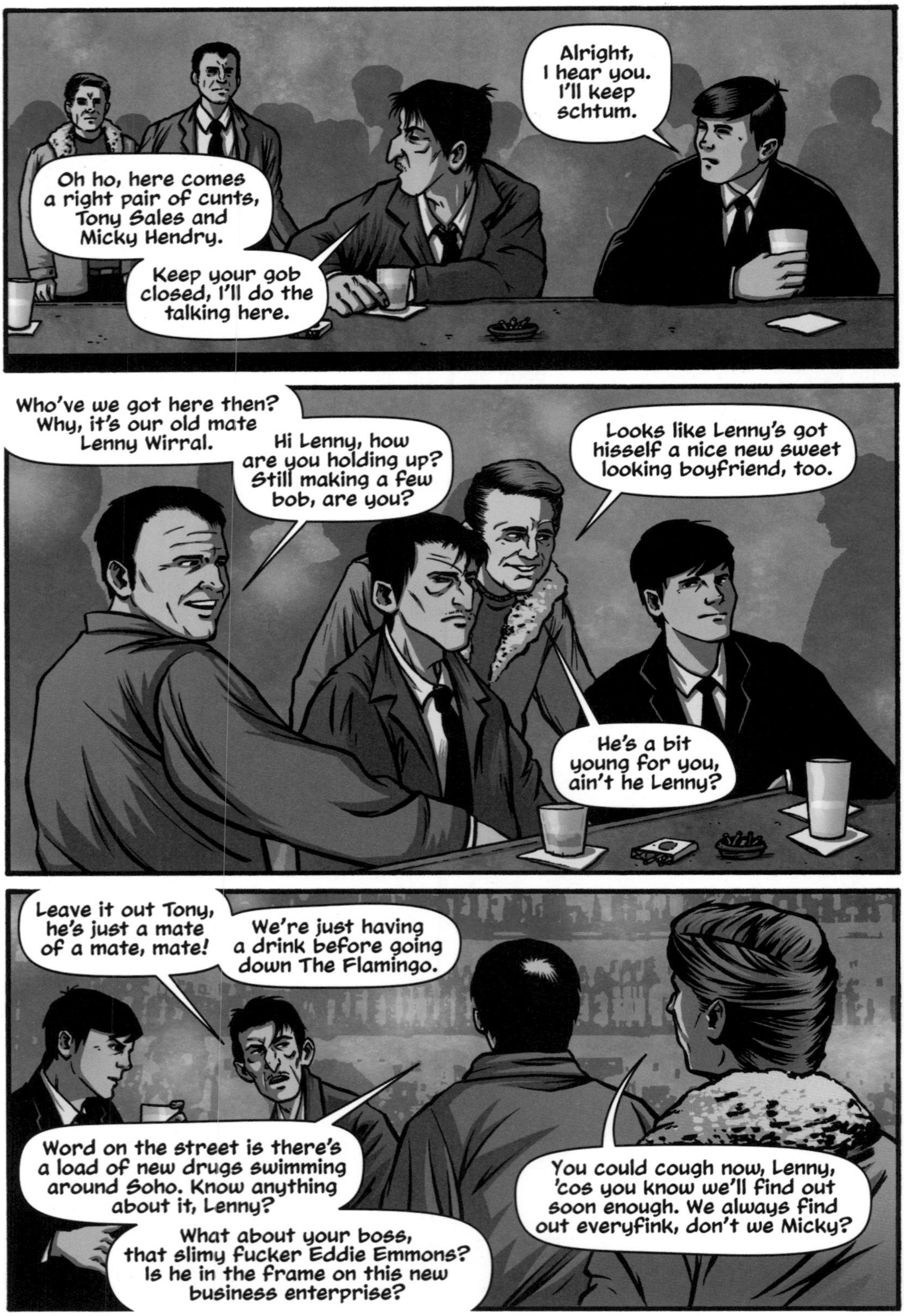
Alright, I hear you. I'll keep schtum.
Oh ho, here comes a right pair of cunts, Tony Sales and Micky Hendry.
Keep your gob closed, I'll do the talking here.
Who've we got here then? Why, it's our old mate Lenny Wirral.
Hi Lenny, how are you holding up? Still making a few bob, are you?
Looks like Lenny's got hisself a nice new sweet looking boyfriend, too.
He's a bit young for you, ain't he Lenny?
Leave it out Tony, he's just a mate of a mate, mate!
We're just having a drink before going down The Flamingo.
Word on the street is there's a load of new drugs swimming around Soho. Know anything about it, Lenny?
What about your boss, that slimy fucker Eddie Emmons? Is he in the frame on this new business enterprise?
You could cough now, Lenny, 'cos you know we'll find out soon enough. We always find out everyfink, don't we Micky?

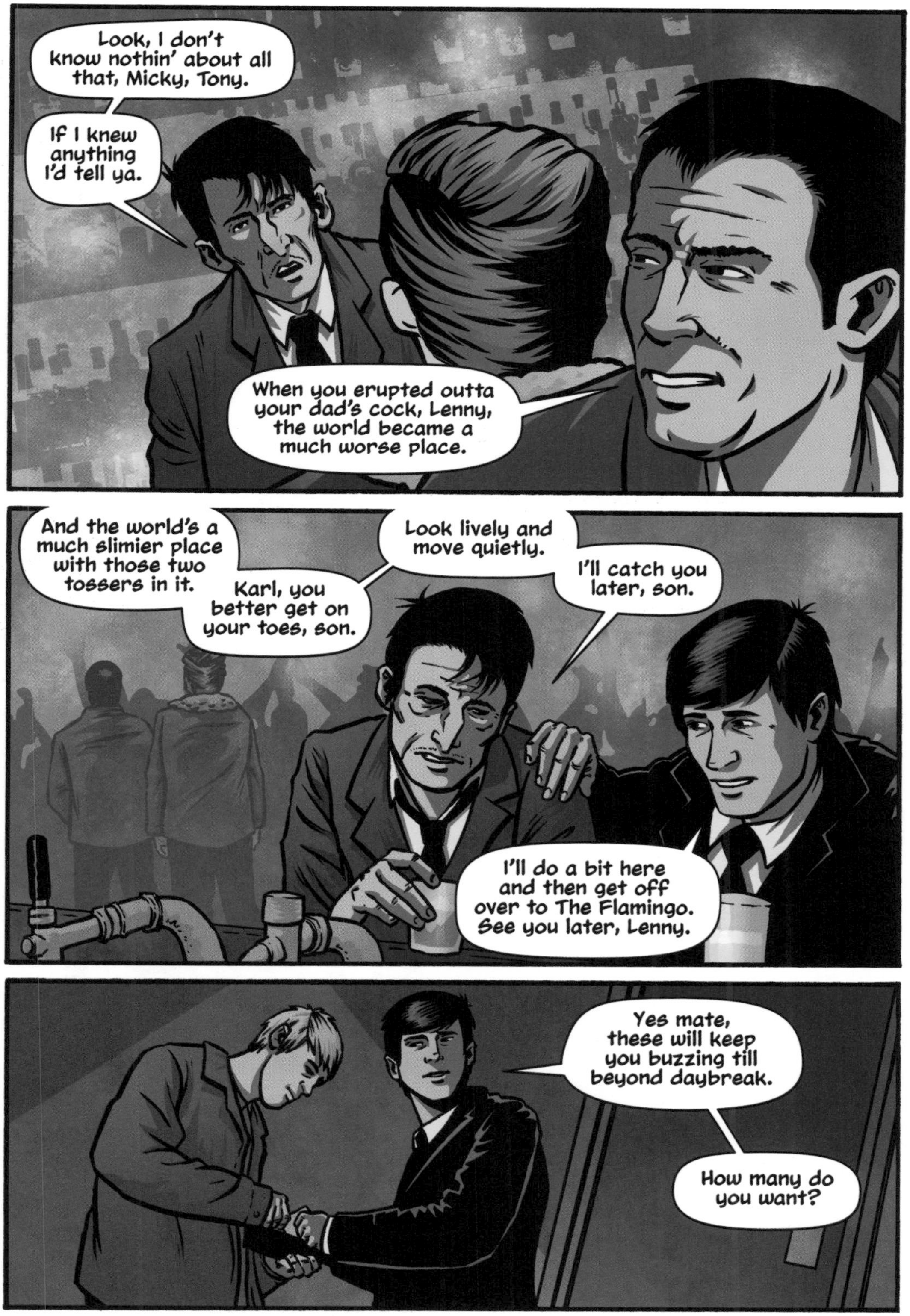
Look, I don't know nothin' about all that, Micky, Tony.
If I knew anything I'd tell ya.
When you erupted outta your dad's cock, Lenny, the world became a much worse place.
And the world's a much slimier place with those two tossers in it.
Look lively and move quietly.
Karl, you better get on your toes, son.
I'll catch you later, son.
I'll do a bit here and then get off over to The Flamingo. See you later, Lenny.
Yes mate, these will keep you buzzing till beyond daybreak.
How many do you want?

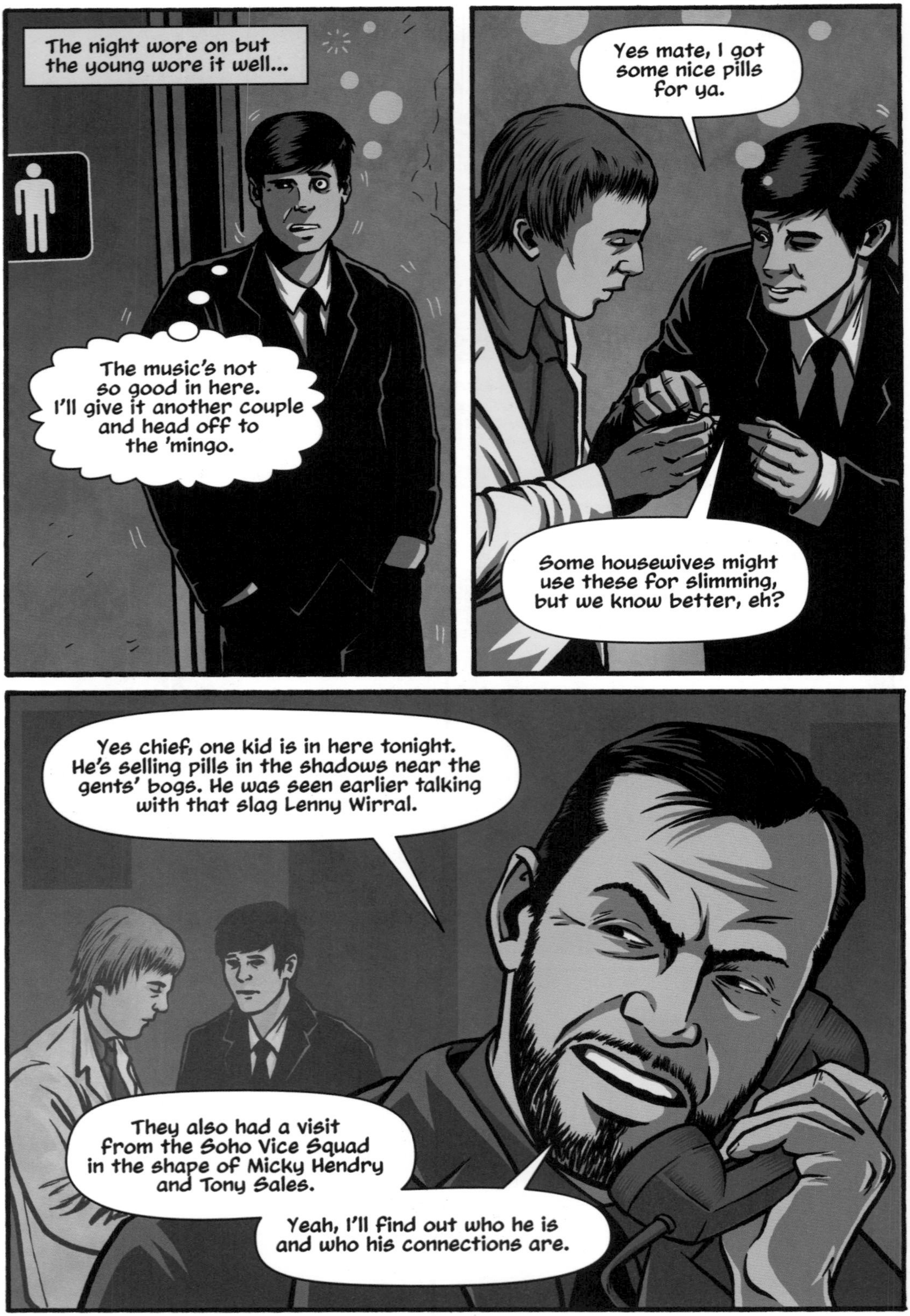
The night wore on but the young wore it well...
The music's not so good in here. I'll give it another couple and head off to the 'mingo.
Yes mate, I got some nice pills for ya.
Some housewives might use these for slimming, but we know better, eh?
Yes chief, one kid is in here tonight. He's selling pills in the shadows near the gents' bogs. He was seen earlier talking with that slag Lenny Wirral.
They also had a visit from the Soho Vice Squad in the shape of Micky Hendry and Tony Sales.
Yeah, I'll find out who he is and who his connections are.

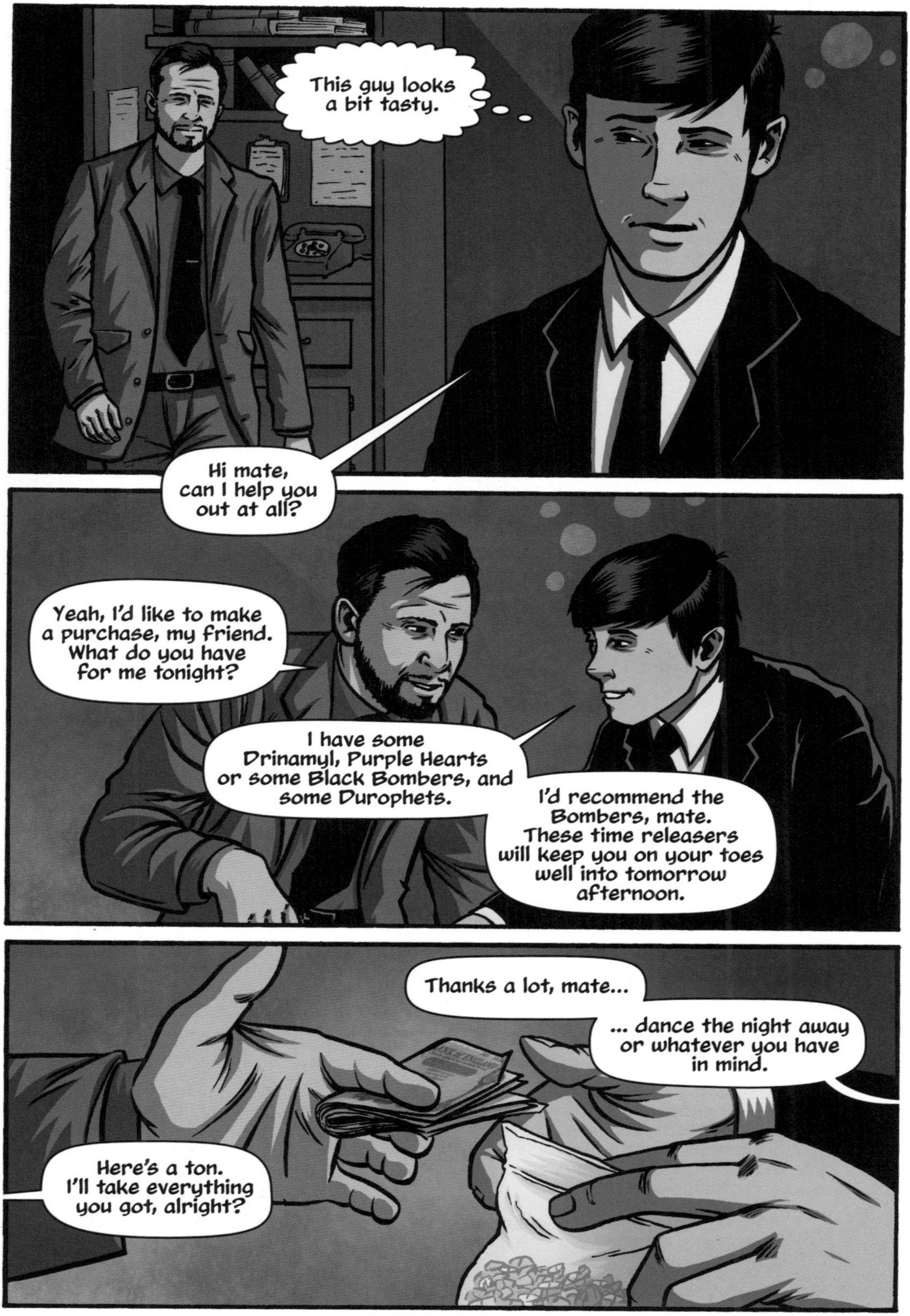
This guy looks a bit tasty.
Hi mate, can I help you out at all?
Yeah, I'd like to make a purchase, my friend. What do you have for me tonight?
I have some Drinamyl, Purple Hearts or some Black Bombers, and some Durophets.
I'd recommend the Bombers, mate. These time releasers will keep you on your toes well into tomorrow afternoon.
Thanks a lot, mate...
... dance the night away or whatever you have in mind.
Here's a ton. I'll take everything you got, alright?

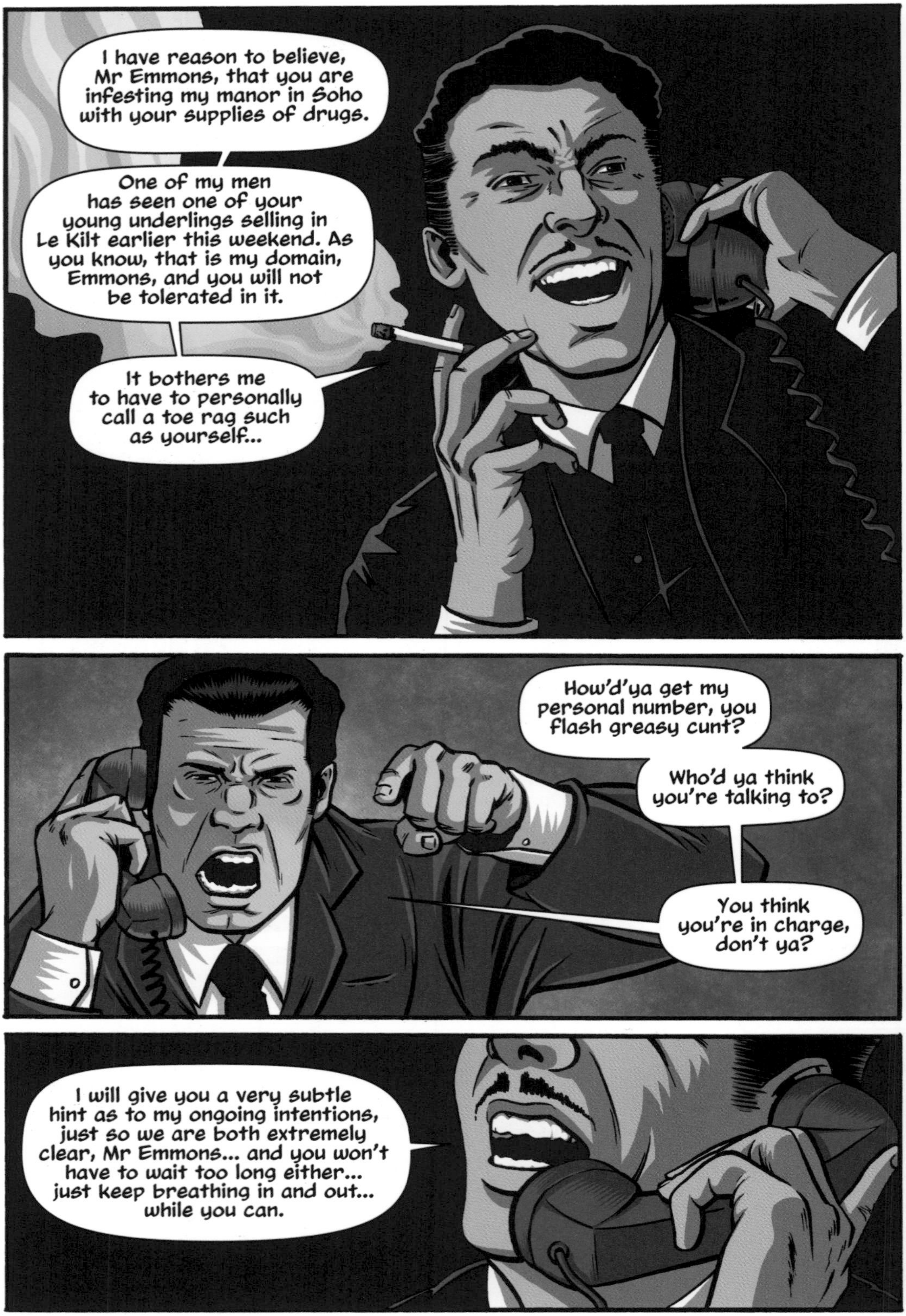

I have reason to believe, Mr Emmons, that you are infesting my manor in Soho with your supplies of drugs.
One of my men has seen one of your young underlings selling in Le Kilt earlier this weekend. As you know, that is my domain, Emmons, and you will not be tolerated in it.
It bothers me to have to personally call a toe rag such as yourself...
How'd'ya get my personal number, you flash greasy cunt?
Who'd ya think you're talking to?
You think you're in charge, don't ya?
I will give you a very subtle hint as to my ongoing intentions, just so we are both extremely clear, Mr Emmons... and you won't have to wait too long either... just keep breathing in and out... while you can.

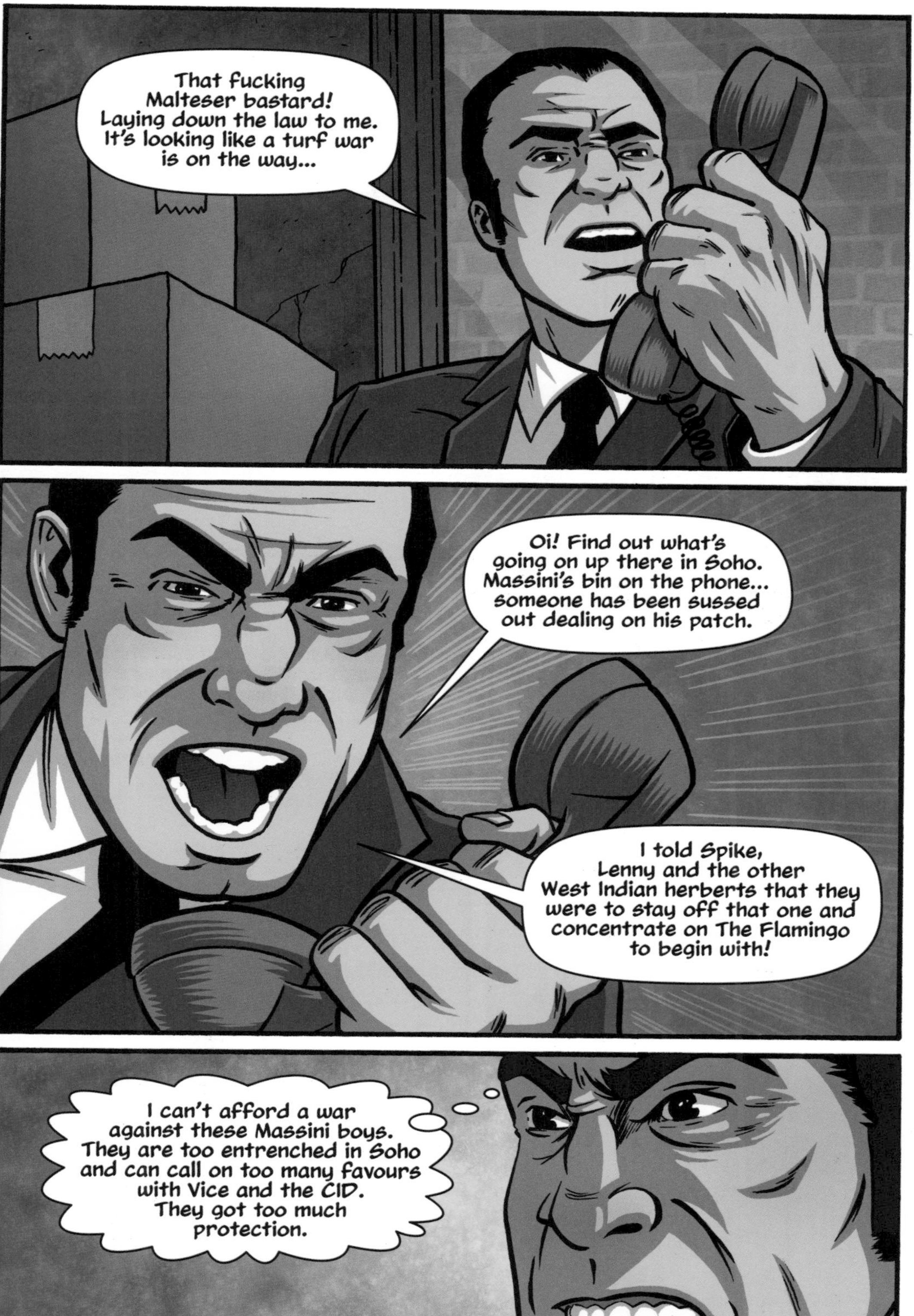

That fucking Malteser bastard! Laying down the law to me. It's looking like a turf war is on the way...
Oi! Find out what's going on up there in Soho. Massini's bin on the phone... someone has been sussed out dealing on his patch.
I told Spike, Lenny and the other West Indian herberts that they were to stay off that one and concentrate on The Flamingo to begin with!
I can't afford a war against these Massini boys. They are too entrenched in Soho and can call on too many favours with Vice and the CID. They got too much protection.

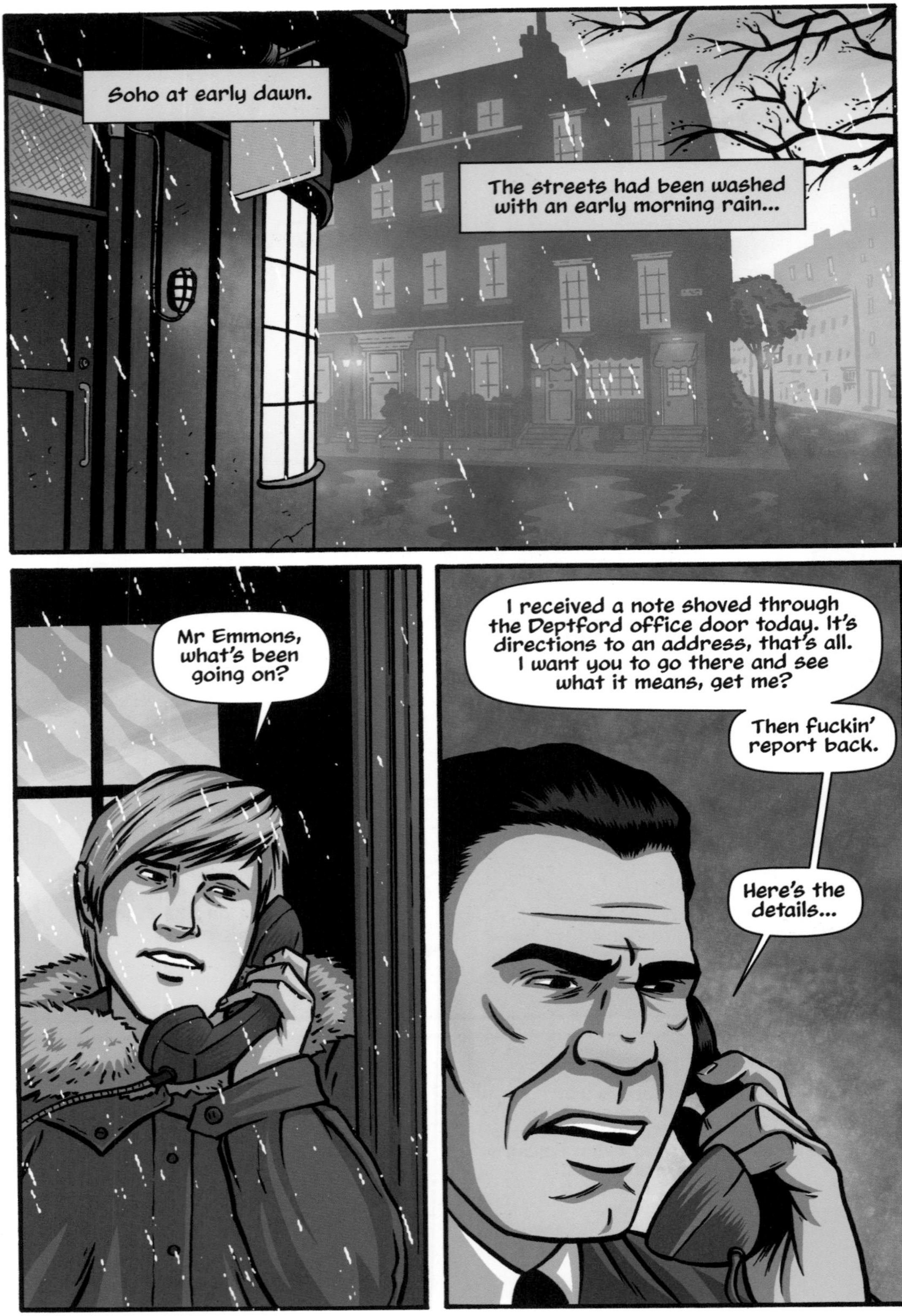
Soho at early dawn.
The streets had been washed with an early morning rain...
Mr Emmons, what's been going on?
I received a note shoved through the Deptford office door today. It's directions to an address, that's all. I want you to go there and see what it means, get me?
Then fuckin' report back.
Here's the details...

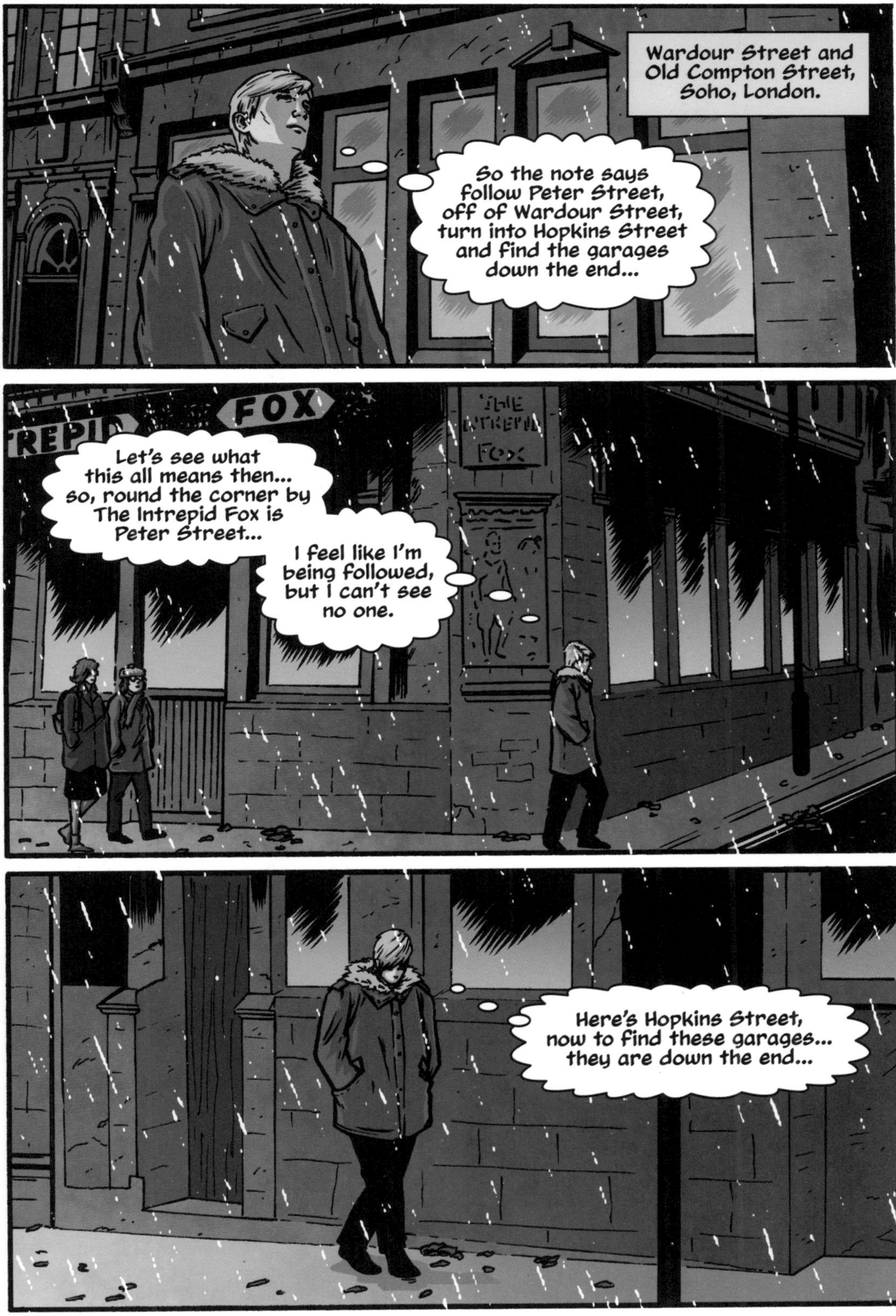

Wardour Street and Old Compton Street, Soho, London.
So the note says follow Peter Street, off of Wardour Street, turn into Hopkins Street and find the garages down the end...
FOX
Let's see what this all means then... so, round the corner by The Intrepid Fox is Peter Street...
I feel like I'm being followed, but I can't see no one.
Here's Hopkins Street, now to find these garages... they are down the end...

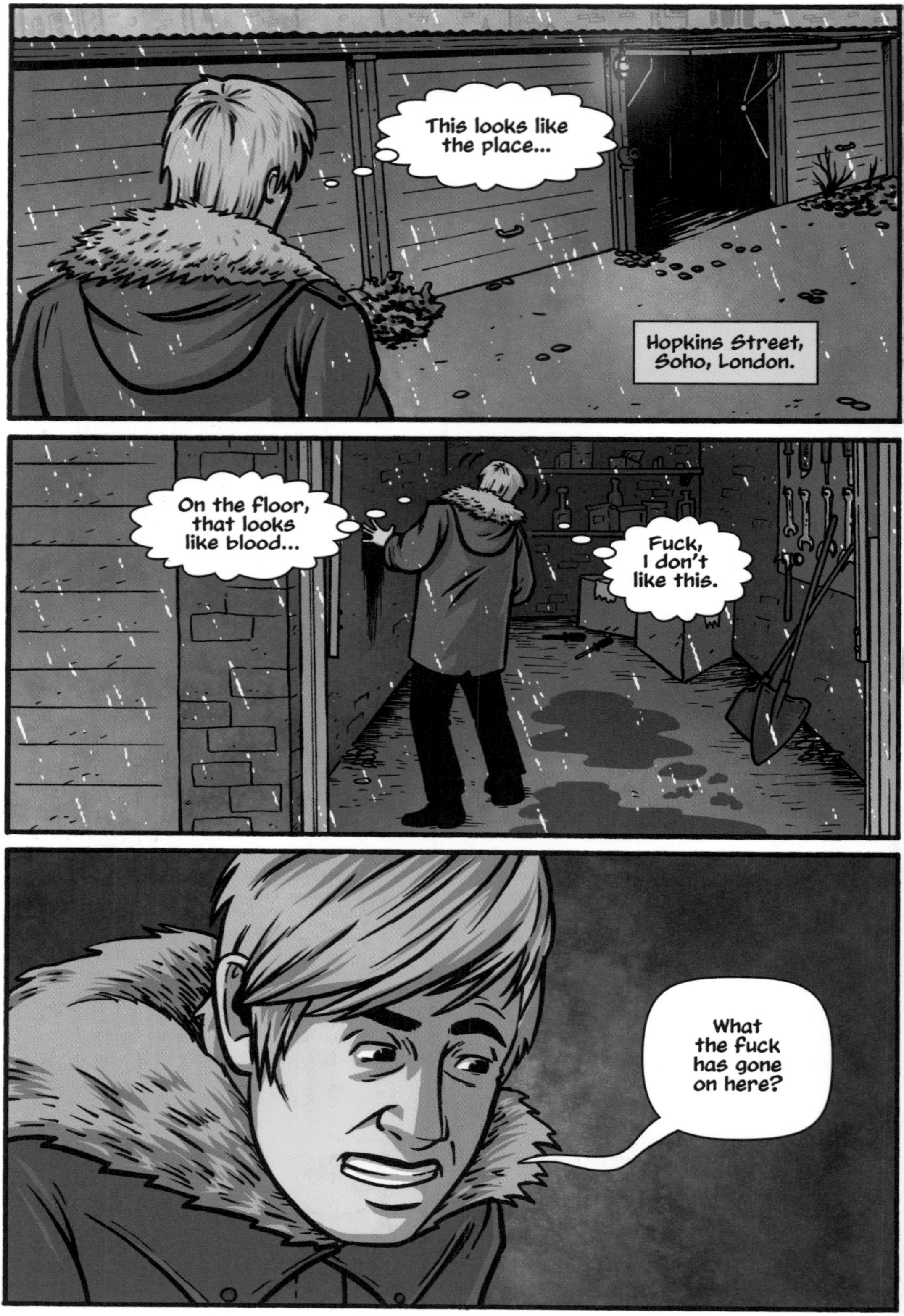
This looks like the place...
Hopkins Street, Soho, London.
On the floor, that looks like blood...
Fuck, I don't like this.
What the fuck has gone on here?

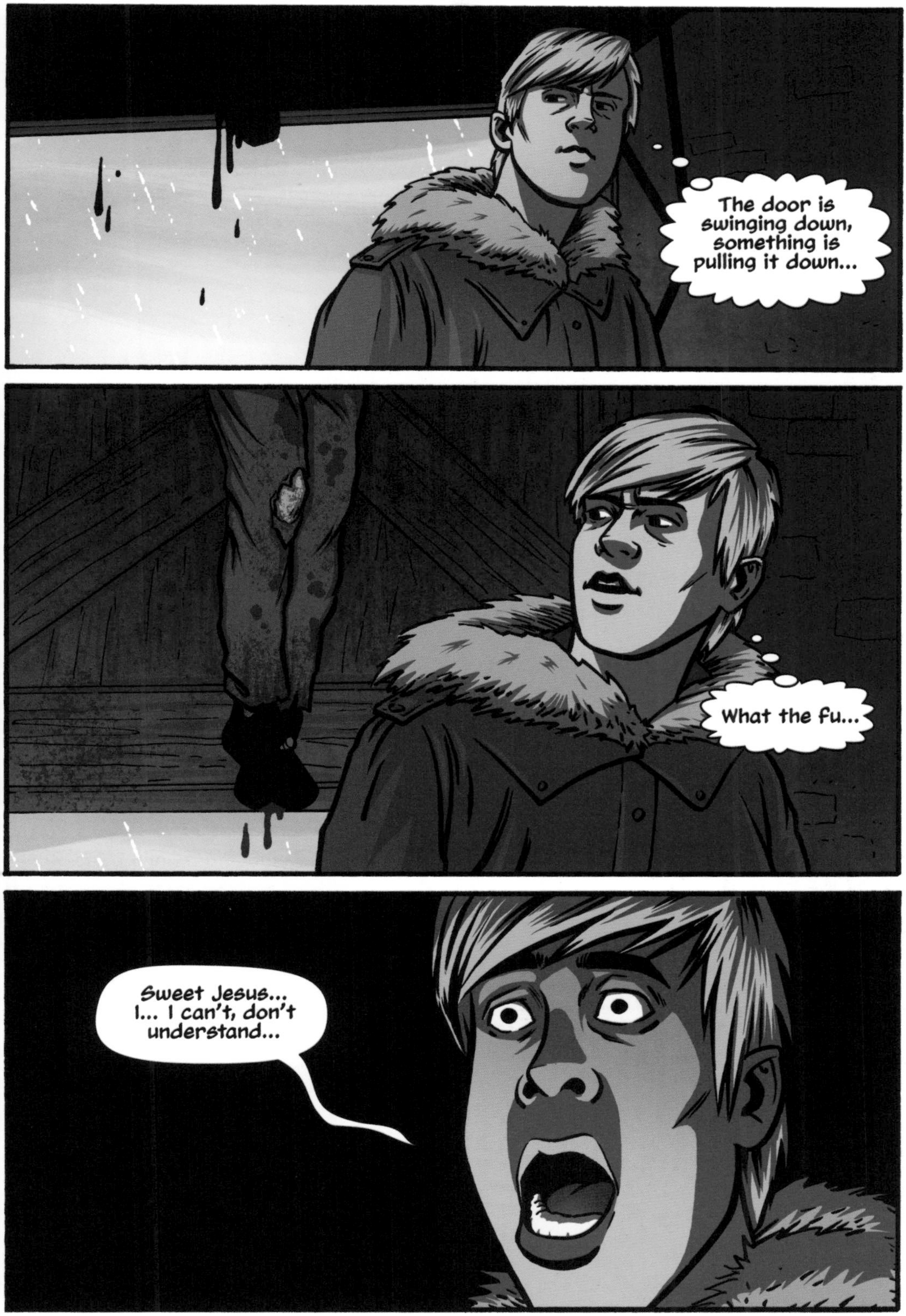
The door is swinging down, something is pulling it down...
What the fu...
Sweet Jesus... I... I can't, don't understand...

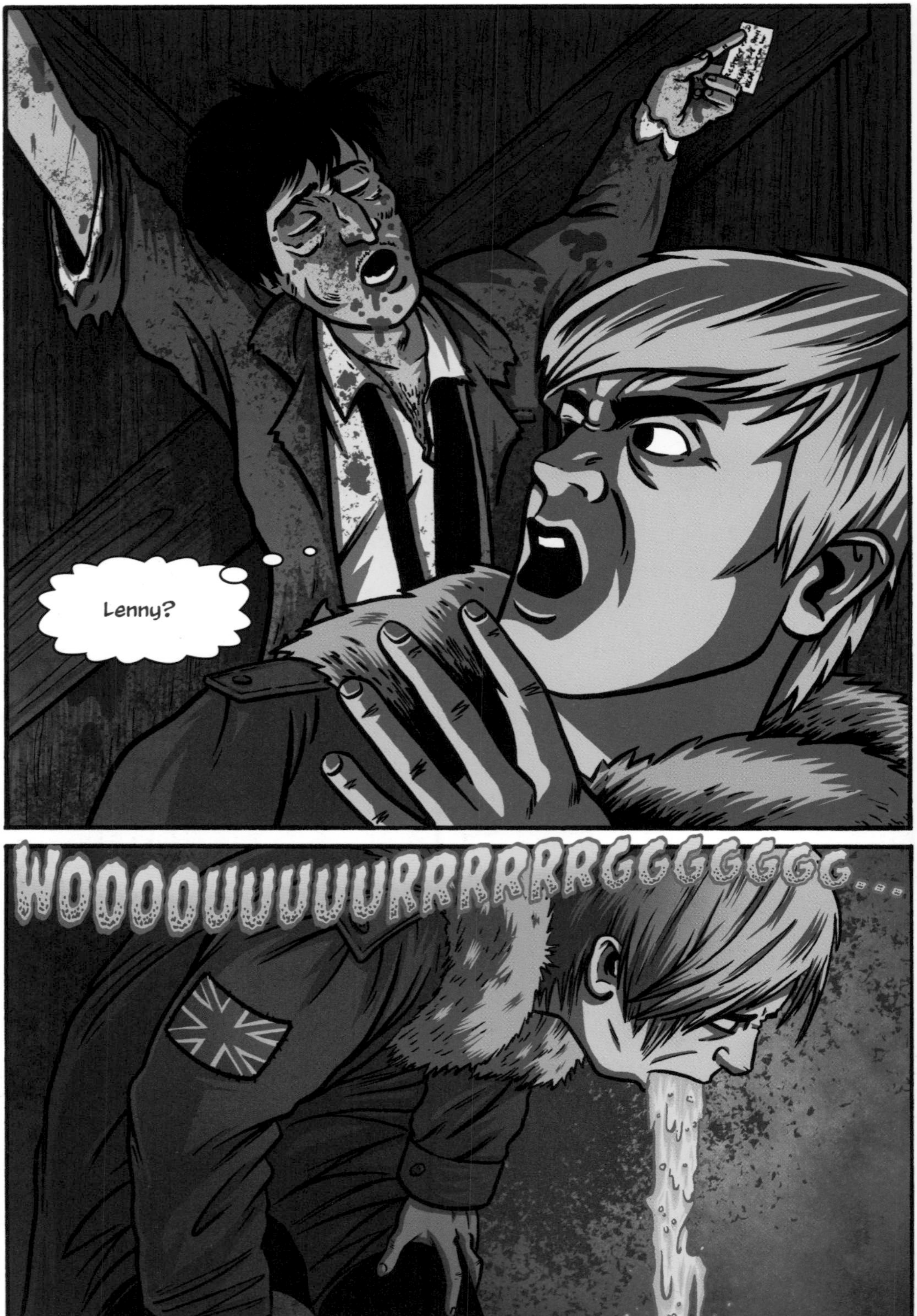
Lenny?
WOOOOUUUUURRRRRRRGGGGGGG...

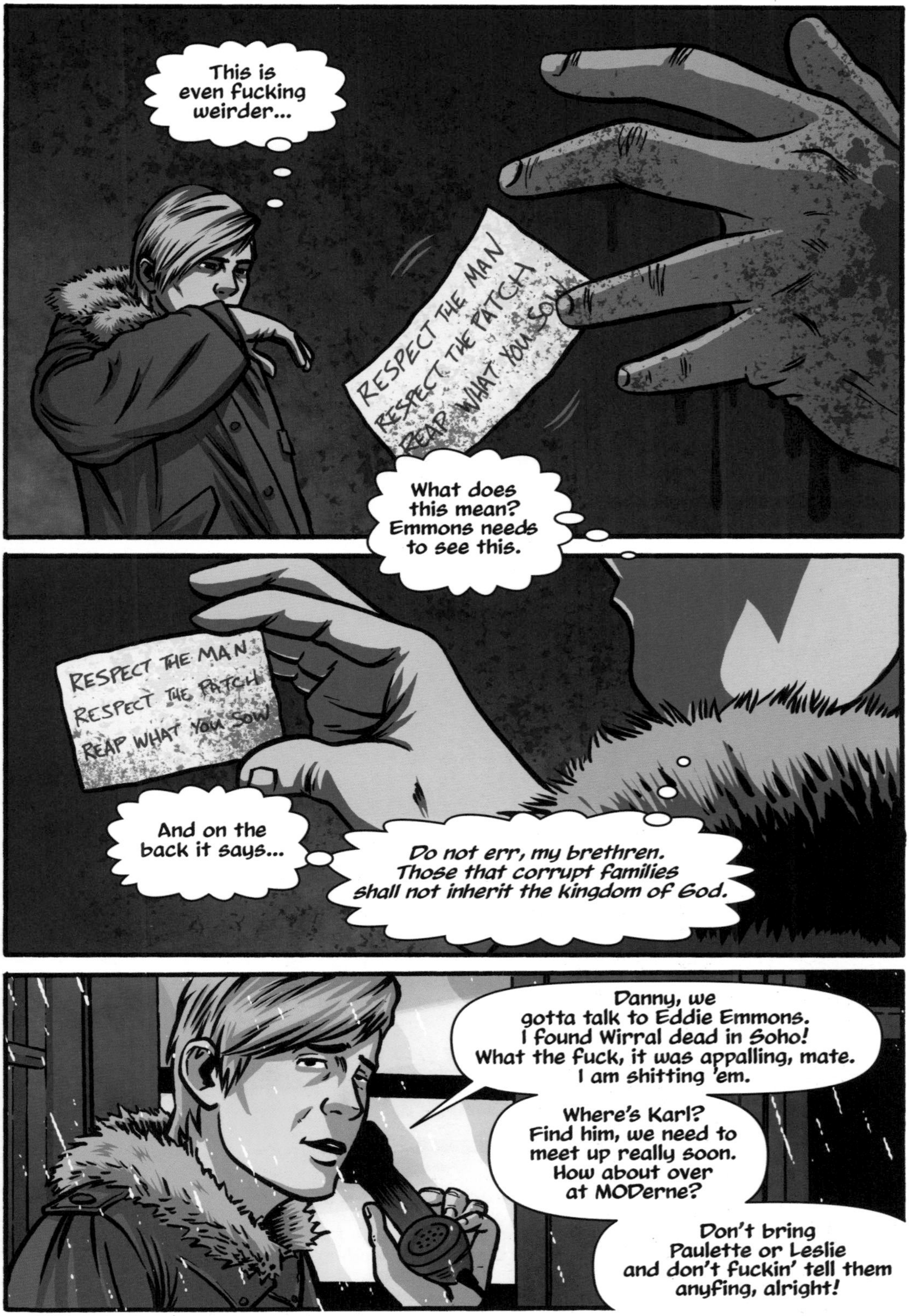
This is even fucking weirder...
RESPECT THE MAN
RESPECT THE PATCH
REAP WHAT YOU SOW
What does this mean? Emmons needs to see this.
RESPECT THE MAN
RESPECT THE PATCH
REAP WHAT YOU SOW
And on the back it says...
Do not err, my brethren. Those that corrupt families shall not inherit the kingdom of God.
Danny, we gotta talk to Eddie Emmons. I found Wirral dead in Soho! What the fuck, it was appalling, mate. I am shitting 'em.
Where's Karl? Find him, we need to meet up really soon. How about over at MODerne?
Don't bring Paulette or Leslie and don't fuckin' tell them anyfing, alright!

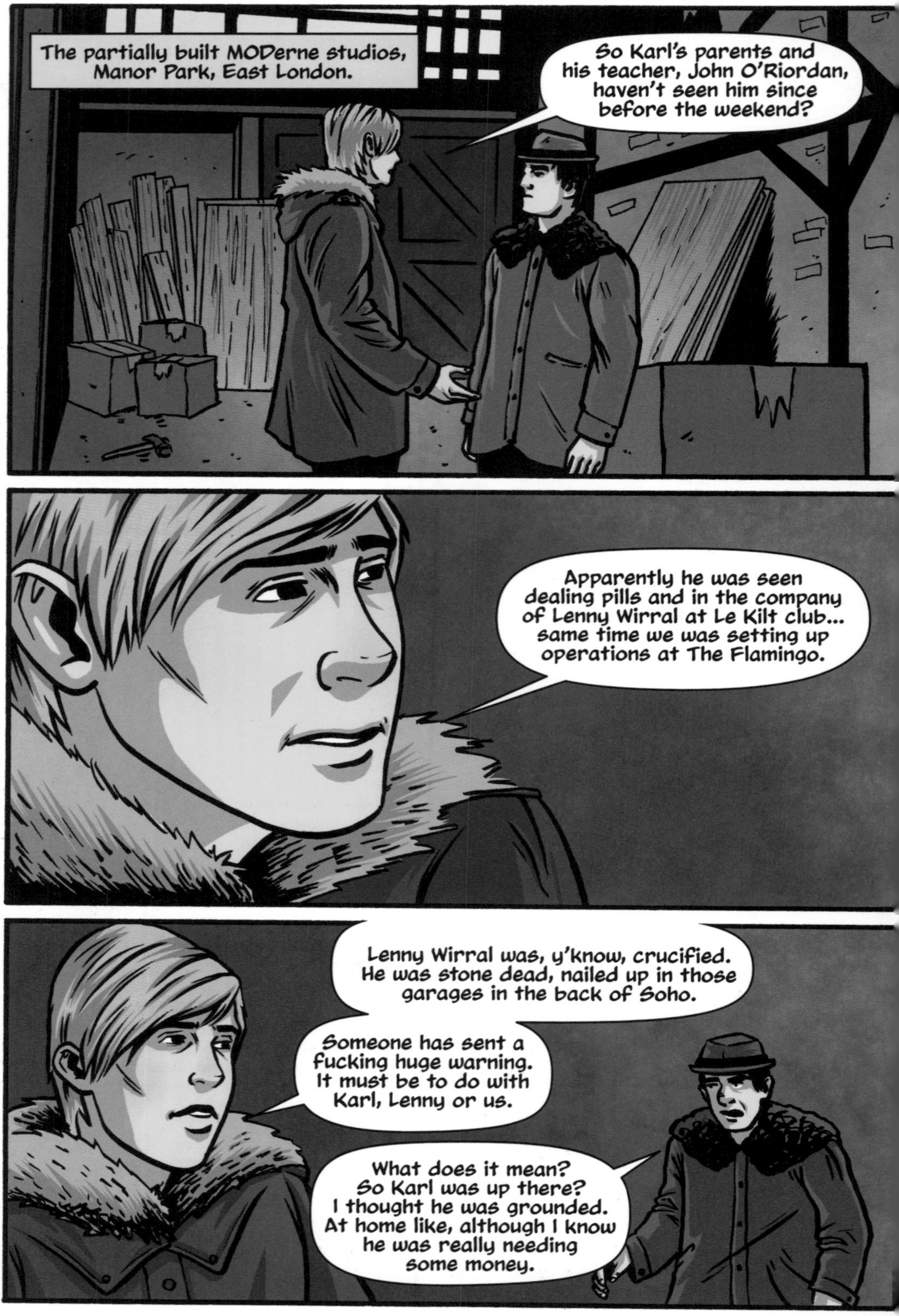

The partially built MODerne studios, Manor Park, East London.
So Karl's parents and his teacher, John O'Riordan, haven't seen him since before the weekend?
Apparently he was seen dealing pills and in the company of Lenny Wirral at Le Kilt club... same time we was setting up operations at The Flamingo.
Lenny Wirral was, y'know, crucified. He was stone dead, nailed up in those garages in the back of Soho.
Someone has sent a fucking huge warning. It must be to do with Karl, Lenny or us.
What does it mean? So Karl was up there? I thought he was grounded. At home like, although I know he was really needing some money.

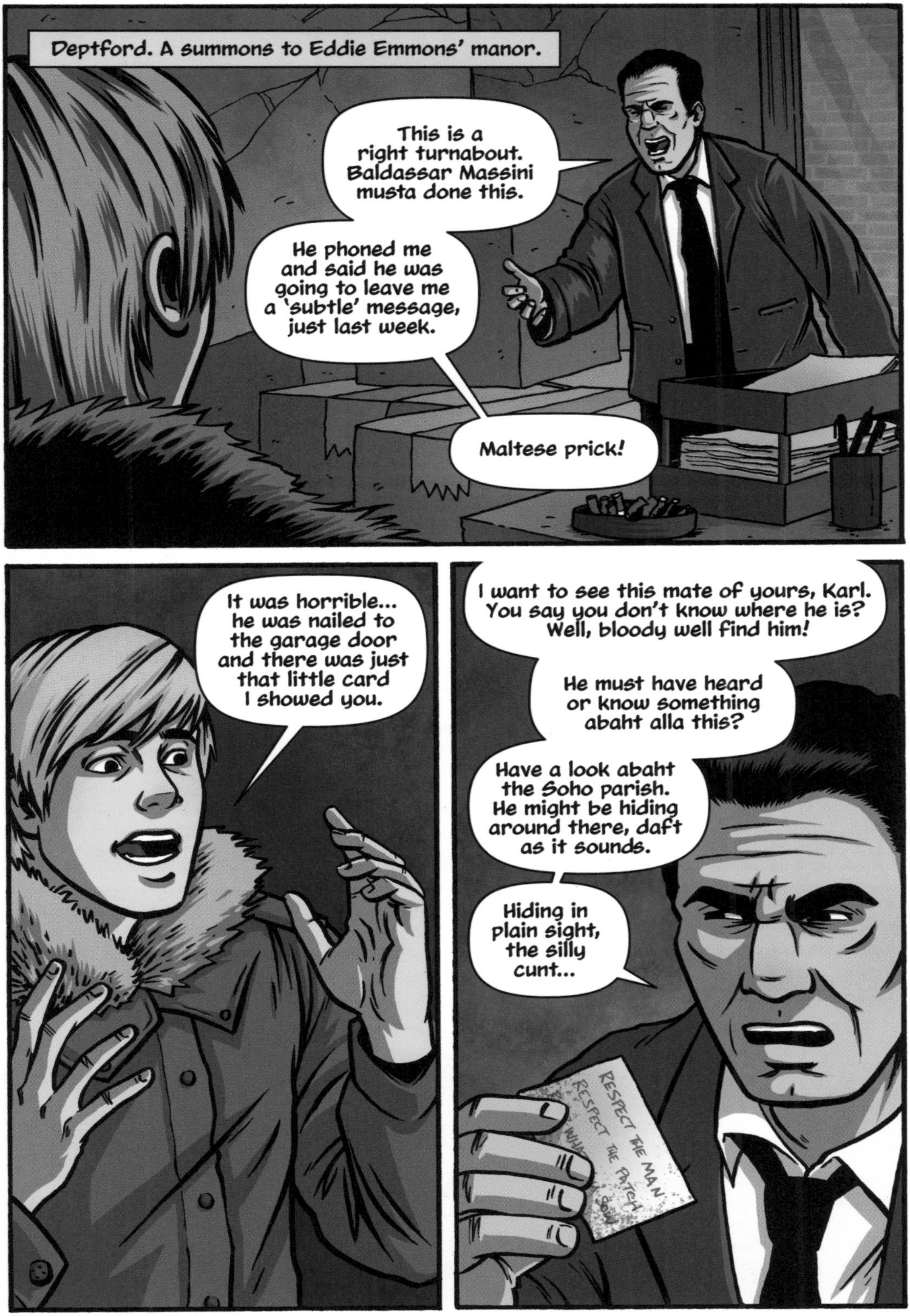
Deptford. A summons to Eddie Emmons' manor.
This is a right turnabout. Baldassar Massini musta done this.
He phoned me and said he was going to leave me a 'subtle' message, just last week.
Maltese prick!
It was horrible... he was nailed to the garage door and there was just that little card I showed you.
I want to see this mate of yours, Karl. You say you don't know where he is? Well, bloody well find him!
He must have heard or know something abaht alla this?
Have a look abaht the Soho parish. He might be hiding around there, daft as it sounds.
Hiding in plain sight, the silly cunt...
RESPECT THE MAN
RESPECT THE PATCH

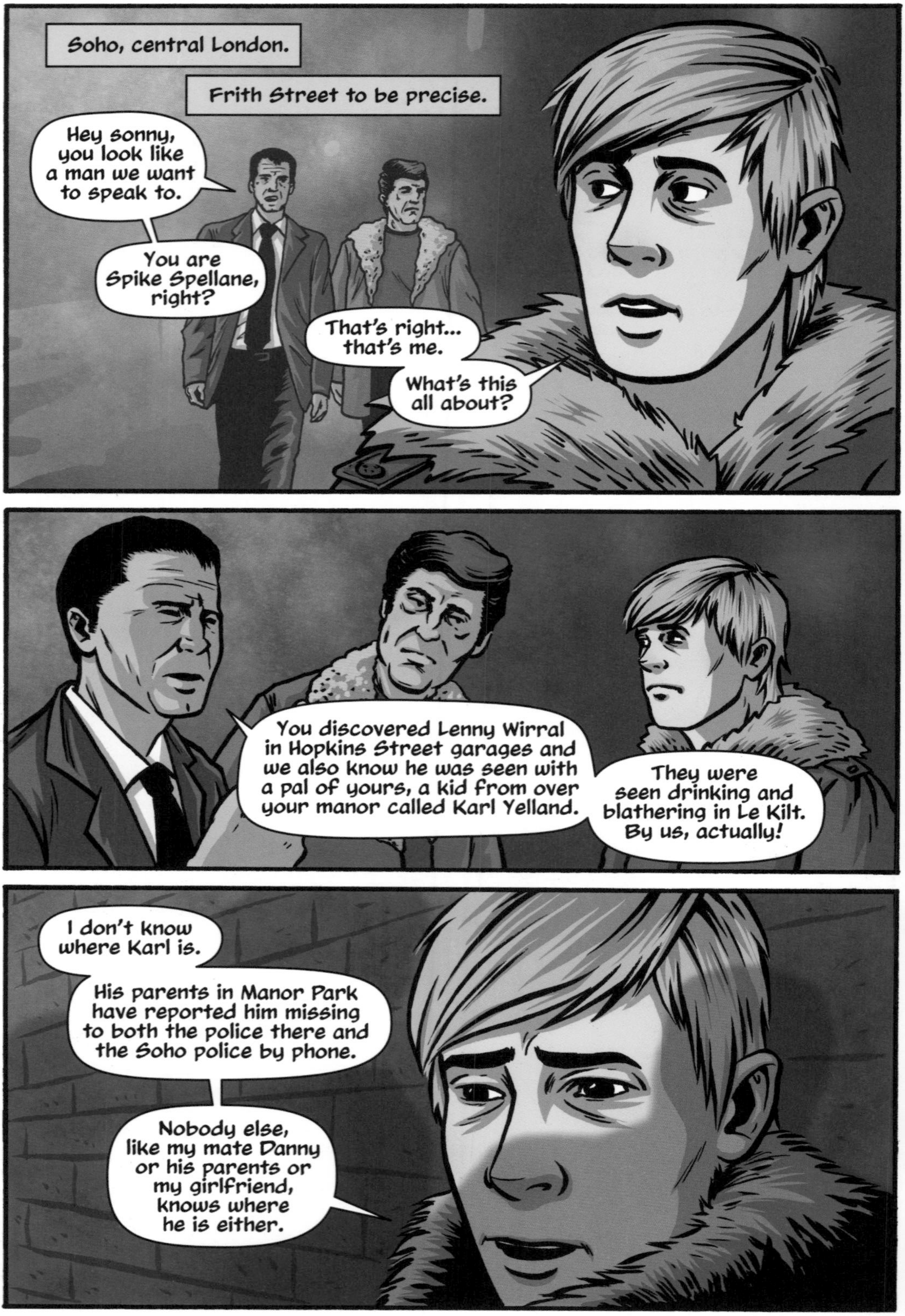
Soho, central London.
Frith Street to be precise.
Hey sonny, you look like a man we want to speak to.
You are Spike Spellane, right?
That's right... that's me.
What's this all about?
You discovered Lenny Wirral in Hopkins Street garages and we also know he was seen with a pal of yours, a kid from over your manor called Karl Yelland.
They were seen drinking and blathering in Le Kilt. By us, actually!
I don't know where Karl is.
His parents in Manor Park have reported him missing to both the police there and the Soho police by phone.
Nobody else, like my mate Danny or his parents or my girlfriend, knows where he is either.

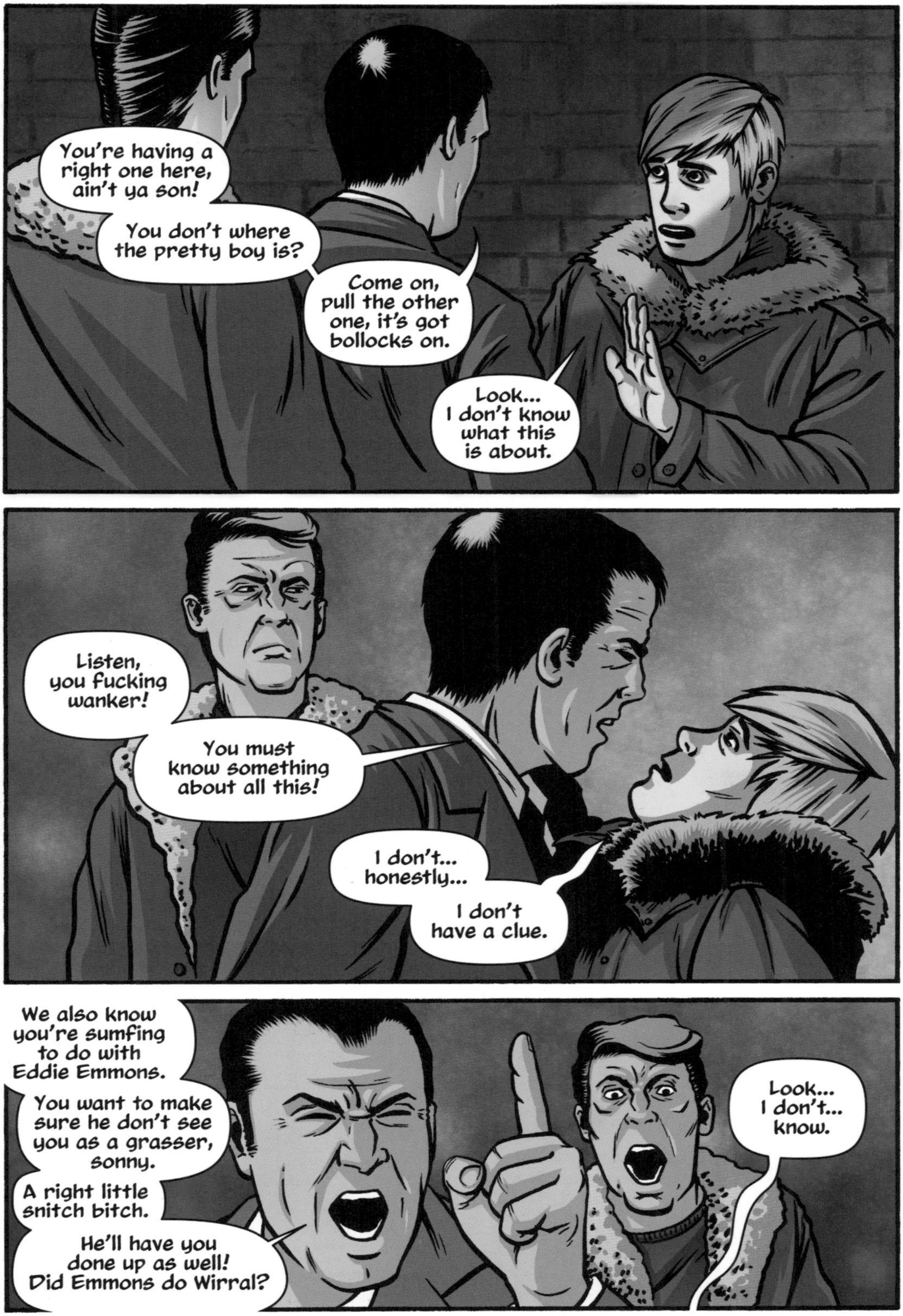
You're having a right one here, ain't ya son!
You don't where the pretty boy is?
Come on, pull the other one, it's got bollocks on.
Look... I don't know what this is about.
Listen, you fucking wanker!
You must know something about all this!
I don't... honestly...
I don't have a clue.
We also know you're sumfing to do with Eddie Emmons.
You want to make sure he don't see you as a grasser, sonny.
A right little snitch bitch.
He'll have you done up as well! Did Emmons do Wirral?
Look... I don't... know.

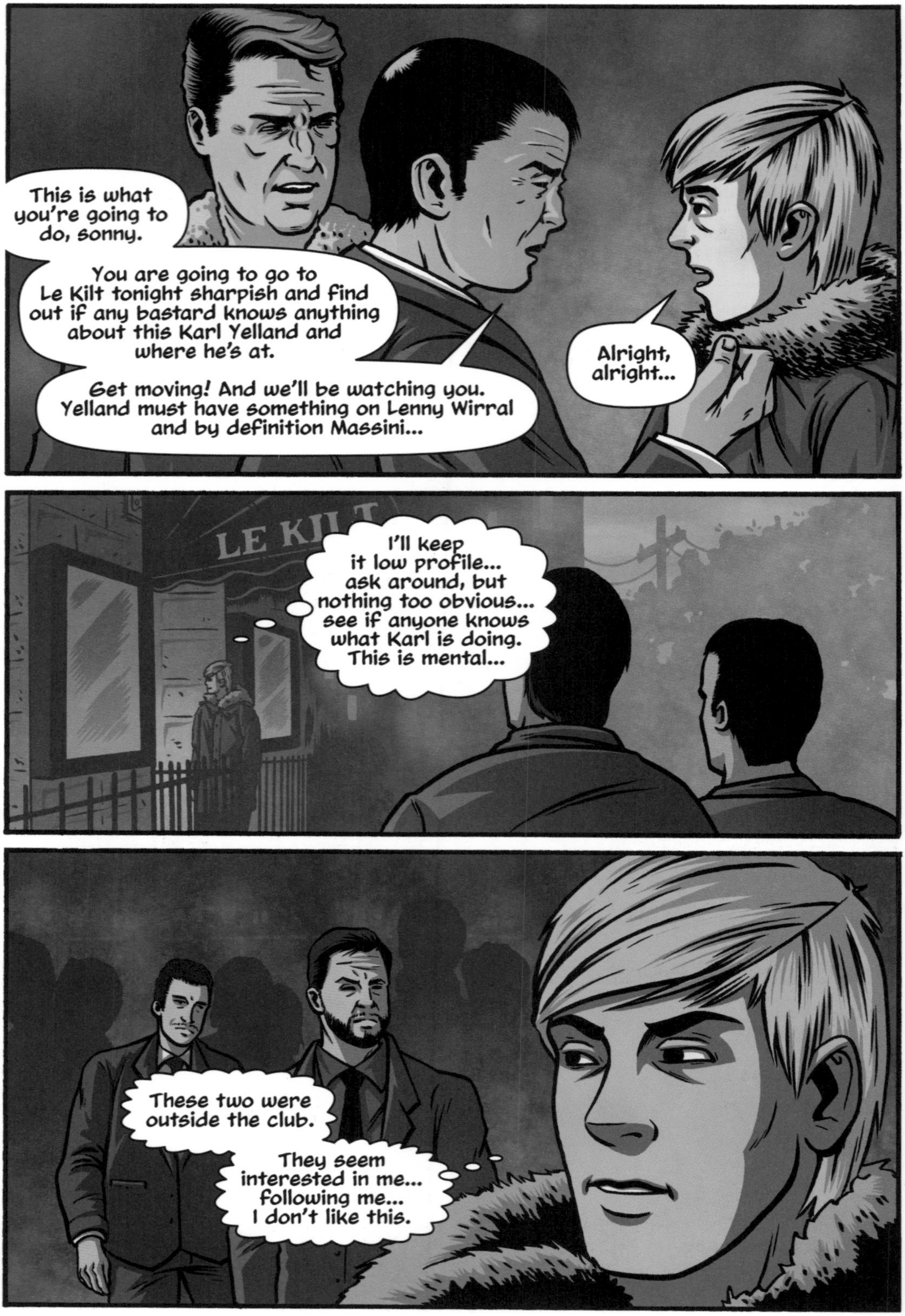

This is what you're going to do, sonny.
You are going to go to Le Kilt tonight sharpish and find out if any bastard knows anything about this Karl Yelland and where he's at.
Get moving! And we'll be watching you. Yelland must have something on Lenny Wirral and by definition Massini...
Alright, alright...
LE KILT
I'll keep it low profile... ask around, but nothing too obvious... see if anyone knows what Karl is doing. This is mental...
These two were outside the club.
They seem interested in me... following me... I don't like this.

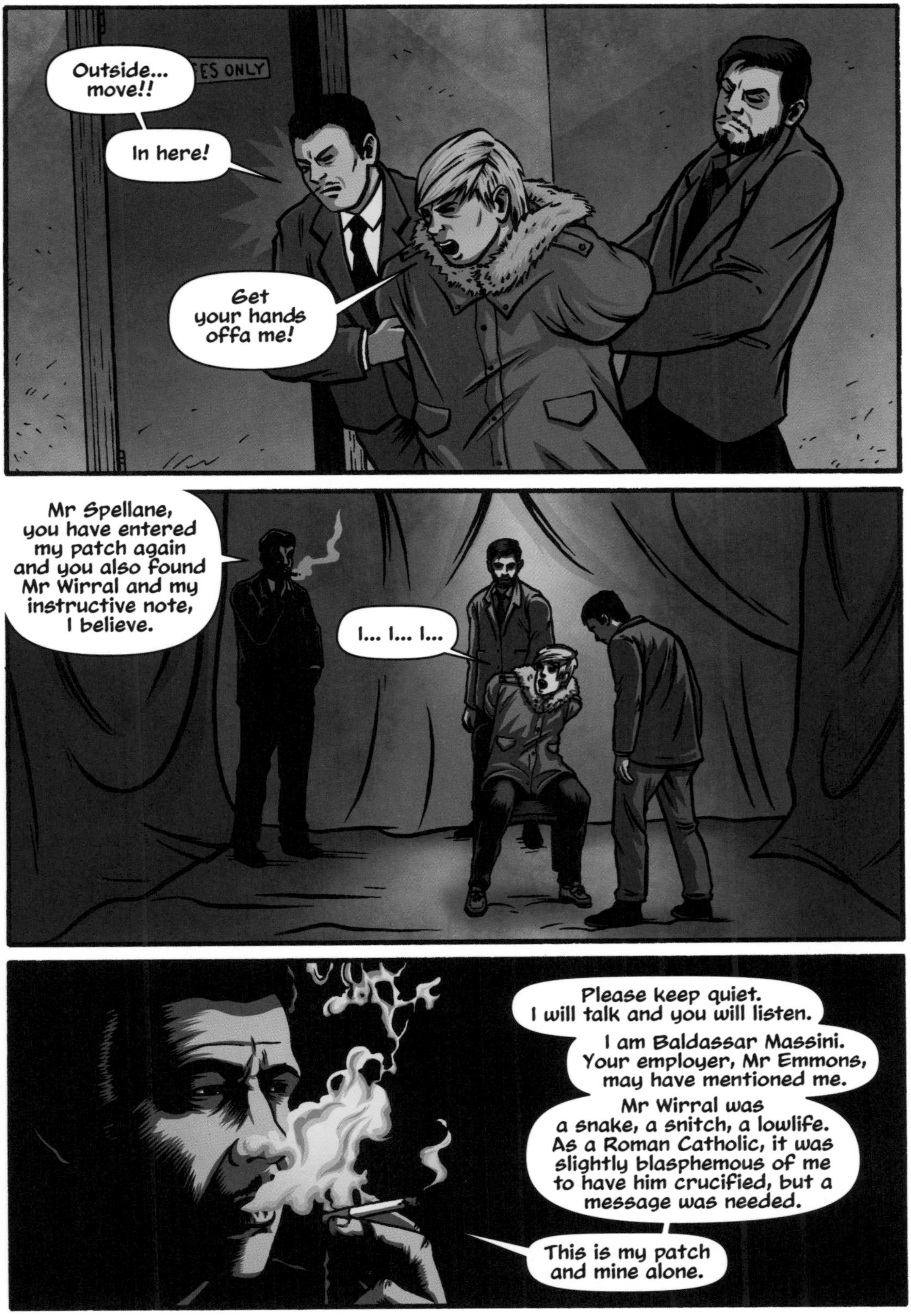

Outside... move!!
In here!
Get your hands offa me!
Mr Spellane, you have entered my patch again and you also found Mr Wirral and my instructive note, I believe.
I... I... I...
Please keep quiet. I will talk and you will listen.
I am Baldassar Massini. Your employer, Mr Emmons, may have mentioned me.
Mr Wirral was a snake, a snitch, a lowlife. As a Roman Catholic, it was slightly blasphemous of me to have him crucified, but a message was needed.
This is my patch and mine alone.

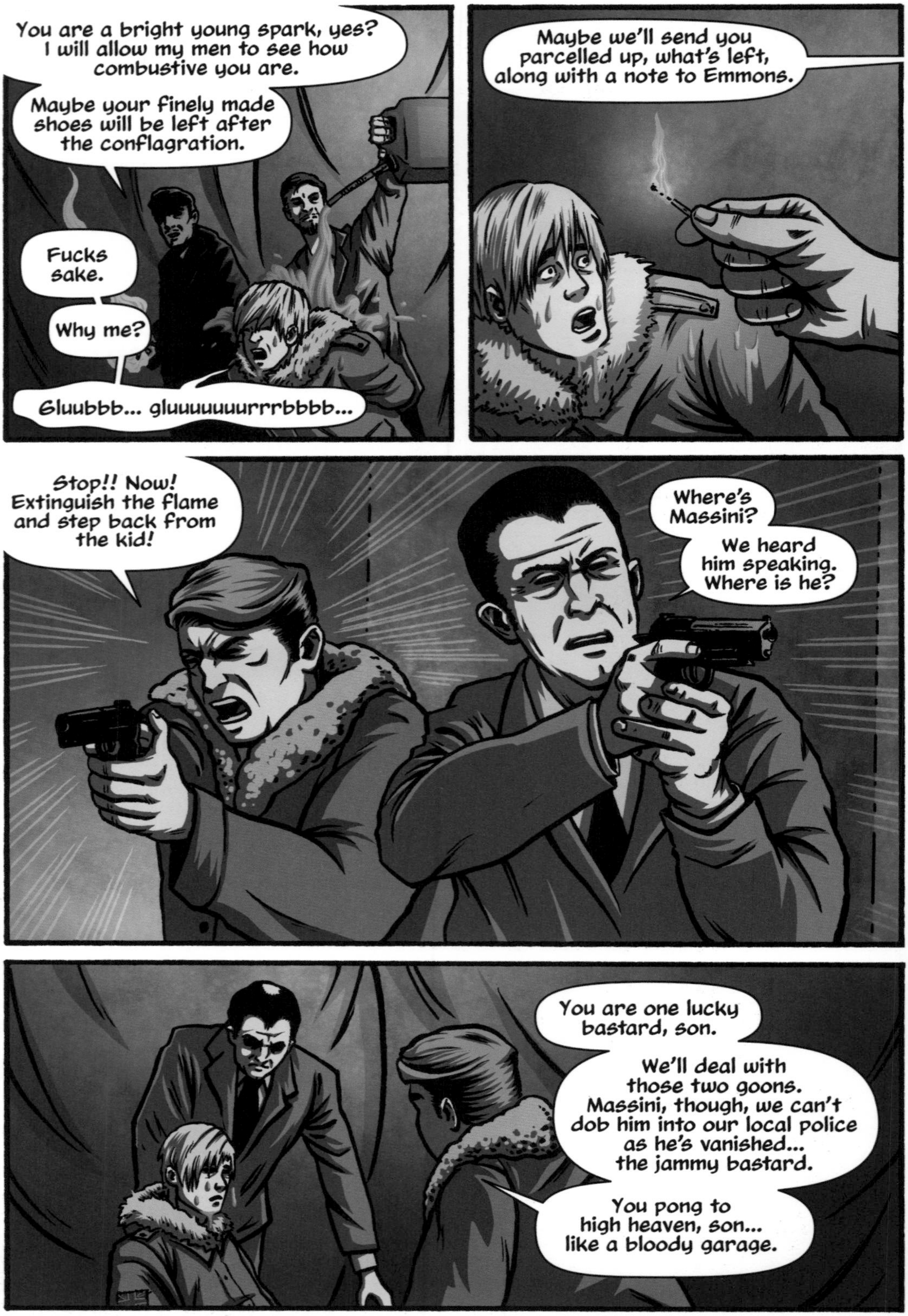
You are a bright young spark, yes? I will allow my men to see how combustive you are.
Maybe your finely made shoes will be left after the conflagration.
Fucks sake.
Why me?
Gluubbb... gluuuuuuurrrbbbb...
Maybe we'll send you parcelled up, what's left, along with a note to Emmons.
Stop!! Now! Extinguish the flame and step back from the kid!
Where's Massini?
We heard him speaking. Where is he?
You are one lucky bastard, son.
We'll deal with those two goons. Massini, though, we can't dob him into our local police as he's vanished... the jammy bastard.
You pong to high heaven, son... like a bloody garage.

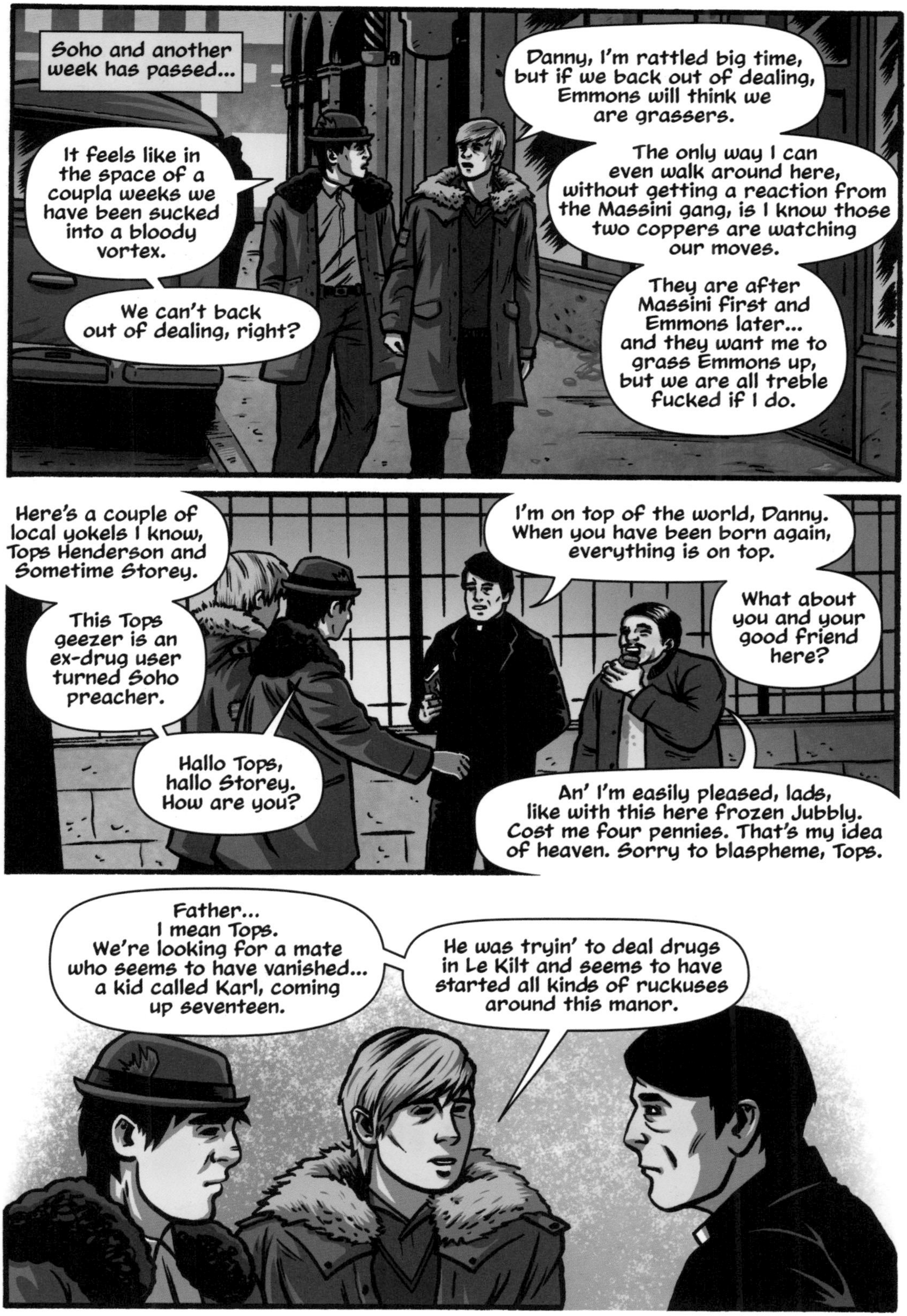
Soho and another week has passed...
It feels like in the space of a coupla weeks we have been sucked into a bloody vortex.
We can't back out of dealing, right?
Danny, I'm rattled big time, but if we back out of dealing, Emmons will think we are grassers.
The only way I can even walk around here, without getting a reaction from the Massini gang, is I know those two coppers are watching our moves.
They are after Massini first and Emmons later... and they want me to grass Emmons up, but we are all treble fucked if I do.
Here's a couple of local yokels I know, Tops Henderson and Sometime Storey.
This Tops geezer is an ex-drug user turned Soho preacher.
Hallo Tops, hallo Storey. How are you?
I'm on top of the world, Danny. When you have been born again, everything is on top.
What about you and your good friend here?
An' I'm easily pleased, lads, like with this here frozen Jubbly. Cost me four pennies. That's my idea of heaven. Sorry to blaspheme, Tops.
Father... I mean Tops. We're looking for a mate who seems to have vanished... a kid called Karl, coming up seventeen.
He was tryin' to deal drugs in Le Kilt and seems to have started all kinds of ruckuses around this manor.

Well, it's funny you say that, as we heard the weirdest thing from some of the ladies that frequent the streets here, where I preach, in my ordained fashion.

As God is my judge, we heard that a young man is working as a different version of himself, so to speak, in a strip club or clip joint somewhere behind Old Compton Street.

Sorry, hold up! Spike, look at this prick, what a herbert.

Did you injure your arms during the war, mate?

What the fuck... I know... you had that suit made to measure at Burton's... you fucking haddock!

Bollocks!

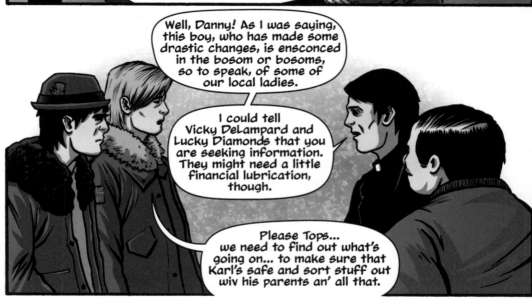

Well, Danny! As I was saying, this boy, who has made some drastic changes, is ensconced in the bosom or bosoms, so to speak, of some of our local ladies.

I could tell Vicky DeLampard and Lucky Diamonds that you are seeking information. They might need a little financial lubrication, though.

Please Tops... we need to find out what's going on... to make sure that Karl's safe and sort stuff out wiv his parents an' all that.

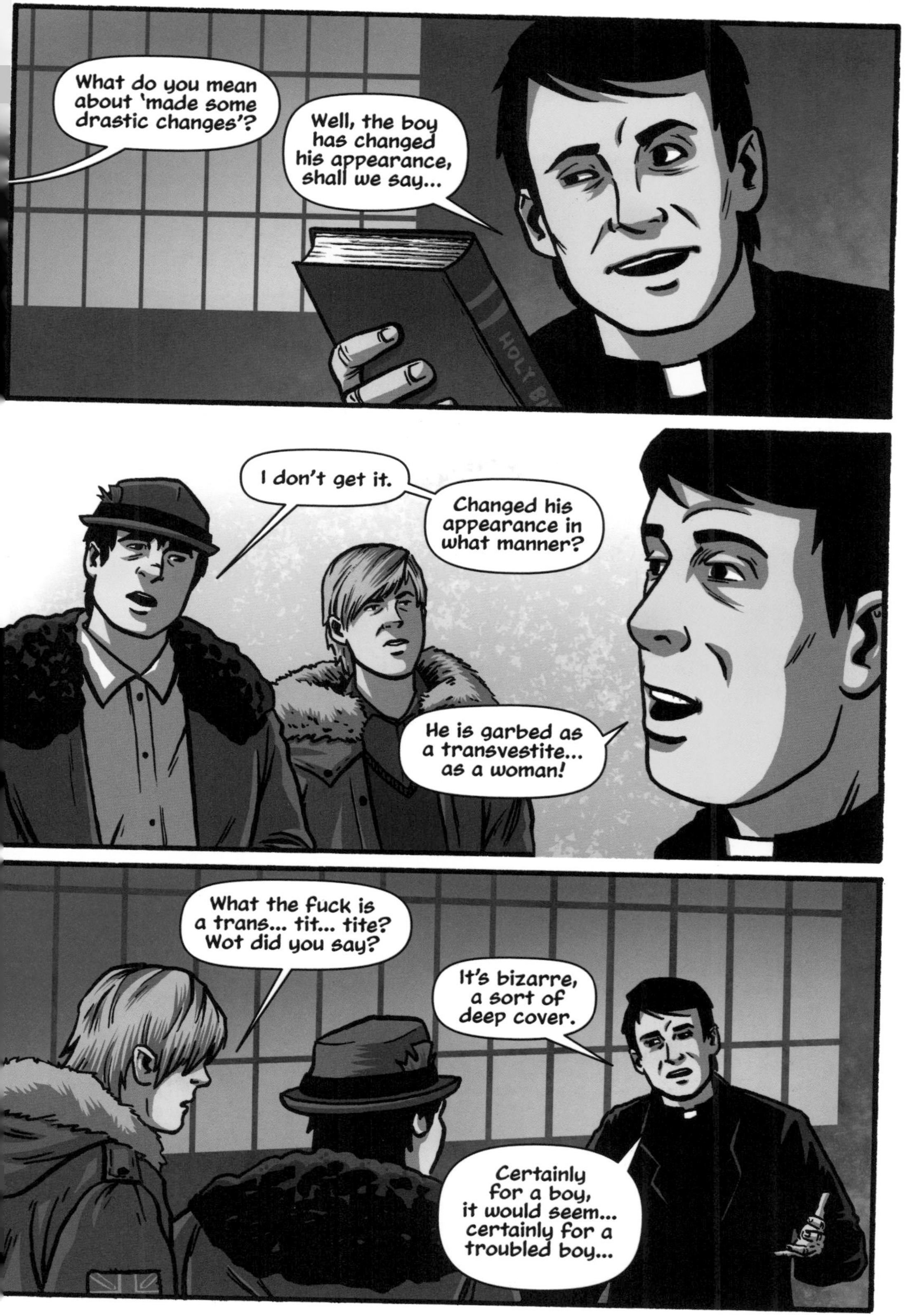
What do you mean about 'made some drastic changes'?
Well, the boy has changed his appearance, shall we say...
HOLY BI
I don't get it.
Changed his appearance in what manner?
He is garbed as a transvestite... as a woman!
What the fuck is a trans... tit... tite? Wot did you say?
It's bizarre, a sort of deep cover.
Certainly for a boy, it would seem... certainly for a troubled boy...

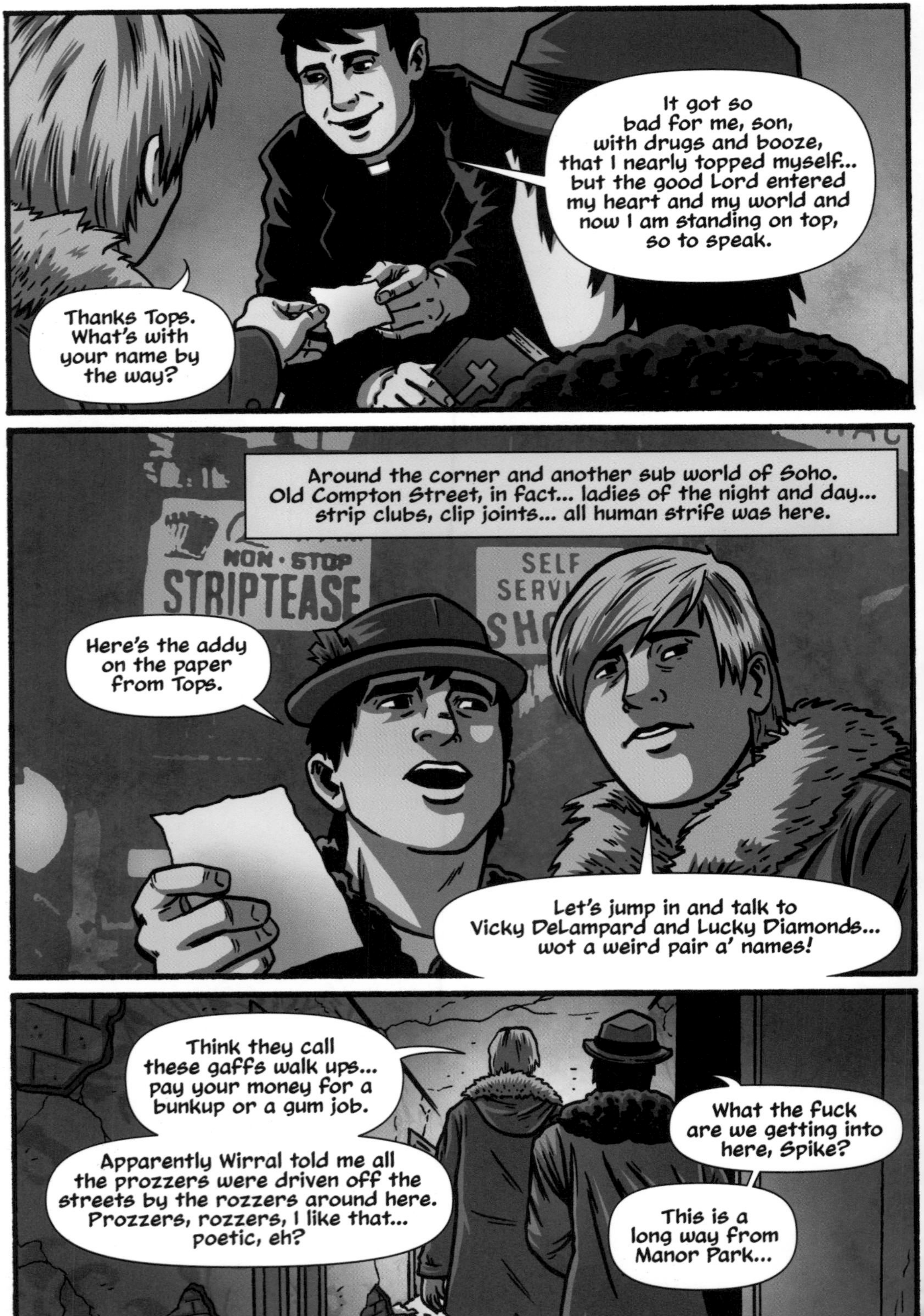

It got so bad for me, son, with drugs and booze, that I nearly topped myself... but the good Lord entered my heart and my world and now I am standing on top, so to speak.
Thanks Tops. What's with your name by the way?
Around the corner and another sub world of Soho. Old Compton Street, in fact... ladies of the night and day... strip clubs, clip joints... all human strife was here.
NON · STOP
STRIPTEASE
SELF SERVI
SHO
Here's the addy on the paper from Tops.
Let's jump in and talk to Vicky DeLampard and Lucky Diamonds... wot a weird pair a' names!
Think they call these gaffs walk ups... pay your money for a bunkup or a gum job.
Apparently Wirral told me all the prozzers were driven off the streets by the rozzers around here. Prozzers, rozzers, I like that... poetic, eh?
What the fuck are we getting into here, Spike?
This is a long way from Manor Park...

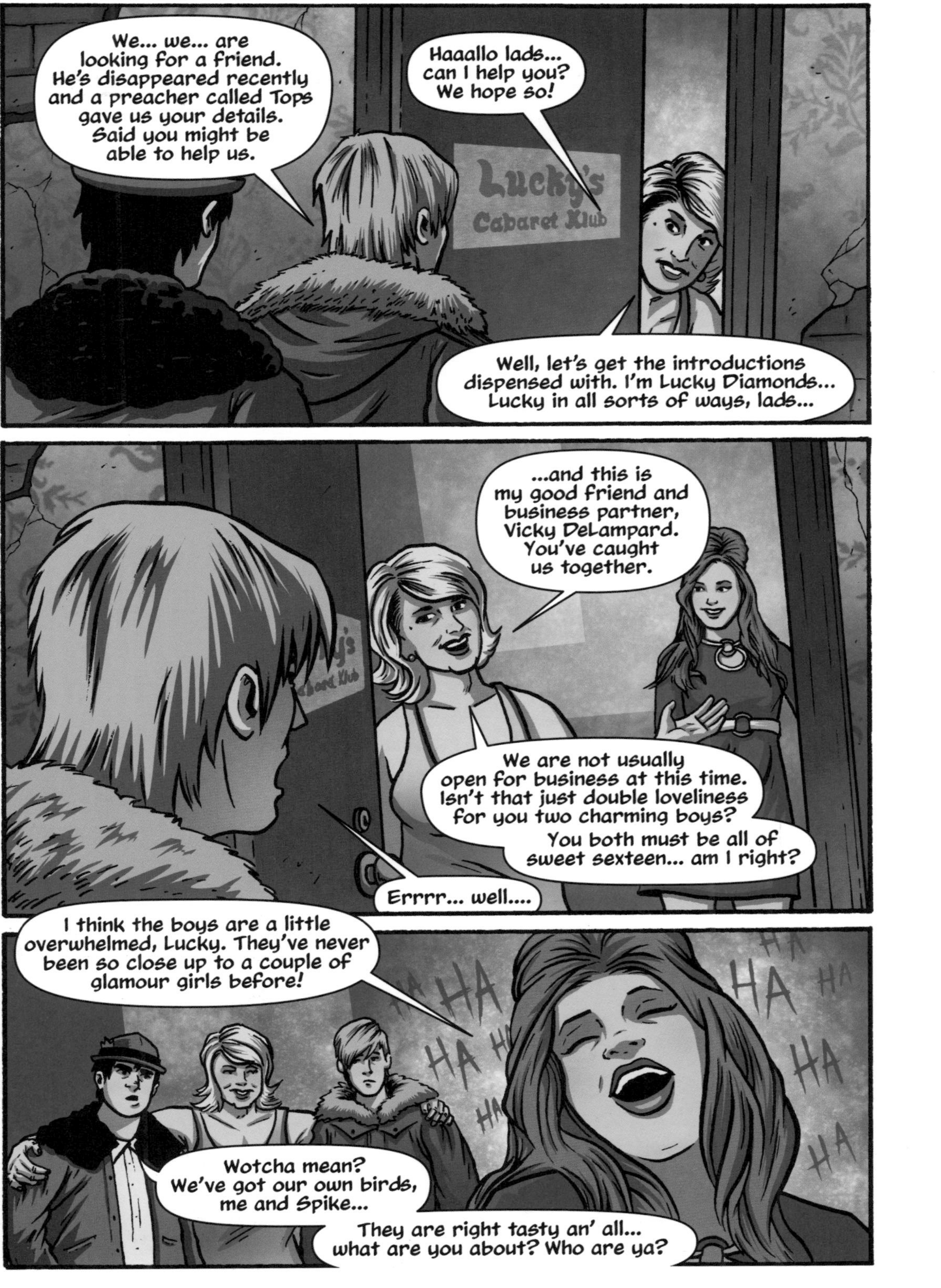
We... we... are looking for a friend. He's disappeared recently and a preacher called Tops gave us your details. Said you might be able to help us.
Haaallo lads... can I help you? We hope so!
Lucky's Cabaret Klub
Well, let's get the introductions dispensed with. I'm Lucky Diamonds... Lucky in all sorts of ways, lads...
...and this is my good friend and business partner, Vicky DeLampard. You've caught us together.
We are not usually open for business at this time. Isn't that just double loveliness for you two charming boys?
You both must be all of sweet sexteen... am I right?
Errrr... well....
I think the boys are a little overwhelmed, Lucky. They've never been so close up to a couple of glamour girls before!
HA HA HA HA HA HA HA HA HA HA HA
Wotcha mean? We've got our own birds, me and Spike...
They are right tasty an' all... what are you about? Who are ya?

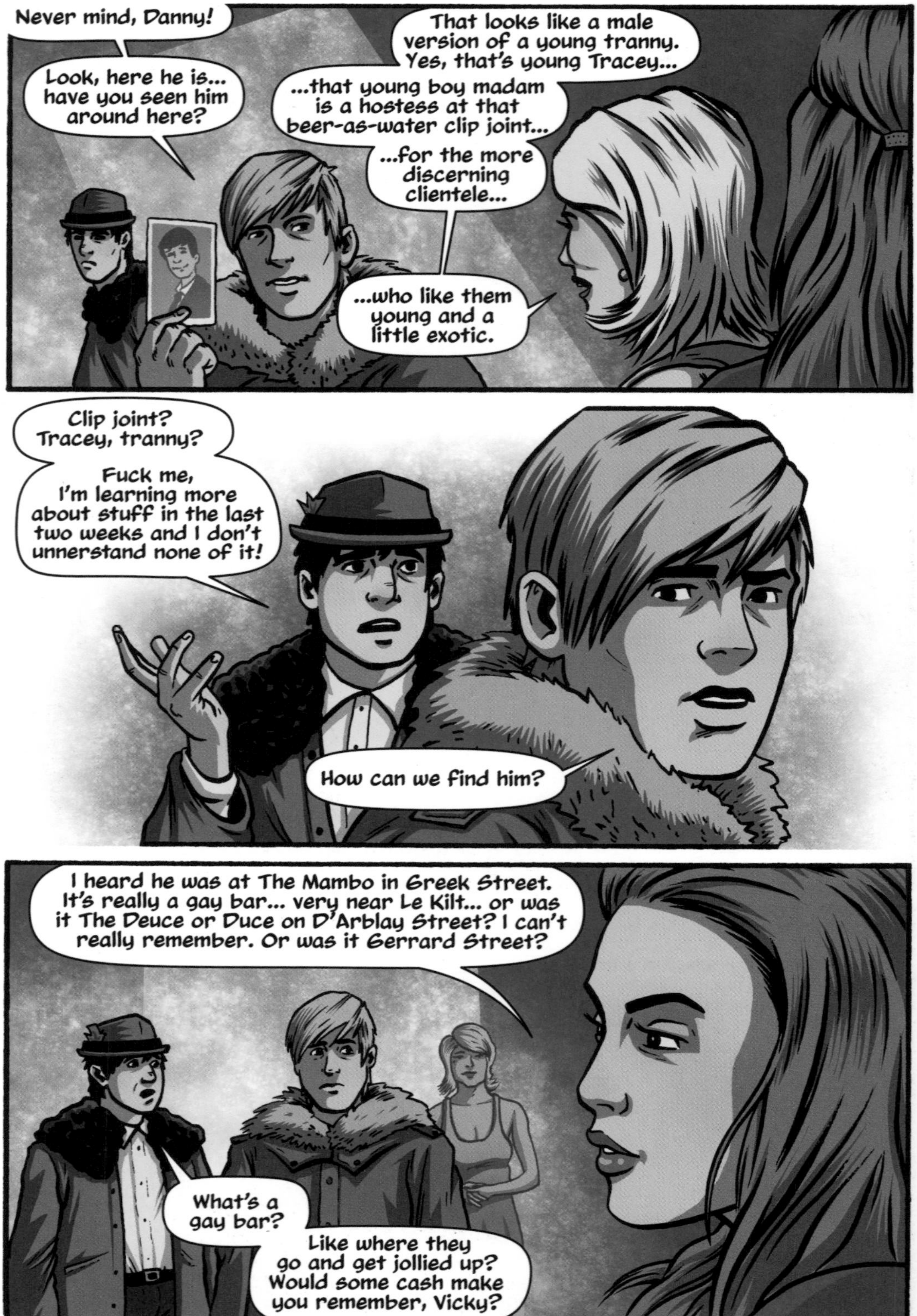

Never mind, Danny!
Look, here he is... have you seen him around here?
That looks like a male version of a young tranny. Yes, that's young Tracey...
...that young boy madam is a hostess at that beer-as-water clip joint...
...for the more discerning clientele...
...who like them young and a little exotic.
Clip joint? Tracey, tranny?
Fuck me, I'm learning more about stuff in the last two weeks and I don't unnerstand none of it!
How can we find him?
I heard he was at The Mambo in Greek Street. It's really a gay bar... very near Le Kilt... or was it The Deuce or Duce on D'Arblay Street? I can't really remember. Or was it Gerrard Street?
What's a gay bar?
Like where they go and get jollied up? Would some cash make you remember, Vicky?

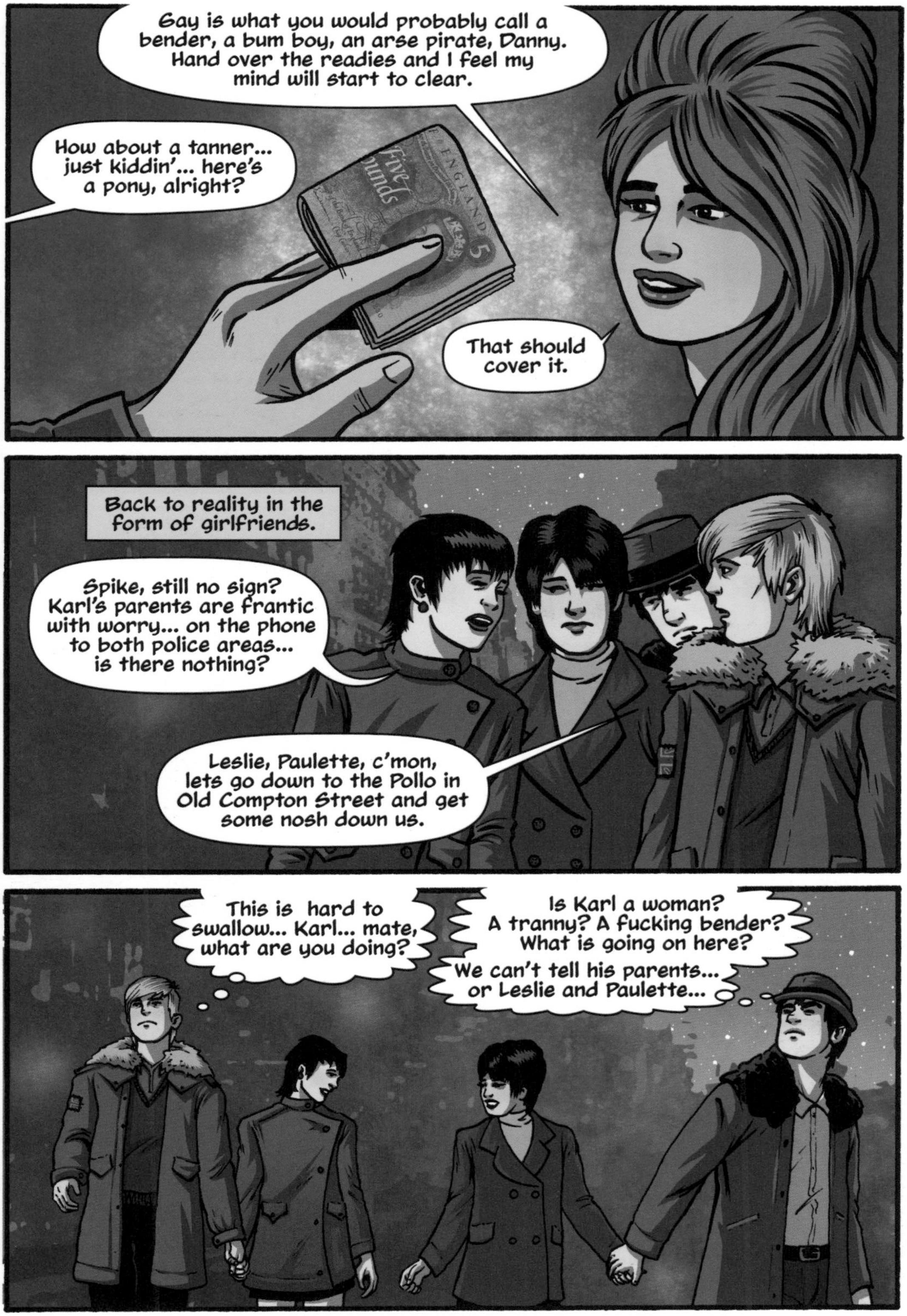
Gay is what you would probably call a bender, a bum boy, an arse pirate, Danny. Hand over the readies and I feel my mind will start to clear.
How about a tanner... just kiddin'... here's a pony, alright?
That should cover it.
Back to reality in the form of girlfriends.
Spike, still no sign? Karl's parents are frantic with worry... on the phone to both police areas... is there nothing?
Leslie, Paulette, c'mon, lets go down to the Pollo in Old Compton Street and get some nosh down us.
This is hard to swallow... Karl... mate, what are you doing?
Is Karl a woman? A tranny? A fucking bender? What is going on here?
We can't tell his parents... or Leslie and Paulette...

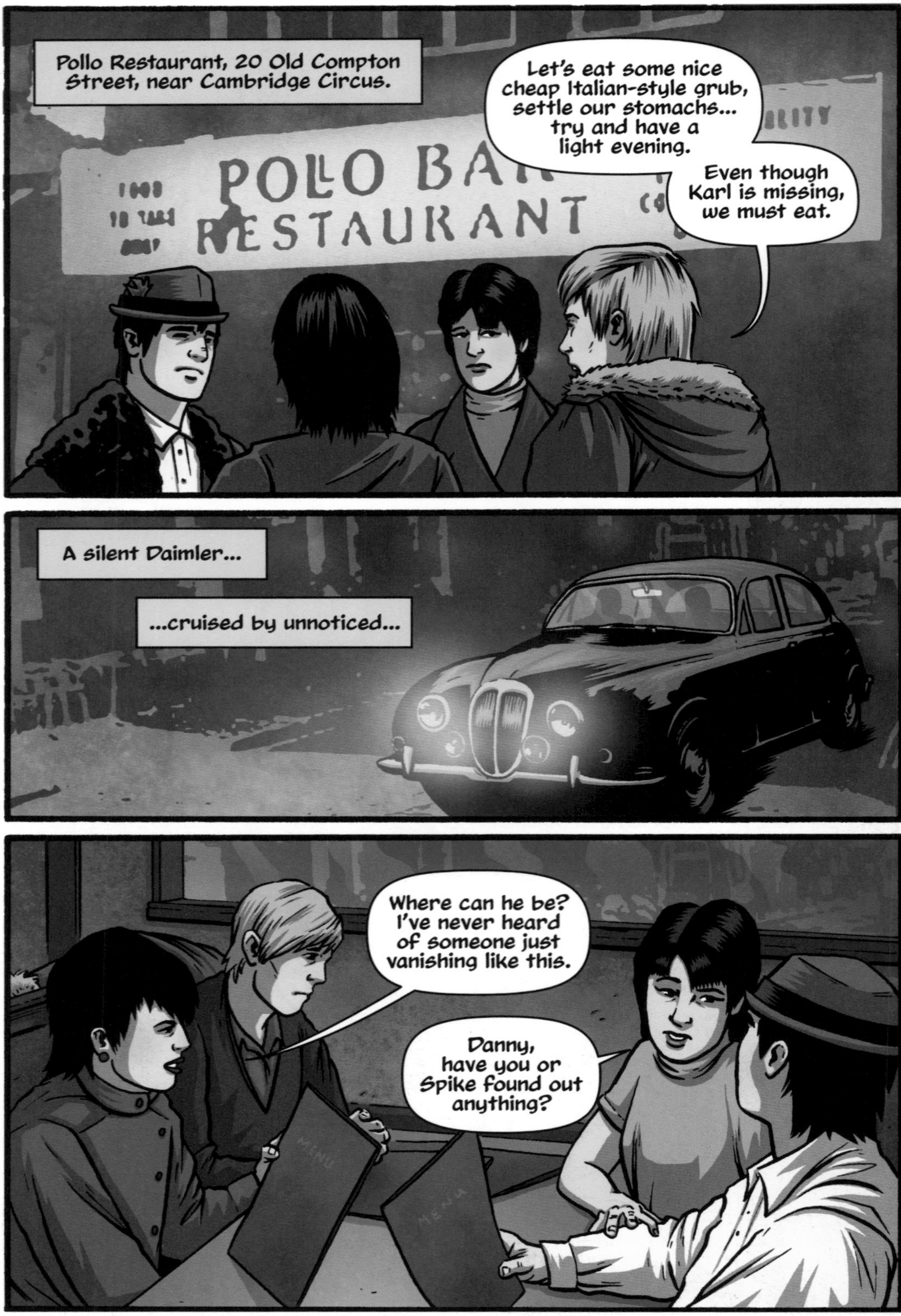

Pollo Restaurant, 20 Old Compton Street, near Cambridge Circus.
Let's eat some nice cheap Italian-style grub, settle our stomachs... try and have a light evening.
Even though Karl is missing, we must eat.
POLLO BAR
RESTAURANT
A silent Daimler...
...cruised by unnoticed...
Where can he be? I've never heard of someone just vanishing like this.
Danny, have you or Spike found out anything?
MENU
MENU

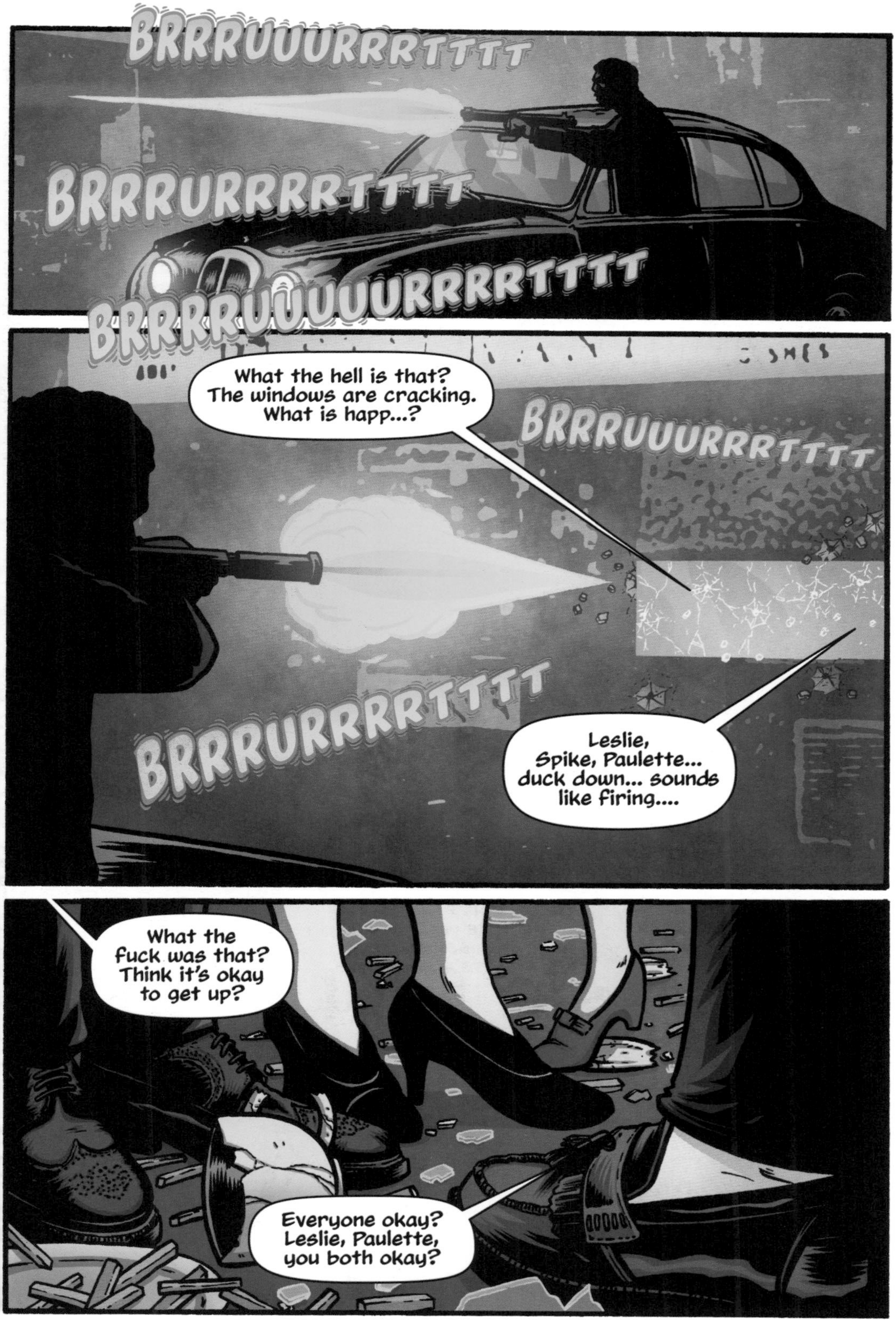
BRRRUUURRRTTTT
BRRRURRRRTTTT
BRRRRUUUUURRRRTTTTT
What the hell is that? The windows are cracking. What is happ...?
BRRRUUURRRTTTT
BRRRURRRRTTTT
Leslie, Spike, Paulette... duck down... sounds like firing....
What the fuck was that? Think it's okay to get up?
Everyone okay? Leslie, Paulette, you both okay?

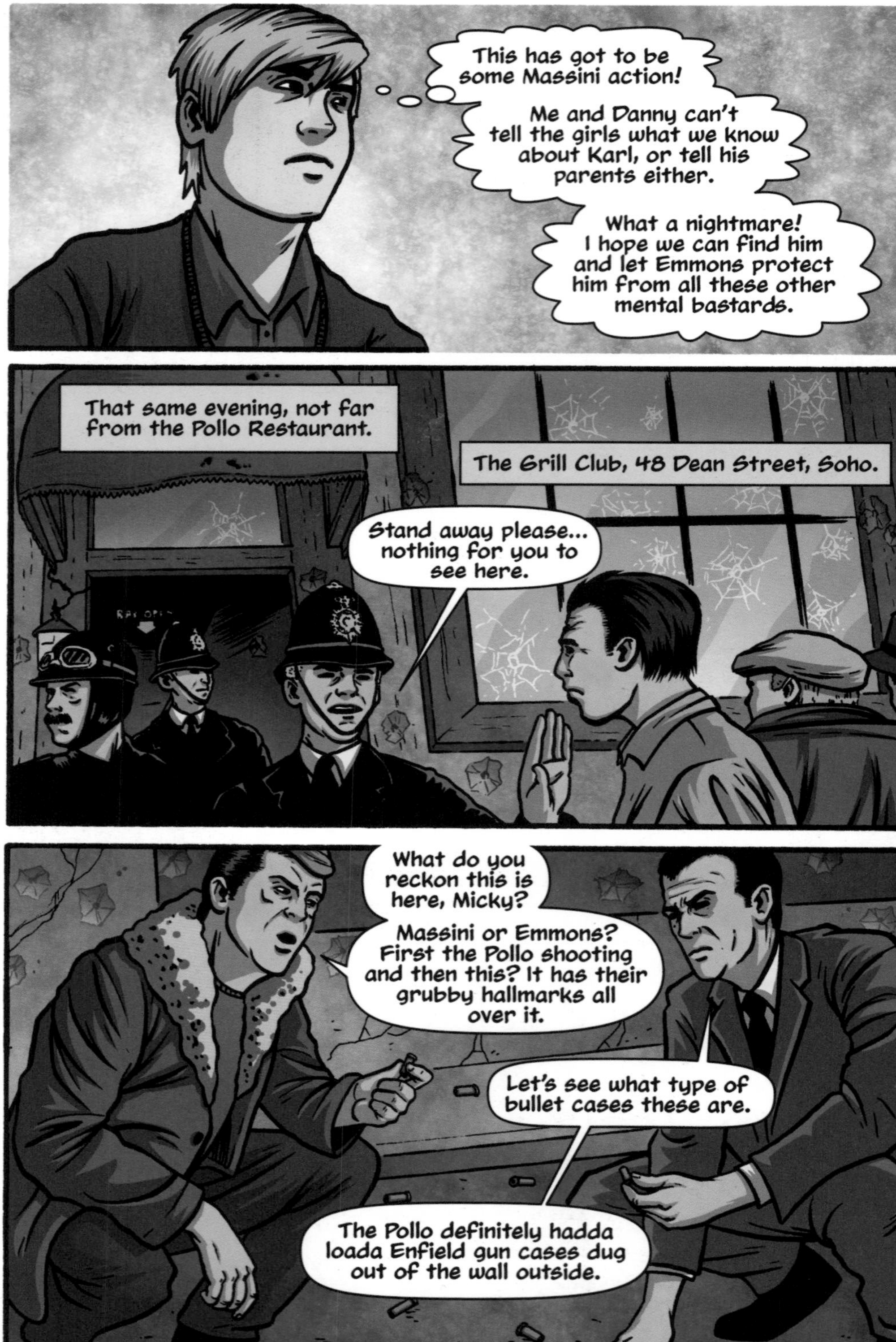
This has got to be some Massini action!
Me and Danny can't tell the girls what we know about Karl, or tell his parents either.
What a nightmare! I hope we can find him and let Emmons protect him from all these other mental bastards.
That same evening, not far from the Pollo Restaurant.
The Grill Club, 48 Dean Street, Soho.
Stand away please... nothing for you to see here.
What do you reckon this is here, Micky?
Massini or Emmons? First the Pollo shooting and then this? It has their grubby hallmarks all over it.
Let's see what type of bullet cases these are.
The Pollo definitely hadda loada Enfield gun cases dug out of the wall outside.

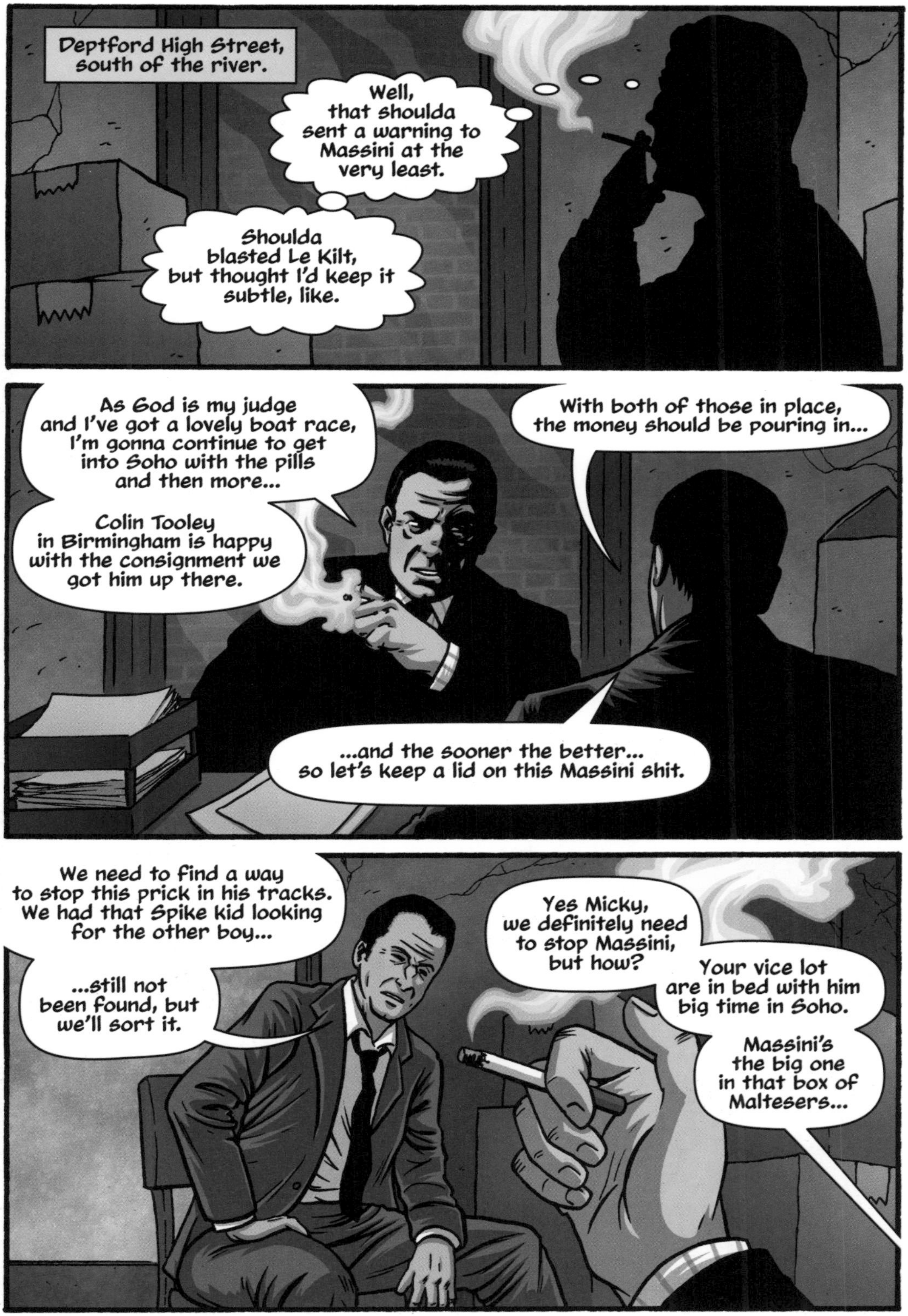
Deptford High Street, south of the river.
Well, that shoulda sent a warning to Massini at the very least.
Shoulda blasted Le Kilt, but thought I'd keep it subtle, like.
As God is my judge and I've got a lovely boat race, I'm gonna continue to get into Soho with the pills and then more...
Colin Tooley in Birmingham is happy with the consignment we got him up there.
With both of those in place, the money should be pouring in...
...and the sooner the better... so let's keep a lid on this Massini shit.
We need to find a way to stop this prick in his tracks. We had that Spike kid looking for the other boy...
...still not been found, but we'll sort it.
Yes Micky, we definitely need to stop Massini, but how?
Your vice lot are in bed with him big time in Soho.
Massini's the big one in that box of Maltesers...

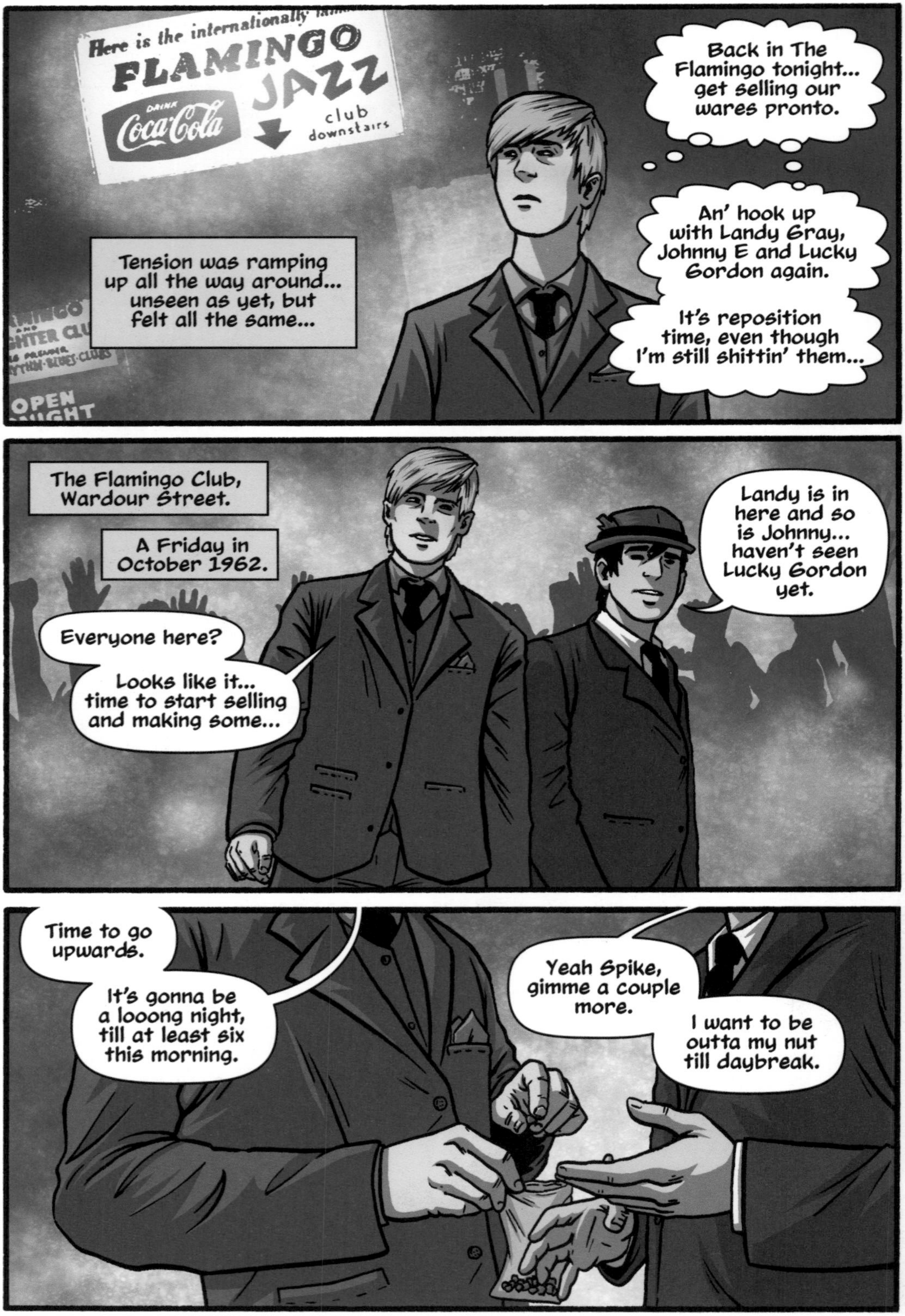

Here is the internationally fam...
FLAMINGO
FLAMINGO JAZZ club downstairs
DRINK Coca-Cola
Back in The Flamingo tonight... get selling our wares pronto.
An' hook up with Landy Gray, Johnny E and Lucky Gordon again.
It's reposition time, even though I'm still shittin' them...
Tension was ramping up all the way around... unseen as yet, but felt all the same...
OPEN
The Flamingo Club, Wardour Street.
A Friday in October 1962.
Landy is in here and so is Johnny... haven't seen Lucky Gordon yet.
Everyone here?
Looks like it... time to start selling and making some...
Time to go upwards.
It's gonna be a looong night, till at least six this morning.
Yeah Spike, gimme a couple more.
I want to be outta my nut till daybreak.

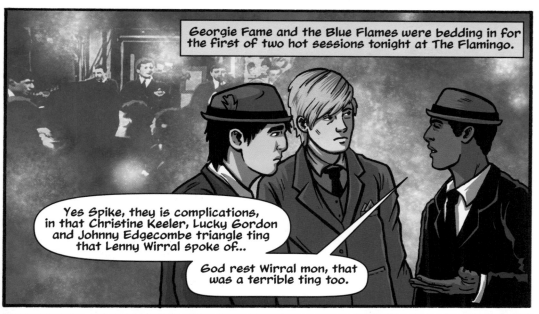

Georgie Fame and the Blue Flames were bedding in for the first of two hot sessions tonight at The Flamingo.

Yes Spike, they is complications, in that Christine Keeler, Lucky Gordon and Johnny Edgecombe triangle ting that Lenny Wirral spoke of...

God rest Wirral mon, that was a terrible ting too.

Landy, what the fuck else can go wrong?

It's too much, all this shit in the last few weeks.

Well, Keeler was buying some weed from Lucky, and she was dating himself too, for a moment. Johnny has heard this and is none too happy, mon... then Keeler breaks it off with Lucky... he goes fuckin' mad, mon, and held her hostage in a flat, wielding an axe and all kinds of ting.

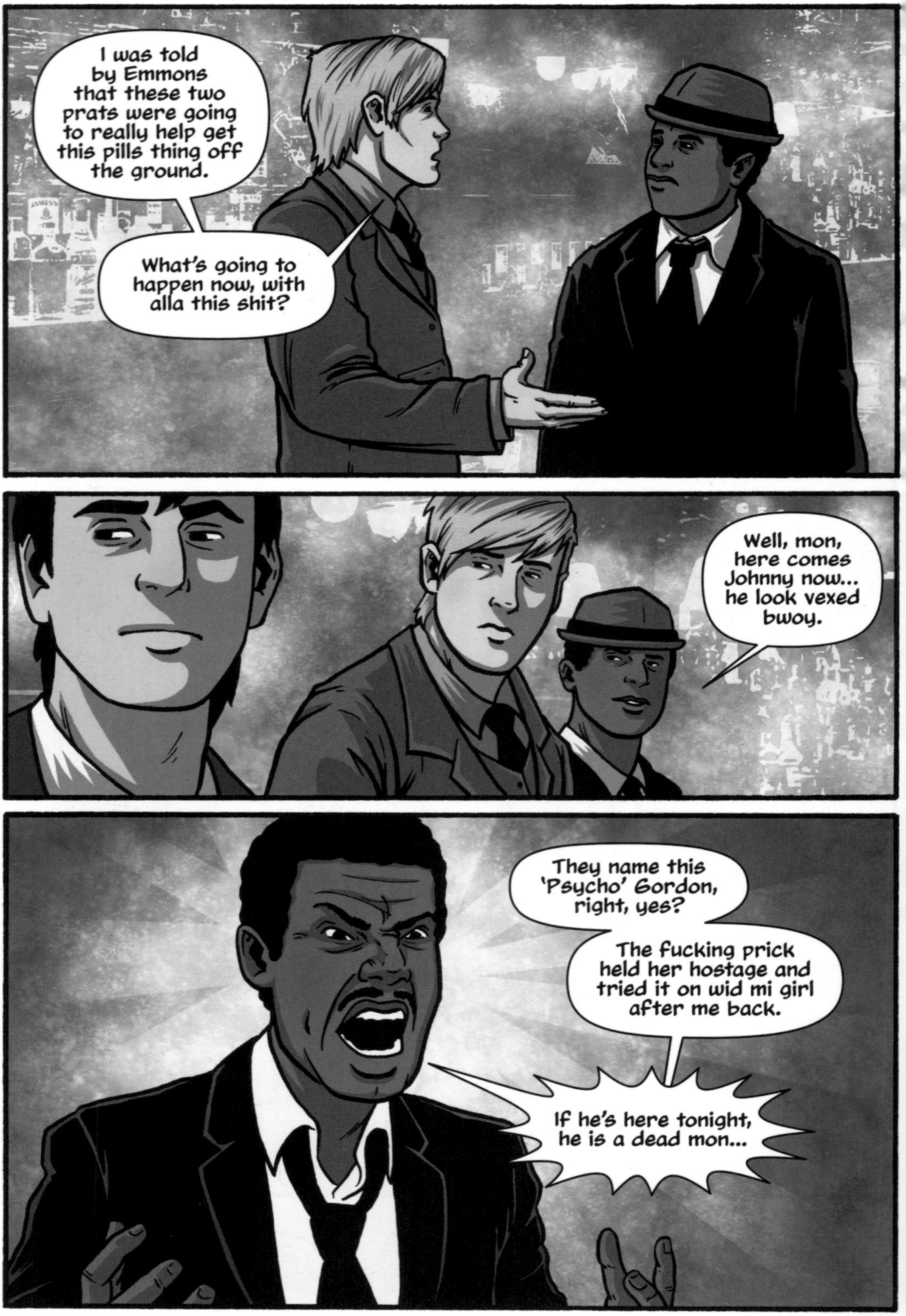
I was told by Emmons that these two prats were going to really help get this pills thing off the ground.
What's going to happen now, with alla this shit?
Well, mon, here comes Johnny now... he look vexed bwoy.
They name this 'Psycho' Gordon, right, yes?
The fucking prick held her hostage and tried it on wid mi girl after me back.
If he's here tonight, he is a dead mon...

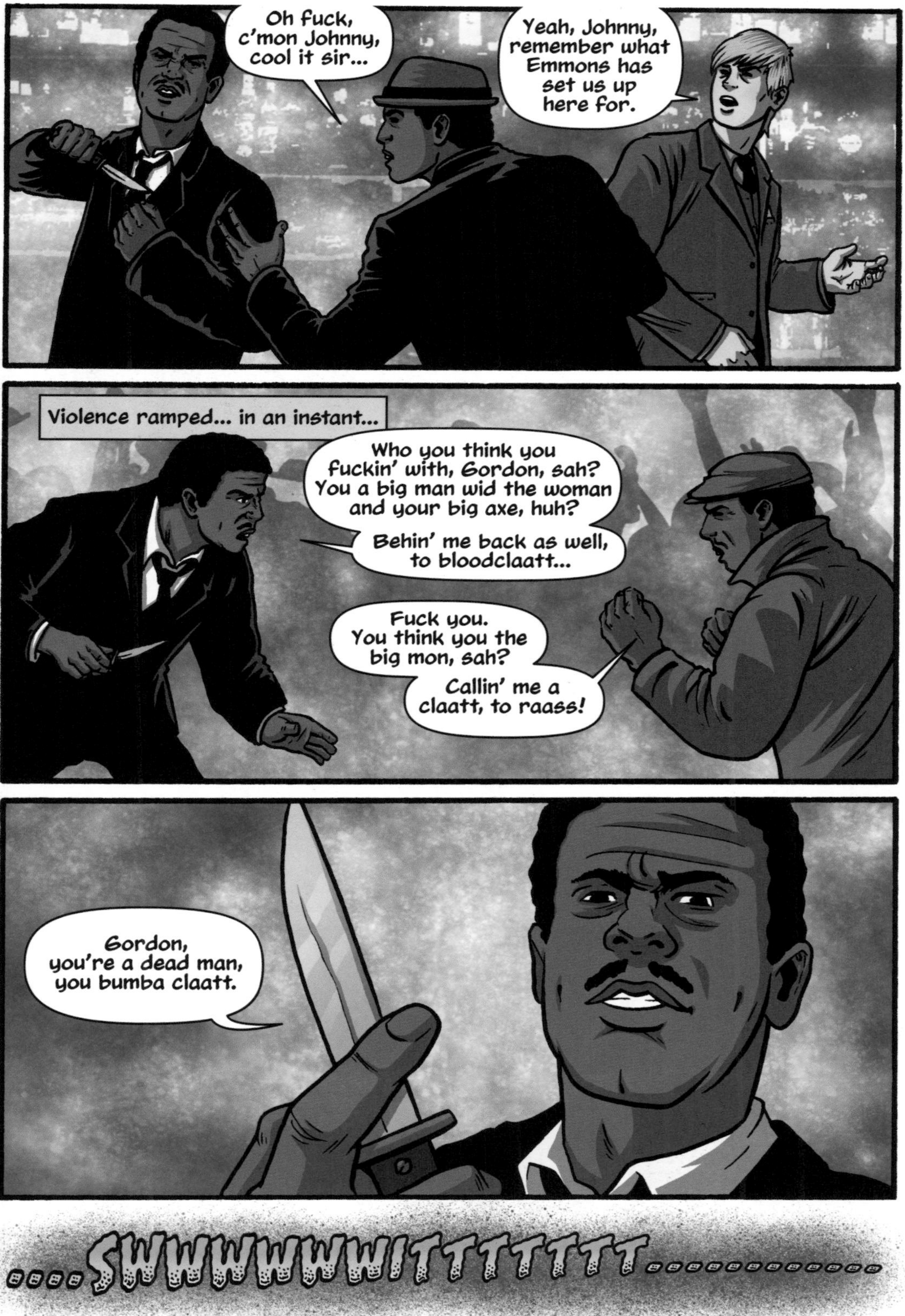
Oh fuck, c'mon Johnny, cool it sir...
Yeah, Johnny, remember what Emmons has set us up here for.
Violence ramped... in an instant...
Who you think you fuckin' with, Gordon, sah? You a big man wid the woman and your big axe, huh?
Behin' me back as well, to bloodclaatt...
Fuck you. You think you the big mon, sah?
Callin' me a claatt, to raass!
Gordon, you're a dead man, you bumba claatt.
....SWWWWWWITTTTTTT.............

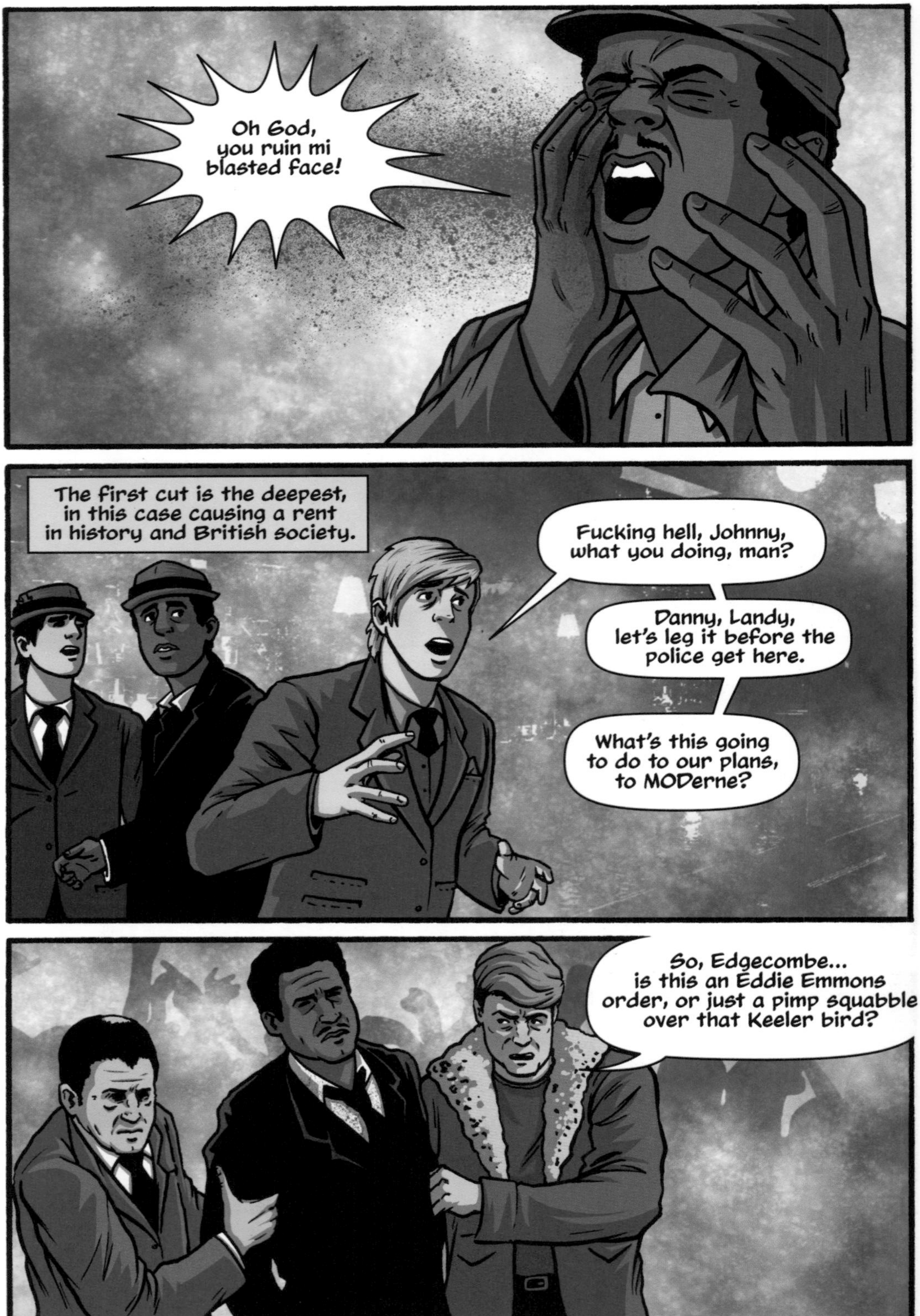

Oh God, you ruin mi blasted face!
The first cut is the deepest, in this case causing a rent in history and British society.
Fucking hell, Johnny, what you doing, man?
Danny, Landy, let's leg it before the police get here.
What's this going to do to our plans, to MODerne?
So, Edgecombe... is this an Eddie Emmons order, or just a pimp squabble over that Keeler bird?

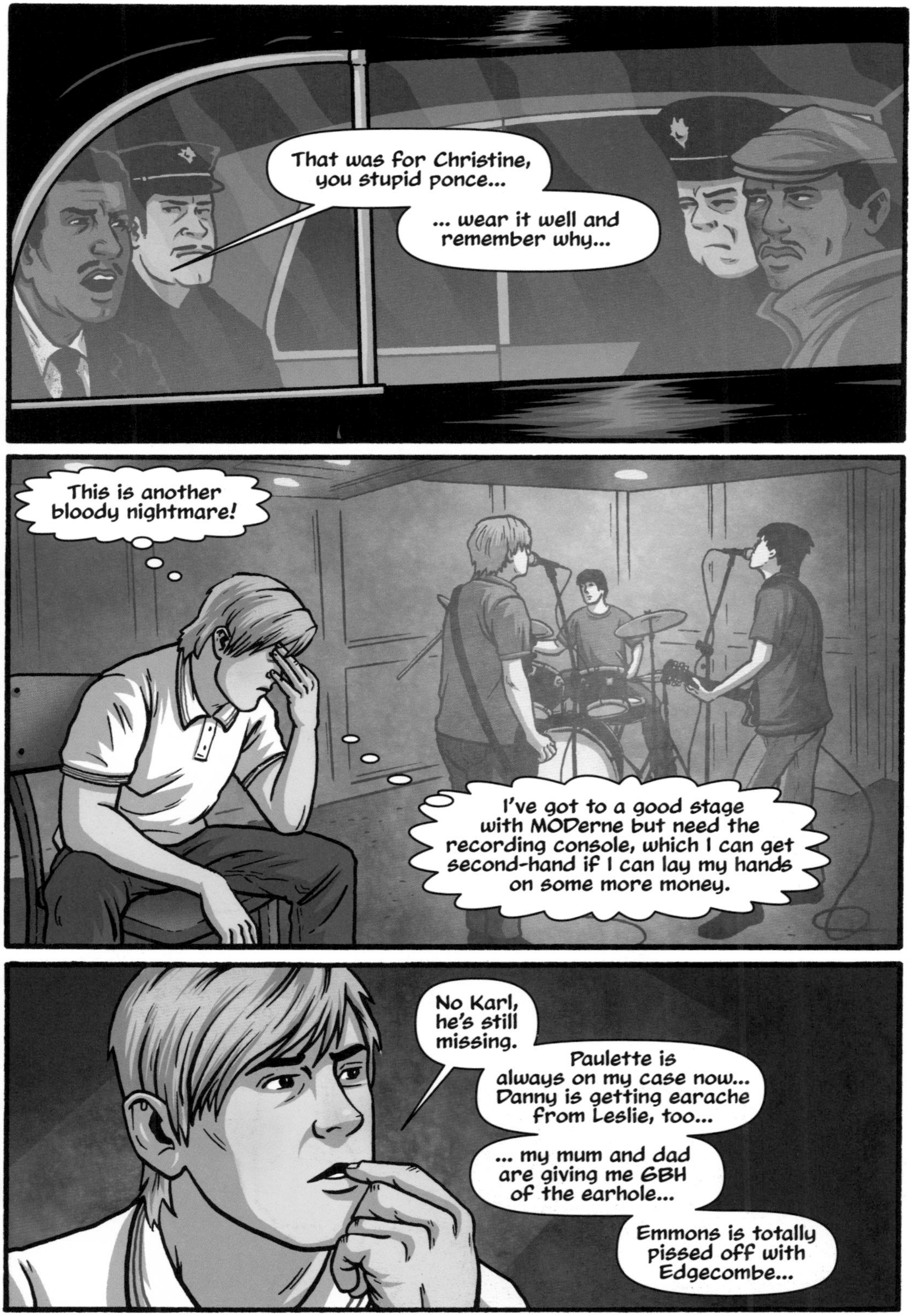
That was for Christine, you stupid ponce...
... wear it well and remember why...
This is another bloody nightmare!
I've got to a good stage with MODerne but need the recording console, which I can get second-hand if I can lay my hands on some more money.
No Karl, he's still missing.
Paulette is always on my case now... Danny is getting earache from Leslie, too...
... my mum and dad are giving me GBH of the earhole...
Emmons is totally pissed off with Edgecombe...

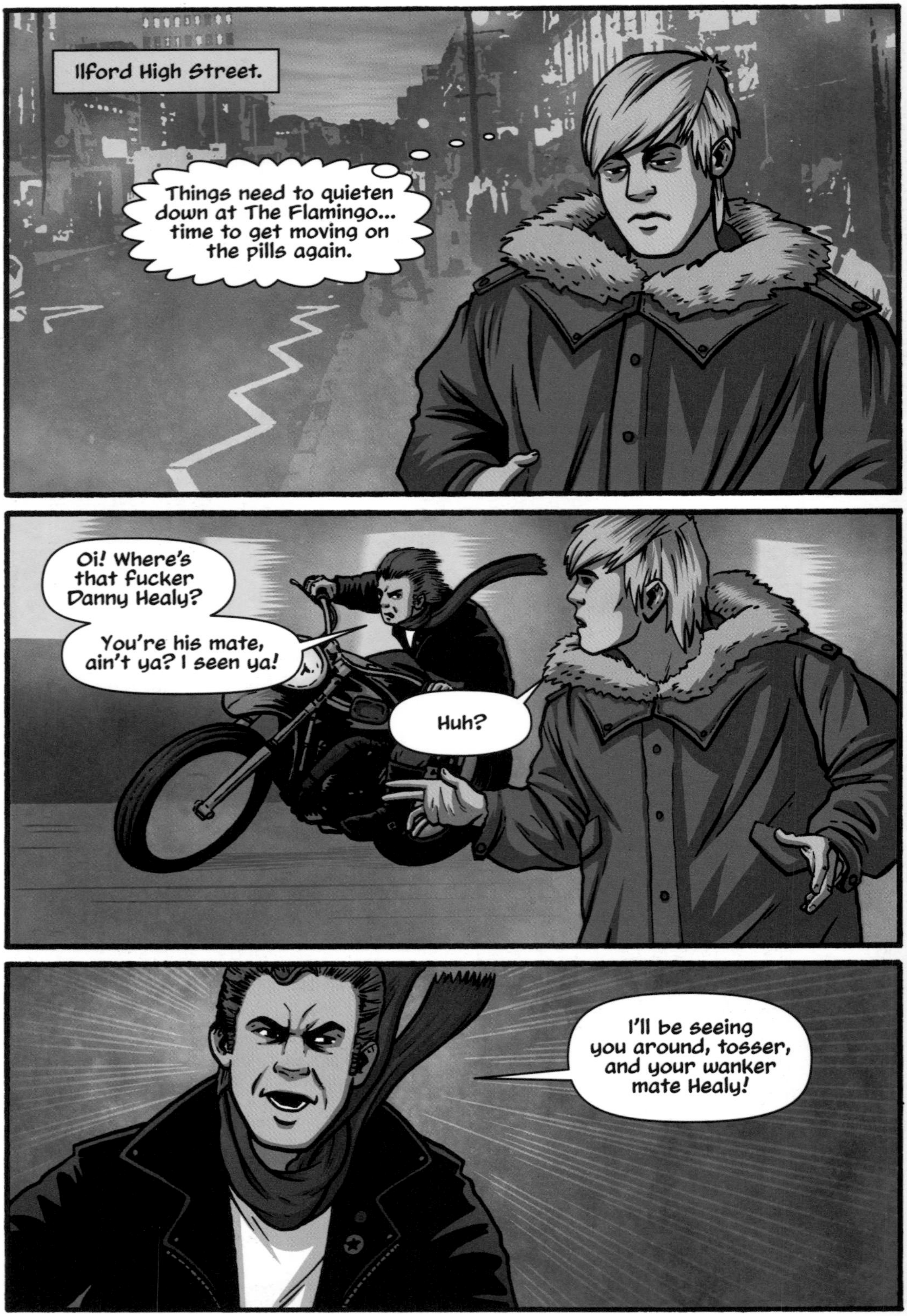
Ilford High Street.
Things need to quieten down at The Flamingo... time to get moving on the pills again.
Oi! Where's that fucker Danny Healy?
You're his mate, ain't ya? I seen ya!
Huh?
I'll be seeing you around, tosser, and your wanker mate Healy!

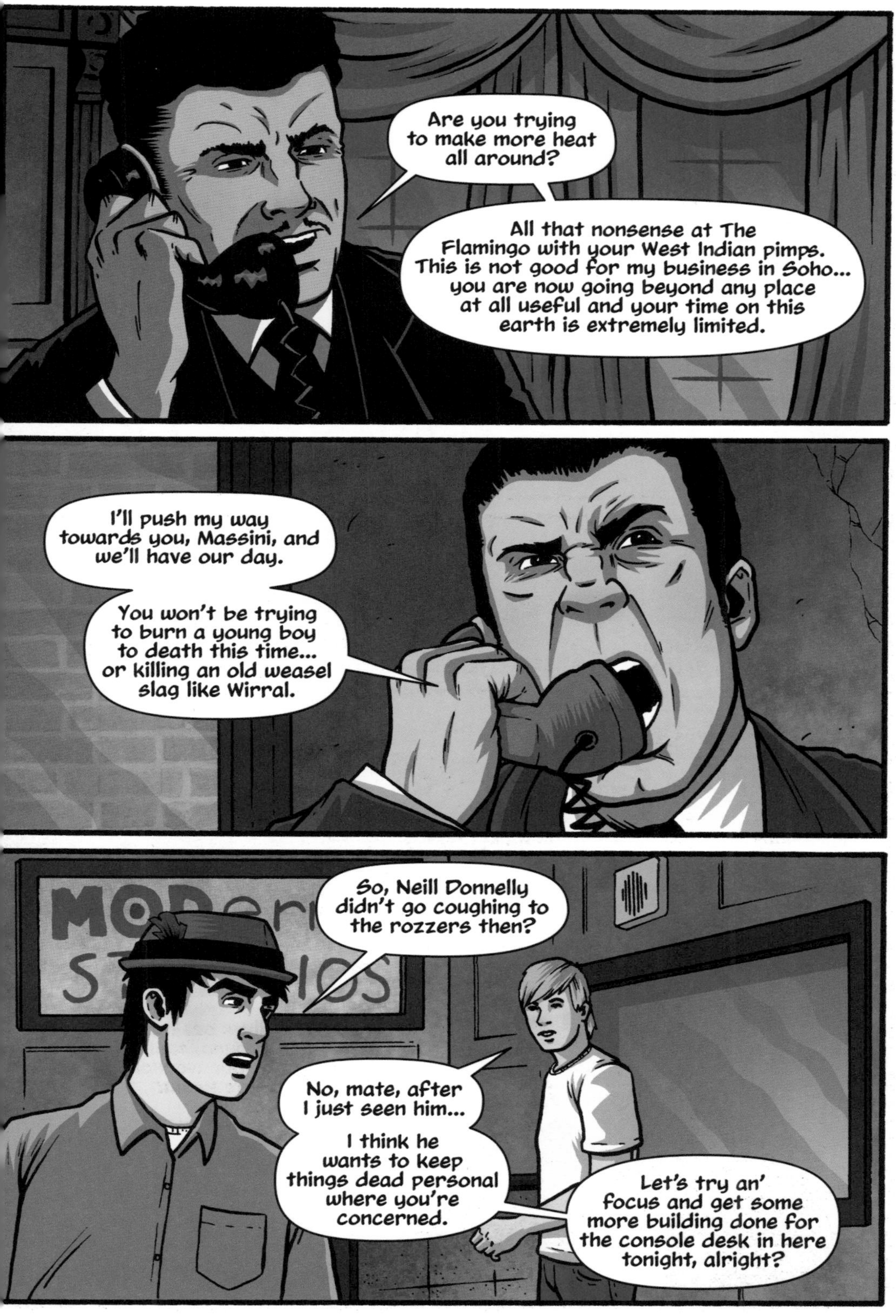
Are you trying to make more heat all around?
All that nonsense at The Flamingo with your West Indian pimps. This is not good for my business in Soho... you are now going beyond any place at all useful and your time on this earth is extremely limited.
I'll push my way towards you, Massini, and we'll have our day.
You won't be trying to burn a young boy to death this time... or killing an old weasel slag like Wirral.
MODern
So, Neill Donnelly didn't go coughing to the rozzers then?
No, mate, after I just seen him...
I think he wants to keep things dead personal where you're concerned.
Let's try an' focus and get some more building done for the console desk in here tonight, alright?

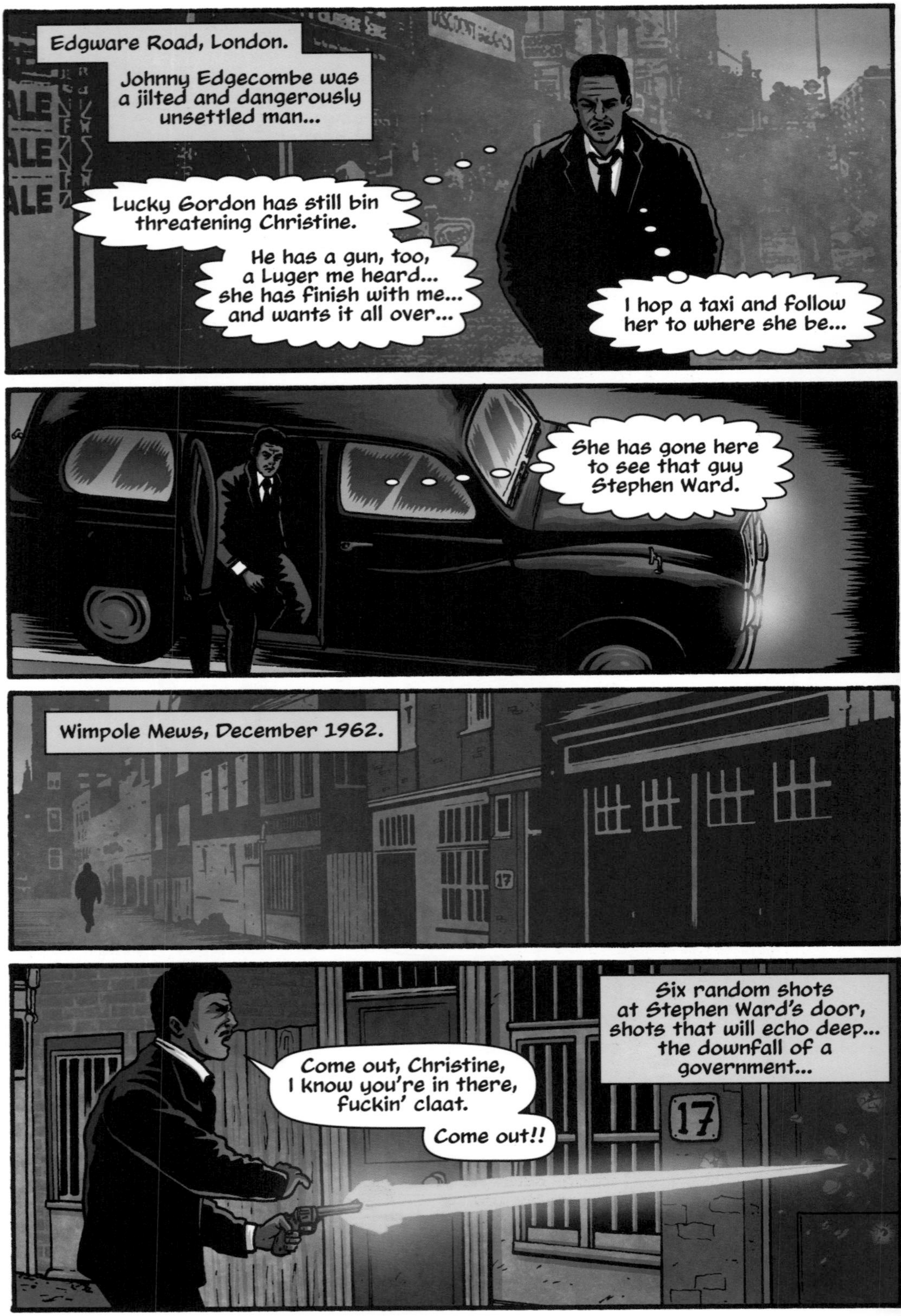
Edgware Road, London.
Johnny Edgecombe was a jilted and dangerously unsettled man...
Lucky Gordon has still bin threatening Christine.
He has a gun, too, a Luger me heard... she has finish with me... and wants it all over...
I hop a taxi and follow her to where she be...
She has gone here to see that guy Stephen Ward.
Wimpole Mews, December 1962.
17
Six random shots at Stephen Ward's door, shots that will echo deep... the downfall of a government...
Come out, Christine, I know you're in there, fuckin' claat.
Come out!!
17

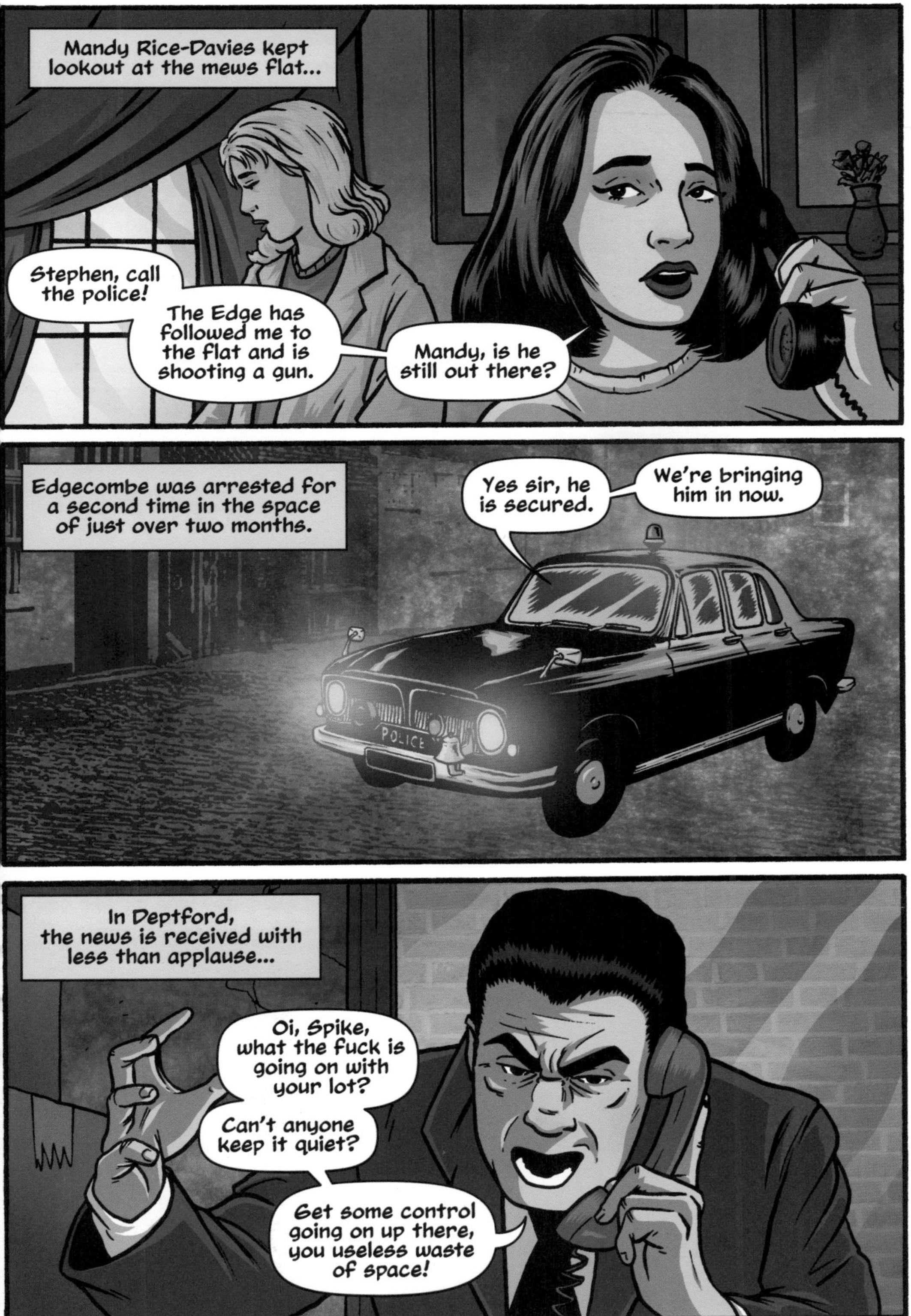
Mandy Rice-Davies kept lookout at the mews flat...
Stephen, call the police!
The Edge has followed me to the flat and is shooting a gun.
Mandy, is he still out there?
Edgecombe was arrested for a second time in the space of just over two months.
Yes sir, he is secured.
We're bringing him in now.
POLICE
In Deptford, the news is received with less than applause...
Oi, Spike, what the fuck is going on with your lot?
Can't anyone keep it quiet?
Get some control going on up there, you useless waste of space!

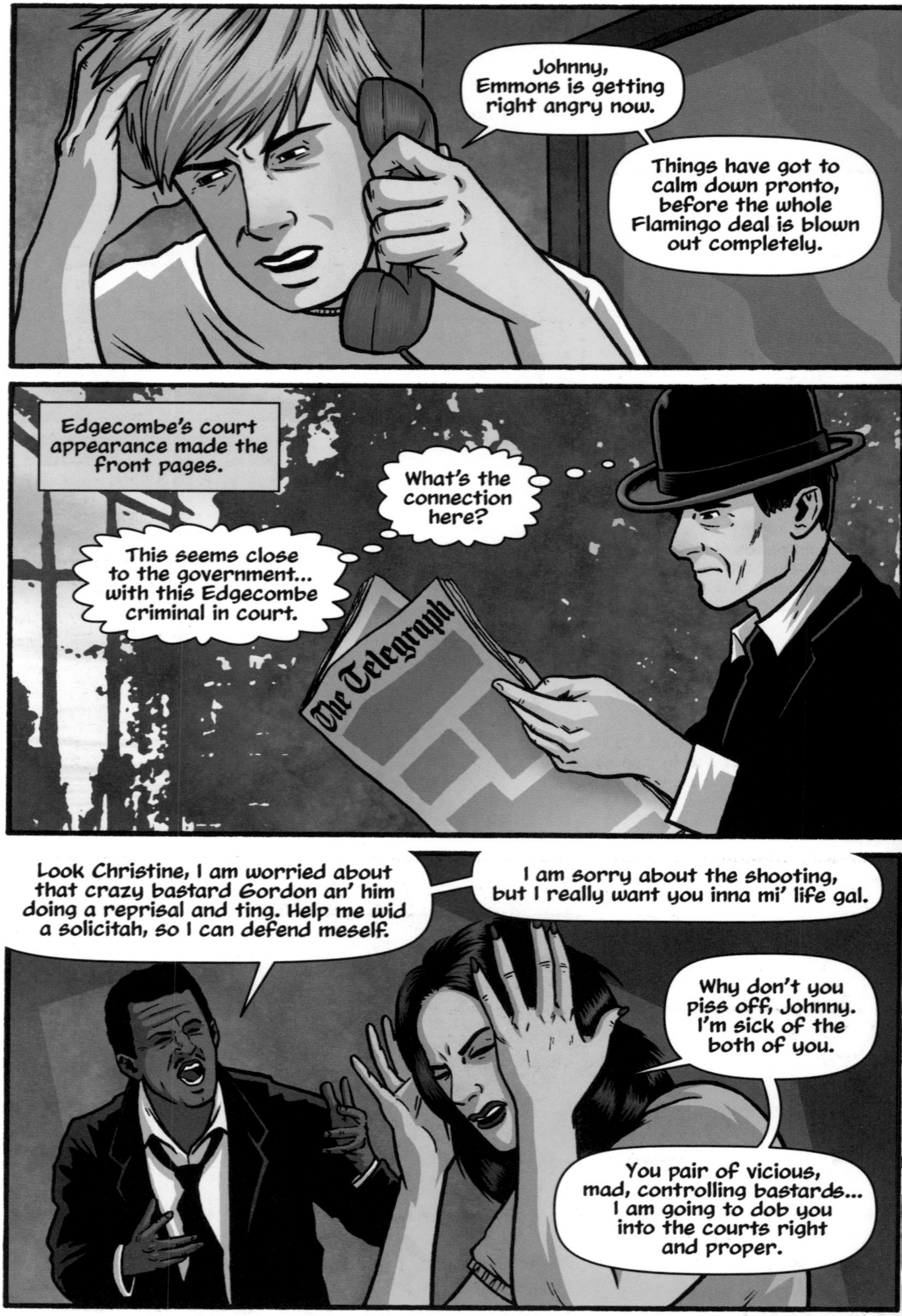
Johnny, Emmons is getting right angry now.
Things have got to calm down pronto, before the whole Flamingo deal is blown out completely.
Edgecombe's court appearance made the front pages.
What's the connection here?
This seems close to the government... with this Edgecombe criminal in court.
The Telegraph
Look Christine, I am worried about that crazy bastard Gordon an' him doing a reprisal and ting. Help me wid a solicitah, so I can defend meself.
I am sorry about the shooting, but I really want you inna mi' life gal.
Why don't you piss off, Johnny. I'm sick of the both of you.
You pair of vicious, mad, controlling bastards... I am going to dob you into the courts right and proper.

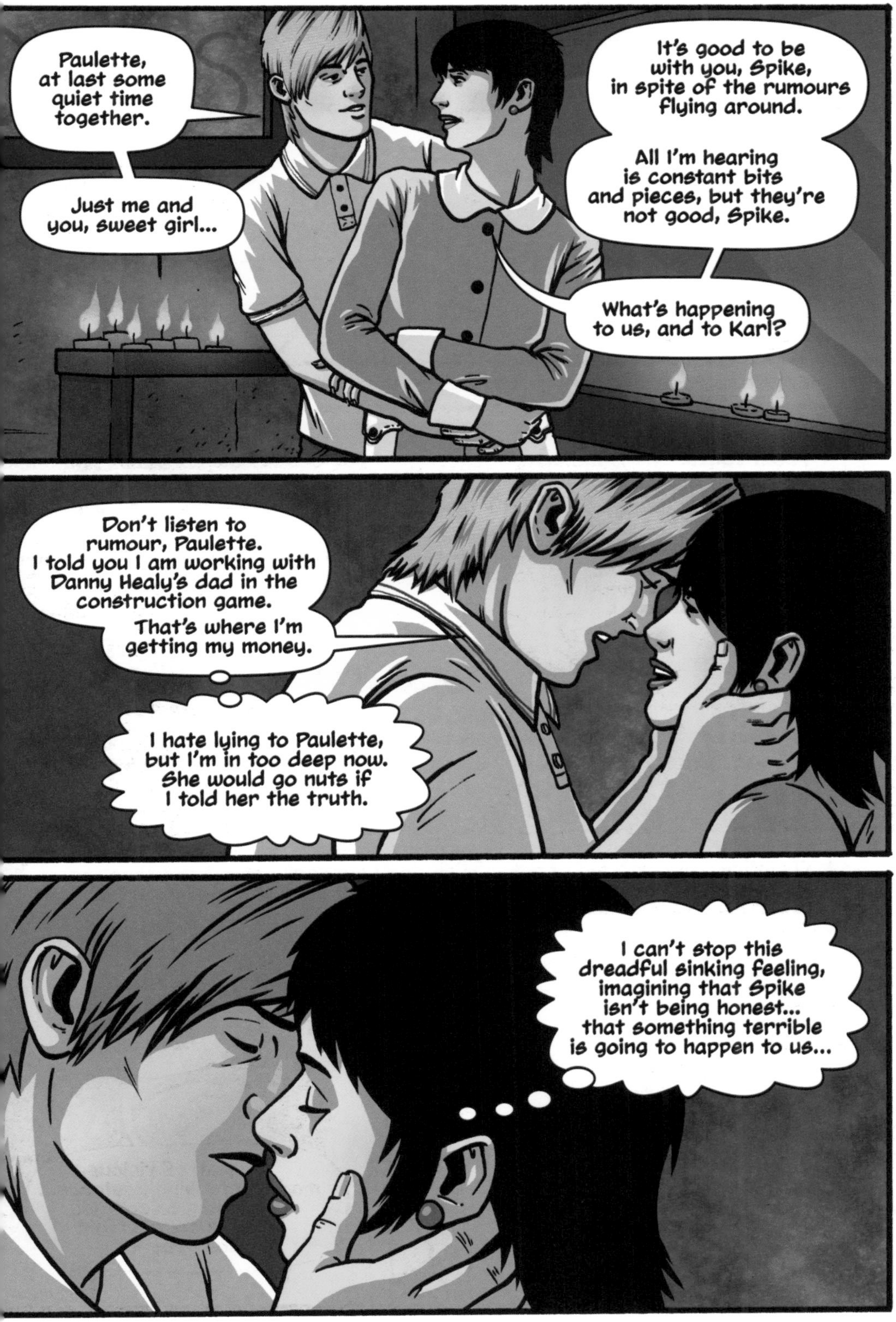
Paulette, at last some quiet time together.
Just me and you, sweet girl...
It's good to be with you, Spike, in spite of the rumours flying around.
All I'm hearing is constant bits and pieces, but they're not good, Spike.
What's happening to us, and to Karl?
Don't listen to rumour, Paulette. I told you I am working with Danny Healy's dad in the construction game.
That's where I'm getting my money.
I hate lying to Paulette, but I'm in too deep now. She would go nuts if I told her the truth.
I can't stop this dreadful sinking feeling, imagining that Spike isn't being honest... that something terrible is going to happen to us...

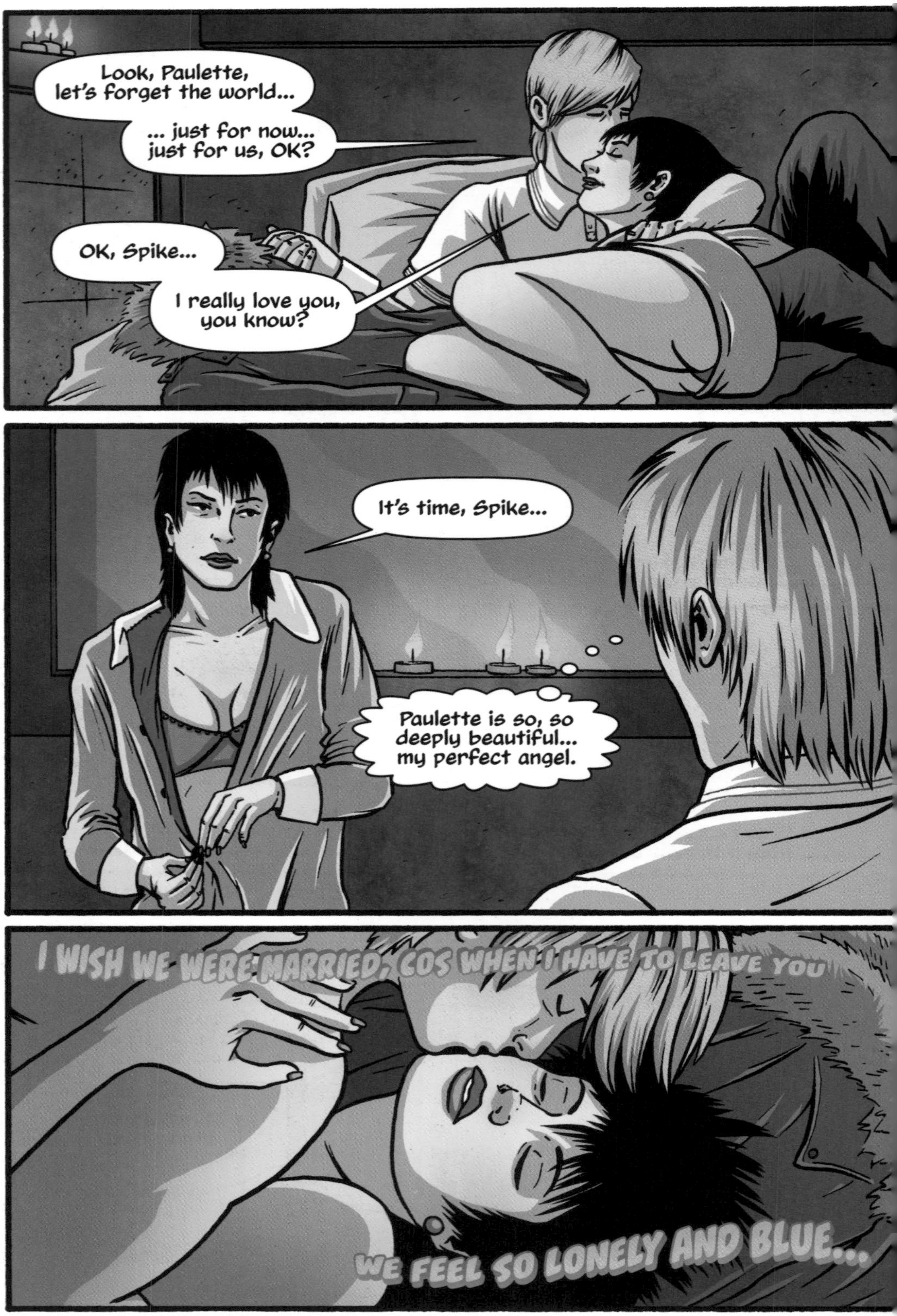
Look, Paulette, let's forget the world...
... just for now... just for us, OK?
OK, Spike...
I really love you, you know?
It's time, Spike...
Paulette is so, so deeply beautiful... my perfect angel.
I WISH WE WERE MARRIED, COS WHEN I HAVE TO LEAVE YOU
WE FEEL SO LONELY AND BLUE...

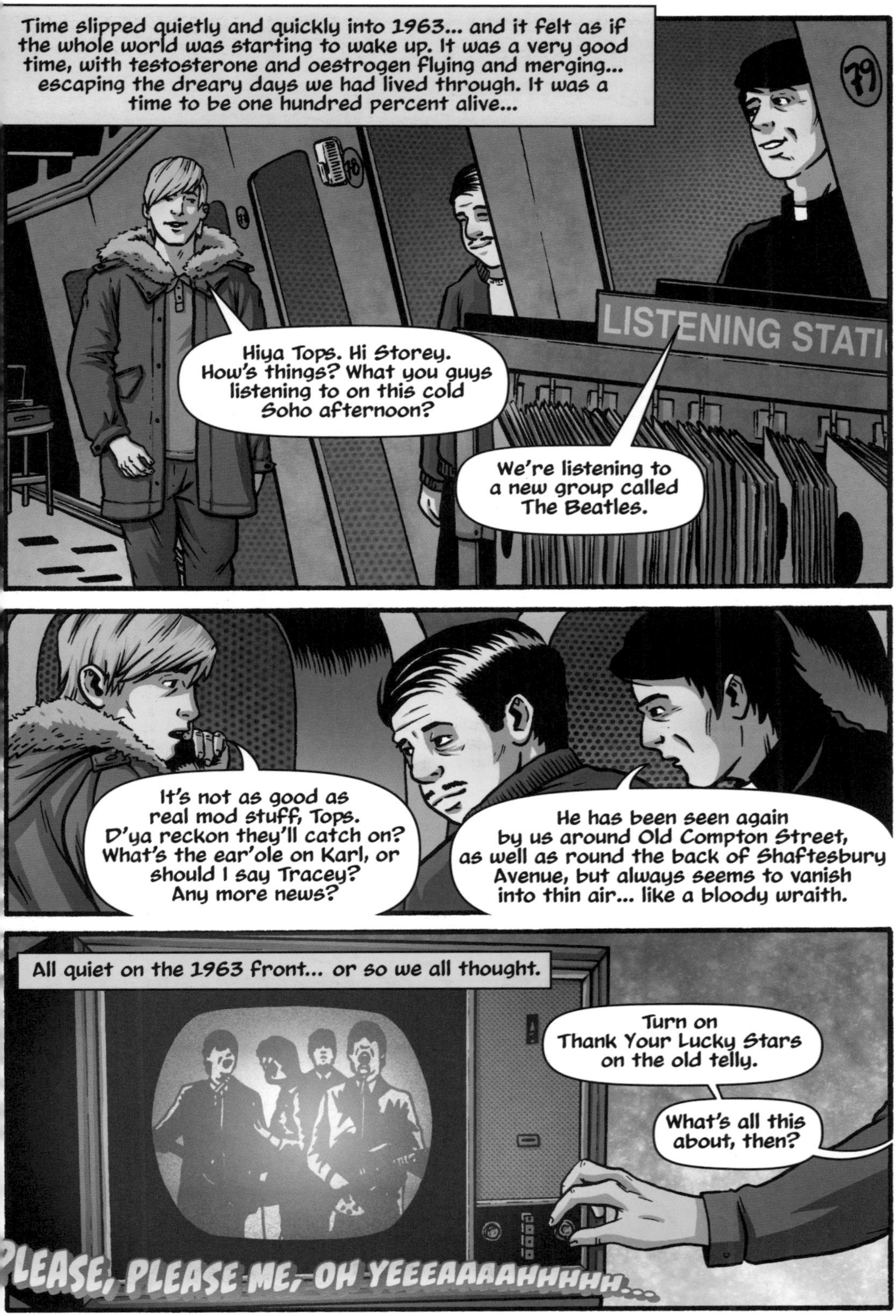

Time slipped quietly and quickly into 1963... and it felt as if the whole world was starting to wake up. It was a very good time, with testosterone and oestrogen flying and merging... escaping the dreary days we had lived through. It was a time to be one hundred percent alive...
79
LISTENING STATI
Hiya Tops. Hi Storey. How's things? What you guys listening to on this cold Soho afternoon?
We're listening to a new group called The Beatles.
It's not as good as real mod stuff, Tops. D'ya reckon they'll catch on? What's the ear'ole on Karl, or should I say Tracey? Any more news?
He has been seen again by us around Old Compton Street, as well as round the back of Shaftesbury Avenue, but always seems to vanish into thin air... like a bloody wraith.
All quiet on the 1963 front... or so we all thought.
Turn on Thank Your Lucky Stars on the old telly.
What's all this about, then?
PLEASE, PLEASE ME, OH YEEEAAAAHHHHH...

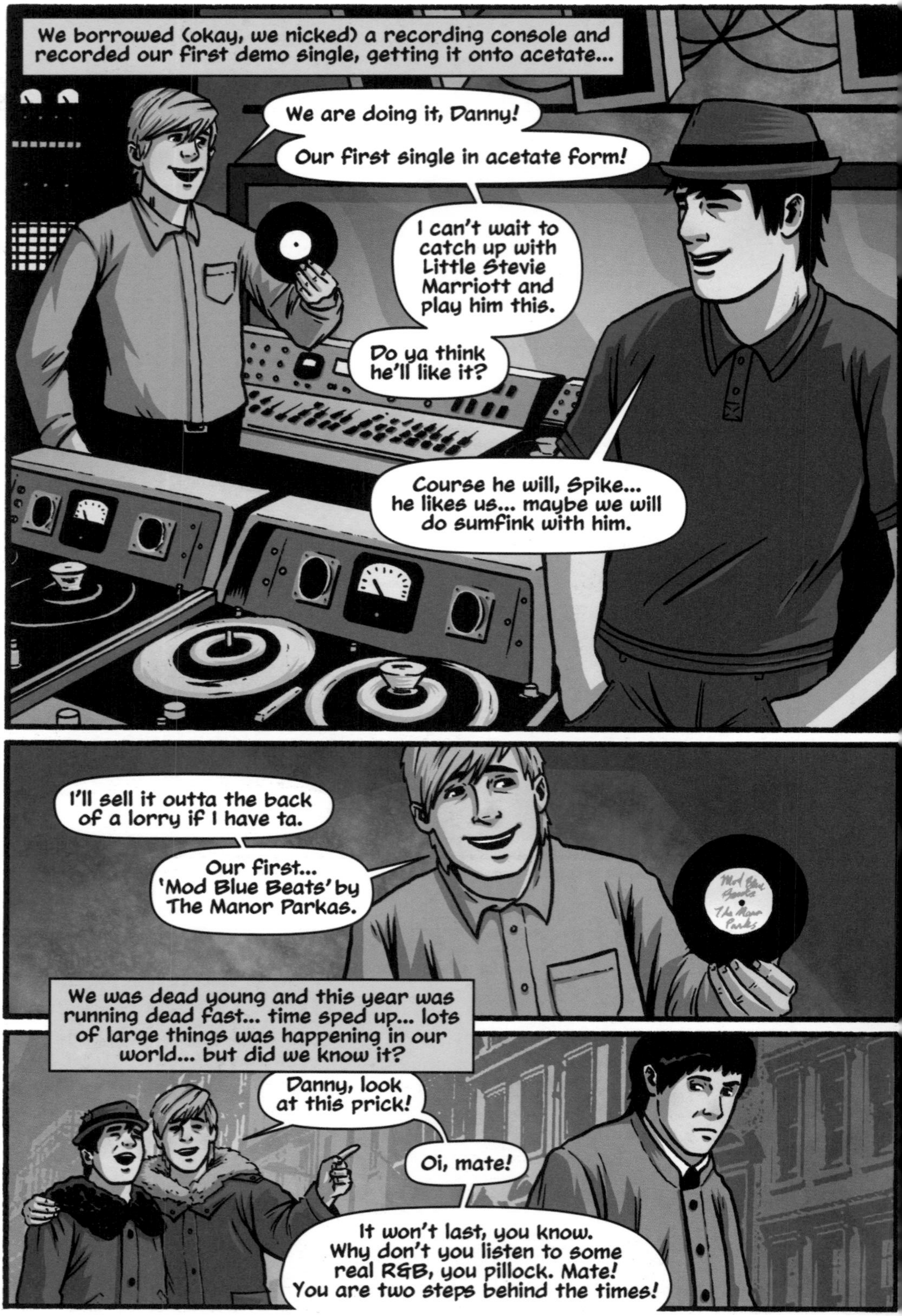
We borrowed (okay, we nicked) a recording console and recorded our first demo single, getting it onto acetate...
We are doing it, Danny!
Our first single in acetate form!
I can't wait to catch up with Little Stevie Marriott and play him this.
Do ya think he'll like it?
Course he will, Spike... he likes us... maybe we will do sumfink with him.
I'll sell it outta the back of a lorry if I have ta.
Our first... 'Mod Blue Beats' by The Manor Parkas.
We was dead young and this year was running dead fast... time sped up... lots of large things was happening in our world... but did we know it?
Danny, look at this prick!
Oi, mate!
It won't last, you know. Why don't you listen to some real R&B, you pillock. Mate! You are two steps behind the times!

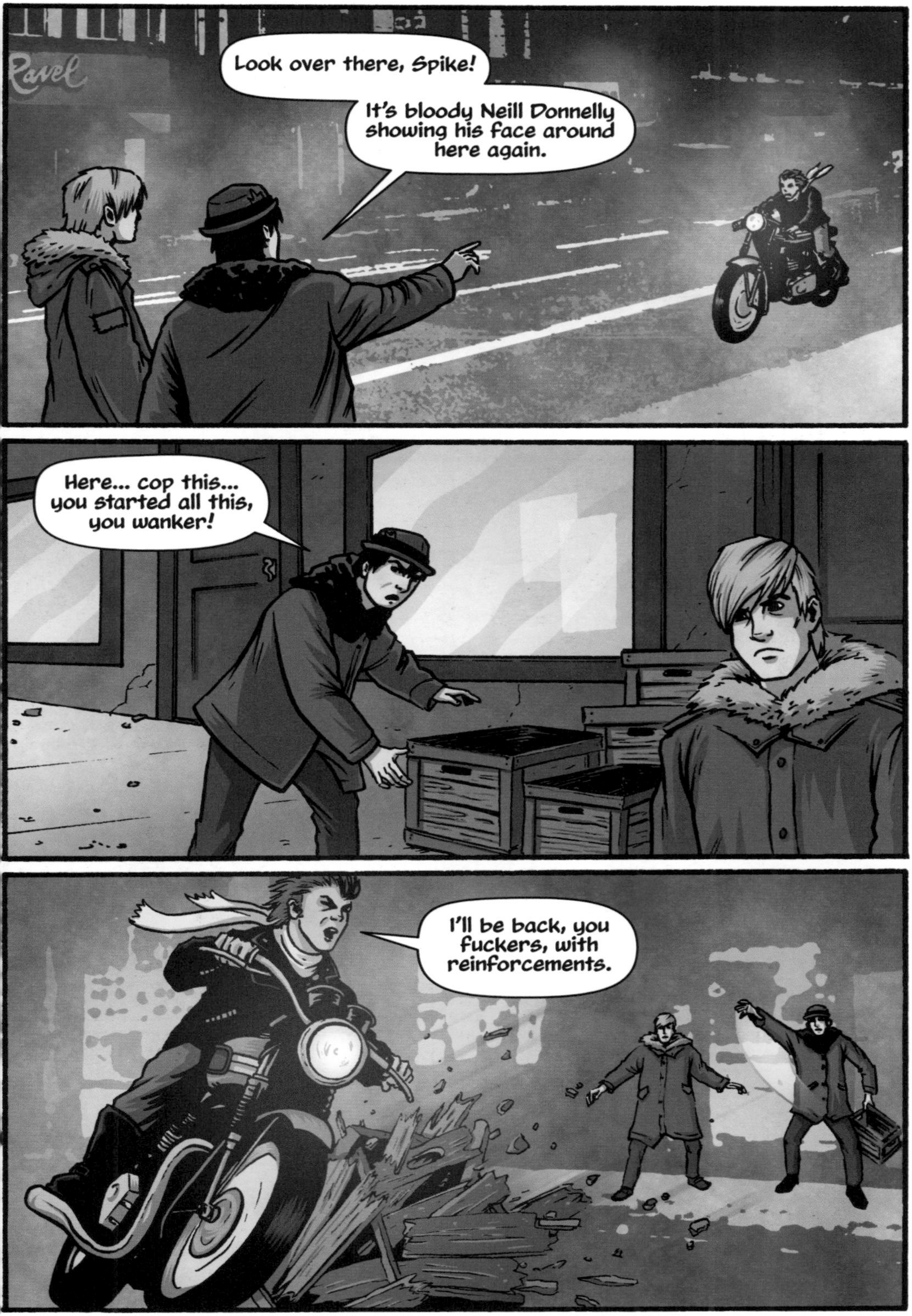
Ravel
Look over there, Spike!
It's bloody Neill Donnelly showing his face around here again.
Here... cop this... you started all this, you wanker!
I'll be back, you fuckers, with reinforcements.

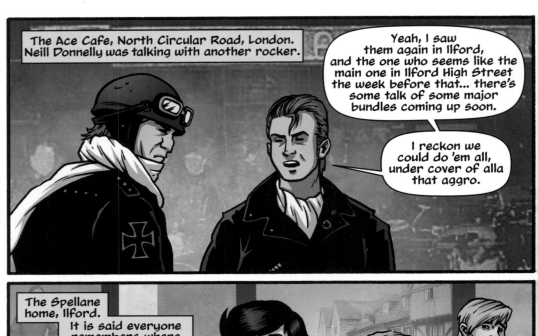

The Ace Cafe, North Circular Road, London. Neill Donnelly was talking with another rocker.

Yeah, I saw them again in Ilford, and the one who seems like the main one in Ilford High Street the week before that... there's some talk of some major bundles coming up soon.

I reckon we could do 'em all, under cover of alla that aggro.

The Spellane home, Ilford. It is said everyone remembers where they were... exactly.

It has been announced that President John Fitzgerald Kennedy has been fatally shot in Dallas, Texas. He died at Parkland Hospital in Dallas at 1:00pm American time.

The historic date is 22nd November 1963.

Jasus, that's the beginning of the bleddy end for all of us... if they can shoot the President in broad daylight!

Maybe Dad's right. There has been a sort of shift in the world.

I will certainly remember this moment... a chilling minute...

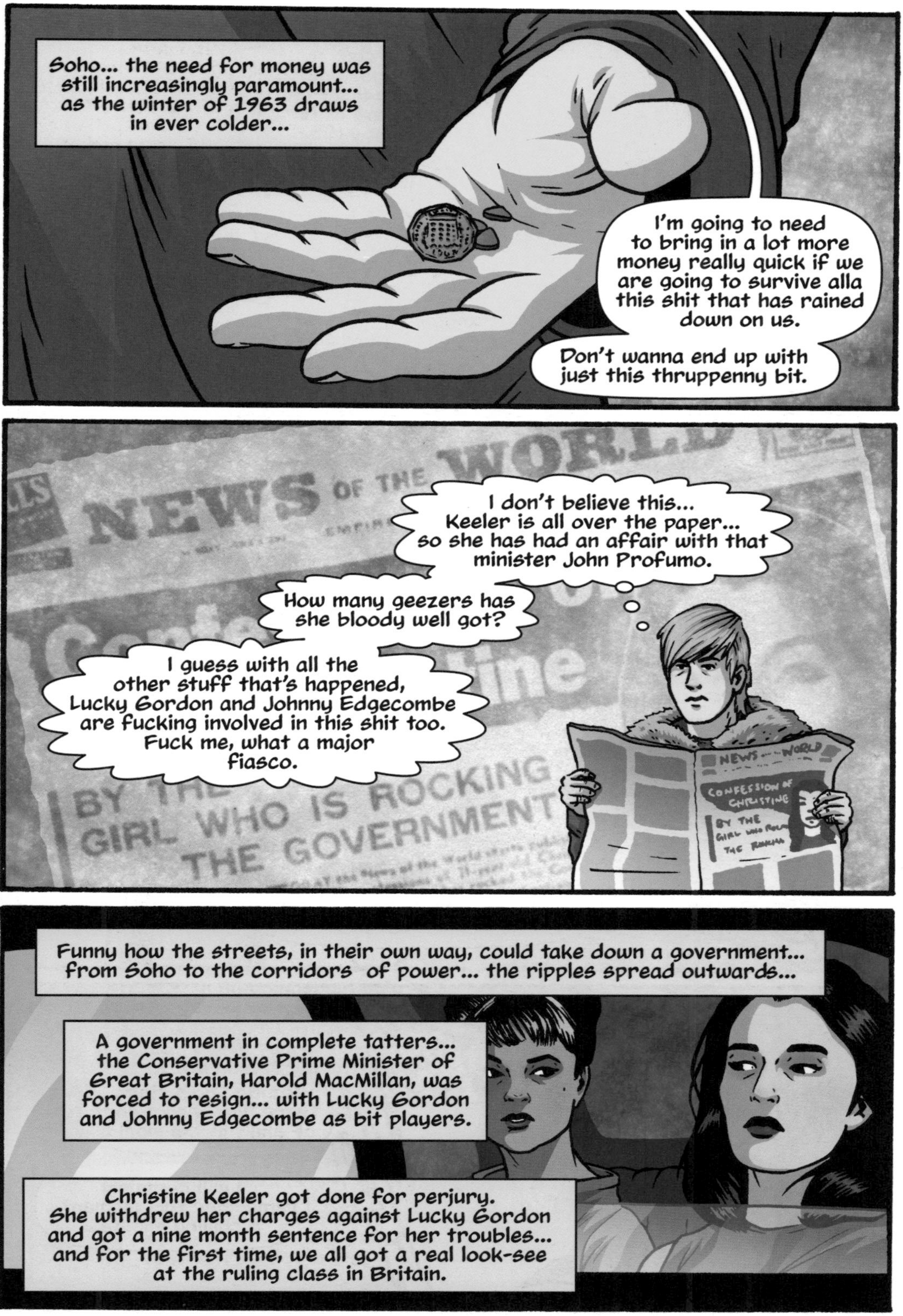
Soho... the need for money was still increasingly paramount... as the winter of 1963 draws in ever colder...
I'm going to need to bring in a lot more money really quick if we are going to survive alla this shit that has rained down on us.
Don't wanna end up with just this thruppenny bit.
NEWS OF THE WORLD
I don't believe this... Keeler is all over the paper... so she has had an affair with that minister John Profumo.
How many geezers has she bloody well got?
I guess with all the other stuff that's happened, Lucky Gordon and Johnny Edgecombe are fucking involved in this shit too. Fuck me, what a major fiasco.
BY THE
GIRL WHO IS ROCKING
THE GOVERNMENT
Funny how the streets, in their own way, could take down a government... from Soho to the corridors of power... the ripples spread outwards...
A government in complete tatters... the Conservative Prime Minister of Great Britain, Harold MacMillan, was forced to resign... with Lucky Gordon and Johnny Edgecombe as bit players.
Christine Keeler got done for perjury. She withdrew her charges against Lucky Gordon and got a nine month sentence for her troubles... and for the first time, we all got a real look-see at the ruling class in Britain.

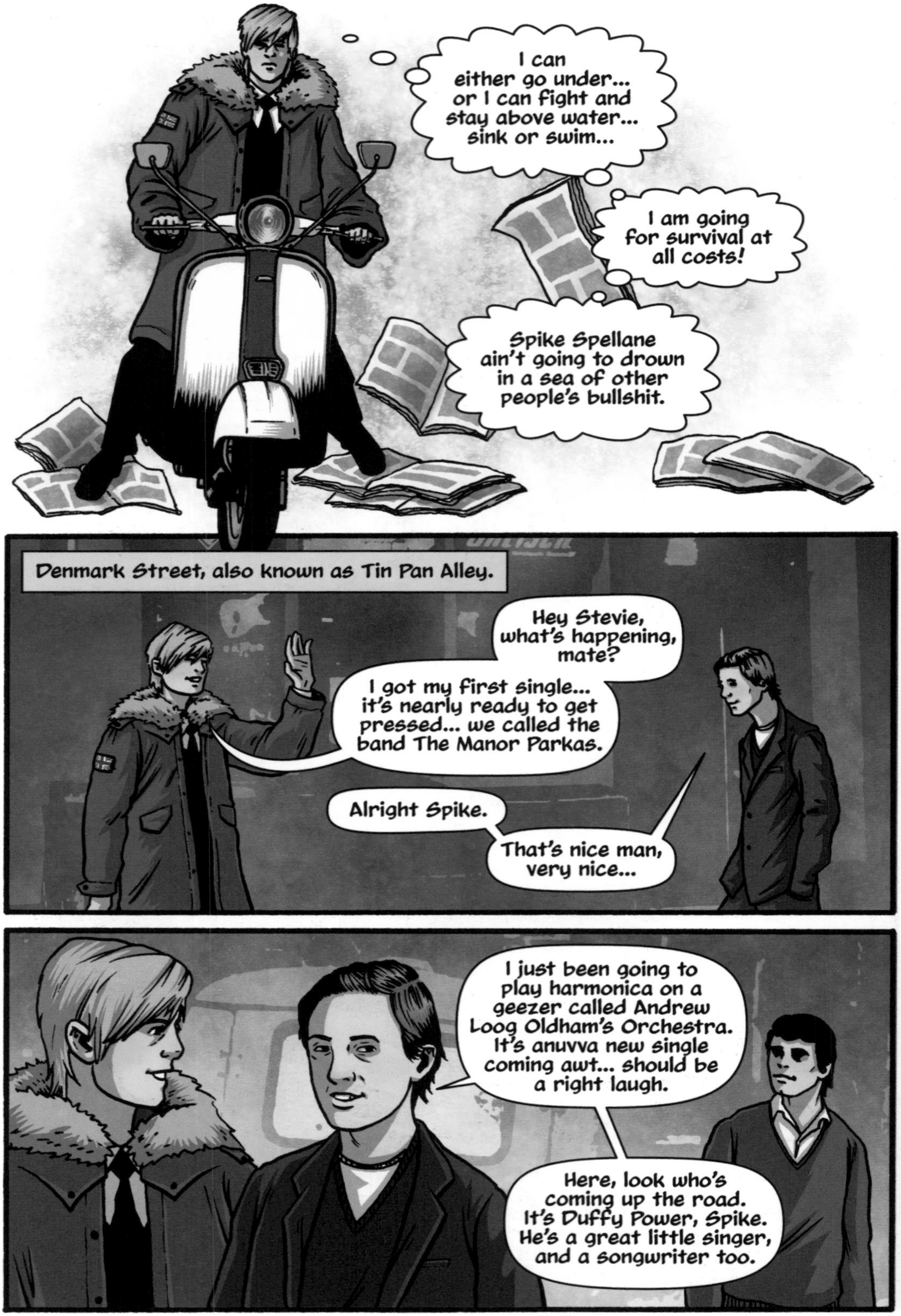
I can either go under... or I can fight and stay above water... sink or swim...
I am going for survival at all costs!
Spike Spellane ain't going to drown in a sea of other people's bullshit.
Denmark Street, also known as Tin Pan Alley.
Hey Stevie, what's happening, mate?
I got my first single... it's nearly ready to get pressed... we called the band The Manor Parkas.
Alright Spike.
That's nice man, very nice...
I just been going to play harmonica on a geezer called Andrew Loog Oldham's Orchestra. It's anuvva new single coming awt... should be a right laugh.
Here, look who's coming up the road. It's Duffy Power, Spike. He's a great little singer, and a songwriter too.

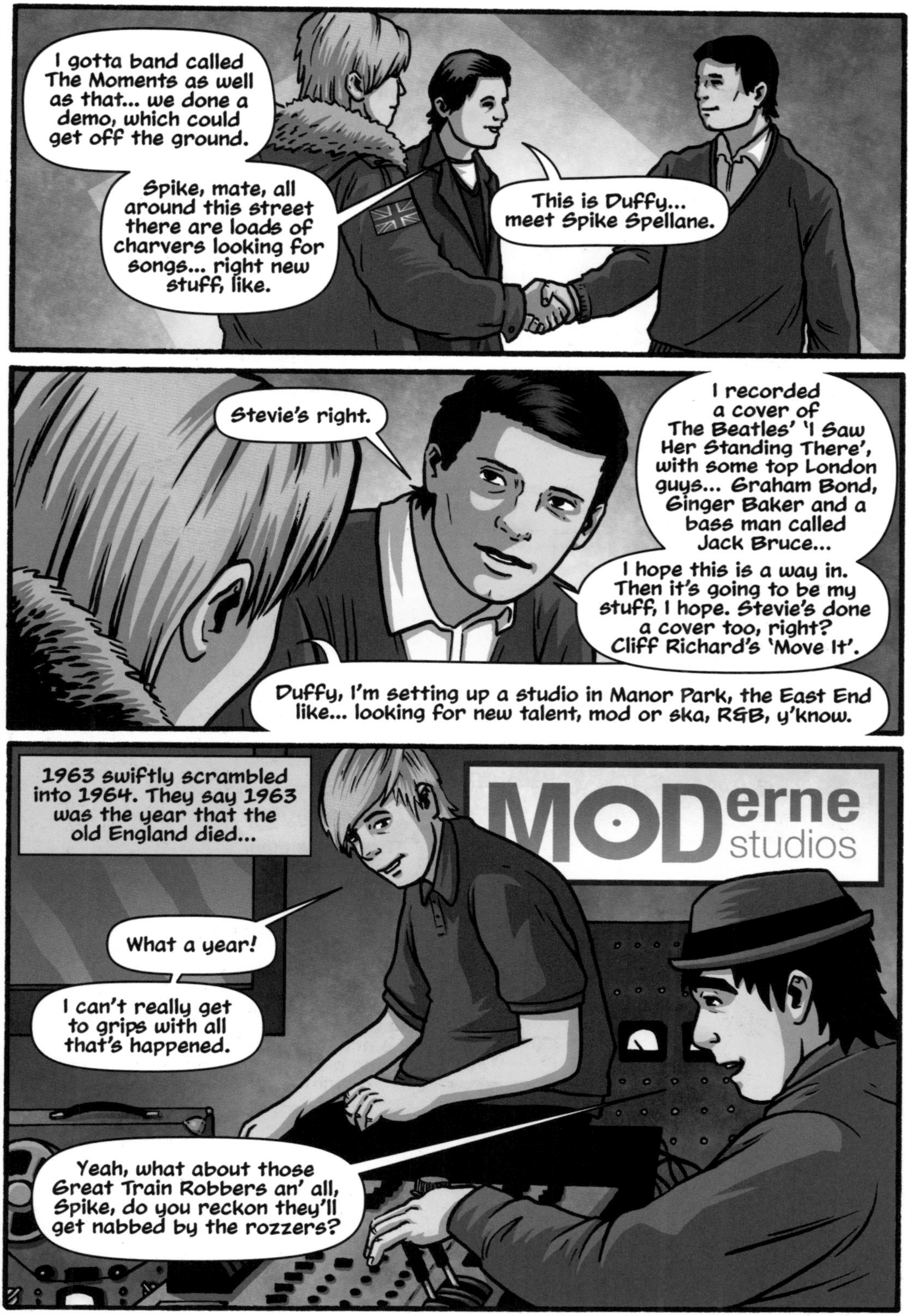
I gotta band called The Moments as well as that... we done a demo, which could get off the ground.
Spike, mate, all around this street there are loads of charvers looking for songs... right new stuff, like.
This is Duffy... meet Spike Spellane.
Stevie's right.
I recorded a cover of The Beatles' 'I Saw Her Standing There', with some top London guys... Graham Bond, Ginger Baker and a bass man called Jack Bruce...
I hope this is a way in. Then it's going to be my stuff, I hope. Stevie's done a cover too, right? Cliff Richard's 'Move It'.
Duffy, I'm setting up a studio in Manor Park, the East End like... looking for new talent, mod or ska, R&B, y'know.
1963 swiftly scrambled into 1964. They say 1963 was the year that the old England died...
MODerne studios
What a year!
I can't really get to grips with all that's happened.
Yeah, what about those Great Train Robbers an' all, Spike, do you reckon they'll get nabbed by the rozzers?

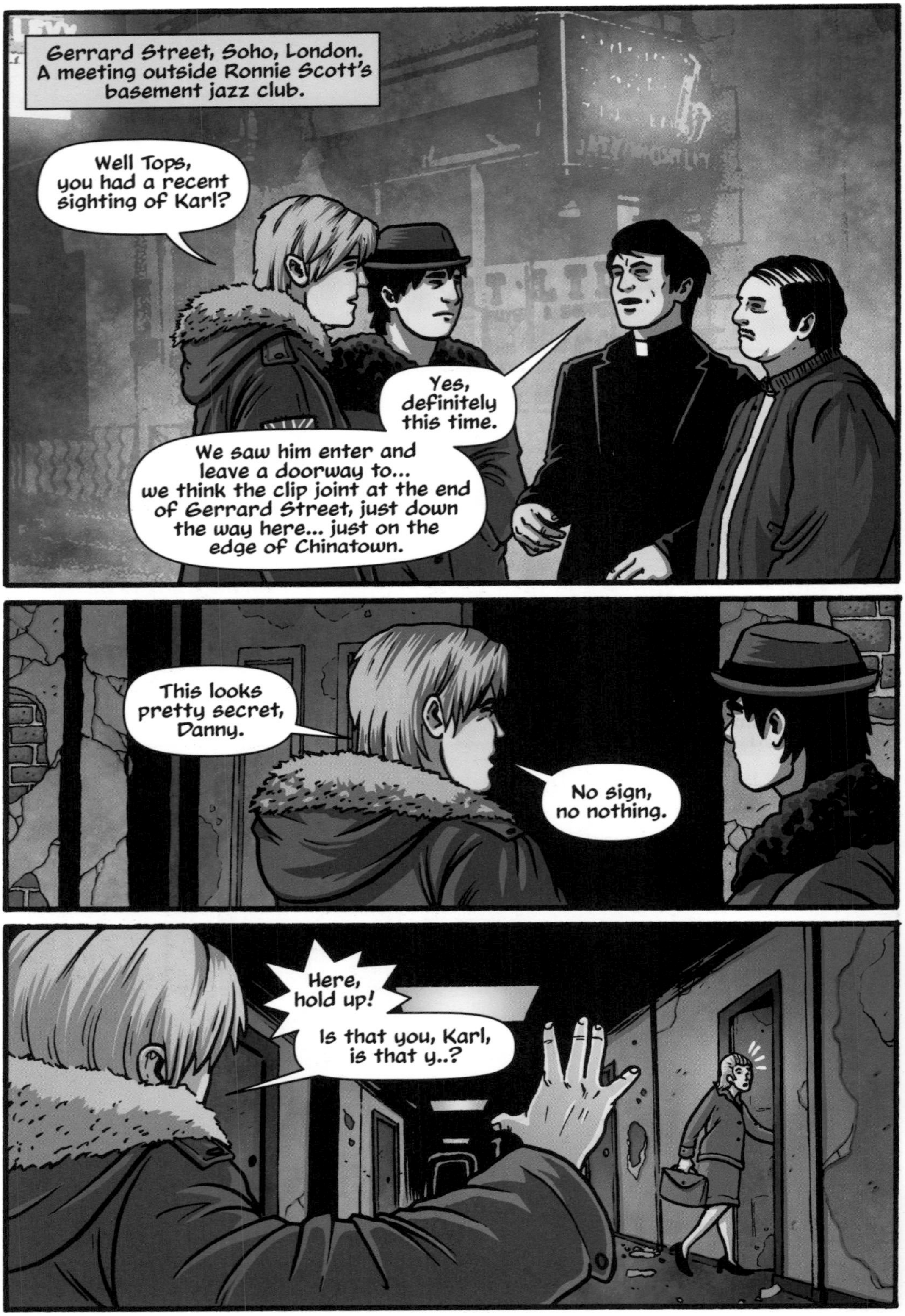
Gerrard Street, Soho, London. A meeting outside Ronnie Scott's basement jazz club.
Well Tops, you had a recent sighting of Karl?
Yes, definitely this time.
We saw him enter and leave a doorway to... we think the clip joint at the end of Gerrard Street, just down the way here... just on the edge of Chinatown.
This looks pretty secret, Danny.
No sign, no nothing.
Here, hold up!
Is that you, Karl, is that y..?

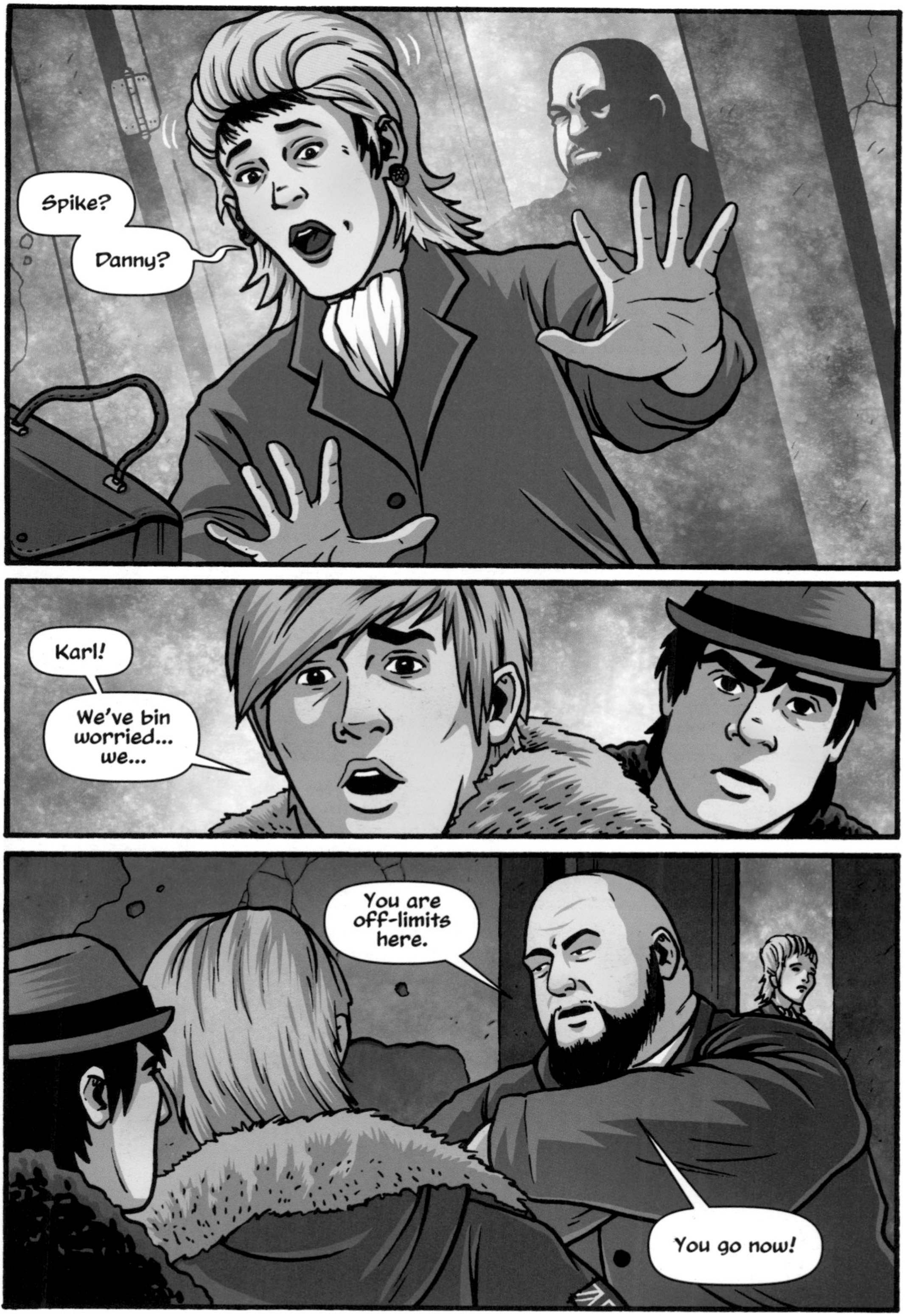
Spike?
Danny?
Karl!
We've bin worried... we...
You are off-limits here.
You go now!

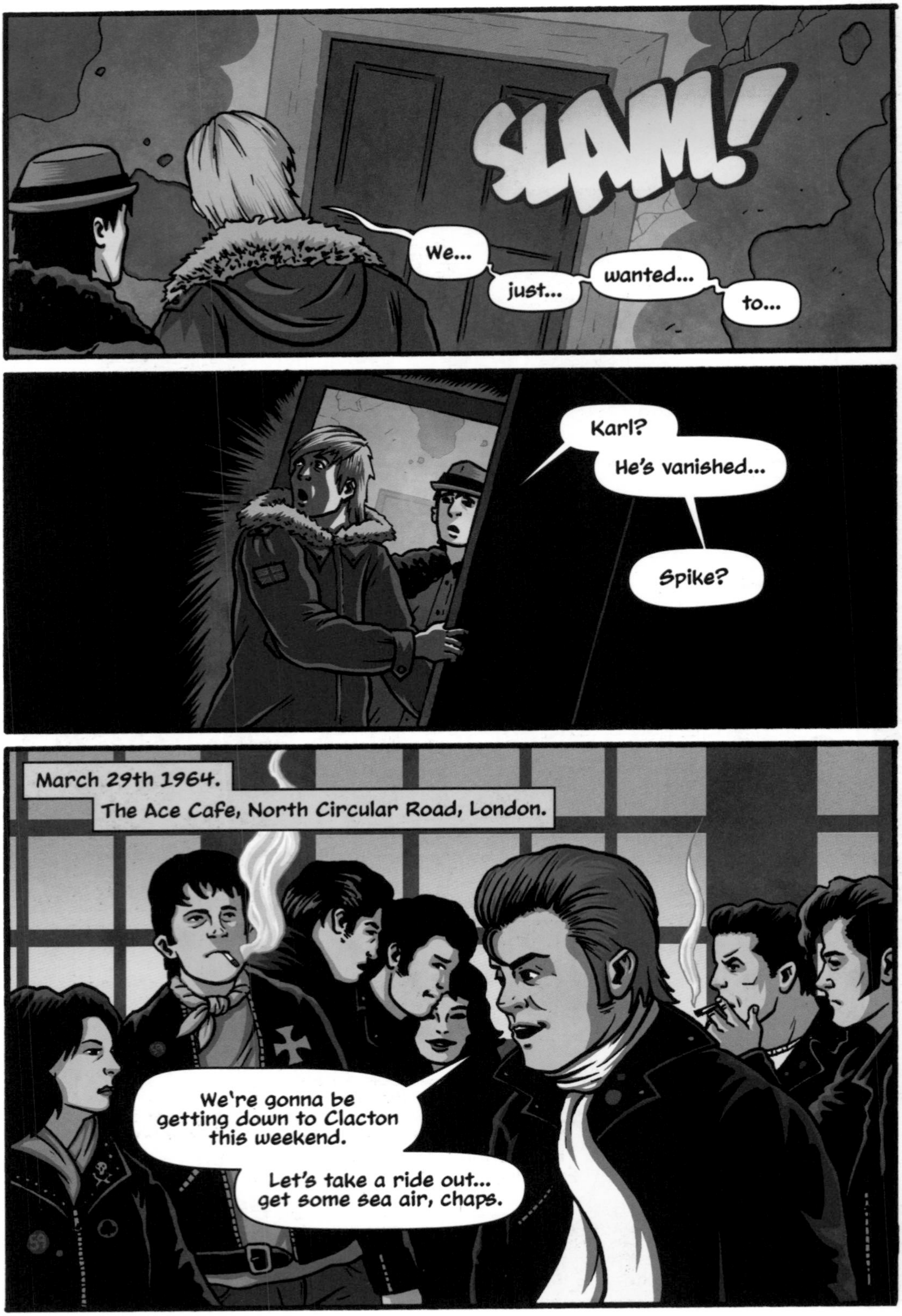
SLAM!
We...
just...
wanted...
to...
Karl?
He's vanished...
Spike?
March 29th 1964.
The Ace Cafe, North Circular Road, London.
We're gonna be getting down to Clacton this weekend.
Let's take a ride out... get some sea air, chaps.

Clacton, an Essex seaside resort.

The coldest Easter Bank Holiday since 1863.

Monday, March 30th 1964.

Some of us had arrived already, but there was nothing happening. Well, not yet, anyway...

Off you go, sonny Jim!

We don't want your sort in our resort, out here to cause bloody trouble.

Call this a resort?

You're jokin', ain't ya?

I've been in better mortuaries than this... what a fucking dump!

An' my name ain't Jim, you prize prat!

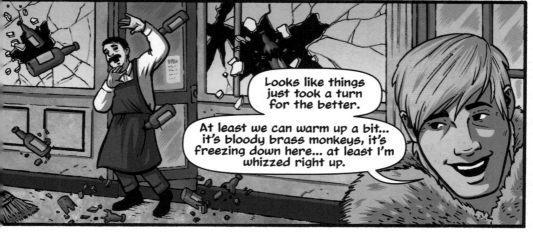

Looks like things just took a turn for the better.

At least we can warm up a bit... it's bloody brass monkeys, it's freezing down here... at least I'm whizzed right up.

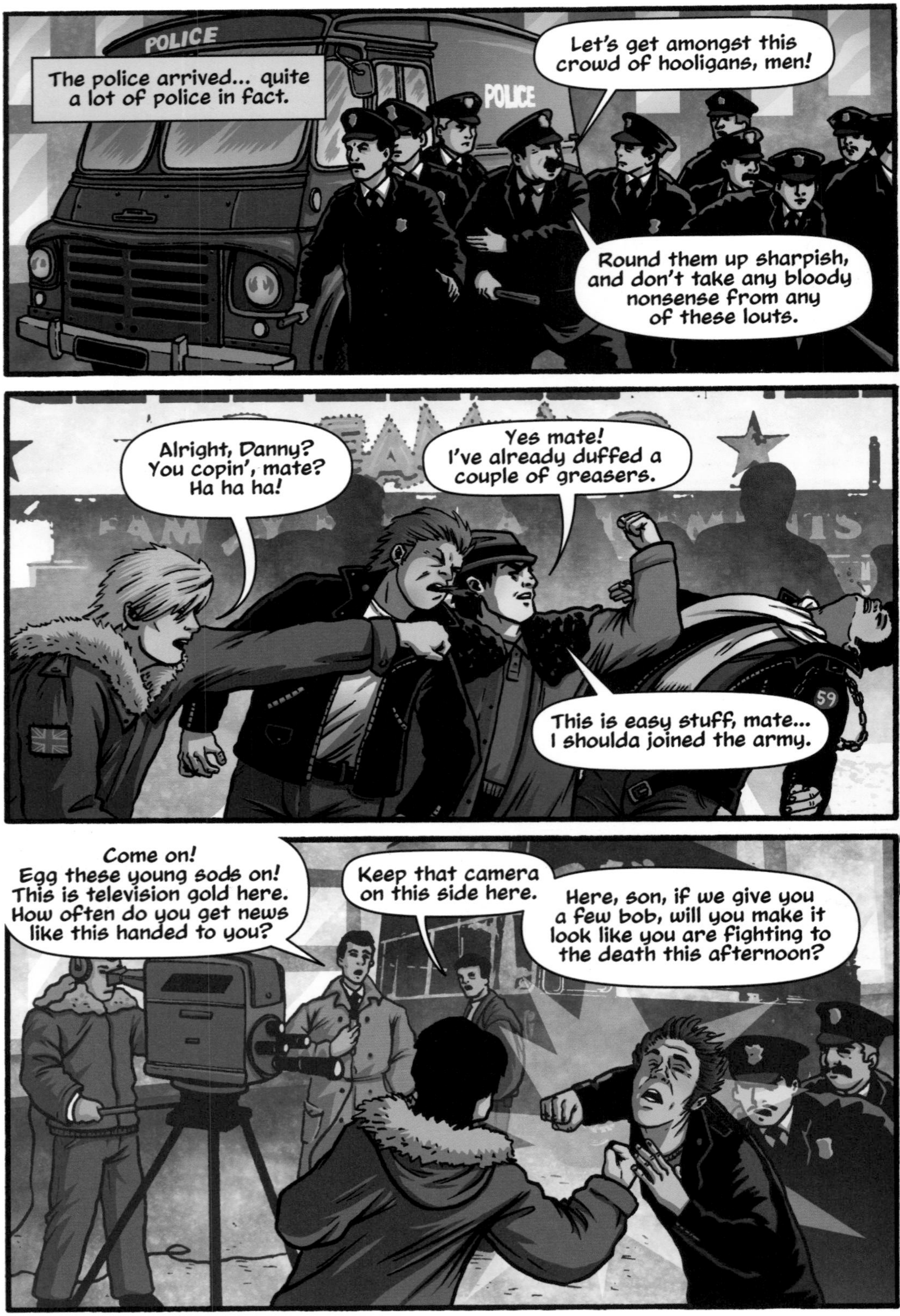
POLICE
The police arrived... quite a lot of police in fact.
POLICE
Let's get amongst this crowd of hooligans, men!
Round them up sharpish, and don't take any bloody nonsense from any of these louts.
Alright, Danny? You copin', mate? Ha ha ha!
Yes mate! I've already duffed a couple of greasers.
This is easy stuff, mate... I shoulda joined the army.
Come on! Egg these young sods on! This is television gold here. How often do you get news like this handed to you?
Keep that camera on this side here.
Here, son, if we give you a few bob, will you make it look like you are fighting to the death this afternoon?

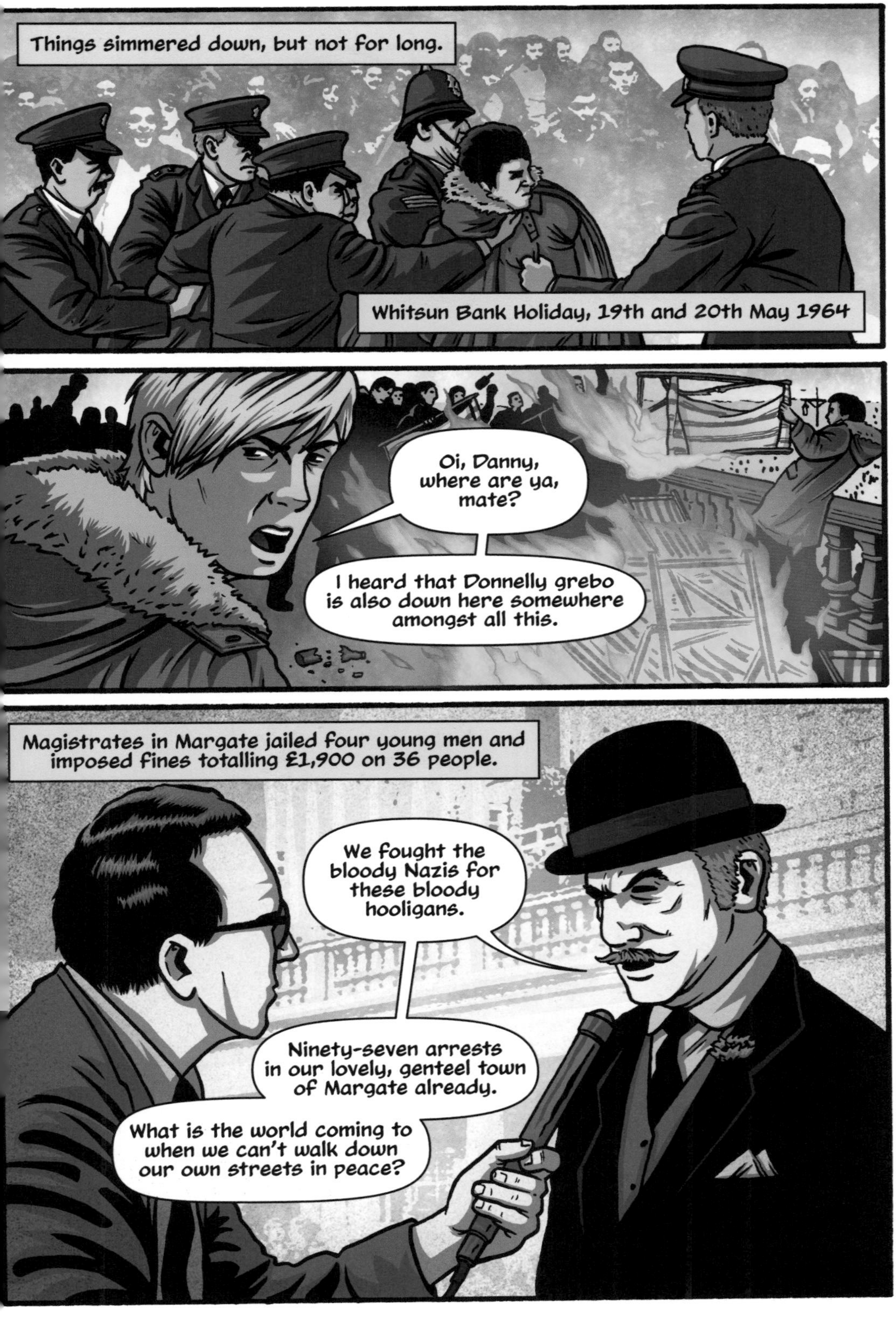
Things simmered down, but not for long.
Whitsun Bank Holiday, 19th and 20th May 1964
Oi, Danny, where are ya, mate?
I heard that Donnelly grebo is also down here somewhere amongst all this.
Magistrates in Margate jailed four young men and imposed fines totalling £1,900 on 36 people.
We fought the bloody Nazis for these bloody hooligans.
Ninety-seven arrests in our lovely, genteel town of Margate already.
What is the world coming to when we can't walk down our own streets in peace?

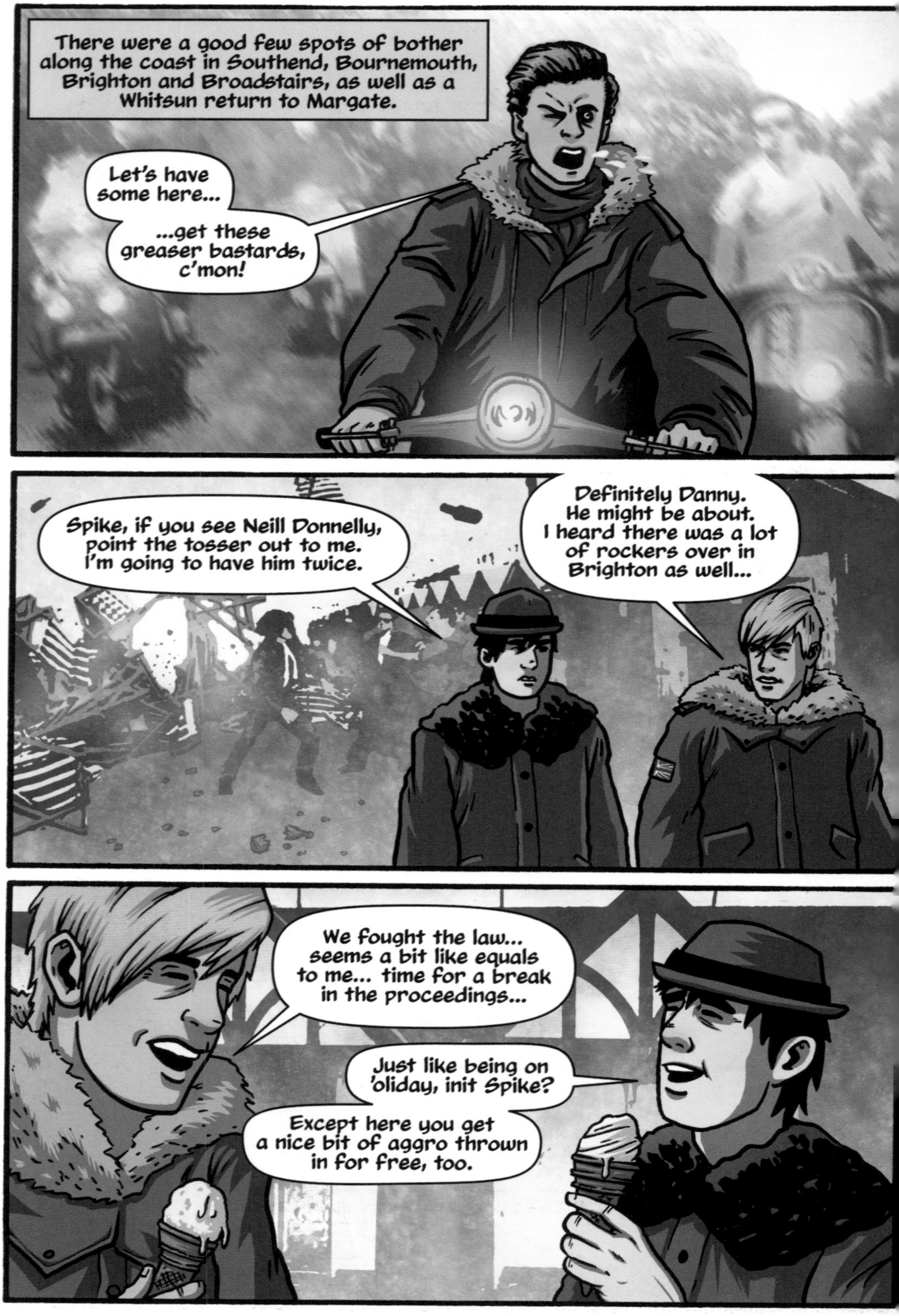
There were a good few spots of bother along the coast in Southend, Bournemouth, Brighton and Broadstairs, as well as a Whitsun return to Margate.
Let's have some here...
...get these greaser bastards, c'mon!
Spike, if you see Neill Donnelly, point the tosser out to me. I'm going to have him twice.
Definitely Danny. He might be about. I heard there was a lot of rockers over in Brighton as well...
We fought the law... seems a bit like equals to me... time for a break in the proceedings...
Just like being on 'oliday, init Spike?
Except here you get a nice bit of aggro thrown in for free, too.

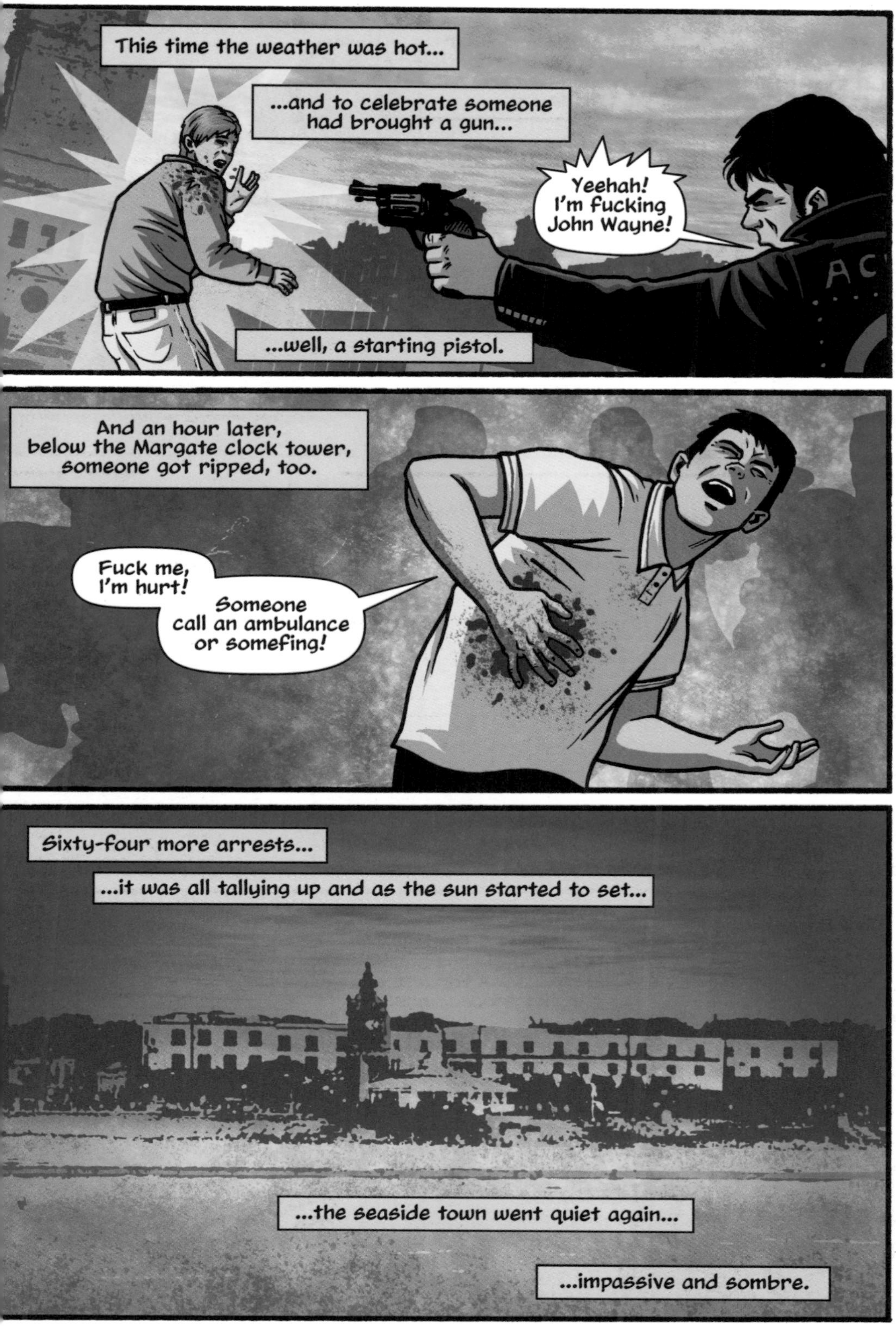
This time the weather was hot...
...and to celebrate someone had brought a gun...
Yeehah! I'm fucking John Wayne!
...well, a starting pistol.
And an hour later, below the Margate clock tower, someone got ripped, too.
Fuck me, I'm hurt!
Someone call an ambulance or somefing!
Sixty-four more arrests...
...it was all tallying up and as the sun started to set...
...the seaside town went quiet again...
...impassive and sombre.

There were a good few bundles all over: Bognor, Southend... forty arrests in Bournemouth... and back in Margate, Dr George Simpson doled out summary fines and punishments to the arrested mods.

It is not likely that the air of this town has ever been so polluted by hordes of hooligans, male and female, such as we have seen this weekend, and of whom you are an example. These long haired, mentally unstable, petty little sawdust Caesars seem to only find courage like rats by hunting in packs. We shall discourage you and other thugs of your kind who are infected with this vicious virus. Margate will not tolerate louts like you.

In Brighton, on the Sussex coast, mods had gathered in even larger throngs to do battle with their enemy.

May 18th 1964. Seventeen year-old Barry Prior took a walk.

What a weekend! It's a bloody lot different to the time The Who played down here about a month ago.

At 7:00am next morning, Barry's mates found him lying at the bottom of Telscombe Cliffs, Saltdean, Sussex.

No one saw nothing during the night and there was no screams or nothing.

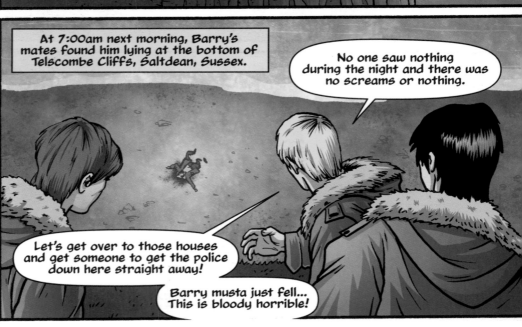

Let's get over to those houses and get someone to get the police down here straight away!

Barry musta just fell... This is bloody horrible!

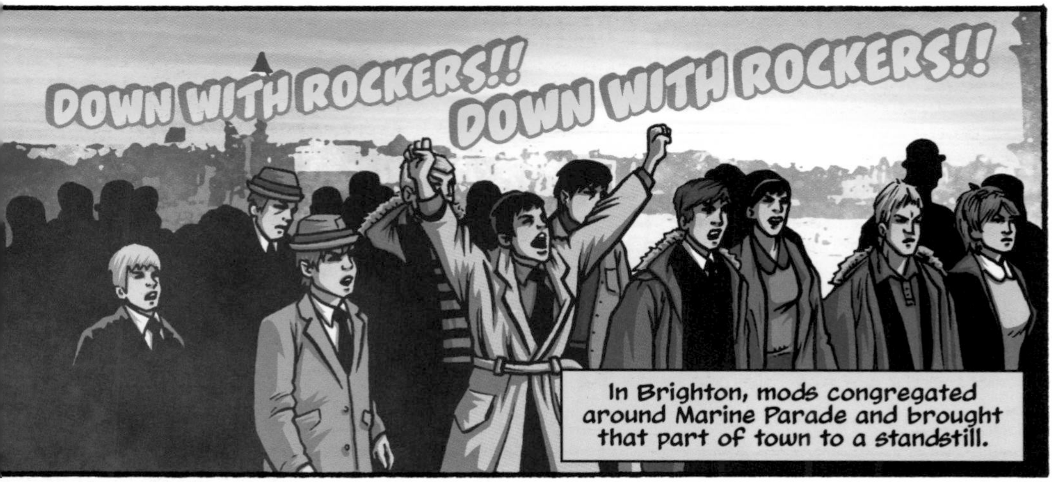

DOWN WITH ROCKERS!!
DOWN WITH ROCKERS!!
In Brighton, mods congregated around Marine Parade and brought that part of town to a standstill.

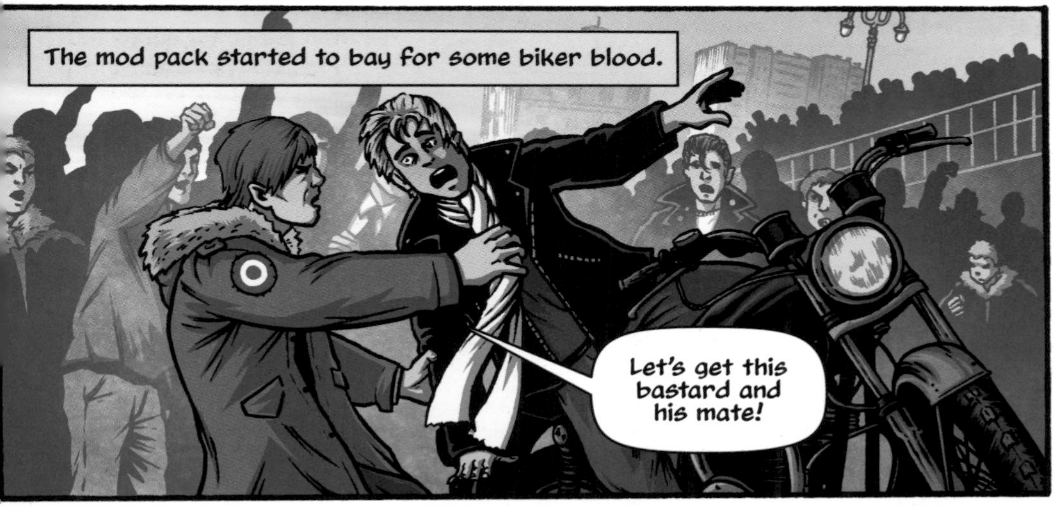

The mod pack started to bay for some biker blood.
Let's get this bastard and his mate!

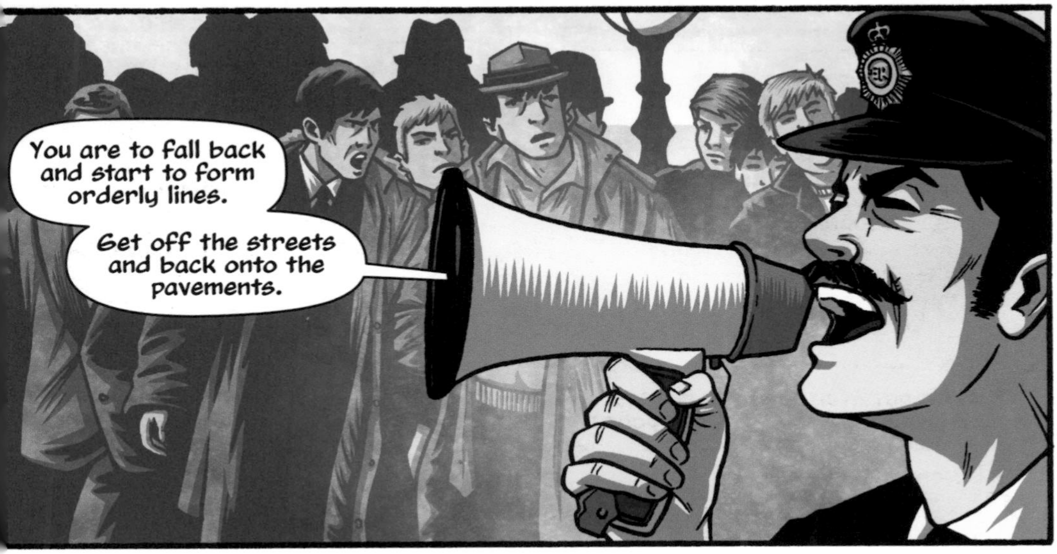

You are to fall back and start to form orderly lines.
Get off the streets and back onto the pavements.

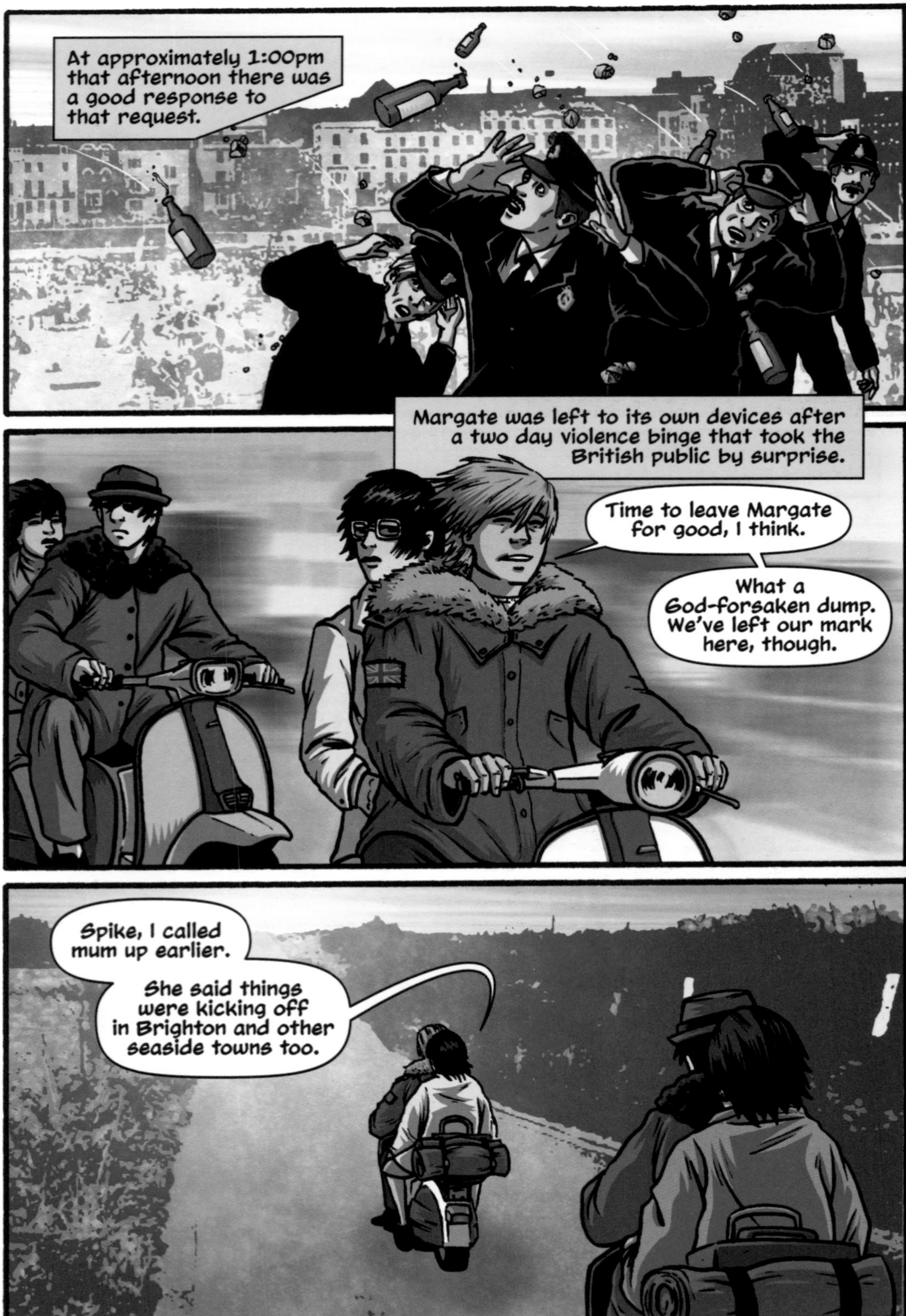

At approximately 1:00pm that afternoon there was a good response to that request.
Margate was left to its own devices after a two day violence binge that took the British public by surprise.
Time to leave Margate for good, I think.
What a God-forsaken dump. We've left our mark here, though.
Spike, I called mum up earlier.
She said things were kicking off in Brighton and other seaside towns too.

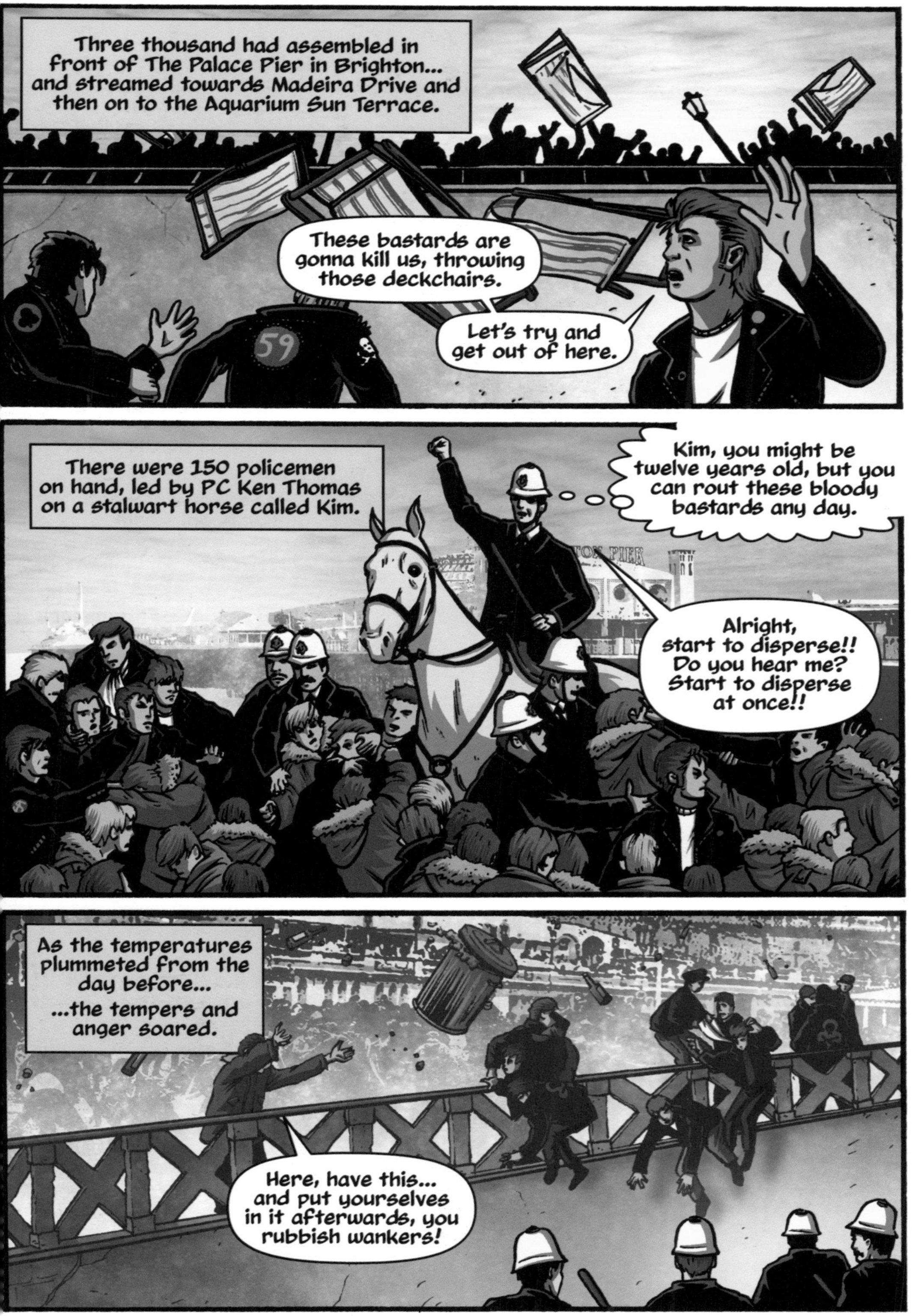

Three thousand had assembled in front of The Palace Pier in Brighton... and streamed towards Madeira Drive and then on to the Aquarium Sun Terrace.
These bastards are gonna kill us, throwing those deckchairs.
Let's try and get out of here.
There were 150 policemen on hand, led by PC Ken Thomas on a stalwart horse called Kim.
Kim, you might be twelve years old, but you can rout these bloody bastards any day.
Alright, start to disperse!! Do you hear me? Start to disperse at once!!
As the temperatures plummeted from the day before...
...the tempers and anger soared.
Here, have this... and put yourselves in it afterwards, you rubbish wankers!

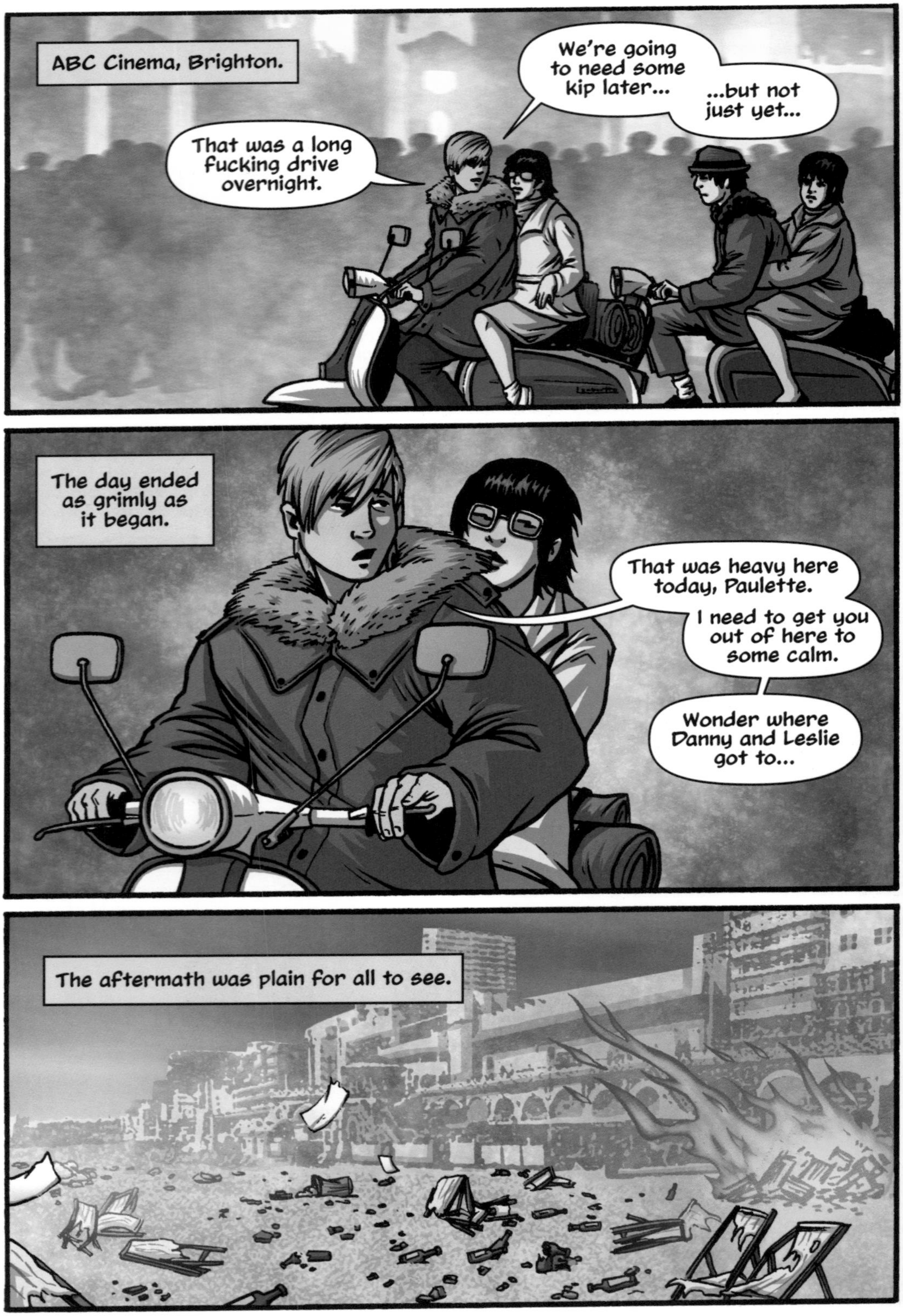
ABC Cinema, Brighton.
That was a long fucking drive overnight.
We're going to need some kip later...
...but not just yet...
The day ended as grimly as it began.
That was heavy here today, Paulette.
I need to get you out of here to some calm.
Wonder where Danny and Leslie got to...
The aftermath was plain for all to see.

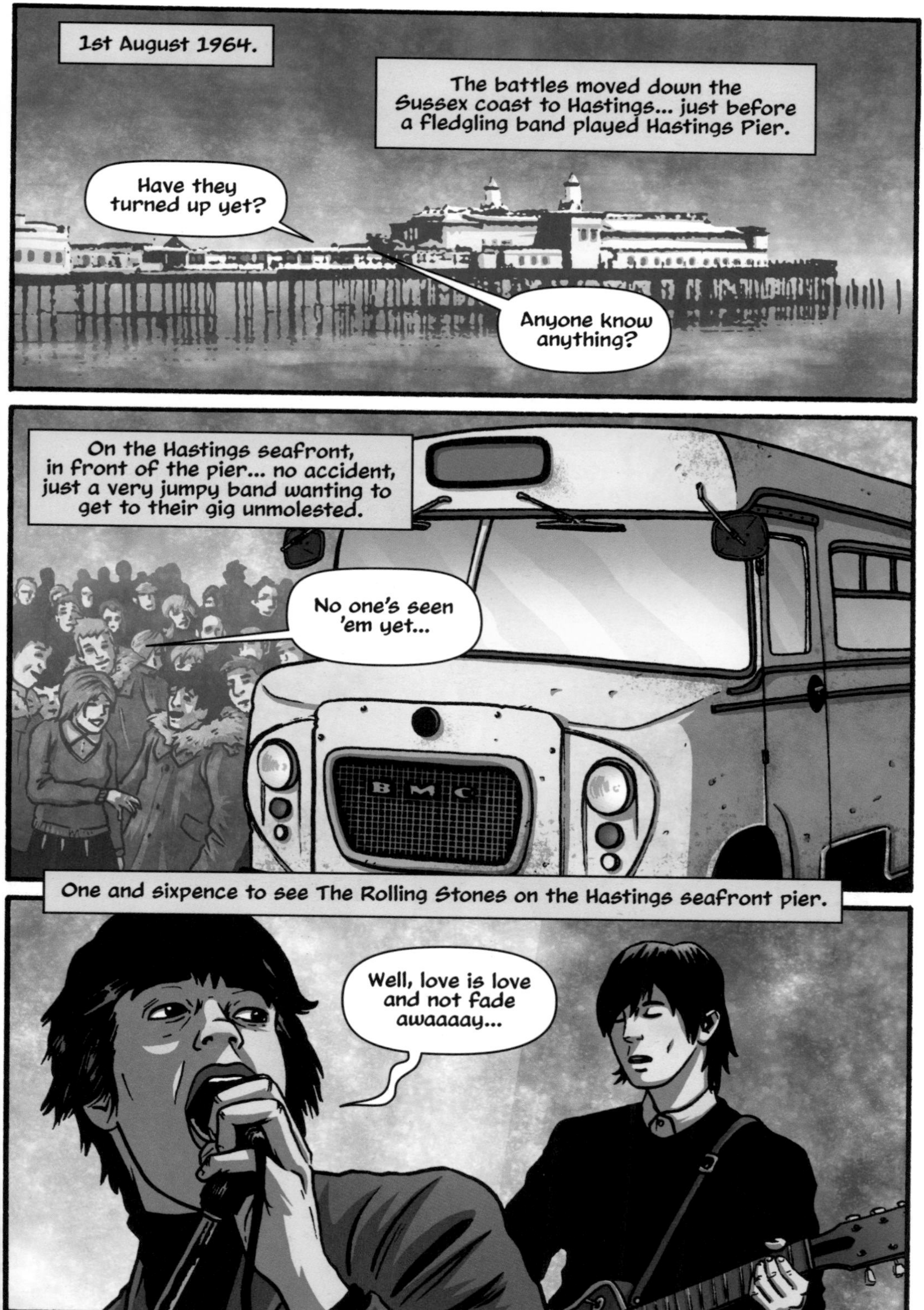
1st August 1964.
The battles moved down the Sussex coast to Hastings... just before a fledgling band played Hastings Pier.
Have they turned up yet?
Anyone know anything?
On the Hastings seafront, in front of the pier... no accident, just a very jumpy band wanting to get to their gig unmolested.
No one's seen 'em yet...
BMC
One and sixpence to see The Rolling Stones on the Hastings seafront pier.
Well, love is love and not fade awaaaay...

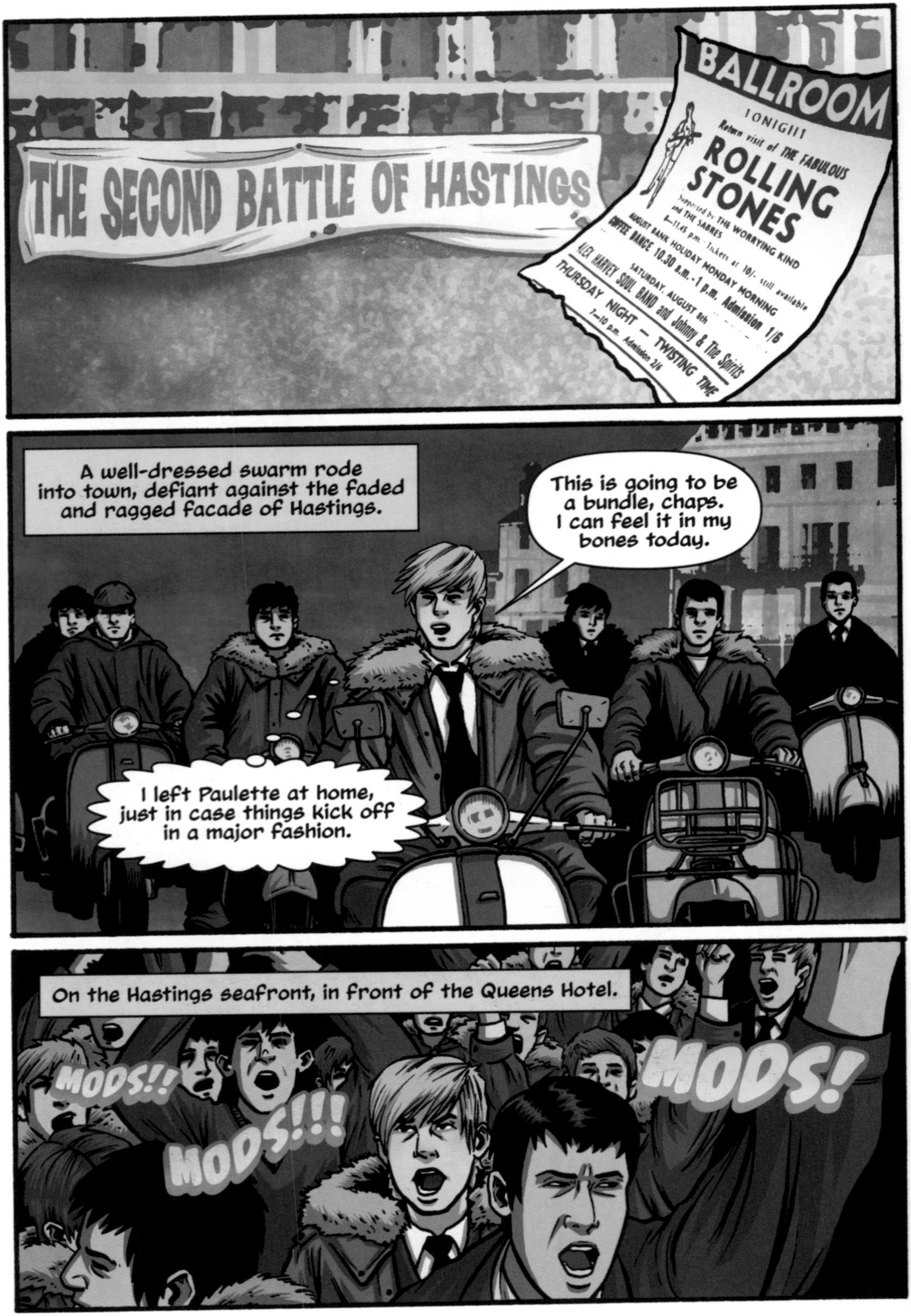
THE SECOND BATTLE OF HASTINGS
BALLROOM
TONIGHT
Return visit of THE FABULOUS
ROLLING STONES
Supported by THE WORRYING KIND and THE SABRES
8—11.45 p.m. · Tickets at 10/- still available
AUGUST BANK HOLIDAY MONDAY MORNING
COFFEE DANCE 10.30 a.m.-1 p.m. Admission 1/6
SATURDAY, AUGUST 8th
ALEX HARVEY SOUL BAND and Johnny & The Spirits
THURSDAY NIGHT — TWISTING TIME
7—10 p.m. Admission 2/6
A well-dressed swarm rode into town, defiant against the faded and ragged facade of Hastings.
This is going to be a bundle, chaps. I can feel it in my bones today.
I left Paulette at home, just in case things kick off in a major fashion.
On the Hastings seafront, in front of the Queens Hotel.
MODS!!
MODS!!!
MODS!

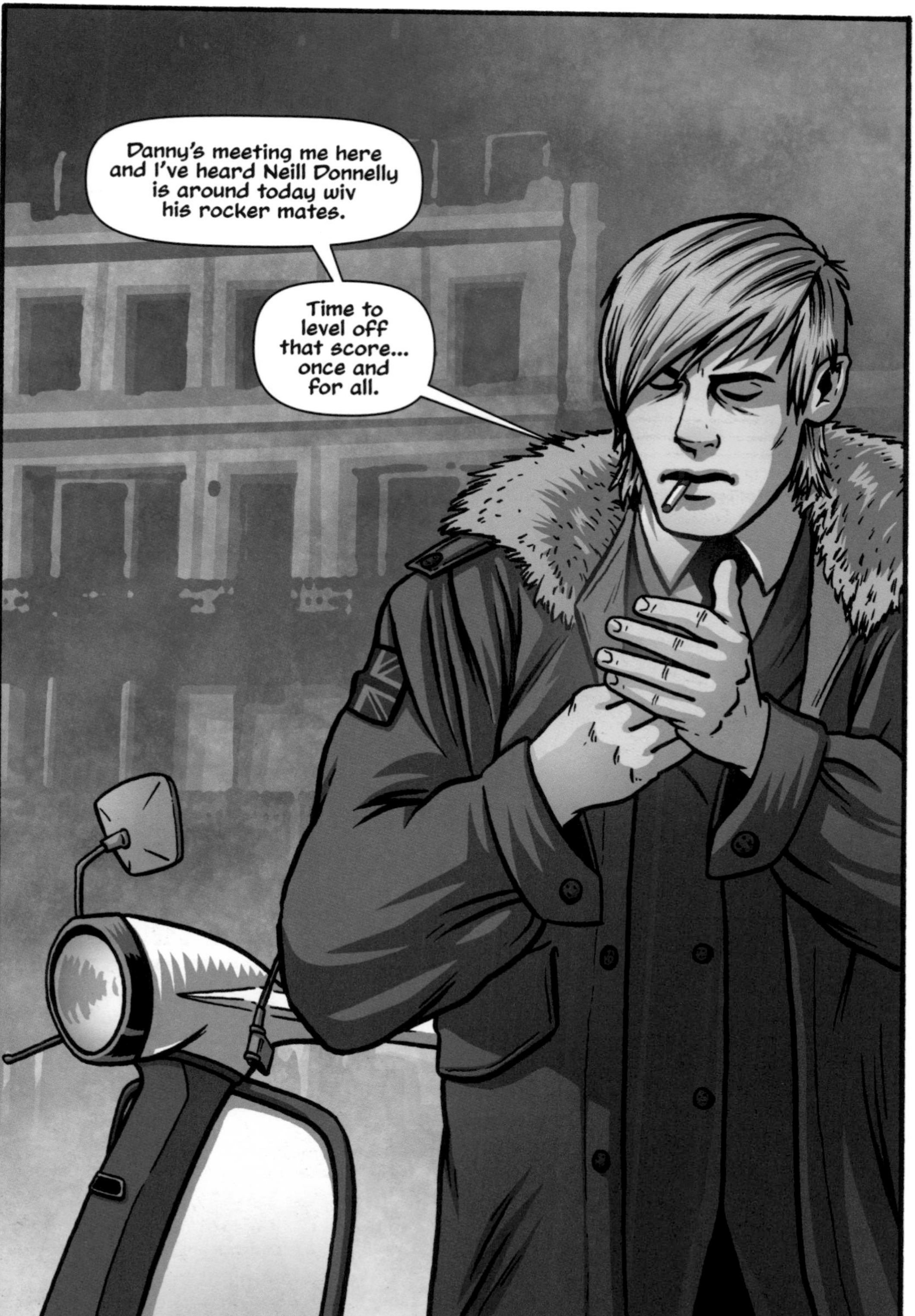
Danny's meeting me here and I've heard Neill Donnelly is around today wiv his rocker mates.
Time to level off that score... once and for all.

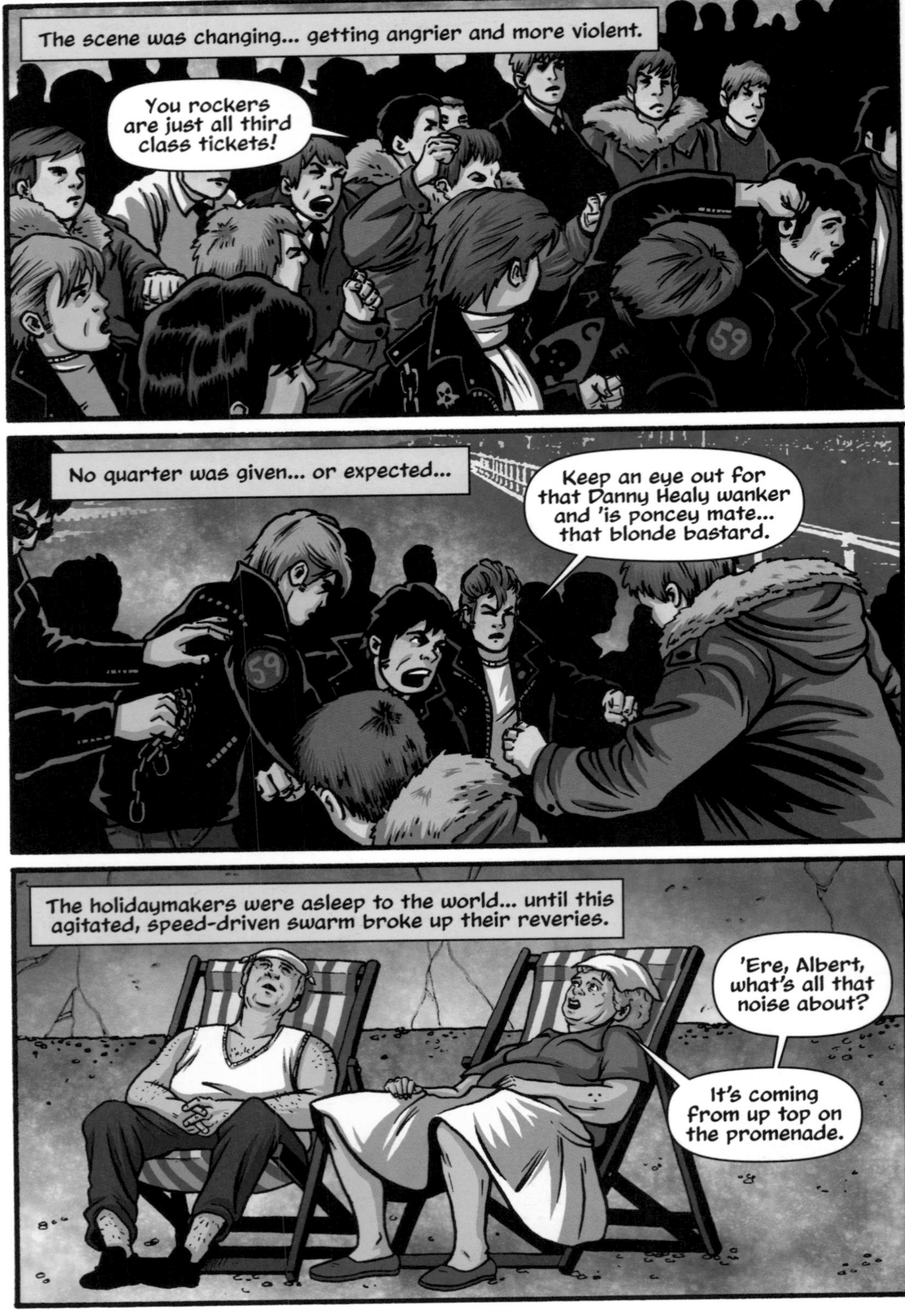
The scene was changing... getting angrier and more violent.
You rockers are just all third class tickets!
No quarter was given... or expected...
Keep an eye out for that Danny Healy wanker and 'is poncey mate... that blonde bastard.
The holidaymakers were asleep to the world... until this agitated, speed-driven swarm broke up their reveries.
'Ere, Albert, what's all that noise about?
It's coming from up top on the promenade.

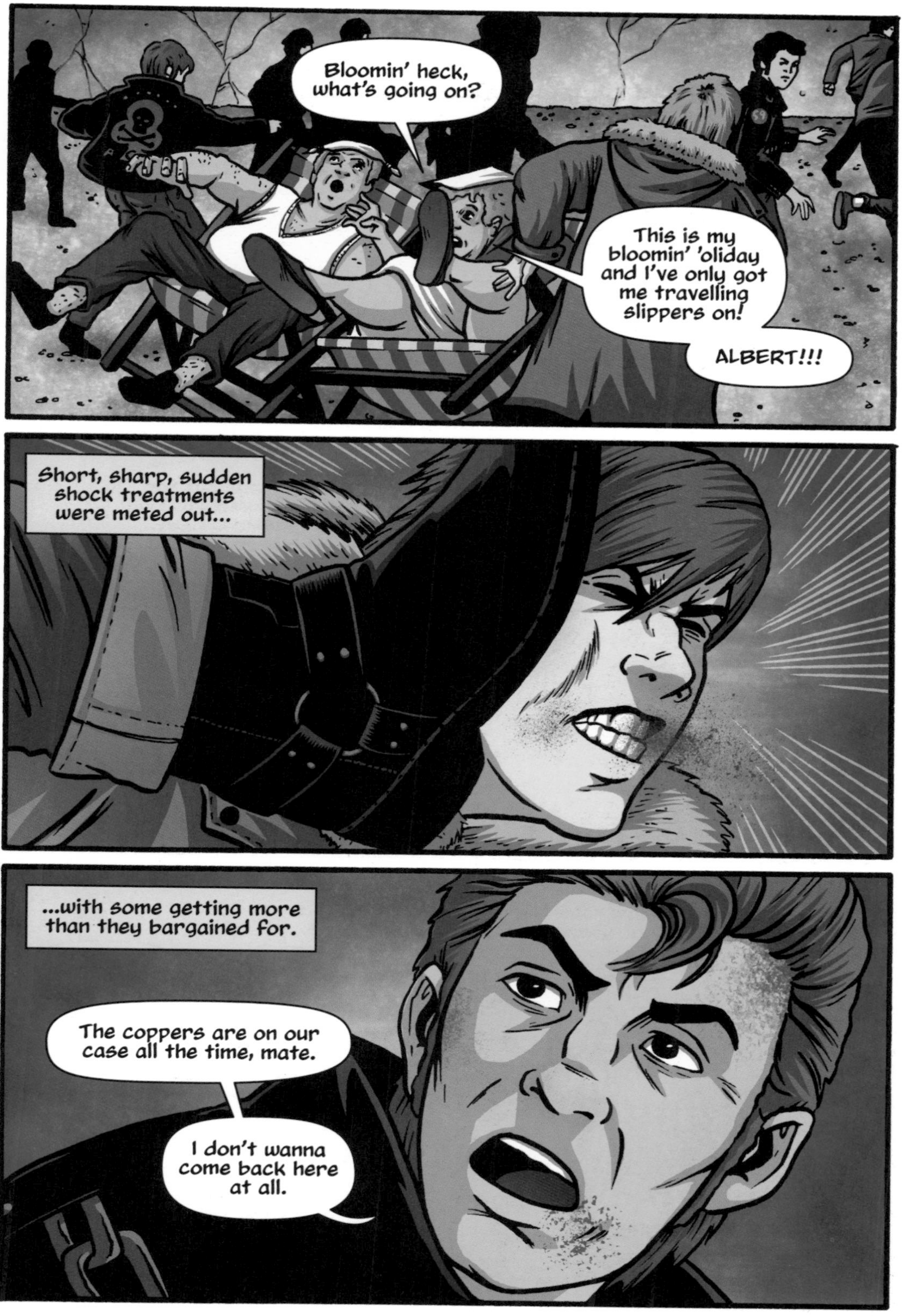
Bloomin' heck, what's going on?
This is my bloomin' 'oliday and I've only got me travelling slippers on!
ALBERT!!!
Short, sharp, sudden shock treatments were meted out...
...with some getting more than they bargained for.
The coppers are on our case all the time, mate.
I don't wanna come back here at all.

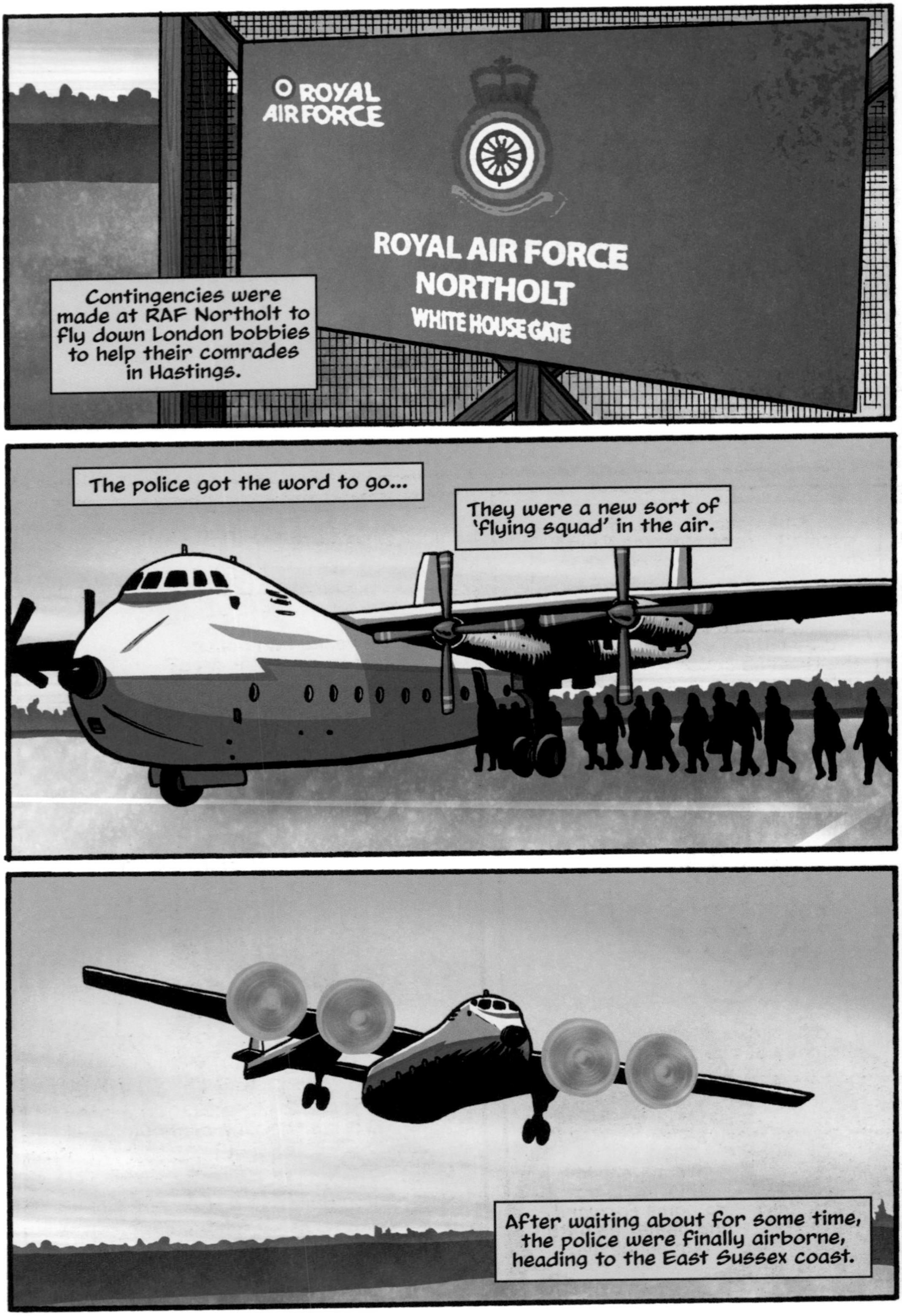
ROYAL AIR FORCE
ROYAL AIR FORCE
NORTHOLT
WHITE HOUSE GATE
Contingencies were made at RAF Northolt to fly down London bobbies to help their comrades in Hastings.
The police got the word to go...
They were a new sort of 'flying squad' in the air.
After waiting about for some time, the police were finally airborne, heading to the East Sussex coast.

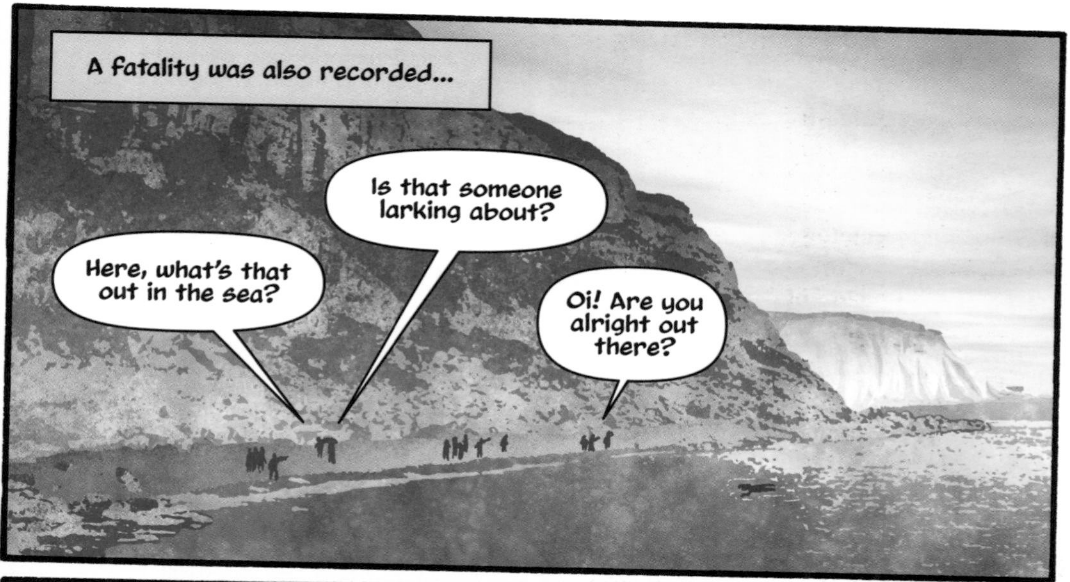
A fatality was also recorded...
Here, what's that out in the sea?
Is that someone larking about?
Oi! Are you alright out there?

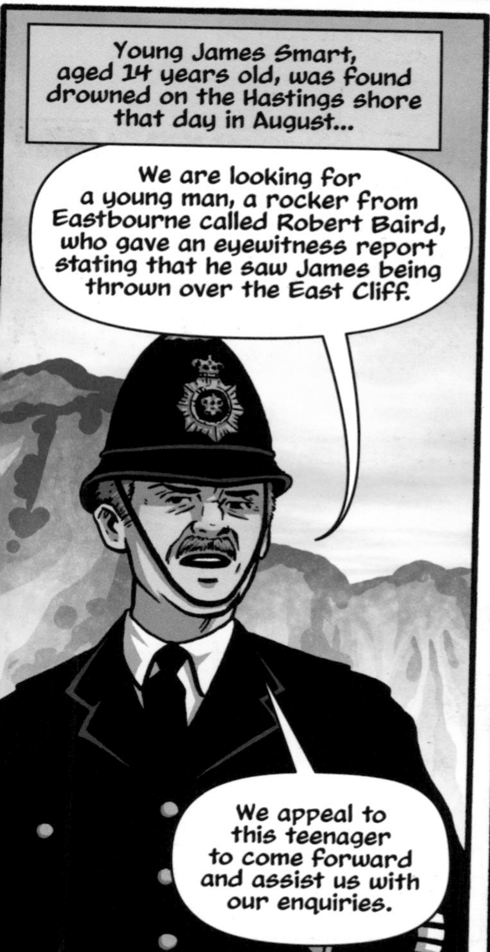
Young James Smart, aged 14 years old, was found drowned on the Hastings shore that day in August...
We are looking for a young man, a rocker from Eastbourne called Robert Baird, who gave an eyewitness report stating that he saw James being thrown over the East Cliff.
We appeal to this teenager to come forward and assist us with our enquiries.

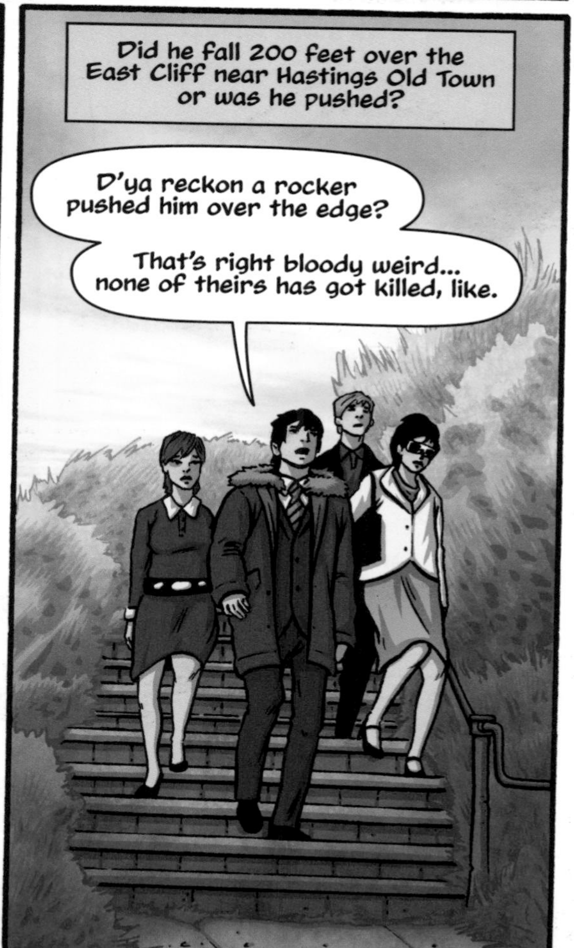
Did he fall 200 feet over the East Cliff near Hastings Old Town or was he pushed?
D'ya reckon a rocker pushed him over the edge?
That's right bloody weird... none of theirs has got killed, like.

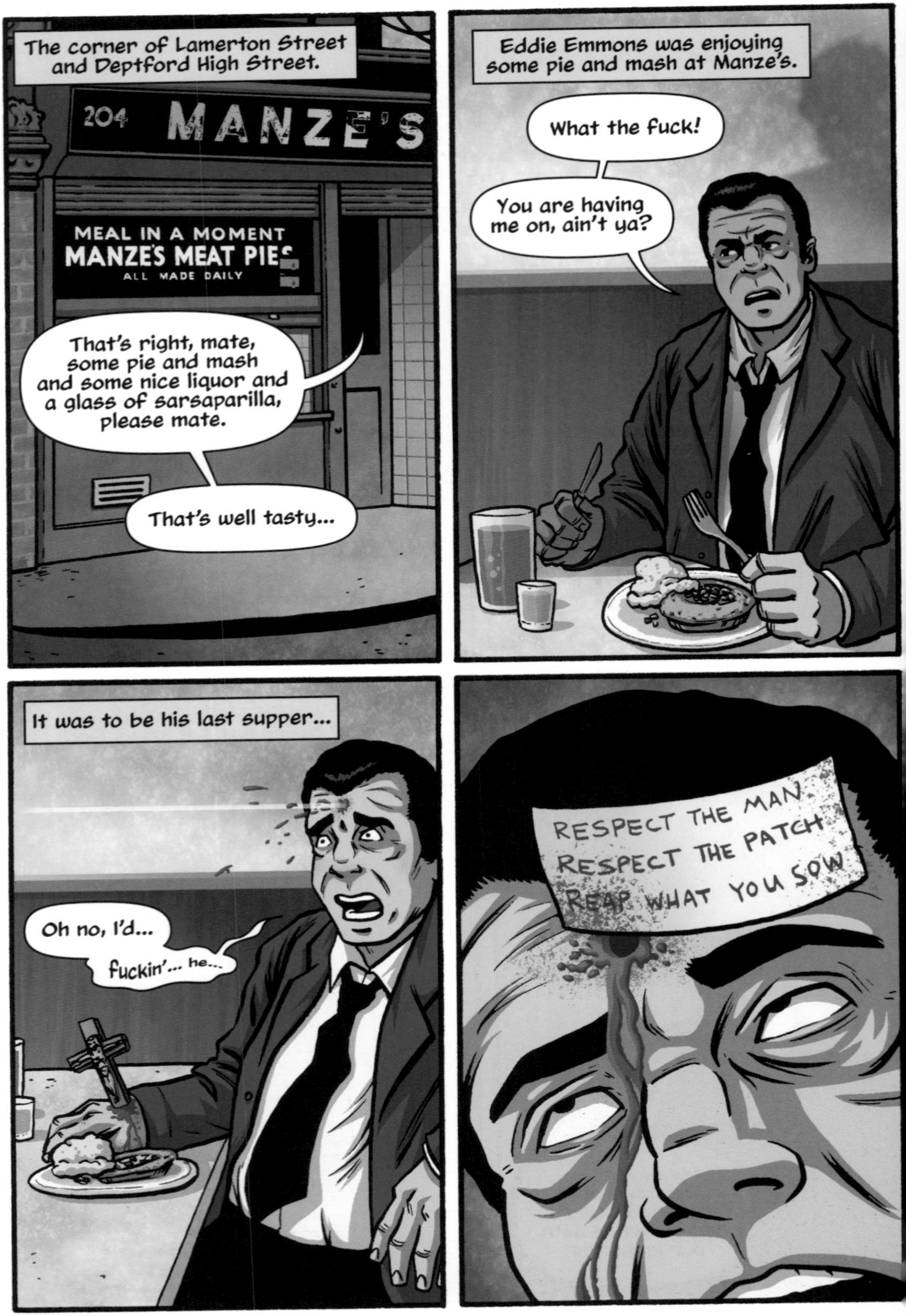
The corner of Lamerton Street and Deptford High Street.
204 MANZE'S
MEAL IN A MOMENT
MANZE'S MEAT PIES
ALL MADE DAILY
That's right, mate, some pie and mash and some nice liquor and a glass of sarsaparilla, please mate.
That's well tasty...
Eddie Emmons was enjoying some pie and mash at Manze's.
What the fuck!
You are having me on, ain't ya?
It was to be his last supper...
Oh no, I'd...
fuckin'... he...
RESPECT THE MAN
RESPECT THE PATCH
REAP WHAT YOU SOW

Hastings, the fighting continued... the skies darkened...

I've lost Danny and me mates and nearly got cornered... I'm going to head for the Old Town in Hastings.

Past Claremont to the seafront... past Peter Jackson's shop that sold good mod clobber...

Sorry mates, where are you guys from?

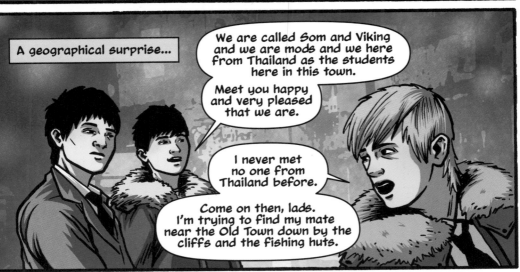

A geographical surprise...

We are called Som and Viking and we are mods and we here from Thailand as the students here in this town.

Meet you happy and very pleased that we are.

I never met no one from Thailand before.

Come on then, lads. I'm trying to find my mate near the Old Town down by the cliffs and the fishing huts.

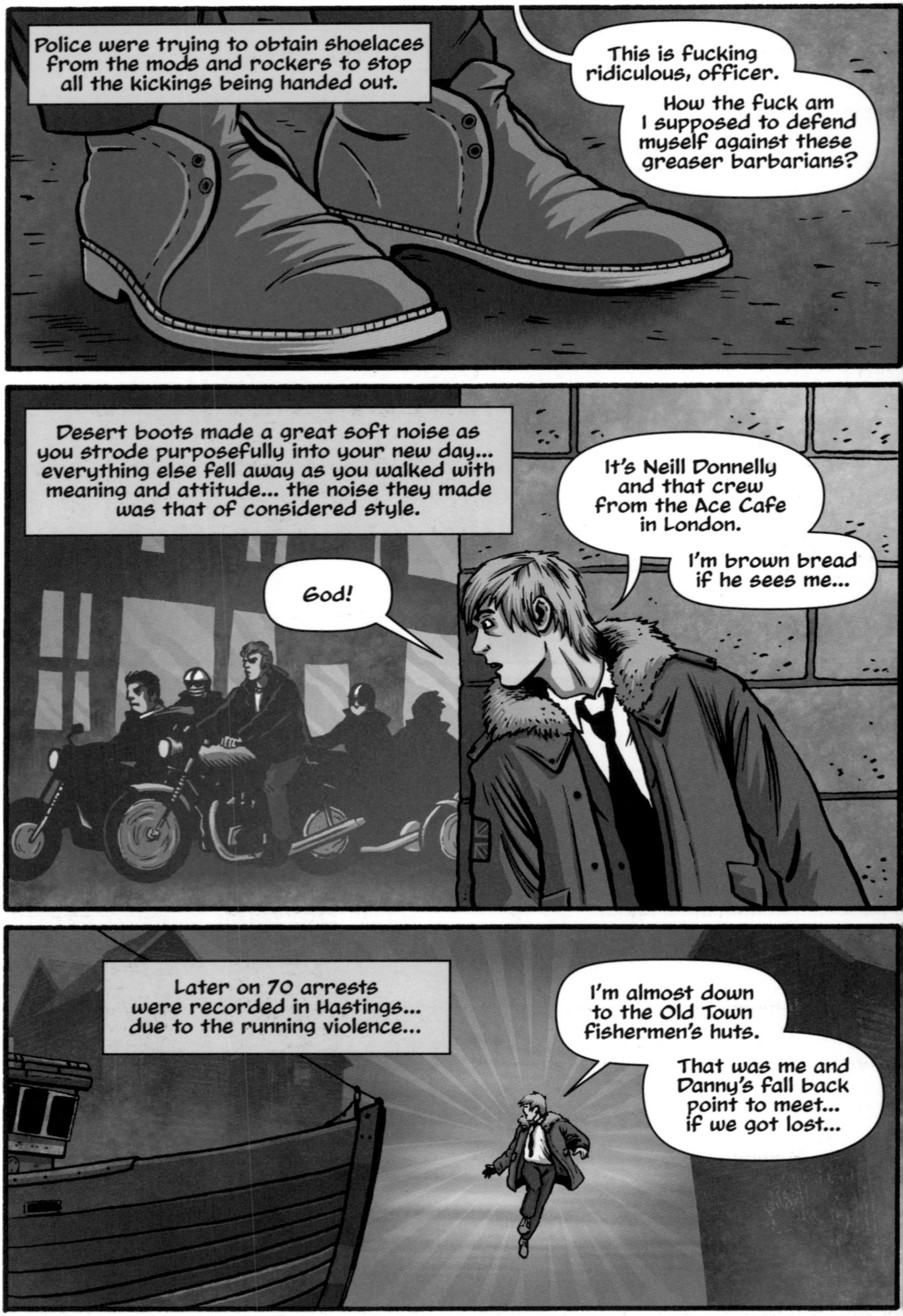
Police were trying to obtain shoelaces from the mods and rockers to stop all the kickings being handed out.
This is fucking ridiculous, officer.
How the fuck am I supposed to defend myself against these greaser barbarians?
Desert boots made a great soft noise as you strode purposefully into your new day... everything else fell away as you walked with meaning and attitude... the noise they made was that of considered style.
It's Neill Donnelly and that crew from the Ace Cafe in London.
I'm brown bread if he sees me...
God!
Later on 70 arrests were recorded in Hastings... due to the running violence...
I'm almost down to the Old Town fishermen's huts.
That was me and Danny's fall back point to meet... if we got lost...

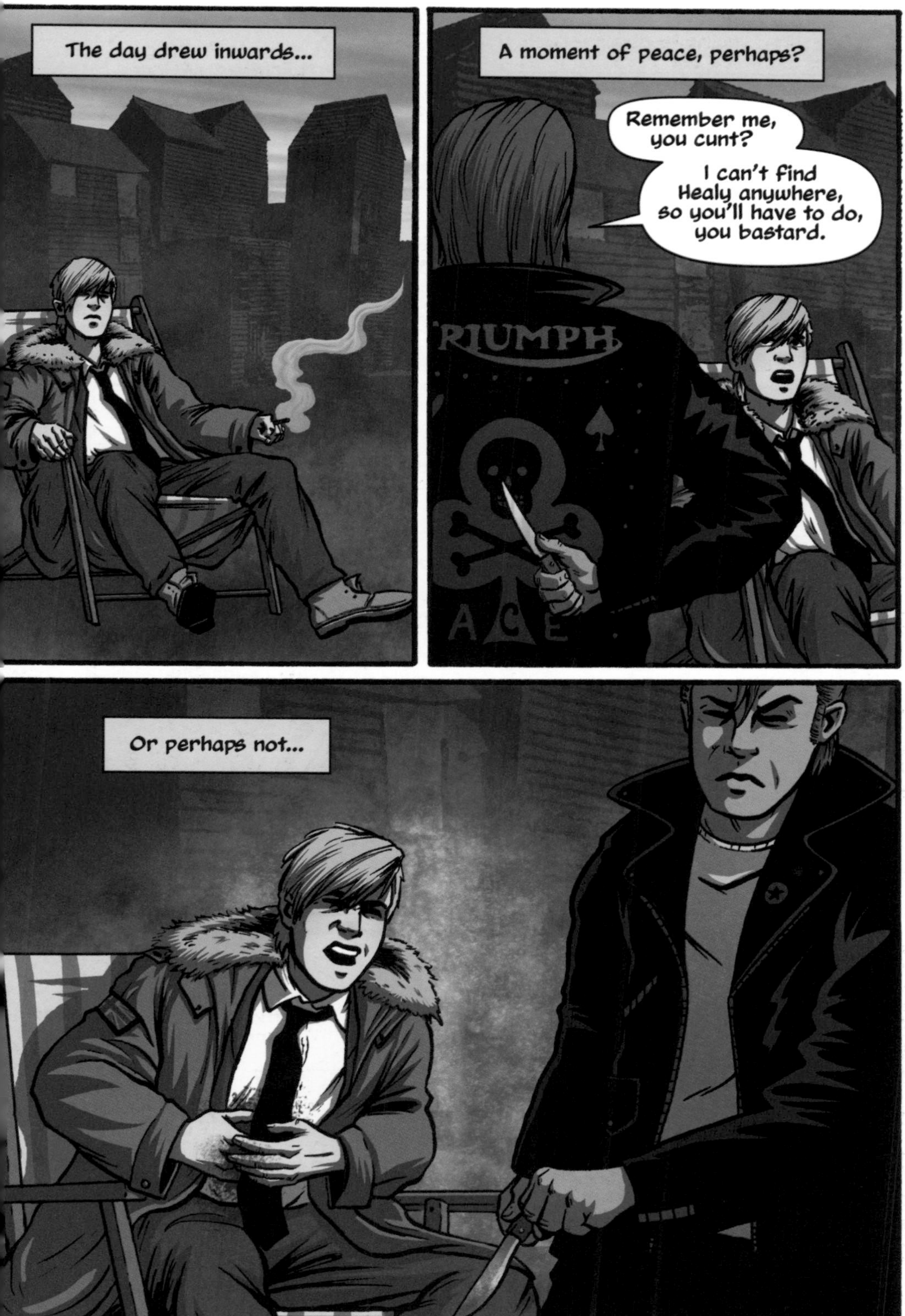
The day drew inwards...
A moment of peace, perhaps?
Remember me, you cunt?
I can't find Healy anywhere, so you'll have to do, you bastard.
RIUMPH
ACE
Or perhaps not...

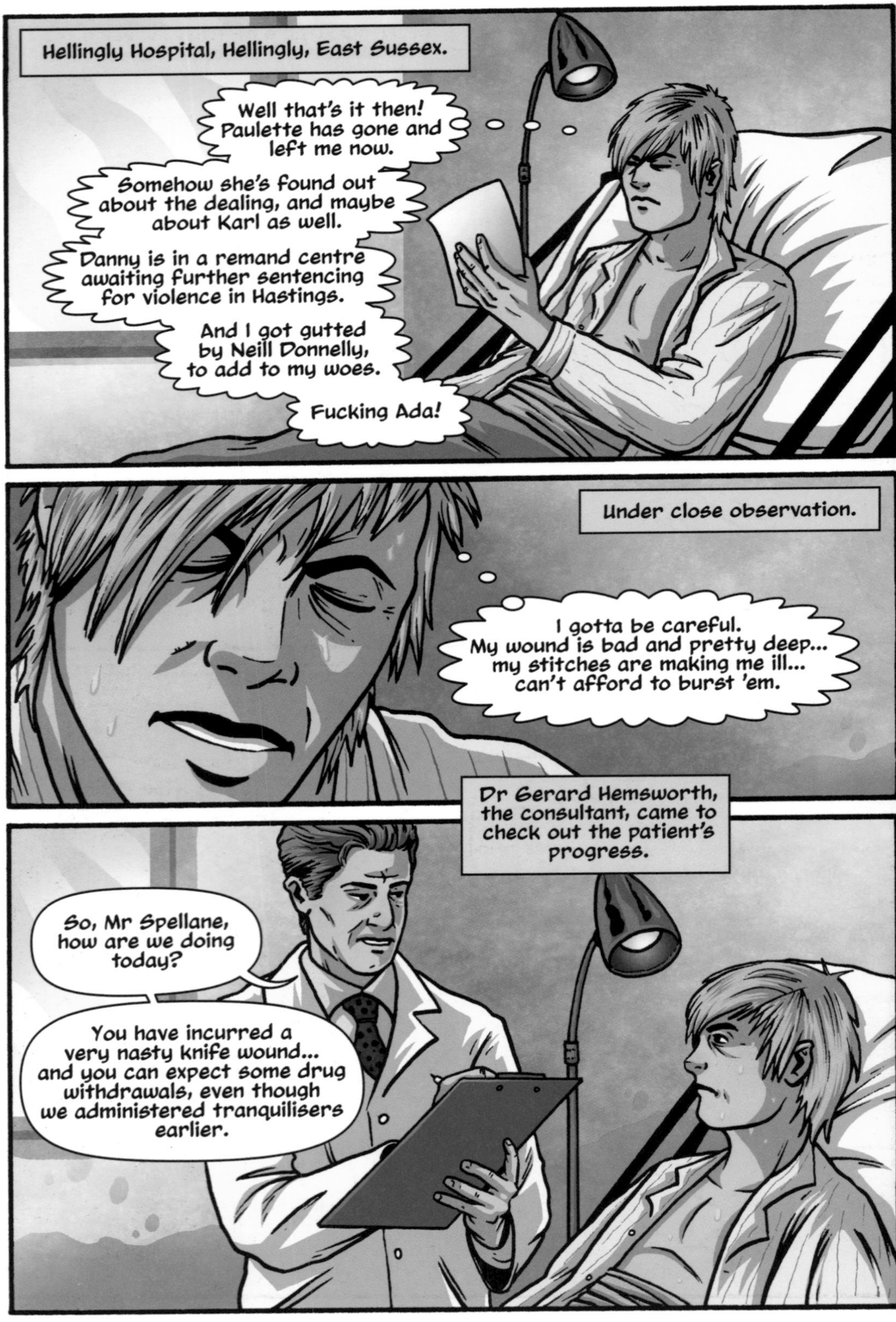
Hellingly Hospital, Hellingly, East Sussex.
Well that's it then! Paulette has gone and left me now.
Somehow she's found out about the dealing, and maybe about Karl as well.
Danny is in a remand centre awaiting further sentencing for violence in Hastings.
And I got gutted by Neill Donnelly, to add to my woes.
Fucking Ada!
Under close observation.
I gotta be careful. My wound is bad and pretty deep... my stitches are making me ill... can't afford to burst 'em.
Dr Gerard Hemsworth, the consultant, came to check out the patient's progress.
So, Mr Spellane, how are we doing today?
You have incurred a very nasty knife wound... and you can expect some drug withdrawals, even though we administered tranquilisers earlier.

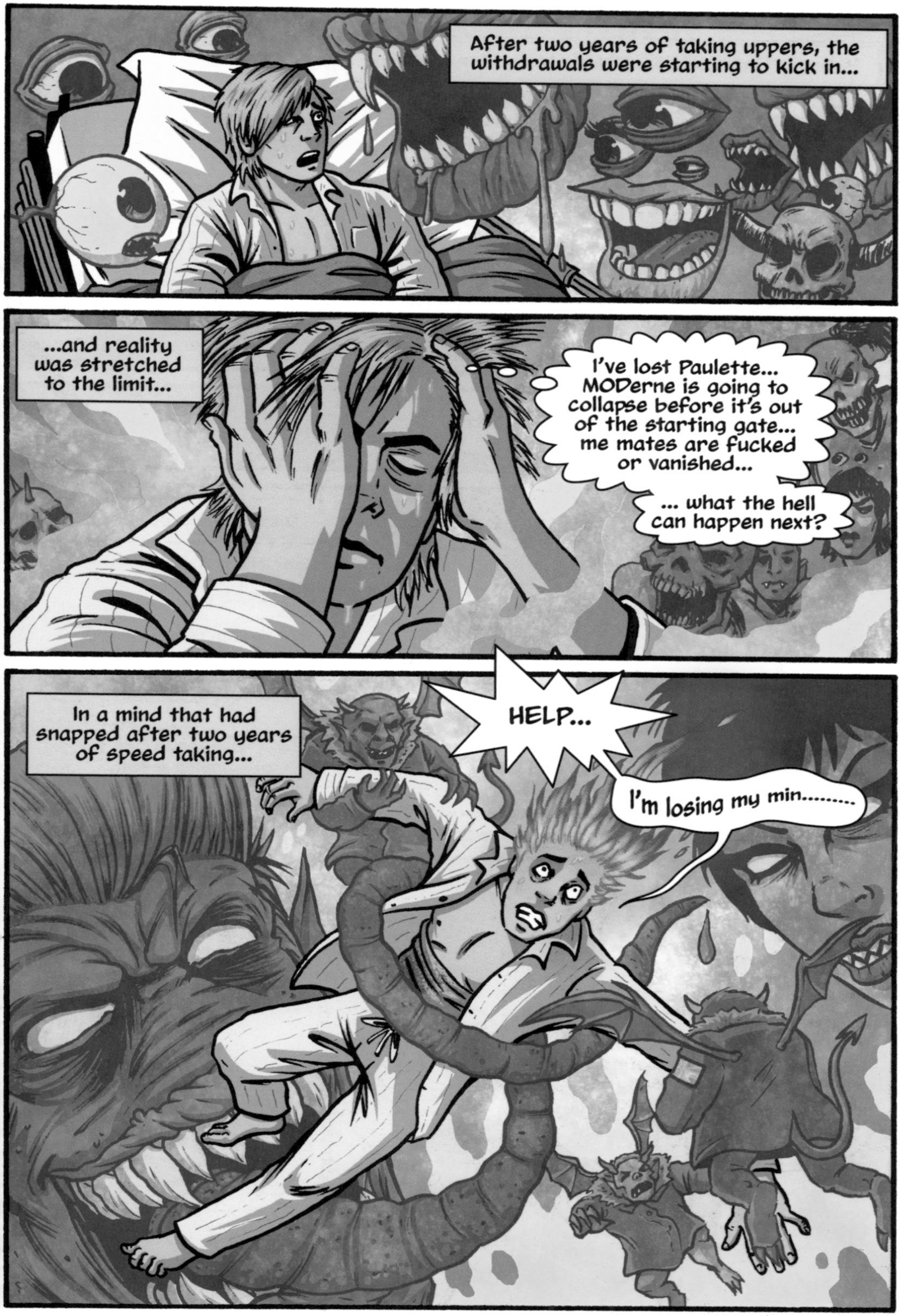
After two years of taking uppers, the withdrawals were starting to kick in...
...and reality was stretched to the limit...
I've lost Paulette... MODerne is going to collapse before it's out of the starting gate... me mates are fucked or vanished...
... what the hell can happen next?
In a mind that had snapped after two years of speed taking...
HELP...
I'm losing my min.........

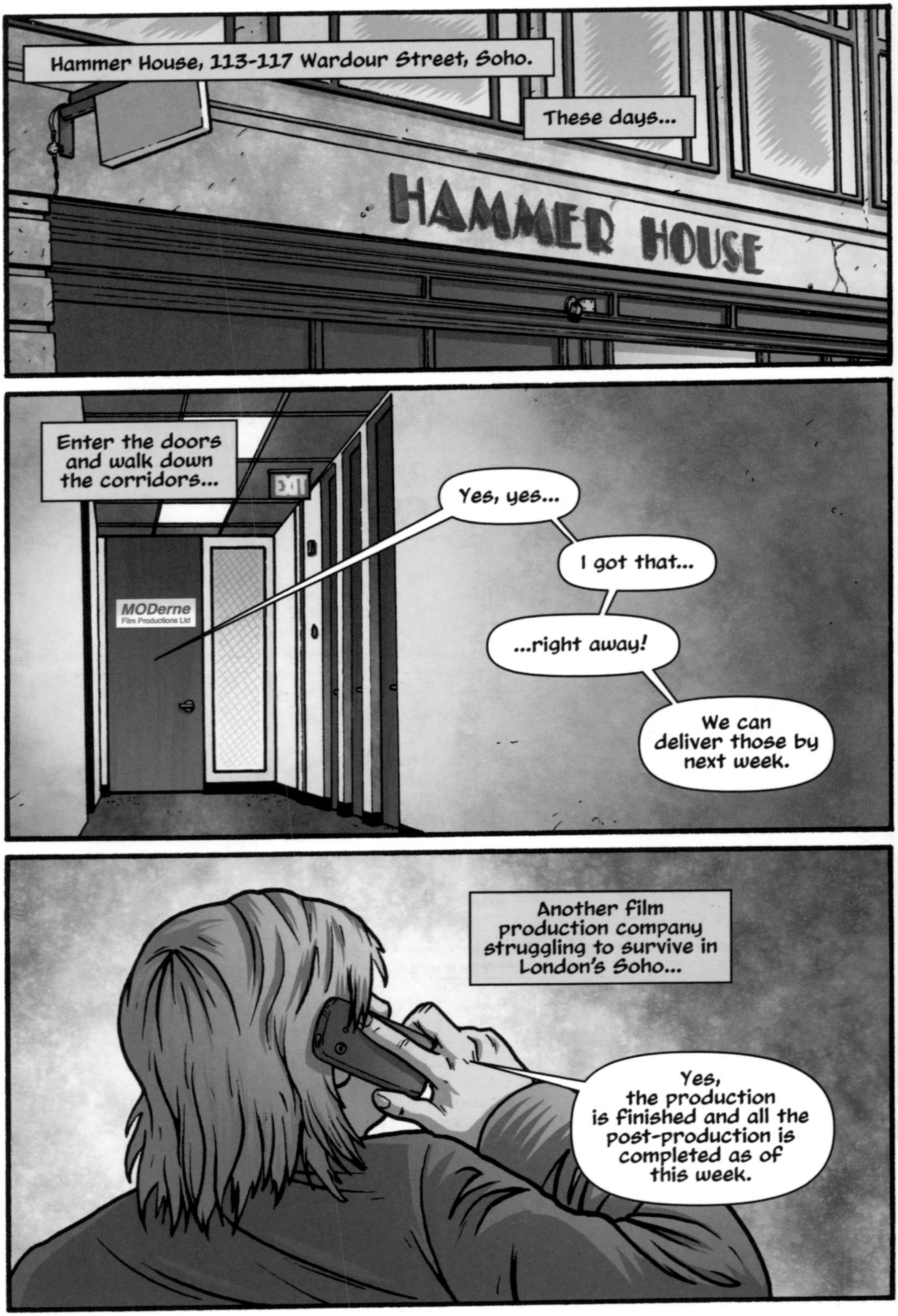
Hammer House, 113-117 Wardour Street, Soho.
These days...
HAMMER HOUSE
Enter the doors and walk down the corridors...
EXIT
MODerne Film Productions Ltd
Yes, yes...
I got that...
...right away!
We can deliver those by next week.
Another film production company struggling to survive in London's Soho...
Yes, the production is finished and all the post-production is completed as of this week.

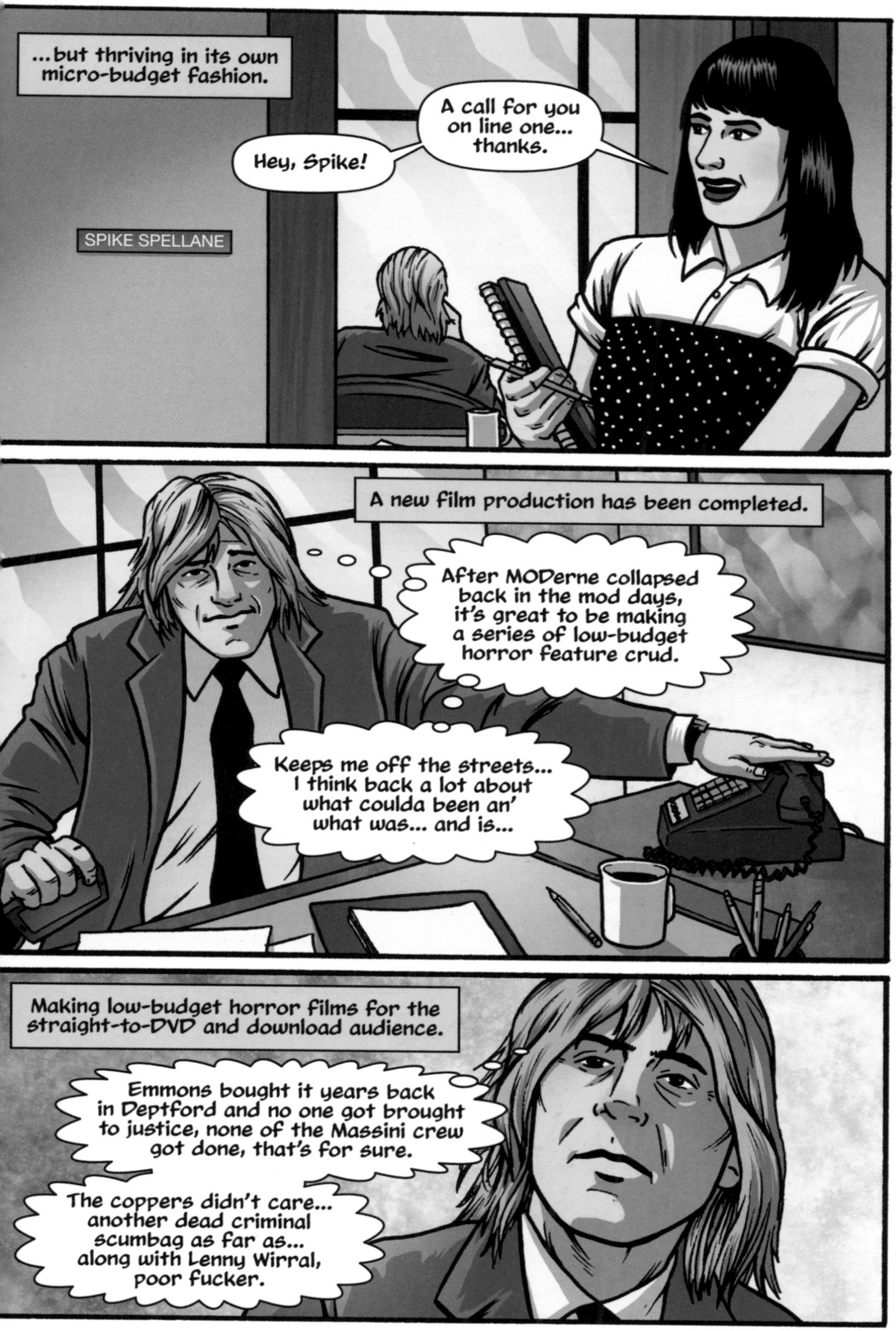
...but thriving in its own micro-budget fashion.
A call for you on line one... thanks.
Hey, Spike!
SPIKE SPELLANE
A new film production has been completed.
After MODerne collapsed back in the mod days, it's great to be making a series of low-budget horror feature crud.
Keeps me off the streets... I think back a lot about what coulda been an' what was... and is...
Making low-budget horror films for the straight-to-DVD and download audience.
Emmons bought it years back in Deptford and no one got brought to justice, none of the Massini crew got done, that's for sure.
The coppers didn't care... another dead criminal scumbag as far as... along with Lenny Wirral, poor fucker.

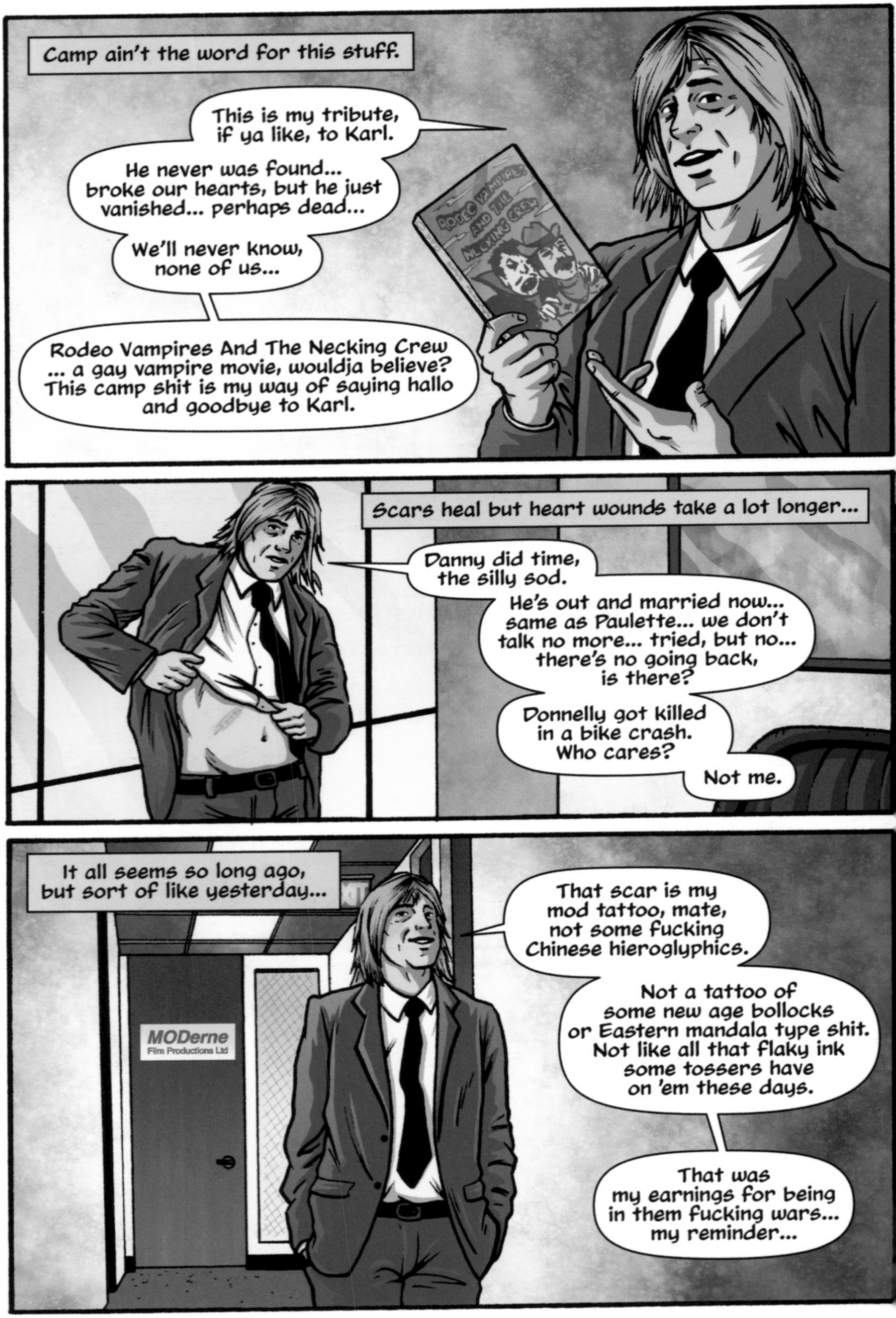
Camp ain't the word for this stuff.
This is my tribute, if ya like, to Karl.
He never was found... broke our hearts, but he just vanished... perhaps dead...
We'll never know, none of us...
Rodeo Vampires And The Necking Crew ... a gay vampire movie, wouldja believe? This camp shit is my way of saying hallo and goodbye to Karl.
Scars heal but heart wounds take a lot longer...
Danny did time, the silly sod.
He's out and married now... same as Paulette... we don't talk no more... tried, but no... there's no going back, is there?
Donnelly got killed in a bike crash. Who cares?
Not me.
It all seems so long ago, but sort of like yesterday...
MODerne
Film Productions Ltd
That scar is my mod tattoo, mate, not some fucking Chinese hieroglyphics.
Not a tattoo of some new age bollocks or Eastern mandala type shit. Not like all that flaky ink some tossers have on 'em these days.
That was my earnings for being in them fucking wars... my reminder...

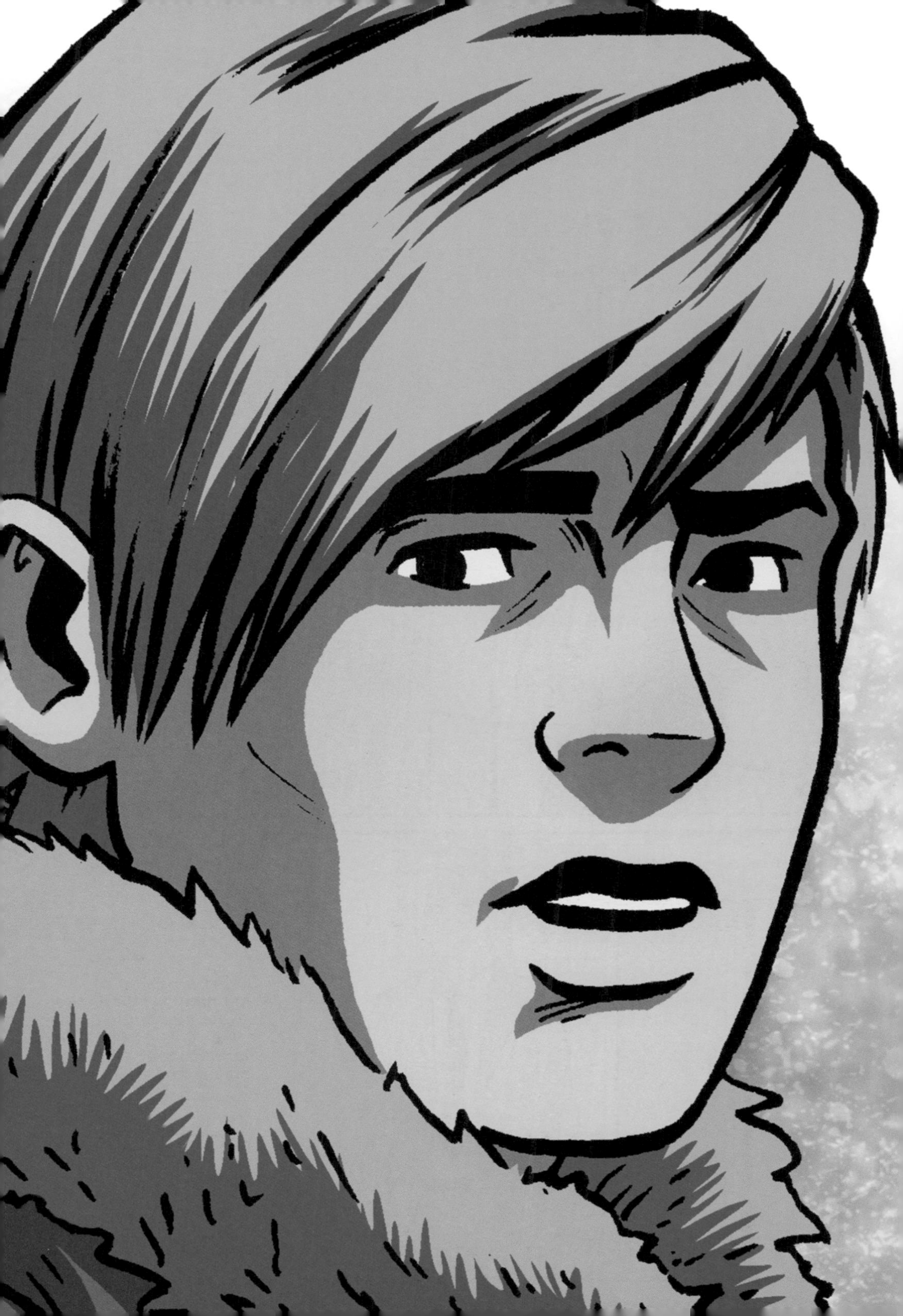

the cast of **Living for Kicks**

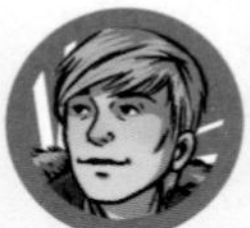

Spike Spellane: A 16-year-old good-looking alpha male. Our story's main protagonist, anti-hero and mod survivor.

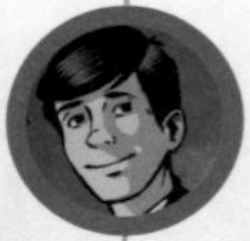

Karl Yelland: Spike's good friend, a pretty boy, with a secret and confused gay sexuality. This leads to his eventual disappearance.

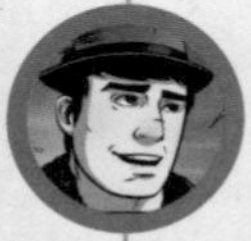

Danny Healy: Spike's good friend, also 16 years of age. Shorter, dark haired, pugilistic, loyal, temperamental and very hotheaded.

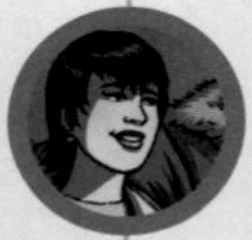

Paulette Harrison: Spike's girlfriend, stable, cool, sexual, alluring, determined. Her need for early stability and Spike's lies drive the lovelorn couple apart.

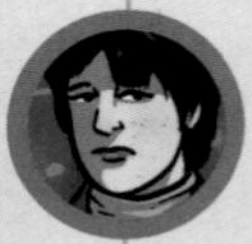

Leslie Milligan: Danny Healy's girlfriend, faithful, sexual, friendship-orientated. She is Paulette's best friend and they form a mod foursome.

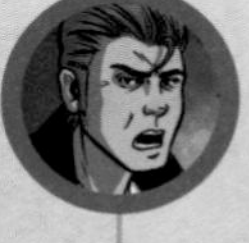

Neill Donnelly: A rocker in his late twenties, who is the main biker figure in the story. Has a violence-based vendetta against Danny Healy in particular.

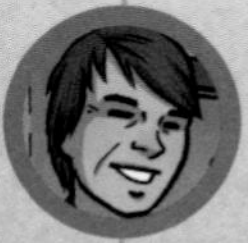

John O'Riordan: Karl Yelland's art teacher, a young, foppish, trendy and secretly gay man. An extra curricular visit from Karl will set a chain of events in motion.

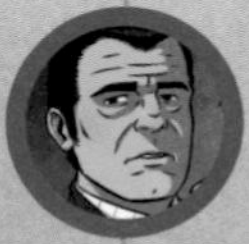

Eddie Emmons: Deptford-based gangster trying to gain ground in the Soho drugs and extortion rackets. Uses Spike to head up a speed-dealing team in Soho.

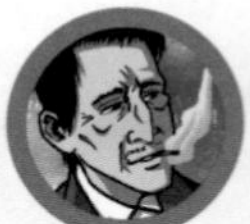

Lenny Wirral: Eddie Emmons' lackey and general dogsbody. The hapless and seedy gangster Wirral becomes a target in a horrific Soho killing. Knows where all the bodies are buried.

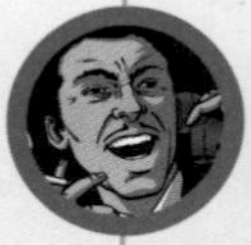

Baldassar Massini: Maltese gang crime head, runs Soho crime, silently and ruthlessly. A more traditional and efficient old-school gangster.

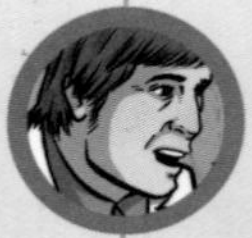

Colin Tooley: Birmingham and Midlands based crime boss. Has links to Eddie Emmo and runs various drug and other crime racke from the Constitution Hill area of Birminghar

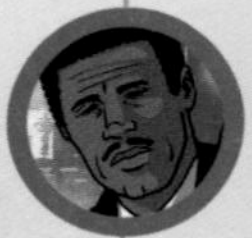

Johnny Edgecombe (real-life characte West Indian hustler, mover and shaker and face about Soho. Briefly Christine Keeler's boyfriend and also a habitué of the feted Flamingo Club. Involved in the infamous Profumo affair. Died aged 77 in 2010.

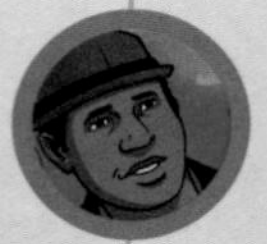

Landy Gray: Young West Indian boy, who wears a trademark pork pie hat. Landy is a young scenester with a humorous and adaptable personality.

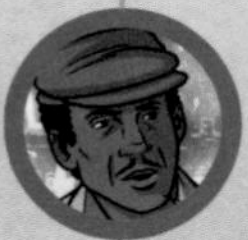

Lucky Gordon (real-life character)**:** West Indian with an unstable mien, a hustler, who briefly dates and also attempts to kill Christine Keeler. Peripherally involved in the infamous Profumo affair.

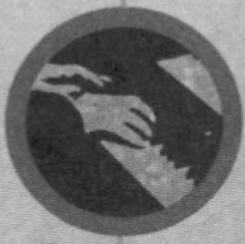

Psycho Gordon (real-life character)**:** Piano-playing brother of Lucky Gordon, who also hung out at The Flamingo. He played and sat in with Georgie Fame And The Blue Flames.

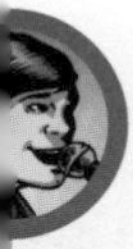

Stevie Marriott (real-life character)**:** Original face and scene maker. Went on to lead the glorious Small Faces. An original and totally unique talent. Died in an Essex house fire in 1991.

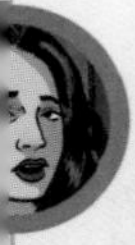

Christine Keeler (real-life character)**:** Call girl. Sexually alluring, she became embroiled in the infamous John Profumo scandal that brought down the Harold Macmillan government of the day.

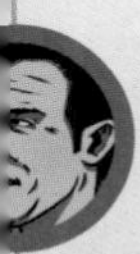

Micky Hendry: Vice Squad undercover and plainclothes copper on the make. Machievellian, scheming and totally underhanded.

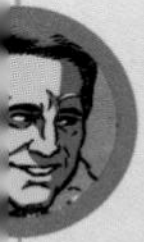

Tony Sales: Vice Squad plainclothes copper. Sly, nefarious, shifty and nasty. In professional and personal competition with Micky Hendry.

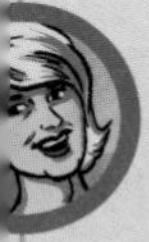

Lucky Diamonds: A young man in his late twenties, very sexualized. A cross-dressing and extremely camp fantasist.

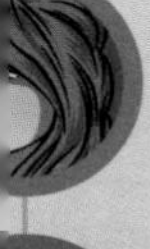

Vicky DeLampard: A beautiful female stripper in her early twenties. Unsure, troubled, social, tempestuous.

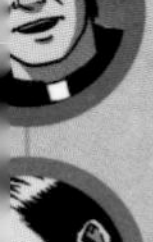

Tops Henderson: Funny, stand-alone, Christian and God fearing. Tops was a Soho based street-style preacher.

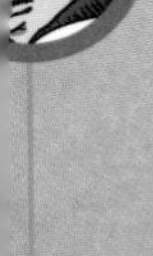

Sometime Storey: Hanger-on and friend of Tops Henderson. He is young and nerdy with learning difficulties.

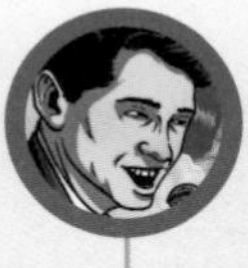

Georgie Fame (real-life character)**:** Renowned Hammond B3 keyboardist and a young hipster in the Soho scene. Led the popular band The Blue Flames with a (now) legendary late-night weekend residency at The Flamingo Club.

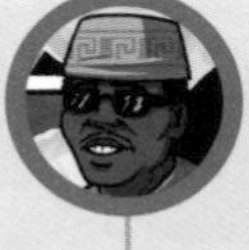

Speedy Acquaye (real-life character)**:** Georgie Fame's exotic Ghanaian conga drummer, an early proponent of Soho-based worldbeat and an unusual musical sight in the early 1960s.

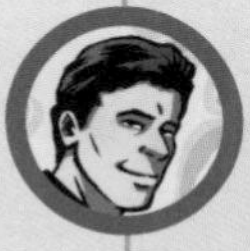

John McLaughlin (real-life character)**:** Superb guitarist who went on to form The Mahavishnu Orchestra and other lightning-fast guitar-based jazz fusion ensembles. He was also a member of Georgie Fame's band.

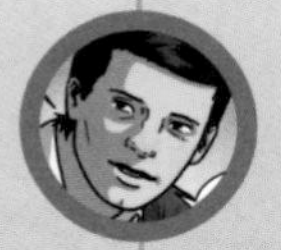

Duffy Power (real-life character)**:** Soulful singer and songwriter who never quite made the upper echelons of the music business. Revered by other musicians in his day. Died in 2014.

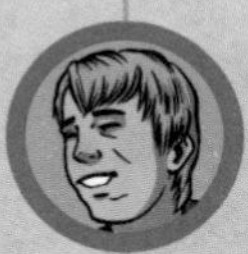

Ace Kefford (real-life character)**:** A young and up-and-coming face on the early sixties Birmingham scene, he formed The Move. The group were infamously sued by Harold Wilson, the British Prime Minister, in 1967. Ace cracked up after bad drug experiences and now lives in Leamington Spa.

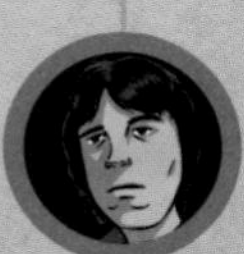

Trevor Burton (real-life character)**:** Formed The Move with Ace Kefford, as two young upstart mods. Burton was a talented and rebelliously fiery musician. Still playing the Midland blues clubs circuit.

mods slang **glossary**

Addy: Address.

Aggro: Aggravation or violence.

Arse pirate: A homosexual.

Barnet: Hair or hairstyle.

Bender: A homosexual.

Bird: Girl or young woman, girlfriend.

Black Bombers: Amphetamines, time release pills and powerful. Branded as Philon.

Blag: To obtain by dodgy means.

Bleddy: Irish for bloody.

Blood claat: A blood cloth/ sanitary towel used as a Jamaican derogatory term. Variation on bumba claat.

Boat race: Rhyming slang for face.

Bob: Term for a shilling used in old pre-decimal UK currency (what would be 5p in today's currency).

Bogs: Toilets.

Bollocks: Testicles, balls or sometimes knackers.

Boost: To take some speed.

Brass: From brass nail, aka tail. A whore. A call girl.

Brass monkeys: Really cold, freezing.

Breadbasket: Head or noggin.

Brown bread: Rhyming slang for dead.

Bumba claat: A blood cloth/ sanitary towel used as a Jamaican derogatory term. An ass wipe.

Bunce: Money, a bundle of money.

Bung: Receive some money in a dodgy fashion. A bribe.

Bunkup: Sex usually in the missionary position.

Buzzing: Speeding or high on speed or other drugs.

Bwoy: Jamaican term for man or boy.

Chaps: One of the men.

Charver: A dodgy/nasty geezer or woman.

Choice: Variation on tasty, very appropriate.

Clobber: Clothes, nice threa[ds]

Cough: To talk, spill the bea[ns] to tell the truth.

Crud: Rubbish, crap, low-level output.

Dob: To turn someone into the police.

Dog's nuts: The dog's bollo[cks] aka the very best.

Face: Noted hip individual in their locale.

Fecking: Irish for fucking.

Firm: A local gang on your m[anor]

Flakey ink: Crappy or badly done tattoos.

Flash: Sharply dressed, up front and very showy.

Foggy: A kind of thick smog of pollution prevalent in UK cities in the 1960s.

Garrity: Going absolutely me[ntal]

Geezer: One of the lads. On[e of] the chaps. A righteous man. The American equivalent would be dude.

Grass: To fit up, to inform on someone.

Greaser: Biker.

Grebo: Derogatory term for a biker.

Grub: Food.

Guineas: Old pre-decimal money worth twenty-one shi[llings] (or £1.05 in today's currency)

addock: Useless pratt or loser.

andsome: Spot on.

erberts: Hooligans or idiotic ...sers who get everything wrong.

eep schtum: Keep your mouth ...rmly shut; to say nothing.

arking about: Fooling or ...essing about.

ugholes: Ears or earholes.

altesers: Derogatory term ...sed by Eddie Emmons for ...altese people.

inging: Out of one's head, ...eeding. Unsavoury or smelly.

ingo: Abbreviated term for ...e Flamingo Club.

iscreant: Dodgy, a law breaker.

on: Jamaican term for man.

onkey's uncle: Amazement ...d surprise (not like "Couldn't ...ve a monkeys").

ush: Mate or good friend.

eck: Swallow it down.

ccurring: Happening.

llock: An inept idiot, a total fool.

once: Someone always on ...e take. Poser or fey wannabe.

oncey: Frilly and useless, ...t worth it. Pretentious.

ong: A rank smell.

at: Idiotic person, hapless idiot.

ick: A worthless dickhead, a ...nstant irritant socially.

onto: Urgent, as in NOW!

ozzers: Prostitutes.

urple Hearts: Amphetamines, ...a speed. Branded as Dexamyl.

ass: A Jamaican derogatory term ...r arse. Shortened version of ...ss claat.

eadies: Money in your hand.

ozzers: Police.

Sah: Jamaican term for man.

Scarper: Run off very fast, to flee the scene.

Serving up: Selling drugs.

Shag bandy: Bow legged from too much sex.

Sharpish: On the double, to get it done quick.

Slag: A whore, a lowlife.

Smarties: Drugs of various kinds.

Snitch: A grass, a stool pigeon in American terms.

Sods: Idiots, a light expression.

Soppy: Soft, wet, feeble and completely prat-like.

Spazzy: Hyper or manic, an old-time and pre-PC expression.

Spielers: Glib talk, also a secret drinking den.

Tasty: Nice, cool, very appealing.

Third class tickets: Cheap and scruffy.

Thruppenny bit: A threepenny piece, also rhyming slang for tits.

Ting: Jamaican term for thing.

Toerag: A complete turd, a snivelling wretch of a person.

Ton: A hundred pounds.

Tosser: Also known as wanker or puller, a masturbator.

Tranny: Transvestite.

Wanker: Also known as a tosser, a puller, a masturbator.

Weasel: A rodent, a snivelling person.

Whizz: Speed.

Whoor: Irish for whore.

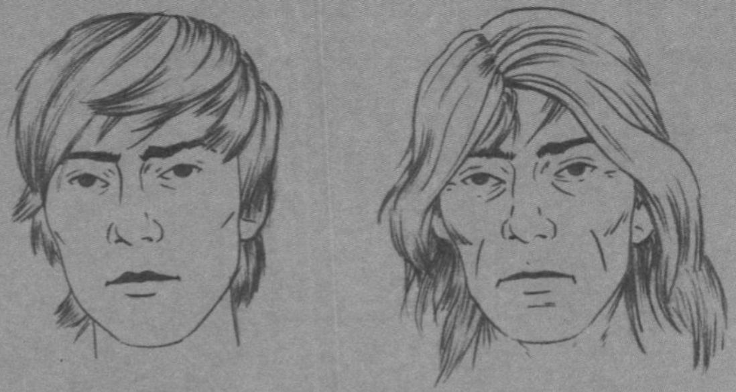

Living for Kicks gallery

Over the past few years, my work has become increasingly more cartoony, for lack of a better term. Looking at these sketches now that the book is done, I can see that I was trying to force my style to be a tad more realistic while retaining the cartoony aspects which come more naturally.

The final head sketches of a young Spike Spellane and his aged counterpart look foreign to me. Not my style at all. The interior pages of this book are evidence of the struggle, and eventual compromise, between what normally comes out of the end of my pencil and what was probably more appropriate for this book. I learned a lot making the pages and I hope the end result does justice to Jim's words.

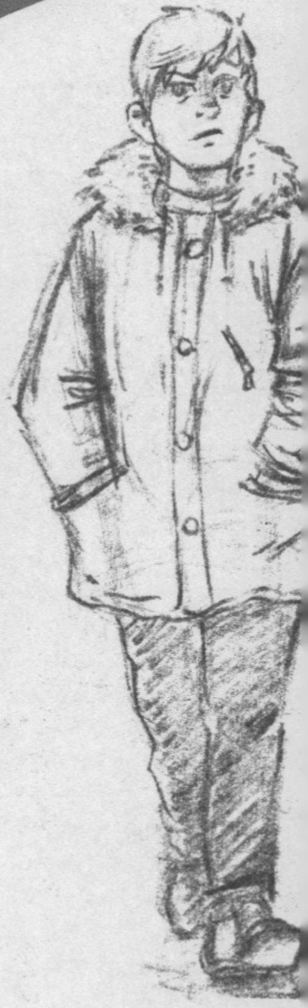

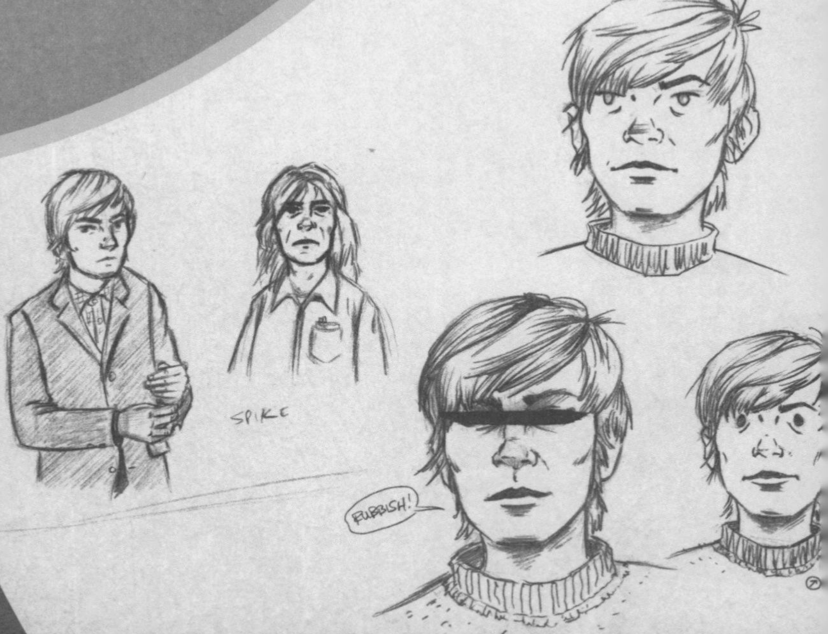
SPIKE
RUBBISH!

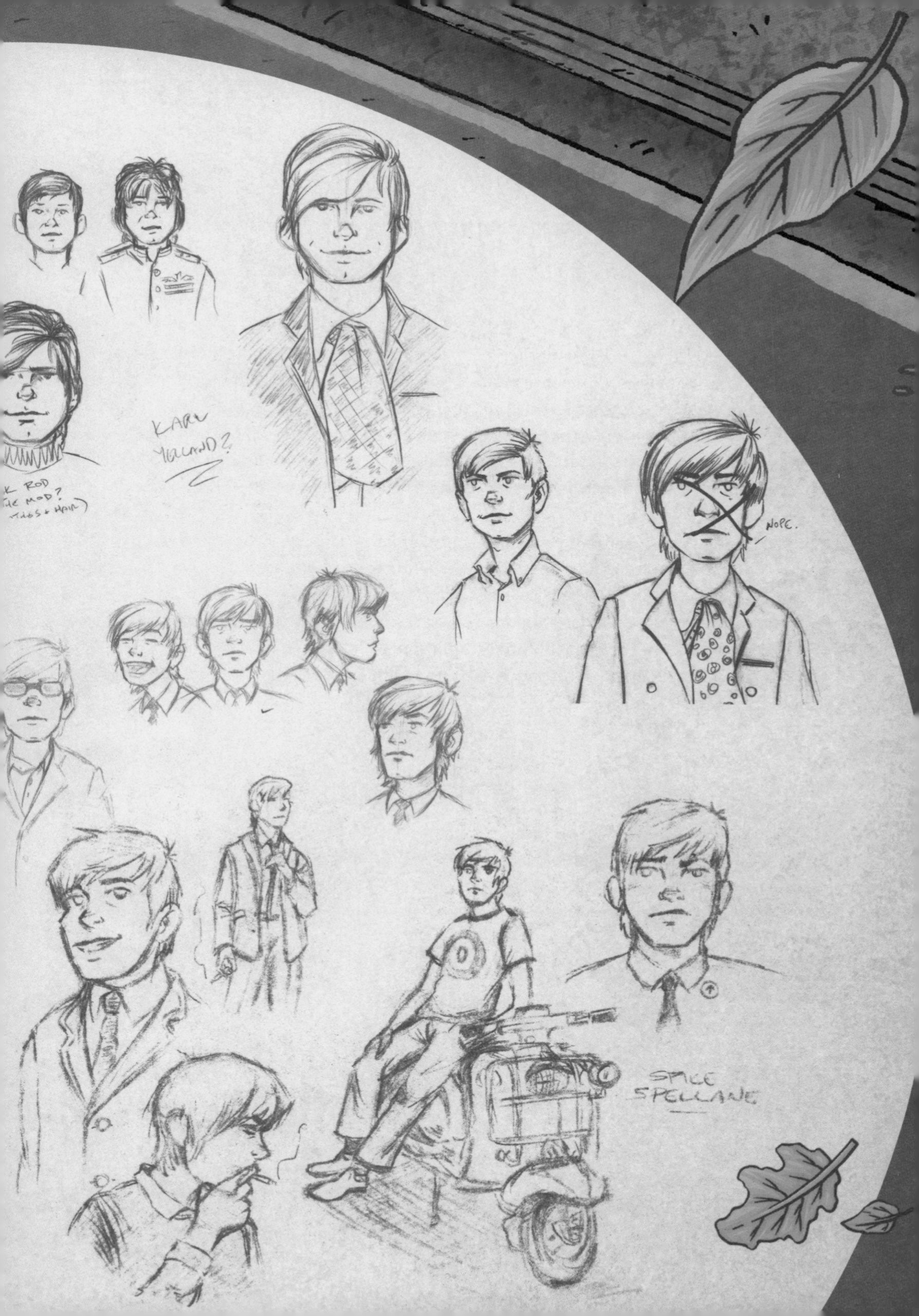
KARN YELLAND?
NOPE.
SPICE SPELLANE

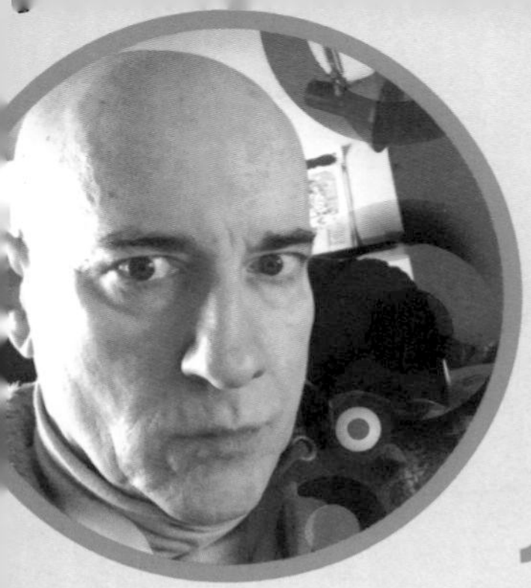

Jim McCarthy

Living For Kicks is Jim's first original graphic novel for Omnibus Press, following his successful series of music biographies, which includes *Reckless Life: The Guns N' Roses Graphic* and *Metallica: Nothing Else Matters.* Among Jim's other titles are *Gabba Gabba Hey: The Graphic Story of the Ramones*, *Neverland: The Life And Death Of Michael Jackson*, three Bad Company paperback collections, *Godspeed: The Kurt Cobain Graphic*, *Death Rap: Tupac Shakur*, *Eminem: In My Skin*, *How To Draw Monsters For Kids* and *The Sex Pistols Graphic*.

Jim's first book, *Voices Of Latin Rock*, was published by Hal Leonard in North America and was the first in-depth examination of Santana, Latin rock culture and the Mission District of San Francisco, the area where this nascent political and musical art form emerged.

Jim's books have been translated and published in numerous foreign rights countries, including Russia, Czechoslovakia, Spain, Norway, Italy, Poland, France, Croatia, Germany and Japan.

www.jimmccarthy.co.uk

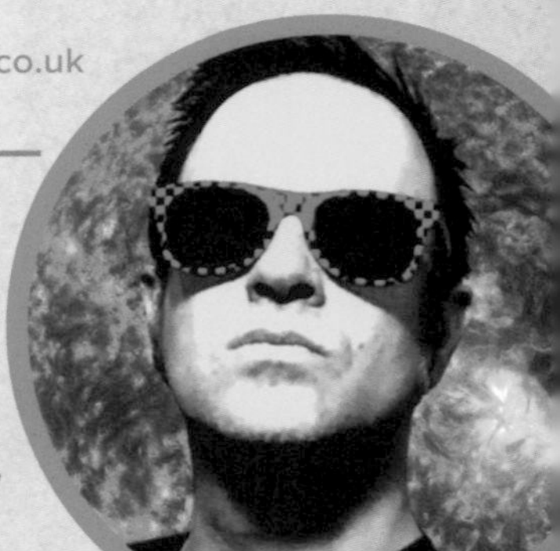

Kevin Cross

San Francisco Bay Area native Kevin Cross is currently living in Portland, Oregon with his rad daughter. He has been playing guitar, and occasionally screaming, in hardcore punk bands for over 30 years. Most notably Big Rig (Lookout! Records), The Nerve Agents (Revelation Records), and Pitch Black (Lookout! Records and Revelation Records).

Coupled with the creativity of the punk rock scene and his disdain for day jobs, Kevin stepped onto the path towards a career as an illustrator and cartoonist just over 15 years ago. He has undertaken a wide variety of work, including skateboard graphics, children's books, comics and storyboarding, to name just a few.

When he's not fighting the establishment through his music or making pictures for cash, Kevin stays up later than everyone else to work on his passion comic book project, *The Monkey Mod & Friends Show.* Additionally, Kevin likes to destroy his body skateboarding and enjoys a nice piece of lemon meringue pie.

www.kevincross.net